A Lon

William Shakespeare's

HENRY IV

Parts One and Two

Edited by

Ronald L. Levao
Rutgers University

PEARSON
Longman

New York   Boston   San Francisco
London   Toronto   Sydney   Tokyo   Singapore   Madrid
Mexico City   Munich   Paris   Cape Town   Hong Kong   Montreal

Vice President and Editor-in-Chief: Joseph P. Terry
Executive Marketing Manager: Ann Stypuloski
Production Coordinator: Scarlett Lindsay
Project Coordination, Text Design, and Electronic Page Makeup:
    Grapevine Publishing Services, Inc.
Cover Designer/Manager: John Callahan
Cover Illustration: *Portrait of King Henry IV of England (1367–1413)* (oil on
    canvas). Private Collection/The Bridgeman Art Library.
Manufacturing Buyer: Lucy Hebard
Printer and Binder: R. R. Donnelly & Sons Company / Harrisonburg
Cover Printer: Coral Graphics Services, Inc.

Library of Congress Cataloging-in-Publication Data

Shakespeare, William, 1564–1616.
    [King Henry IV]
    William Shakespeare's Henry IV, parts one and two / edited by Ronald L. Levao.
        p. cm. — (A Longman cultural edition)
    Includes bibliographical references.
    1. Henry IV, King of England, 1367–1413—Drama. 2. Great Britain—History—
Henry IV, 1399–1413—Drama. 3. Shakespeare, William, 1564–1616. King Henry IV.
I. Levao, Ronald. II. Title.

PR2809.A2L48 2007
822.3'3—dc22
                                                            2006034093

Please visit our Web site at www.ablongman.com

ISBN 0-321-18274-X

2 3 4 5 6 7 8 9 10—DOH—09 08 07

Contents

List of Illustrations

About Longman Cultural Editions

Reading always seems to vibrate with the transformation of the day—now, yesterday, and centuries ago, when the presses first put printed language into wide circulation. Correspondingly, literary culture has always been a matter of change: of new practices confronting established traditions; of texts transforming under the pressure of new techniques of reading and new perspectives of understanding; of canons shifting and expanding; of informing traditions getting reviewed and renewed, recast and reformed by emerging cultural interests and concerns; of culture, too, as a variable "text"—a reading. Inspired by the innovative *Longman Anthology of British Literature*, Longman Cultural Editions respond creatively to the changes, past and recent, by presenting key texts in contexts that illuminate the lively intersections of literature, tradition, and culture. A principal work is made more interesting by materials that place it in relation to its past, present, and future, enabling us to see how it may be reworking traditional debates and practices, how it appears amid the conversations and controversies of its own historical moment, how it gains new significances in subsequent eras of reading and reaction. Readers new to the work will discover attractive paths for exploration, while those more experienced will encounter fresh perspectives and provocative juxtapositions.

Longman Cultural Editions serve not only several kinds of readers but also (appropriately) their several contexts, from various courses of study to independent adventure. Handsomely produced and affordably priced, our volumes offer appealing companions to *The Longman Anthology of British Literature*, in some cases enriching and expanding units originally developed for the *Anthology*, and in other cases presenting this wealth for the first time. The logic and composition of the contexts vary across the series. The constants are the complete text of an important literary work, reliably edited, headed by an inviting introduction, and supplemented by helpful annotation; a table of dates to track its composition, publication, and public reception in relation to biographical, cultural, and historical events; and a guide for further inquiry and study. With these common measures and uncommon assets, Longman Cultural Editions encourage your literary pleasures with resources for lively reflection and adventurous inquiry.

SUSAN J. WOLFSON
General Editor
Professor of English
Princeton University

About This Edition

This edition offers a resource rare in paperback: the two parts of *Henry IV* in one volume, together with relevant contextual and critical materials.

Henry IV, Part One, written in 1596 or 1597, is widely regarded as the greatest of English history plays. Its contemporary publication record (a remarkable nine quarto editions, two after the First Folio), the frequent allusions to it (especially to its chief comic character, Falstaff), and its modern reception confirm its status as one of Shakespeare's most popular works. Less so is *Part Two*, written in 1597 or 1598, with only one quarto edition before the 1623 Folio. But if this darker and more cynical play has been less popular than *Part One*, its admirers are no less avid about it and place it on the same level of importance, especially for its complex, powerful, and controversial final two acts.

We do not know at what point Shakespeare decided to write a two-part drama—before, during, or after the writing of *Part One*. (The most influential discussion remains Harold Jenkins', cited in Further Reading.) Although the plays were probably not acted successively until the nineteenth century, modern discussion almost always assumes familiarity with both, and productions occasionally conflate them, beginning with a private performance in the 1620s and continuing to the recent Lincoln Center offering that featured Kevin Kline as Falstaff. Among critics and playgoers, the two plays have become, if not a "single organism" (as E. M. W. Tillyard once called them), then something like conjoined twins, distinctive yet inseparable.

The texts in this edition are those established by David Bevington for *The Complete Works of Shakespeare*, fifth edition (Longman,

2004); his copy texts are primarily the Quartos of 1598 and 1600 for *Part One* and *Part Two*, respectively (see his textual notes in that edition, pp. A-112 and A-113, for further detail). The extensive and valuable footnotes are also his, except for rare supplements indicated by [RL], which are mine, as are the summaries at the start of each scene, intended for readers new to these plays and to their numerous characters and events.

The Contexts section includes historical, poetic, and dramatic sources, as well as texts representing wider aspects of Shakespeare's intellectual world—political, religious, and philosophical. I have modernized all texts in the belief that presenting a modernized Shakespeare while retaining older forms for contextual material may sacrifice more than it gains. A range of positions, religious and secular, orthodox and subversive, marks out the contradictory forces that Shakespeare exploits in creating dramatic conflict.

A substantial Contexts section is devoted to one of Shakespeare's most famous characters, Falstaff. There are historical and literary materials concerning Sir John Oldcastle, after whom Shakespeare originally named this character. Shakespeare's altering of his name has interested modern scholars, both for what this reveals about Elizabethan censorship as well as for what the original might tell us about Shakespeare's political and religious sympathies. The primary interest in this section, however, concerns Falstaff as a literary figure, a vital presence whenever he is on stage and one whose disruptive energies are felt throughout critical thought as much as they are felt in the plays themselves. Especially important are the remarks of eighteenth-, nineteenth-, and early twentieth-century critics who were uninhibited practitioners of what we broadly call "character criticism." Maurice Morgann, William Hazlitt, A. C. Bradley, and others had prejudices, as do we; even so, they are remarkably penetrating readers, opening perspectives on the plays that remain fundamental to, and valuable for, modern debate and performance.

It is with pleasure that I acknowledge my deep appreciation and admiration for Dianne Hall and Chrysta Meadowbrooke for their extraordinary attentiveness and resourceful suggestions, and for Susan Wolfson, for her advice, encouragement, and so much more.

RONALD LEVAO
Rutgers University

Introduction

The two parts of *Henry IV* align and undermine quests for personal and national identity. A young heir passes through what looks like a phase of youthful rebellion, acting out his resentment at an unwanted destiny, having to "pay the debt I never promisèd" (*Part One*, 1.2.188), until finally accepting, even embracing, his adult obligations. On a broader front, England struggles with wildness at its borders and rebellion from within, until military and political victories temporarily secure the integrity of an emerging nation. Yet even as the psychological and the political reflect each other, Shakespeare complicates the histories at hand. A dense network of repetitions, analogies, and parodies within and across the two plays encourages multiple perspectives on character and incident, entertaining, engaging, and challenging its original audience with rival versions about its own past. From linguistic nuance to broad structure, we find Elizabethan triumphalism crossed by skeptical doubt, a world where loyalists and usurpers alike produce excitingly eloquent, deeply flawed, and ultimately irreconcilable claims to the moral high ground—even as we are repeatedly mesmerized by "a gross fat man" whose wit threatens to undo the very idea of a moral high ground. The result is one of Shakespeare's richest, most evocative theatrical inventions, instantly and durably popular.

Part One

Shakespeare's audience would likely have known some version of the history of Henry IV's rise to, and struggle to maintain, power. For those who hadn't read the accounts of Edward Hall, Raphael Holinshed, or Samuel Daniel, Shakespeare's *Richard II* (staged a year or two earlier) had set the scene, and the characters of the *Henry IV* plays repeatedly recall and are haunted by the troubling past. The

THE

HISTORY OF
HENRIE THE
FOVRTH;

With the battell at Shrewsburie,
betweene the King and Lord
Henry Percy, furnamed
Henrie Hotfpur of
the North,

With the humorous conceits of Sir
Iohn Falftalffe.

AT LONDON,
Printed by *P. S.* for *Andrew Wife,* dwelling
in Paules Churchyard,at the figne of
the Angell. 1598.

Title page of First Quarto (1598). The earliest surviving complete text, Q1 was pre-ceded by what is now a fragment (Q0). Featured prominently here is the climactic, his-torical battle at Shrewsbury with its opposing leaders, and a separate advertisement for Falstaff's "humorous conceits." Conspicuous by absence are the names of the play's "central" figure, Prince Hal, and of the author. The latter absence is sometimes taken to reflect differences between Elizabethan and modern notions of authorship, but a 1599 reprint (Q2) does note the work as "Newly corrected by W. Shake-speare." Both Shakespeare and Hal (as "Henrie the Fift") appear on the title page of the 1600 quarto of *Part Two* (see p. xxi).

chief event was Henry's overthrow of a corrupt and increasingly eccentric Richard II—an action regarded as both justifiable and dishonorable, even treasonous. The powerful Percy family (Northumberland, Worcester, Hotspur) that helped Henry seize the crown from his cousin now chafes at the new King's lack of gratitude and remuneration; continuing conflicts with Wales and Scotland are a further aggravation to Henry; and a rival claimant, Sir Edmund Mortimer, is linked by marriage to both internal and external foes: Hotspur is married to Mortimer's sister, and Mortimer is married to the daughter of the Welsh rebel, Owen Glendower. Most personally distressing to Shakespeare's Henry is his son's riotous misbehavior.

As *Part One* opens, we hear an exhausted and demoralized King ("So shaken as we are, so wan with care" [1.1.1]) longing for clarity and singularity of purpose as he dreams of subsuming his violent times within a larger, providential narrative of Christian history. Yet the romantic tinge of his language as he imagines a redemptive crusade fought on "strands afar remote" exposes the distance of this fantasy from the immediate reality of power politics, betrayal, and civil conflict. The ideal of a phalanx of like-minded warriors, marching all one way to liberate the Holy Land, is compromised even as it is uttered; it is an enterprise "To be commenced" (1.1.4), a dream already deferred twelve months. It seems "bootless" even to speak of it (1.1.29). The fracture between providential and secular history troubles Shakespeare's kings no less than it does Renaissance philosophers and historians.

For all its uncertainty, however, the play never sinks into despair. It burgeons with life in complex, multiple structures that generate rather than stifle its energy. High solemnity, intrigue, and boisterous comedy occur where we might expect—respectively, in court, noble houses, and tavern—but these elements also intermingle within single scenes. Centuries of admirers, however opposite their readings, laud the "variety," "amplitude," and "polyvocal" quality of this world, the most comprehensive and nuanced image of social and political life the English stage had yet produced. Shakespeare achieves these effects both through sharp juxtaposition—as when the proud, aristocratic conspiracy ending of 1.3 gives way to the carrier's complaint about missing chamber pots at the start of 2.1— and through the prismatic quality of individual deeds, enacted by an array of characters.

This very array is a broad structure of meaning—at once dramatic, linguistic, political, and moral. In this masterful elaboration of parallels and parodies, of serious and comic action commenting implicitly on each other, Shakespeare is drawing on venerable conventions of English drama. Even so, his dramatic counterpoint of rulers, rebels, and revelers shows unprecedented resourcefulness.[1] At different junctures, King Henry and Falstaff become alternative fathers and kings; Hal and Hotspur, alternative "sons" of dishonor and honor; Hal and Francis, reluctant apprentices of high and low position; Francis and Hotspur, comical "parrot" and "paraquito" with equally predictable obsessions; Hotspur and Falstaff, horse-obsessed knights given to epic hyperbole or outrageous tall tales; squabbling highwaymen and suspicious rebels, reminders that there's no honor among thieves; and so on. Dyads also build to triads, a configuration that beckons some to imagine Hal learning and progressing toward a golden mean—between, say, the joyless Henry IV and the carnivalesque Falstaff, or between the compulsive chivalry of Hotspur and the corpulent self-indulgence of Falstaff. Shakespeare even has Hotspur and Falstaff sprawled before Hal at the end of the battle of Shrewsbury in a momentary tableau.

But such arrangements are deceptively neat. While they may reflect Shakespeare's fondness for morality plays, Aristotelian ethics, psychological analysis, or the more abstract pleasures of geometry, the vitality of the individuals involved breaks free of the schematic, like baroque statues gesturing beyond their architectural niches. Much of the play's power lies in the way Shakespeare forges an illusion of complex inner lives. These creations swell beyond predictable doctrine, engaging us in the urgency and irony of human motivation and aspiration.

The effect is achieved, in part, through a *discordia concors* of materials, the modeling of multifaceted beings who hint at, while frustrating, a full understanding. Prince Hal is intriguingly elusive in his first scene. His soliloquy at the end of 1.2 ("I know you all") establishes an intimacy with the audience, as soliloquies early in a play often do; but the "impure" mode of Elizabethan drama—shifting between symbolic and realistic—highlights our uncertainty about him. Is Hal stepping outside the moment, assuring us that he

---

[1]For concise summaries, see entries under Empson, *Pastoral*; Humphreys, *First Part*; and Mack in Further Reading.

is living out a "Wild Prince" fable (an apocryphal account that early became part of the Henry V legend), that he is only biding his time before mending his ways? Or is he revealing a more unsavory determination to exploit his present companions for his own greater glory? We may recognize a daunting intelligence and resolved will, but we can never be sure, even at Hal's greatest moments, of his sincerity toward others, or his understanding of himself.

Hotspur appears a simpler figure, but he has his own intricacy. The historical Hotspur was thirty-nine, two years older than the thirty-seven-year-old King, Hal's father. Hal is a mere sixteen. Shakespeare's decision (following Samuel Daniel's innovation) to make Hal and Hotspur the same age, and have the King wish they had been exchanged at birth, turns them into alter egos. In this pairing, Hotspur is no mere foil. A proud, frustrated aristocrat (a volatile and dangerous social type in Elizabethan England), he yearns for the glory of a chivalric past. An immediately engaging, charismatic dreamer who pictures himself "pluck[ing] bright honor from the pale-faced moon" (1.3.202), he is also intemperate, self-indulgent, and narcissistic. He evokes comparison to such troubled Shakespearean idealists as Hamlet and Brutus, but his extroverted compulsiveness also evokes an incongruously comic figure: Mercutio from *Romeo and Juliet*. They baffle their cooler-minded companions and fearlessly satirize their rivals; but their hyperkinetic imaginations, whether dreaming of fairy lore or of chivalric war, apprehend a world of figures whose outlet in high-spirited self-assertion makes tragedy inevitable. Hotspur will, appropriately, be recalled in *Part Two* both as a "mark and glass, copy and book, / That fashioned others" (2.3.31–32) and as one driven by "great imagination / Proper to madmen" which "led his powers to death" (1.3.31–32).

The character of Hotspur is further qualified by those with whom he interacts. Owen Glendower's self-mythologizing portents and prophecies make Hotspur look skeptically rational by contrast, even as he recklessly (and rudely) tweaks his important ally. Glendower, too, despite his limited time on stage, is richly suggestive: mystical, credulous, but also highly cultured and shrewd, angrily defensive one moment (3.1.118–23) and exquisitely lyrical the next (3.1.209–17), his range of tones anticipating those of a later magician, Prospero, as he leads the female characters on stage. As for the play's women, they are notoriously scarce—especially in the cold, loveless court of Henry IV. Yet they are impressive when they do appear, especially Lady Percy ("Kate"), who shows both strength of mind and reluctant subservience in her seriocomic quarrel with Hotspur (2.3). Occasionally the "feminine" is reduced to an ideological foil, a threat to masculine heroism, as in the early report of the Welshwomen's mutilation of the dead English (1.1.43–46). But Lady Percy, in two and a half rueful lines—"I fear my brother Mortimer doth stir / About his title, and hath sent for you / To line his enterprise" (2.3.77–79)—opens a humane, alternative perspective on the destructive, aristocratic ambition that drives the large movements of the day.

The play's greatest figure, in girth and reputation, is Falstaff (one of the Contexts sections is dedicated to the long fascination with his stupendous and unruly presence). Although there are numerous literary antecedents, none takes his measure. Even his supposed function as "misleader of youth" is misleading. His parodies of cultural voices—the court's dandified Euphuism, the Puritan's sanctimonious quotations and iterations—protect him, at least temporarily, from moral solemnity, even if they expose his unfitness for serious times. An audience supposedly wary of the world, the flesh, and the devil may welcome this "white-bearded Satan" (2.4.423) as much as it values the joy of life itself ("banish plump Jack, and banish all the world" [2.4.438]).[2] We are delighted and appalled by his inversion of the ideal *puer senex*—the humanist fusion of youthful energy with prudential wisdom—by his joining of infantile irresponsibility with decrepit decadence. Our engagement is only intensified when Falstaff triggers our ambivalence. His "catechism" on the emptiness of honor (5.1.129–39) and his claims for survival as the only legitimacy (5.4.114–20) evoke discomfort at their corrosive skepticism of all nonegoistic impulses; yet the demystifying bluntness also compels assent. Even Falstaff's depraved indifference to battlefield losses, a dark consequence of his greedy self-centeredness, reminds us that the war was not his idea to begin with. That was the achievement of more sober-blooded men.

---

[2]W. H. Auden goes further: Falstaff is "a comic symbol for the supernatural order of charity . . . until he is rejected he radiates happiness as Hal radiates power, and this happiness is without apparent cause, this untiring devotion to making others laugh becomes a comic image for a love which is absolutely self-giving" (*The Dyer's Hand*, 1963).

Shakespeare plots the dramatic action to be as multihued as its participants, even when the play appears headed for structural decisiveness. Hal's crucial reckonings with his two father figures, famously performed in jest in the tavern in 2.4 and in earnest before the King in 3.2, are prime examples.

The episode in the Boar's Head tavern begins by reminding us of Hal's simultaneous capacity for good fellowship and petty cruelty as he dangles false hopes before the eager-to-please apprentice, Francis. Falstaff's theatrics after the botched mugging on Gadshill—deploying, and milking laughs for, his role as braggart warrior—show his resourcefulness, his willingness even to court exposure in order to please. His hilariously subversive, metatheatrical conceits win the Hostess's peals of laughter at the "play extempore" no less than ours. Yet we never forget that sporting with the Prince of Wales is like toying with a big cat whose claws, as many have noted, can wound at any moment. Hal's seizing control of the game by exchanging roles—"Do thou stand for me, and I'll play my father" (2.4.394–95)—threatens the illusion of Falstaff's verbal omnipotence, his capacity for endless hyperbole, parody, and metamorphic wit. And it is psychologically pregnant. Assuming the voice of paternal anger, Hal both sharpens a condemnation of himself and deepens the usual mockery he indulges at his friend's expense. Falstaff's comic swagger becomes a fight for his life, a fight that Hal predicts, both in jest and in earnest, is doomed: "Banish plump Jack, and banish all the world." "I do, I will" (2.4.438–39).

The meeting of actual father and son two scenes later works, in a broad sense, as a "serious" version, its depth and power set off by its parodic anticipation in the tavern. Yet the contrast is also more nuanced. The Boar's Head contains a frisson of real danger, as we have seen, while Hal's confrontation with the King, for all its earnest political consequence, has its own distinctive mix of solemnity and playacting. The son's disingenuous self-excuse to the father's bitter, tearful reproach, matched to the King's sense of personal and political injury that will not be mollified until the Prince produces a high rhetorical vow to "redeem all this on Percy's head" (3.2.132), create a scene that is by turns pious and sanctimonious, heroic and calculating, moving and manipulative, redemptive and inauthentic. The King's pride in his own image management (a histrionic savviness that links him to his son more than he realizes) is curiously unnoted or only indirectly acknowledged by Hal, further accentuating, at the very moment of rapprochement, the silence between them. And if, by this scene's end, young Hal has pledged himself to the greater "business" of state, what can he possibly mean in the very next scene by his gloating remark, "I am good friends with my father and may do anything" (3.3.167–68)?

We might regard this announcement as a loose end or momentary slip on Shakespeare's part; but it is in such discontinuities—what the critic A. P. Rossiter calls the "ambivalence" or "dialectic" of Shakespeare's histories—that the play's most basic structure is revealed. Consider, for example, the decisive Battle of Shrewsbury. As the opposing forces mass, we witness the rebels' deterioration through defection and internal division, a process that began almost as soon as the conspiracy itself: the reluctant lord of 2.3; the comic bickering in the map scene of 3.1; Northumberland's suspicious illness and Glendower's delay of 4.1; Worcester's lie to Hotspur in 5.2. Yet, the action halts twice, not to instruct us once again that there is no honor among thieves but to remind us that perfectly coherent counter-narratives validate the rebel's claims (4.3 and 5.1), claims that the royalists scorn but never really refute. And finally, when we are granted the dramatic and symbolic satisfaction of a one-on-one combat between the two "Harrys," a climactic meeting of enemy twins or alter egos, Shakespeare makes the long-awaited encounter share the stage with Falstaff—first as cheerleader, then as floundering, overmatched combatant against "the Douglas."

The mingling of high and low, of kings and clowns, is a breach of stage decorum that Sir Philip Sidney complains of in one of the conservative moments of *An Apology for Poetry* (c. 1581–83, pub. 1595). Shakespeare places at the climax a most outrageous example. Comic and serious scenes have alternated up to now, but at this decisive moment, the modes are daringly simultaneous. Even that tableau of Hal bidding a rueful farewell to the two bodies stretched out at his feet, as if allegorizing the ethical mean shunning extremes, mutates into something else—grotesque farce or mythological parody. And if the wound Falstaff inflicts on the dead Hotspur's thigh recalls the Welshwomen's mutilation of corpses (reported in the opening scene), our sense of climactic closure is thrown open yet again.

This is only one of the play's many centrifugal forces. Of the King's closing speech, nineteenth-century critic Hartley Coleridge writes, "It is a conclusion in which nothing is concluded." We could say as much for the play as a whole. Yet, the final movement of *Henry IV, Part One* is as expansive as it is skeptical. If the practical, battlefield strategy of royal decoys reminds us, yet again, of the mere theatricality of power ("The King hath many marching in his coats" [5.3.25]; "I fear thou art another counterfeit" [5.4.35]), the tough, old King impresses us as an ambitious and pugnacious player. On the morning of the great battle, the bloody sun and blustery wind spell no fatal portents to him, but defiance: "Then with the losers let it sympathize, / For nothing can seem foul to those that win" (5.1.7–8). And while the Prince's deeper motives remain murky, his battlefield heroism—far beyond anything found in Holinshed—earns him the approval he has longed for and has promised us since his early soliloquy: "Thou hast *redeemed* thy lost opinion" (5.4.48, emphasis added). Shakespeare writes this redemption not to advance an ideology, Tudor or otherwise, but to show the combined powers of human will and mythmaking in action, the forces that make history.

Part Two

Henry IV, Part Two can stand on its own as a dramatic work, but it also keeps looking back to its predecessor. Critical comparison is inevitable—first for tone, and ultimately for aesthetic value. *Part Two* is darker and more cynical; its imagery of disease and disorder characterizes a generation of aging, limping, sleepless figures—Northumberland, Falstaff, Shallow, the King—no less than a fevered polity: "The commonwealth is sick," intones the Archbishop of York, who goes on to compare its populace to the proverbial sick dog that "wouldst eat [its] dead vomit up" (1.3). Some readers see the strangeness of *Part Two* as the unlucky effect of being a sequel to so striking a success. It has less energy, its jokes and situations repeated with less conviction, less fun, less nobility of purpose. The spectacle of Poins and Hal dressed as drawers in *Part Two* (2.4) scarcely matches Falstaff's tall tale of men in Kendal green or the "play extempore" in *Part One* (2.4). The sanctimonious treachery of the victory at Gaultree leaves a sour taste compared to the triumph at Shrewsbury, notwithstanding all the ironies.

And yet the challenges of *Part Two* exert a peculiar fascination. L. C. Knights considers it a breakthrough, "one of the first plays in which we recognize the great Shakespeare," especially for its development of a distinctive paradox: exuberant virtuosity shadowed by mutability and death.

The diversity that was a hallmark of *Part One*, a gloriously messy, quotidian world coexisting with grand deeds of historical import, returns with greater pungency. "Of all the plays, this most richly draws the panorama of national life," enthuses A. R. Humphreys. The tavern is a grittier place; by the play's end "a man or two" has been killed there (5.4.5–6). Yet the expanded female roles—more Mistress Quickly and a new character, prostitute Doll Tearsheet—create amid the new dimensions of decadence, disease, and double entendres surprising, if fleeting, moments of intimacy. First Doll then Quickly halt the squabbling and rough-housing to bid farewell, possibly forever, to the larcenous Falstaff: "Come, I'll be friends with thee, Jack. Thou art going to the wars, and whether I shall ever see thee again or no there is nobody cares"; "I have known thee these twenty-nine years come peascod time, but an honester and truer-hearted man—well, fare thee well" (2.4.59–61, 350–52). Pistol's swaggering may be a sad parody of Hotspur's zeal, but his absurdist jumble of bombast and bawdy tickled playgoers (as the advertisement on the 1600 Quarto's title page shows), lampooning both Shakespeare's dramatic rivals (especially Marlowe) and the serious, and seriously compromised, heroic language elsewhere in this play.

Even apparent digressions become theatrical high points: Falstaff's trip to Gloucestershire, once again to misuse the King's press and to visit his old schoolmate, the modestly corrupt Justice Shallow, produces striking moments. Shallow's exaggerated recollections of a wild youth, his head-shaking repetitions (part reflection, part doddering), and his alternation of melancholy and pragmatism ("Death, as the Psalmist saith, is certain to all, all shall die. How a good yoke of bullocks at Stamford fair?" [3.2.33–35]) are offered in a spirit both keenly satirical and warmly tolerant, thanks to a deftness of characterization. Shallow is a precursor to Polonius—shrewdness still glinting through encroaching senility. Falstaff sizes him up as his next mark—"a philosopher's two stones to me" (3.2.301)—but Shallow, despite his name, is not a complete fool and means to exploit Falstaff's connections at court. Their comic reunion

THE
Second part of Henrie

the fourth, continuing to his death,
and coronation of Henrie
the fift.

With the humours of fir Iohn Fal-
ſtaffe, *and ſwaggering*
Piſtoll.

As it hath been ſundrie times publikely
acted by the right honourable, the Lord
Chamberlaine his ſeruants.

Written by William Shakeſpeare.

LONDON

Printed by V.S. for Andrew Wiſe, and
William Aſpley.
1600.

Title page of 1600 Quarto.

is less a meeting of rogue and gull than of two wily, old operators circling each other for advantage. If only the rebels at Gaultree, caught up in their own optimistic rhetoric, were as alert to fraud.

The Falstaff–Shallow scenes are richly layered: good-humored amidst all the calculation. Falstaff waxes sinister, perhaps, when Pistol arrives with news of Hal's accession: "the laws of England are at my commandment." But he is also reflexively generous with his imagined fortune: "Master Robert Shallow, choose what office thou wilt in the land, 'tis thine" (5.3.129, 116–17). This generosity stands out in a drama where, for the most part, it is in short supply. Rumor is an ill-tempered Prologue who implicates the audience's very interest in plays as part of the world's degraded taste for fakery. The Earl of Northumberland enters next, having betrayed his son with his crafty sickness, then mounting an unconvincing display of grief at the news of his death. The Earl's hyperbolic cry, "Let order die," sounds like an amateur's version of Lear on the heath and deserves Lord Bardolph's comment about his "strainèd passion" (1.1.154, 161). (It will not be long before Shakespeare has Hamlet respond with similar tartness to Laertes' emoting at his sister's grave.) And while the Earl may be truly affected by the dire news (reversing false Rumor) that Hotspur has not really triumphed over Hal, there is a tinniness to his sentiment, a need not only to perform his sorrow for others but also to manufacture a passion for himself. His wife and Lady Percy will soon convince him of the need for discretion again, even as he insists on the vast forces within him, "As with the tide swelled up unto his height" (2.3.63).

This ambivalent, dissociative mood—of characters affecting or exploiting focused passions they cannot quite believe, yet cannot disavow—returns throughout this play. It is marked by the unstable uses of "suppose" and "supposed" at crucial junctures, where characters struggle to inspire conviction in themselves or in others despite continual reversals, betrayed expectations, and mistakes in judgment. Explaining why the failed rebellion might be revived, Morton proposes to his co-conspirators that a new ally, the Archbishop of York, will make all the difference. If their troops had felt dispiriting guilt because of the very word "rebellion," the presence of a Bishop now "Turns insurrection to religion. / Supposed sincere and holy in his thoughts, / He's followed both with body and with mind" (1.1.201–3). Some editions gloss "supposed" as something like "rightly believed"—an odd shunning of the skeptical sense, especially given its later uses in this play, let alone the slippery, self-defining Prologue of George Gascoigne's *Supposes* (1566): "A mistaking or imagination of one thing for another."

"Supposed" sincerity is one of the play's serious indeterminacies. If "supposed" means "rightly believed," one could take heart at the inspiring force of faith, even if the leaders were themselves misguided. If it means "erroneously believed" (*OED* 1), one confronts a bleaker case of commoners duped by the pious fictions of unscrupulous aristocrats. The most we can paraphrase is "believed with assurance" (*OED* 1b), aware that religion, like any legitimating morality, gets invoked because it works. For the soldiers, the cause must be perceived *as* genuine, but for the leaders, it need only be deployed *as if* genuine, a Machiavellian detachment understood by leaders on both sides. Yet even this detachment is not entirely certain. Are Prince John's praises to God and "Christian care" after his ruthless opportunism at Gaultree (4.2.112ff) a victor's unseemly gloating? Or do the praises bespeak so deep a need to believe as to hide a hypocrite's duplicity from himself?

While hypocrisy is omnipresent, it is never unalloyed. The epitome of a recurring wish for stability—or failing that, to take genuine, moral self-reckoning—is King Henry himself. He makes his belated first appearance about halfway through *Part Two*, wracked by insomnia, self-pity ("Uneasy lies the head that wears a crown" [3.1.31]) and strained self-justification ("necessity so bowed the state / That I and greatness were compelled to kiss" [3.1.73–74]). He then begins to consider more deeply the "revolution of the times." Fraught with geological imaginings—of the most substantial, earthly forms of land and sea leveling, melting or swelling out of shape—the King finds a broad context in which to lament a career of broken loyalties and betrayed friendships. If he avoids any direct confession of guilt, he also declines to blame others for his sorrows. He summons his deposed cousin Richard's "foul sin . . . break[ing] into corruption" not as partisan reproach but as a view of the human condition, a melancholy fact about political life and the shifts of fortune that ultimately compromise all parties and all participants.

The King's brooding echoes Shakespeare's sonnets on mutability, and the scene ends, as do the more optimistic of those sonnets, with a renewal of energy and purpose. But it also prepares for the second half of *Part Two*, in which critical scenes involve some of the most complex emotional and psychological material Shakespeare had yet explored. The key scenes are Hal's farewells to his two "fathers," the King and Falstaff, motions that convey both a gathering of future power and the threat of inevitable loss.

Shakespeare makes the first farewell, the passing of the crown (4.5), as uncomfortable as possible. Full of energy, Hal bursts in only to pull up embarrassed when he learns of his father's dire condition (a collapse of health ironically occasioned by news of victory). Hal's mistaken assumption about his father's death and his taking the crown are drawn from the chronicles, but with a difference. In these sources the Prince's share is minimized: other noblemen have already covered the King "with a linen cloth," thinking him dead. Shakespeare revises and expands the scene to give the King a sudden revival and a full, scathing condemnation of Hal's parricidal "wish," an eerie anticipation of Kafka's nightmarish tale "The Judgement." With a defensive, antiseptic claim for an absolute, unstained purity of motive, Hal labors to control the moment, to preserve his long-planned and soon-to-be-public upright image.

It is in both their interests to accept this defense. But after hearing his father's bleak, painful confession of the "indirect crook'd ways" (4.5.182) that brought him the crown and the bloodshed it still demands, Hal pushes the collaboration even further with an astonishing assertion:

> You won it, wore it, kept it, gave it me.
> Then plain and right must my possession be,
> Which I with more than with a common pain
> 'Gainst all the world will rightfully maintain.
> (4.5.219–22)

We know Hal too well by this point to think him inattentive or obtuse. He is using *then . . . must* ambiguously, coyly implying logical entailment but asserting hard, political necessity. Power may unify the realm, but only if legitimizing itself as "plain and right," lineal and continuous.[3]

---

[3]Contrast Holinshed's more terse account (Contexts, p. 251), as well as John Speed's blunt version: "Howsoever it was got," said the Prince, "I mean to keep and defend it . . ." (*The History of Britain*, 1611).

Hal's determination anticipates the heroic resolve and dubious morality of *Henry V*, the last play of the tetralogy. In *Henry IV, Part Two*, his sobriety offers a resting point amidst the turmoils of court and battlefield, though we know rest can be only temporary. When the old King beckons, "Come hither, Harry, sit thou by my bed" (4.5.179), he gives his son both a blessing and a curse. On his deathbed, the King predicts better times even as he recalls restless violence ("Which daily grew to quarrel and to bloodshed, / Wounding supposèd peace"), hollow playacting ("all my reign hath been but as a scene / Acting that argument" [4.5.192–93, 195–96]), and the brutal transformation of civilizing *amicitia*: "all my friends, which thou must make thy friends, / Have but their stings and teeth newly ta'en out" (4.5.202–3). His best advice is to project violence overseas: "Be it thy course to busy giddy minds / With foreign quarrels" (4.5.211–12). His final words voice the play's most notorious "suppose." Learning that the room in which he fainted is called "Jerusalem," Henry IV asks to be returned there:

> Laud be to God! Even there my life must end.
> It hath been prophesied to me many years
> I should not die but in Jerusalem,
> Which vainly I supposed the Holy Land.
> But bear me to that chamber; there I'll lie.
> In that Jerusalem shall Harry die.
>
> (4.5.233–38)

Shakespeare takes this anecdote from Holinshed and makes the most of its irony. Henry's holy praise ("Laud") is his final assertion of the providential frame for which he hoped at the beginning of *Part One*, now fulfilled in name—or, in name only—thanks to the equivocal nature of such predictions. The somber, nominalist jest is not the moment's only shadow. We also learn the hitherto undisclosed motive that has lurked behind the King's repeated insistence on going to Jerusalem, the one place where, it has been prophesied, he will die. Was his impulse political necessity, pious consummation, or guilt-ridden suicide? If Henry's uneasy isolation and insomnia look forward to Macbeth's sufferings, even Macbeth clings to prophecies that promise him continued life.

Hal's second farewell to a father has acquired its own title, thanks to A. C. Bradley's renowned essay, "The Rejection of Falstaff"

(Contexts, p. 356). The necessity of this rejection and the priggishness of the new King's remarks to his supposed "misleaders" may be affirmed, denied, or debated, but one development is generally agreed upon: Falstaff the entertainer faces tougher and tougher audiences.

Having crowned himself the monarch of wit in his first appearance ("I am not only witty in myself, but the cause that wit is in other men" [1.2.8–9]), he stands ready to defend those values (4.3.80–94). Despite hints of illness and impotence, his comic vitality never wavers, and even his need to "turn diseases to commodity" never threatens him with a loss of material. But there is a devolution. His Page sasses him; his symbolic rival, the Chief Justice, barely tolerates him; Prince John eyes him soberly; and the shrewd, resentful Poins nails the tacit bargain: "he will drive you out of your revenge and turn all to a merriment, if you take not the heat" (2.4.271–72). The trick is to silence Falstaff's endless capacity for invention, the "fantastical lies" that charmed us through both plays. And so when Falstaff rushes to meet with his high invention, "King Hal" (5.5.40), surveying his own road-stained, sweaty body as one more commodity to be used to advantage ("this poor show doth better. This doth infer the zeal I had to see him" [5.5.12–13]), King Henry V shuts him down with a cold, public declaration: "I know thee not, old man" (5.5.46). Marking him an outsider and a Pauline allegory of sin (Ephesians 2.4), Hal can't resist a final jesting cruelty: "Know the grave doth gape / For thee thrice wider than for other men" (5.5.52–53).

Falstaff never likes to be reminded of his end, but he sees this verbal *memento mori* as too perfectly set not to cue an endearing rejoinder on his own fatness. But it is also a perfectly laid trap. The King anticipates the joke and counters it before it can be delivered: "Reply not to me with a fool-born jest." It is a demonstration of power and of a new era of decorum, and Falstaff himself is forced to acknowledge it. His cornucopian wit, always "full of nimble, fiery, and delectable shapes," shrinks to bitterly laconic chit: "Master Shallow, I owe you a thousand pound." The deflation of Falstaff—at once a political necessity and an end to the revels so close to the life of the theater itself—brings, despite Prince John's jaunty approval and the patriotic (though unreliable) Epilogue, a stark and disturbing conclusion to *Henry IV*, the two-part sequence that conveys Prince Hal to his destiny as Henry V.

Table of Dates

1459	Sir John Fastolf (who appears in *Henry VI, Part One* and whose name is revived to replace Oldcastle's in *Henry IV, Part One*) dies.

* * *

1558	Elizabeth I becomes Queen of England.
1564	William Shakespeare is born at Stratford-upon-Avon.
1569–70	The failed Northern Rebellion, a politically and religiously motivated attempt to install Mary Queen of Scots as Elizabeth's successor, is led by the still-powerful Percy family (including Henry Percy, eighth Earl of Northumberland).
1582	Shakespeare marries Anne Hathaway.
1583	Shakespeare's first daughter, Susannah, is born six months after his marriage.
1585	Shakespeare's twins, Judith and Hamnet, are born.
1585–92	Shakespeare's "lost years."
1587	Raphael Holinshed's *Chronicles* (first edition, 1577) appears in an expanded and revised second edition, a major source for Shakespeare's *Henry IV* plays and others.
1588	England defeats the Spanish Armada.
1592	Robert Greene resentfully calls Shakespeare an "upstart crow," the earliest extant reference to his career in the London theater.
1594	Shakespeare's acting company, The Lord Chamberlain's Men, is formed.
c. 1594–98	The *Famous Victories of Henry the Fifth* (or some version of it) appears, a probable source for Shakespeare's *Henry IV, Parts One* and *Two* and *Henry V*.
1595	The first version of Samuel Daniel's *The First Four Books of the Civil Wars Between the Two Houses of Lancaster and York* is published, an important source for Shakespeare.
1595–96	Shakespeare's *Richard II* inaugurates what modern critics would call the Second (or Lancastrian) Tetralogy.

1596–97	*Henry IV, Part One* is first performed.
1597–98	*Henry IV, Part Two* is first performed.
1598	The first two quarto editions of *Henry IV, Part One* are published in a single year. This play would eventually appear in nine quarto editions, two after the 1623 Folio—an extraordinary number that, together with numerous contemporary references, confirms its great popularity.
1598–99	*Henry V* is first produced, completing the Second Tetralogy.
1599	The Globe Theatre opens.
1600	*Henry IV, Part Two* is published for the first time; unlike *Part One*, it would not be reprinted until the 1623 Folio.
1601	Followers of the Earl of Essex pay Shakespeare's company to perform a play (probably Shakespeare's) about the deposing of Richard II the day before their doomed attempt to overthrow Queen Elizabeth I; the group includes Charles Percy, a descendent of Hotspur.
1603	Death of Elizabeth I; coronation of James I (James VI of Scotland); Shakespeare's company becomes The King's Men.
1616	William Shakespeare dies at Stratford-upon-Avon.
1623	*Mr William Shakespeares Comedies, Histories, & Tragedies* (now often called the First Folio) is published by two senior actors in Shakespeare's company, for the first time grouping Shakespeare's ten plays concerning medieval English history as a distinct genre.
1649–60	Theaters closed after Puritan revolution, but scenes featuring Falstaff continue to be performed as short entertainments.
1660	Theaters reopen with the Restoration of the monarchy, and *Henry IV, Part One* retains popularity.
1851	Sequential production in Germany of *Henry IV, Parts One* and *Two* and *Henry V* becomes the first recorded staging of a Henriad cycle.

Selective Genealogy[1]

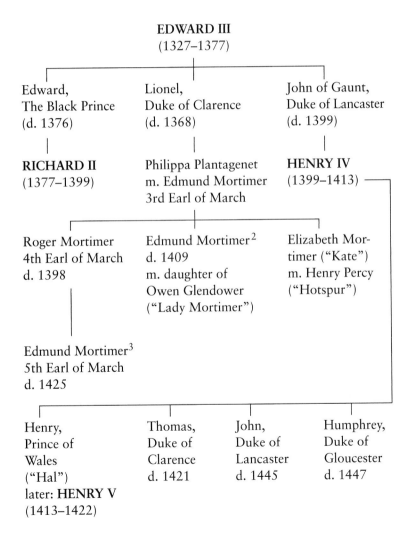

EDWARD III
(1327–1377)

Edward,
The Black Prince
(d. 1376)

Lionel,
Duke of Clarence
(d. 1368)

John of Gaunt,
Duke of Lancaster
(d. 1399)

RICHARD II
(1377–1399)

Philippa Plantagenet
m. Edmund Mortimer
3rd Earl of March

HENRY IV
(1399–1413)

Roger Mortimer
4th Earl of March
d. 1398

Edmund Mortimer[2]
d. 1409
m. daughter of
Owen Glendower
("Lady Mortimer")

Elizabeth Mortimer ("Kate")
m. Henry Percy
("Hotspur")

Edmund Mortimer[3]
5th Earl of March
d. 1425

Henry,
Prince of
Wales
("Hal")
later: **HENRY V**
(1413–1422)

Thomas,
Duke of
Clarence
d. 1421

John,
Duke of
Lancaster
d. 1445

Humphrey,
Duke of
Gloucester
d. 1447

[1]"Edward III had seven sons," John of Gaunt is reminded in *Richard II.* This genealogy traces the descent of the three most relevant to the *Henry IV* plays. Kings are in CAPITALS; dates in parentheses are the years of reign; "d." = died; "m." = married. For more complete tables, see David Bevington, *The Necessary Shakespeare* (Longman, 2001), Peter Saccio, *Shakespeare's English Kings* (Oxford Univ. Press, 1977, 2000), and Oscar James Campbell and Edward Quinn, *The Reader's Encyclopedia of Shakespeare* (Thomas Y. Crowell, 1966).

[2]Shakespeare follows Holinshed's two errors about this Edmund Mortimer, who is defeated by and defects to Glendower's side: conflating him with his nephew, Edmund Mortimer, 5th Earl of March, and mistakenly granting him the title of "Earl of March." Edmund's father, yet another Edmund, was the 3rd Earl of March; his elder brother, Roger, was the 4th, his nephew, the 5th.

[3]This Edmund was named by Richard II as the next in line to the kingship after the death of his father, Roger Mortimer. Edmund was 6 years old at the time.

HIGHLANDS

North
Sea

SCOTLAND

Loch
Lomond
Dunfermline
St. Andrews
Glasgow
Firth of Forth
Edinburgh
Clyde R.

North Channel

Arran
Is.

Holmedon
(Humbleton)
Cheviot Hills
Workworth
Castle

NORTHUMBERLAND
ULSTER
Tyne R.

Solway Firth

△WESTMORELAND

Isle
of Man

Ouse R.
Gaultree
Forest
York

Irish Sea

Anglesey

Humber R.
Ravenspur

Mersey R.
Sherwood
Forest
Trent R.

ENGLAND

Dublin

St. George's Channel

Mt.
Snowdon

The
Fens

The
Wash

WALES

Shrewsbury

Cambrian Mts.

Coventry
Warwick
Ouse R.
Cambridge

Severn R.

Malvern
Hills
Avon R.
Stratford-
on-Avon
St.
Albans

Wye R.
GLOUCESTERSHIRE
Oxford

Milford
Haven

London
Bristol
Greenwich
North
Downs
Canterbury
Bath
Salisbury
Plain
Windsor
Penshurst
Dover

Celtic
Sea

Stonehenge
KENT
Strait of Dover

Salisbury
Winchester
Southampton
Hastings

Dartmoor

Exeter

Isle of
Wight

Blackmoor

Plymouth

Land's
End
Plymouth
Sound

St. Michael's
Mount

English Channel

The First Part of
KING HENRY
THE FOURTH

by William Shakespeare

The First Part of
KING HENRY
THE FOURTH

[*Dramatis Personae*

KING HENRY THE FOURTH
PRINCE HENRY, *Prince of Wales, heir to the throne,*
    also referred to as Hal and Harry } *sons of the King*
PRINCE JOHN OF LANCASTER

EARL OF WESTMORLAND } *loyal to the King*
SIR WALTER BLUNT

EARL OF NORTHUMBERLAND, *Henry Percy*
HARRY PERCY (HOTSPUR), *his son*
EARL OF WORCESTER, *Northumberland's younger brother*
LORD MORTIMER, *Edmund Mortimer, also referred to as the*
    Earl of March, named by Richard II heir to the throne } *rebels against the King*
OWEN GLENDOWER
EARL OF DOUGLAS, *Archibald Douglas*
SIR RICHARD VERNON
ARCHBISHOP OF YORK, *Richard Scroop*
SIR MICHAEL, *a member of the Archbishop's household*

LADY PERCY, *Hotspur's wife and Mortimer's sister, also referred to*
    as Kate
LADY MORTIMER, *Mortimer's wife and Glendower's daughter*

SIR JOHN FALSTAFF

NED POINS

BARDOLPH

PETO

GADSHILL, *arranger of the highway robbery*

HOSTESS OF THE TAVERN, *Mistress Quickly*

FRANCIS, *a drawer, or tapster*

VINTNER, *or tavern keeper*

FIRST CARRIER

SECOND CARRIER

OSTLER, *or stable groom*

CHAMBERLAIN

FIRST TRAVELER

SHERIFF

SERVANT *to Hotspur*

MESSENGER

SECOND MESSENGER

Soldiers, Travelers, Lords, Attendants

SCENE: *England and Wales*]

ACT 1
SCENE 1

*Enter the King, Lord John of Lancaster, [the] Earl of
Westmorland, [Sir Walter Blunt,] with others*

KING   So shaken as we are, so wan with care,
    Find we° a time for frighted° peace to pant,
    And breathe short-winded accents° of new broils°

1.1. Location: The royal court. Summary: Exhausted by conflict with neighboring
Wales and Scotland, King Henry anticipates a deferred crusade to Jerusalem.
Hopeful news, however, is crossed by frustration and doubt. His powerful allies, the
Percy family, have their own agenda, refusing to deliver their Scottish prisoners, and
their success on his behalf, credited to young Harry Percy (called Hotspur), further
torments him by recalling the dishonor of his own son, also named Harry.
2 Find we let us find | **frighted** frightened   **3 breathe short-winded accents** speak,
even though we are out of breath | **accents** words | **broils** battles

To be commenced in strands afar remote.°
No more the thirsty entrance° of this soil   5
Shall daub° her lips with her own children's blood;
No more shall trenching° war channel her fields
Nor bruise her flowerets with the armèd hoofs
Of hostile paces.° Those opposèd eyes,
Which, like the meteors of a troubled heaven,°   10
All of one nature, of one substance bred,
Did lately meet in the intestine° shock
And furious close° of civil° butchery,
Shall now in mutual well-beseeming ranks
March all one way and be no more opposed   15
Against acquaintance, kindred, and allies.
The edge of war, like an ill-sheathèd knife,
No more shall cut his° master. Therefore, friends,
As far as to the sepulcher of Christ—
Whose soldier now, under whose blessèd cross   20
We are impressèd° and engaged to fight—
Forthwith a power° of English shall we levy,
Whose arms were molded in their mother's° womb
To chase these pagans in those holy fields
Over whose acres walked those blessèd feet   25
Which fourteen hundred years ago were nailed
For our advantage on the bitter cross.
But this our purpose now is twelve month old,
And bootless° 'tis to tell you we will go.
Therefore we meet not now.° Then let me hear   30
Of° you, my gentle cousin° Westmorland,
What yesternight our council did decree
In forwarding this dear expedience.°

---

4 **strands afar remote** far-off shores, of the Holy Land (to which, at the end of *Richard II*, Henry has pledged himself to a crusade)   5 **thirsty entrance** parched mouth   6 **daub** coat, smear   7 **trenching** cutting, plowing   9 **paces** horses' tread   10 **heaven** (heavenly anomalies were thought by some to portend earthly disturbances) [RL]   12 **intestine** internal   13 **close** hand-to-hand encounter | **civil** (as in "civil war")   18 **his** its   21 **impressèd** conscripted   22 **power** army   23 **their mother's** England's, but also suggesting *their mothers'*   29 **bootless** useless   30 **Therefore . . . now** that is not the reason for our present meeting   31 **Of** from | **gentle cousin** noble kinsman   33 **dear expedience** urgent expedition

WESTMORLAND   My liege, this haste was hot in question,°
        And many limits of the charge° set down   35
        But yesternight, when all athwart° there came
        A post° from Wales loaden° with heavy news,
        Whose worst was that the noble Mortimer,
        Leading the men of Herefordshire to fight
        Against the irregular and wild° Glendower,   40
        Was by the rude hands of that Welshman taken,
        A thousand of his people butcherèd—
        Upon whose dead corpse° there was such misuse,
        Such beastly shameless transformation,°
        By those Welshwomen done as may not be   45
        Without much shame retold or spoken of.
KING   It seems then that the tidings of this broil
        Brake off our business for the Holy Land.
WESTMORLAND   This matched with other° did, my gracious lord;
        For more uneven° and unwelcome news   50
        Came from the north, and thus it did import:
        On Holy Rood Day,° the gallant Hotspur there,
        Young Harry Percy, and brave Archibald,
        That ever-valiant and approvèd° Scot,
        At Holmedon° met, where they did spend   55
        A sad and bloody hour,
        As by° discharge of their artillery
        And shape of likelihood° the news was told;
        For he that brought them,° in the very heat
        And pride° of their contention did take horse,   60
        Uncertain of the issue any way.
KING   Here is a dear, a true industrious friend,
        Sir Walter Blunt,° new lighted from his horse,

---

34 hot in question being hotly debated   **35 limits . . . charge** particulars of military responsibility   **36 athwart** at cross purposes, contrarily   **37 post** messenger | **loaden** laden   **40 irregular and wild** (*irregular* and *wild* suggest "guerilla" tactics [Kittredge] as well as savagery; cf. *rude*, l. 41, and *beastly*, l. 44) [RL]   **43 corpse** corpses   **44 transformation** mutilation   **49 other** other news   **50 uneven** disconcerting, distressing   **52 Holy Rood Day** September 14   **54 approvèd** proved by experience   **55 Holmedon** Humbleton in Northumberland   **57 by** judging from **58 shape of likelihood** likely outcome   **59 them** the news   **60 pride** height   **62–3 Here . . . Blunt** (whether Blunt enters at the start of the scene, or now, or possibly not at all, is not certain in the original text)

Stained with the variation of each soil
Betwixt that Holmedon and this seat of ours;   65
And he hath brought us smooth° and welcome news.
The Earl of Douglas is discomfited;°
Ten thousand bold Scots, two-and-twenty knights,
Balked° in their own blood, did Sir Walter see
On Holmedon's plains. Of prisoners, Hotspur took   70
Mordake,° Earl of Fife and eldest son
To beaten Douglas, and the Earl of Atholl,
Of Murray, Angus, and Menteith.
And is not this an honorable spoil?
A gallant prize? Ha, cousin, is it not?   75
WESTMORLAND   In faith, it is a conquest for a prince to boast of.
KING   Yea, there thou mak'st me sad, and mak'st me sin
In envy that my lord Northumberland
Should be the father to so blest a son—
A son who is the theme of honor's tongue,   80
Amongst a grove the very straightest plant,°
Who is sweet Fortune's minion° and her pride,
Whilst I, by looking on the praise of him,
See riot° and dishonor stain the brow
Of my young Harry. Oh, that it could be proved   85
That some night-tripping° fairy had exchanged
In cradle clothes our children where they lay,
And called mine Percy, his Plantagenet!°
Then would I have his Harry, and he mine.
But let him° from my thoughts. What think you, coz,°   90
Of this young Percy's pride? The prisoners
Which he in this adventure hath surprised°
To his own use° he keeps, and sends me word
I shall have none but Mordake,° Earl of Fife.

---

66 **smooth** pleasant   67 **discomfited** defeated   69 **Balked** heaped up in balks, or ridges   71 **Mordake** Murdoch, son of the Earl of Albany   81 **plant** young tree   82 **minion** favorite   84 **riot** debauchery   86 **night-tripping** moving nimbly in the night   88 **Plantagenet** (family name of English royalty since Henry II)   90 **let him** let him go | **coz** cousin, kinsman   92 **surprised** ambushed, captured   93 **To . . . use** to collect ransom for them   94 **none but Mordake** (since Mordake was of royal blood, being grandson to Robert II of Scotland, Hotspur could not claim him as his prisoner according to the law of arms)

WESTMORLAND   This is his uncle's teaching. This is Worcester,   95
  Malevolent to you in all aspects,°
  Which makes him prune himself° and bristle up
  The crest of youth against your dignity.
KING   But I have sent for him to answer this;
  And for this cause awhile we must neglect   100
  Our holy purpose to Jerusalem.
  Cousin, on Wednesday next our council we
  Will hold at Windsor. So inform the lords.
  But come yourself with speed to us again,
  For more is to be said and to be done   105
  Than out of anger can be utterèd.
WESTMORLAND   I will, my liege.   *Exeunt*

ACT 1
SCENE 2

Enter Prince of Wales and Sir John Falstaff

FALSTAFF   Now, Hal, what time of day is it, lad?
PRINCE   Thou art so fat-witted with drinking of old sack,° and
  unbuttoning thee after supper, and sleeping upon benches
  after noon, that thou hast forgotten° to demand that truly
  which thou wouldst truly know. What a devil° hast thou to   5
  do with the time of the day? Unless hours were cups of sack,
  and minutes capons, and clocks the tongues of bawds, and
  dials° the signs of leaping houses,° and the blessed sun

96 **Malevolent . . . aspects** (1) implacably hostile to you (2) in astrological terms, a planet in a disobedient orbit, ominous as seen from every angle   97 **Which . . . himself** which teaching makes Hotspur preen himself (as a falcon preens its feathers)
1.2. Location: London, perhaps in an apartment of the Prince's. **Summary:** Prince Hal and Sir John Falstaff banter, perhaps after a late night's revelry. Veering between playful and sharp mockery, an ingratiating Falstaff spars with an amused but cagy Hal. Poins proposes a robbery that will end as a joke at Falstaff's expense. Hal agrees to join in but, once alone, he soliloquizes about his truancy as a ploy to make his later redemption appear more remarkable.
2 **sack** a Spanish white wine (a favorite of Falstaff's; so called from *vin sec* = dry wine; the term also prepares for later word plays on "plunder" and penitential "sackcloth") [RL]   4 **forgotten** forgotten how   5 **a devil** in the devil   8 **dials** clocks | **leaping houses** houses of prostitution

himself a fair hot wench in flame-colored taffeta,° I see no
reason why thou shouldst be so superfluous° to demand the 10
time of the day.

FALSTAFF Indeed, you come near me now,° Hal, for we that
take purses go by° the moon and the seven stars,° and not
by Phoebus, "he, that wandering knight so fair."° And I
prithee, sweet wag, when thou art king, as, God save Thy 15
Grace°—Majesty I should say, for grace thou wilt have
none—

PRINCE What, none?

FALSTAFF No, by my troth,° not so much as will serve to be
prologue to an egg and butter.° 20

PRINCE Well, how then? Come, roundly, roundly.°

FALSTAFF Marry,° then, sweet wag,° when thou art king, let not
us that are squires of the night's body be called thieves of the
day's beauty.° Let us be Diana' foresters,° gentlemen of the
shade, minions° of the moon; and let men say we be men of 25
good government,° being governed, as the sea is, by our
noble and chaste mistress the moon, under whose
countenance° we steal.°

PRINCE Thou sayest well, and it holds well° too, for the fortune
of us that are the moon's men doth ebb and flow like the sea, 30
being governed, as the sea is, by the moon. As, for proof,
now: a purse of gold most resolutely snatched on Monday
night and most dissolutely spent on Tuesday morning, got
with swearing "Lay by"° and spent with crying "Bring in,"°

---

9 **taffeta** (commonly worn by prostitutes) 10 **superfluous** (1) unnecessarily concerned (2) self-indulgent 12 **you . . . now** you've scored a point on me 13 **go by** (1) travel by the light of (2) tell time by | **the seven stars** the Pleiades 14 **Phoebus . . . fair** (Phoebus, god of the sun, is here equated with the wandering knight of a ballad or popular romance) 16 **Grace** royal highness (with pun on spiritual *grace* and also on the *grace* or blessing before a meal) 19 **troth** faith 20 **prologue . . . butter** grace before a brief meal 21 **roundly** out with it 22 **Marry** indeed (literally, "by the Virgin Mary") | **wag** joker 22–4 **let . . . beauty** let not us who are attendants on the goddess of night, members of her household, be blamed for stealing daylight by sleeping in the daytime 24 **Diana's foresters** (an elegant name for thieves by night; Diana is goddess of the moon and the hunt) 25 **minions** favorites 26 **government** (1) conduct (2) commonwealth 28 **countenance** (1) face (2) patronage, approval | **steal** (1) move stealthily (2) rob 29 **it holds well** the comparison is apt 34 **Lay by** (a cry of highwaymen, like "Hands up!") | **Bring in** (an order given to a waiter in a tavern)

now in as low an ebb as the foot of the ladder° and by and by   35
in as high a flow as the ridge° of the gallows.
FALSTAFF   By the Lord, thou say'st true, lad. And is not my
hostess of the tavern a most sweet wench?
PRINCE   As the honey of Hybla,° my old lad of the castle.° And
is not a buff jerkin° a most sweet robe of durance?°   40
FALSTAFF   How now, how now, mad wag, what, in thy quips and
thy quiddities?° What a plague have I to do with a buff jerkin?
PRINCE   Why, what a pox° have I to do with my hostess of the
tavern?
FALSTAFF   Well, thou hast called her to a reckoning° many a   45
time and oft.
PRINCE   Did I ever call for thee to pay thy part?
FALSTAFF   No, I'll give thee thy due, thou hast paid all there.
PRINCE   Yea, and elsewhere, so far as my coin would stretch,
and where it would not I have used my credit.   50
FALSTAFF   Yea, and so used it that, were it not here apparent
that thou art heir apparent—But I prithee, sweet wag, shall
there be gallows standing in England when thou art king?
And resolution° thus fubbed° as it is with the rusty curb of
old father Antic° the law? Do not thou, when thou art king,   55
hang a thief.
PRINCE   No, thou shalt.
FALSTAFF   Shall I? Oh, rare!° By the Lord, I'll be a brave° judge.
PRINCE   Thou judgest false already. I mean, thou shalt have the
hanging of the thieves,° and so become a rare° hangman.   60
FALSTAFF   Well, Hal, well; and in some sort it jumps with my
humor° as well as waiting in the court,° I can tell you.

---

35 **ladder** (1) pier ladder (2) gallows ladder   36 **ridge** crossbar   39 **Hybla** (a town,
famed for its honey, in Sicily near Syracuse) | **old . . . castle** (1) a roisterer (2) the name,
Sir John Oldcastle, borne by Falstaff in an earlier version of this play   40 **buff jerkin** a
leather jacket worn by officers of the law | **durance** (1) imprisonment (2) durability,
durable cloth   42 **quiddities** subtleties of speech   43 **pox** syphilis (here, *what a pox*
is used as an expletive, like "what the devil")   45 **reckoning** settlement of the bill
(with bawdy suggestion that is continued in *pay thy part* and *my coin would stretch*)
54 **resolution** courage (of a highwayman) | **fubbed** cheated   55 **Antic** buffoon
58 **rare** splendid | **brave** excellent   59–60 **have . . . thieves** (1) be in charge of hanging
thieves (or protecting them from hanging) (2) hang like other thieves   60 **rare** (1) rarely
used (2) excellent   61–2 **jumps . . . humor** suits my temperament   62 **waiting in the
court** being in attendance at the royal court

PRINCE   For obtaining of suits?°

FALSTAFF   Yea, for obtaining of suits, whereof the hangman
hath no lean wardrobe. 'Sblood,° I am as melancholy as a   65
gib cat° or a lugged bear.°

PRINCE   Or an old lion, or a lover's lute.

FALSTAFF   Yea, or the drone of a Lincolnshire bagpipe.

PRINCE   What sayest thou to a hare,° or the melancholy of
Moorditch?°   70

FALSTAFF   Thou hast the most unsavory similes, and art indeed
the most comparative,° rascalliest, sweet young prince. But
Hal, I prithee, trouble me no more with vanity.° I would to
God thou and I knew where a commodity° of good names°
were to be bought. An old lord of the council rated° me the   75
other day in the street about you, sir, but I marked him not;
and yet he talked very wisely, but I regarded him not; and
yet he talked wisely, and in the street too.

PRINCE   Thou didst well, for wisdom cries out in the streets and
no man regards it.°   80

FALSTAFF   Oh, thou hast damnable iteration,° and art indeed
able to corrupt a saint. Thou hast done much harm upon
me, Hal, God forgive thee for it. Before I knew thee, Hal, I
knew nothing;° and now am I, if a man should speak truly,
little better than one of the wicked. I must give over this life,   85
and I will give it over. By the Lord, an° I do not I am a
villain. I'll be damned for never a king's son in Christendom.

PRINCE   Where shall we take a purse tomorrow, Jack?

FALSTAFF   Zounds,° where thou wilt, lad, I'll make one.° An I
do not, call me villain and baffle° me.   90

PRINCE   I see a good amendment of life in thee—from praying
to purse taking.

---

63 **suits** petitions (but Falstaff uses the word to mean suits of clothes; clothes
belonging to an executed man were given to the executioner)   65 **'Sblood** by his
(Christ's) blood   66 **gib cat** tomcat | **lugged bear** bear led by a chain and baited
by dogs   69 **hare** (a proverbially melancholy animal)   70 **Moorditch** (a foul
ditch draining Moorfields, outside London walls)   72 **comparative** given to
abusive comparisons   73 **vanity** worldliness   74 **commodity** supply | **names**
reputations   75 **rated** chastised   79–80 **wisdom . . . regards it** (Hal paraphrases
Proverbs 1.20–4, "Wisdom crieth without, and putteth forth her voice in the
streets . . . and no man regarded," in jocose reply to Falstaff's mock
sanctimoniousness)   81 **iteration** repetition (of biblical texts, with a neat twist)
84 **nothing** no evil   86 **an** if   89 **Zounds** by his (Christ's) wounds | **make one**
be one of the party   90 **baffle** publicly disgrace

FALSTAFF Why, Hal, 'tis my vocation,° Hal. 'Tis no sin for a man to labor in his vocation.

Enter Poins

Poins! Now shall we know if Gadshill° have set a match.° 95
Oh, if men were to be saved by merit,° what hole in hell
were hot enough for him? This is the most omnipotent°
villain that ever cried "Stand!"° to a true man.°

PRINCE Good morrow, Ned.

POINS Good morrow, sweet Hal.—What says Monsieur 100
Remorse? What says Sir John, Sack-and-Sugar Jack? How
agrees the devil and thee about thy soul that thou soldest
him on Good Friday last for a cup of Madeira and a cold
capon's leg?

PRINCE Sir John stands to° his word; the devil shall have his 105
bargain, for he was never yet a breaker of proverbs. He will
give the devil his due.

POINS Then art thou damned for keeping thy word with the
devil.

PRINCE Else° he had been damned for cozening° the devil. 110

POINS But my lads, my lads, tomorrow morning, by four
o'clock early, at Gad's Hill,° there are pilgrims going to
Canterbury with rich offerings and traders riding to London
with fat purses. I have vizards° for you all; you have horses
for yourselves. Gadshill lies° tonight in Rochester. I have 115
bespoke° supper tomorrow night in Eastcheap.° We may
do it as secure as sleep. If you will go, I will stuff your
purses full of crowns;° if you will not, tarry at home and
be hanged.

---

93 vocation (a favorite term of the reforming Protestant ministers to describe the function or station to which one is called by God; Falstaff comically misapplies it to justify highway robbing)   **95 Gadshill** (the name of one of the highwaymen) | **set a match** arranged a robbery   **96 by merit** according to their deservings rather than by God's grace   **97 omnipotent** unparalleled, utter   **98 "Stand!"** "stand and deliver!" hand over your money | **true man** honest citizen   **105 stands to** keeps   **110 Else** otherwise | **cozening** cheating   **112 Gad's Hill** (location near Rochester on the road from London to Canterbury; one of the highwaymen is called Gadshill)   **114 vizards** masks   **115 lies** lodges   **116 bespoke** ordered | **Eastcheap** market district in London, with many taverns   **118 crowns** gold coins

FALSTAFF Hear ye, Yedward,° if I tarry at home and go not, I'll   120
hang you for going.°

POINS You will, chops?°

FALSTAFF Hal, wilt thou make one?

PRINCE Who, I rob? I a thief? Not I, by my faith.

FALSTAFF There's neither honesty, manhood, nor good fellowship   125
in thee, nor thou cam'st not of the blood royal, if thou
darest not stand for ten shillings.°

PRINCE Well then, once in my days I'll be a madcap.

FALSTAFF Why, that's well said.

PRINCE Well, come what will, I'll tarry at home.   130

FALSTAFF By the Lord, I'll be a traitor then, when thou art king.

PRINCE I care not.

POINS Sir John, I prithee leave the Prince and me alone. I will
lay him down such reasons for this adventure that he shall go.

FALSTAFF Well, God give thee the spirit of persuasion and him   135
the ears of profiting, that what thou speakest may move
and what he hears may be believed, that the true prince
may, for recreation sake, prove a false thief; for the poor
abuses of the time want countenance.° Farewell. You shall
find me in Eastcheap.   140

PRINCE Farewell, thou latter spring! Farewell, All-hallow
summer!°   [*Exit Falstaff*]

POINS Now, my good sweet honey lord, ride with us
tomorrow. I have a jest to execute that I cannot manage
alone. Falstaff, Peto, Bardolph, and Gadshill shall rob those   145
men that we have already waylaid°—yourself and I will not
be there—and when they have the booty, if you and I do not
rob them, cut this head off from my shoulders.

PRINCE How shall we part with them in setting forth?

POINS Why, we will set forth before or after them and appoint   150
them a place of meeting, wherein it is at our pleasure° to

---

120 **Yedward** (nickname for *Edward*, Poins's first name)   120–1 **if I . . . going**
there's no chance of my not going; sooner than that, I'd see you hanged instead for
going in my place   122 **chops** fat jaws or cheeks   127 **stand . . . shillings** (1) stand
up and fight for booty (2) be worth ten shillings, the value of the *royal*, the gold coin
alluded to in *blood royal* (l. 126)   139 **want countenance** lack sponsorship (from men
of rank)   141–2 **All-hallow summer** a season of clement weather around All
Saints' Day, November 1; the *latter spring* or "Indian summer" of Falstaff's old age
146 **waylaid** set an ambush for   151 **pleasure** choice, discretion

fail; and then will they adventure upon the exploit themselves, which they shall have no sooner achieved but we'll set upon them.

PRINCE Yea, but 'tis like° that they will know us by our horses, 155
by our habits,° and by every other appointment,° to be ourselves.

POINS Tut, our horses they shall not see—I'll tie them in the wood; our vizards we will change after we leave them; and, sirrah,° I have cases of buckram for the nonce,° to immask° 160
our noted° outward garments.

PRINCE Yea, but I doubt° they will be too hard° for us.

POINS Well, for two of them, I know them to be as true-bred cowards as ever turned back;° and for the third, if he fight longer than he sees reason, I'll forswear arms. The virtue of 165
this jest will be the incomprehensible° lies that this same fat rogue will tell us when we meet at supper—how thirty at least he fought with, what wards,° what blows, what extremities he endured; and in the reproof° of this lives the jest.

PRINCE Well, I'll go with thee. Provide us all things necessary 170
and meet me tomorrow night in Eastcheap. There I'll sup. Farewell.

POINS Farewell, my lord.   *Exit Poins*

PRINCE I know you all, and will awhile uphold
The unyoked humor of your idleness.°   175
Yet herein will I imitate the sun,
Who doth permit the base contagious° clouds
To smother up his beauty from the world,
That° when he please again to be himself,
Being wanted° he may be more wondered at   180
By breaking through the foul and ugly mists
Of vapors that did seem to strangle him.
If all the year were playing holidays,

---

155 **like** likely   156 **habits** garments | **appointment** accoutrement   160 **sirrah** (usually addressed to an inferior; here, a sign of intimacy) | **cases . . . nonce** suits of buckram, a stiff-finished heavily sized fabric, for the purpose | **immask** hide, disguise   161 **noted** known   162 **doubt** fear | **too hard** too formidable   164 **turned back** turned their backs and ran away   166 **incomprehensible** boundless   168 **wards** parries   169 **reproof** disproof   175 **unyoked . . . idleness** unbridled inclination of your frivolity   177 **contagious** noxious   179 **That** so that   180 **wanted** missed, lacked

To sport would be as tedious as to work;
But when they seldom come, they wished-for come,   185
And nothing pleaseth but rare accidents.°
So when this loose behavior I throw off
And pay the debt I never promisèd,
By how much better than my word I am,
By so much shall I falsify men's hopes;°   190
And like bright metal on a sullen ground,°
My reformation, glitt'ring o'er my fault,
Shall show more goodly and attract more eyes
Than that which hath no foil° to set it off.
I'll so offend to° make offense a skill,°   195
Redeeming time° when men think least I will.   *Exit*

ACT 1
SCENE 3

Enter the King, Northumberland, Worcester,
Hotspur, Sir Walter Blunt, with others

KING   My blood hath been too cold and temperate,
Unapt to stir at these indignities,
And you have found me,° for accordingly
You tread upon my patience. But be sure
I will from henceforth rather be myself,°   5
Mighty and to be feared, than my condition,°
Which hath been smooth as oil, soft as young down,
And therefore lost that title of respect
Which the proud soul ne'er pays but to the proud.

---

186 accidents events **190 hopes** expectations **191 sullen ground** dark background, like a *foil* (see l. 194) **194 foil** metal sheet laid contrastingly behind a jewel to set off its luster **195 to** as to l **skill** clever tactic, piece of good policy **196 Redeeming time** making amends for lost time

1.3. Location: London. The court (historically at Windsor). Summary: King Henry alienates the Percies, who regard him as ungrateful despite their crucial role in bringing him to power. After dismissing Worcester (Hotspur's uncle) and accusing Mortimer (Hotspur's brother-in-law) of treason, the King exits, leaving the Percies to plan his overthrow. Throughout the scene Hotspur's excitable imagination is at odds with the shrewd political calculators around him.

3 found me found me so   **5 myself** my royal self   **6 my condition** my natural (mild) disposition

WORCESTER   Our house,° my sovereign liege, little deserves   10
   The scourge of greatness to be used on it—
   And that same greatness too which our own hands
   Have holp° to make so portly.°
NORTHUMBERLAND [*to the King*]   My lord—
KING   Worcester, get thee gone, for I do see   15
   Danger and disobedience in thine eye.
   Oh, sir, your presence is too bold and peremptory,
   And majesty might never yet endure
   The moody frontier° of a servant brow.
   You have good leave° to leave us. When we need   20
   Your use and counsel, we shall send for you.
                                   Exit Worcester
   [*To Northumberland*]
   You were about to speak.
NORTHUMBERLAND   Yea, my good lord.
   Those prisoners in Your Highness' name demanded,
   Which Harry Percy here at Holmedon took,
   Were, as he says, not with such strength denied   25
   As is delivered° to Your Majesty.
   Either envy,° therefore, or misprision°
   Is guilty of this fault, and not my son.
HOTSPUR [*to the King*]   My liege, I did deny no prisoners.
   But I remember when the fight was done,   30
   When I was dry with rage and extreme toil,
   Breathless and faint, leaning upon my sword,
   Came there a certain lord, neat and trimly dressed,
   Fresh as a bridegroom, and his chin new reaped°
   Showed° like a stubble land at harvest home.°   35
   He was perfumèd like a milliner,°
   And twixt his finger and his thumb he held
   A pouncet box,° which ever and anon
   He gave his nose and took't away again,

10 **Our house** the Percy family   13 **holp** helped | **portly** majestic, prosperous
19 **moody frontier** angry brow, frown (*frontier* literally means "outwork" or
"fortification")   20 **good leave** full permission   26 **delivered** reported   27 **envy**
malice | **misprision** misunderstanding   34 **chin new reaped** with beard freshly
barbered according to the latest fashion, not like a soldier's beard   35 **Showed**
looked | **harvest home** end of harvest, fields being cut back to stubble   36 **milliner**
dealer in fancy articles, such as gloves and hats   38 **pouncet box** perfume box with
perforated lid

Who° therewith angry, when it next came there,   40
Took it in snuff;° and still° he smiled and talked,
And as the soldiers bore dead bodies by
He called them untaught knaves, unmannerly,
To bring a slovenly unhandsome corpse
Betwixt the wind and his nobility.   45
With many holiday and lady° terms
He questioned me, amongst the rest demanded
My prisoners in Your Majesty's behalf.
I then, all smarting with my wounds being cold,
To be so pestered with a popinjay,°   50
Out of my grief° and my impatience
Answered neglectingly I know not what,
He should, or he should not; for he made me mad
To see him shine so brisk, and smell so sweet,
And talk so like a waiting-gentlewoman   55
Of guns and drums and wounds—God save the mark!°—
And telling me the sovereignest° thing on earth
Was parmacety° for an inward bruise,
And that it was great pity, so it was,
This villainous saltpeter° should be digged   60
Out of the bowels of the harmless earth,
Which many a good tall° fellow had destroyed
So cowardly, and but for these vile guns
He would himself have been a soldier.
This bald° unjointed chat of his, my lord,   65
I answered indirectly,° as I said,
And I beseech you, let not his report
Come current° for an accusation
Betwixt my love and your high majesty.
BLUNT [*to the King*]
    The circumstance considered, good my lord,   70
    Whate'er Lord Harry Percy then had said

40 **Who** his nose   41 **Took it in snuff** (1) inhaled it (2) took offense | **still** continually   46 **holiday and lady** dainty and effeminate   50 **popinjay** parrot   51 **grief** pain   56 **God . . . mark** (probably originally a formula to avert evil omen; here, an expression of impatience)   57 **sovereignest** most efficacious   58 **parmacety** spermaceti, a fatty substance taken from the head of the sperm whale, used as a medicinal ointment   60 **saltpeter** potassium nitrate, used to make gunpowder and also used medicinally   62 **tall** brave   65 **bald** trivial   66 **indirectly** inattentively, offhandedly   68 **Come current** (1) be taken at face value (2) come rushing in

To such a person and in such a place,
At such a time, with all the rest retold,
May reasonably die, and never rise
To do him wrong or any way impeach°   75
What then he said, so° he unsay it now.
KING Why, yet° he doth deny° his prisoners,
But with proviso° and exception
That we at our own charge shall ransom straight°
His brother-in-law, the foolish Mortimer,°   80
Who, on my soul, hath willfully betrayed
The lives of those that he did lead to fight
Against that great magician, damned Glendower,
Whose daughter, as we hear, that Earl of March°
Hath lately married. Shall our coffers then   85
Be emptied to redeem a traitor home?
Shall we buy treason and indent with fears°
When they have lost and forfeited themselves?
No, on the barren mountains let him starve!
For I shall never hold that man my friend   90
Whose tongue shall ask me for one penny cost
To ransom home revolted° Mortimer.
HOTSPUR Revolted Mortimer?
He never did fall off,° my sovereign liege,
But by the chance of war. To prove that true   95
Needs no more but one tongue for all those wounds,
Those mouthèd° wounds, which valiantly he took,
When on the gentle Severn's° sedgy° bank,

---

75 impeach discredit **76 so** provided that **77 yet** (emphatic) even now | **deny** refuse to surrender **78 proviso and exception** (synonymous terms) **79 straight** straightway, at once **80 Mortimer** (there were two Edmund Mortimers; Shakespeare confuses them and combines their stories; it was the uncle [1376–1409?] who was captured by Glendower and married Glendower's daughter; it was the nephew [1391–1425], fifth Earl of March, who was proclaimed heir presumptive to King Richard II after the death of his father, the fourth earl, whom Richard had named as his heir; the uncle was brother to the fourth earl and to Hotspur's wife, Elizabeth, called Kate in this play) **84 Earl of March** (the "Mortimer" of l. 80; see note there) **87 indent with fears** make a bargain or come to terms with traitors whom we have reason to fear **92 revolted** rebellious **94 fall off** change his allegiance **97 mouthèd** gaping and eloquent **98 Severn's** (the Severn River flows from northern Wales and western England into the Bristol Channel) | **sedgy** bordered with reeds

In single opposition, hand to hand,
He did confound° the best part of an hour   100
In changing hardiment° with great Glendower.
Three times they breathed,° and three times did they drink,
Upon agreement, of swift Severn's flood,°
Who° then, affrighted with their bloody looks,
Ran fearfully among the trembling reeds   105
And hid his crisp° head in the hollow bank,
Bloodstainèd with these valiant combatants.
Never did bare° and rotten policy°
Color° her working with such deadly wounds,
Nor never could the noble Mortimer   110
Receive so many, and all willingly.
Then let not him be slandered with revolt.°
KING   Thou dost belie him, Percy, thou dost belie him.
He never did encounter with Glendower.
I tell thee,   115
He durst as well have met the devil alone
As Owen Glendower for an enemy.
Art thou not ashamed? But, sirrah, henceforth
Let me not hear you speak of Mortimer.
Send me your prisoners with the speediest means,   120
Or you shall hear in such a kind° from me
As will displease you.—My lord Northumberland,
We license your departure with your son.
Send us your prisoners, or you will hear of it.
                              Exit King [with Blunt, and train]
HOTSPUR   An if° the devil come and roar for them   125
I will not send them. I will after straight°
And tell him so, for I will ease my heart,
Albeit I make a hazard of my head.°

---

100 **confound** consume   101 **changing hardiment** exchanging blows, matching valor   102 **breathed** paused for breath   103 **flood** river   104 **Who** the river   106 **crisp** curly, rippled   108 **bare** paltry | **policy** cunning   109 **Color** disguise   112 **revolt** the accusation of rebellion   121 **kind** manner   125 **An if** if   126 **will after straight** will go after him immediately   128 **Albeit . . . head** even if I risk being beheaded

NORTHUMBERLAND

What, drunk with choler?° Stay and pause awhile.
Here comes your uncle.

Enter Worcester

HOTSPUR   Speak of Mortimer?   130
Zounds, I will speak of him, and let my soul
Want mercy° if I do not join with him!
Yea, on his part° I'll empty all these veins,
And shed my dear blood drop by drop in the dust,
But I will lift the downtrod Mortimer   135
As high in the air as this unthankful king,
As this ingrate and cankered° Bolingbroke.°

NORTHUMBERLAND

Brother, the King hath made your nephew mad.

WORCESTER   Who struck this heat up after I was gone?

HOTSPUR   He will forsooth have all my prisoners;   140
And when I urged the ransom once again
Of my wife's brother, then his cheek looked pale,
And on my face he turned an eye of death,°
Trembling even at the name of Mortimer.

WORCESTER   I cannot blame him. Was not he° proclaimed   145
By Richard, that dead is, the next of blood?°

NORTHUMBERLAND   He was; I heard the proclamation.
And then it was when the unhappy° king—
Whose wrongs in us° God pardon!—did set forth
Upon his Irish expedition;°   150
From whence he, intercepted,° did return
To be deposed and shortly murderèd.

WORCESTER

And for whose death we in the world's wide mouth
Live scandalized and foully spoken of.

---

129 choler anger   **132 Want mercy** lack mercy, be damned   **133 on his part**
fighting on Mortimer's side   **137 cankered** spoiled, malignant | **Bolingbroke** King
Henry IV (Hotspur pointedly refuses to acknowledge his royalty)   **143 an eye of
death** a fearful look   **145 he** Mortimer   **146 next of blood** heir to the throne
148 unhappy unfortunate   **149 in us** caused by our doings   **150 Irish expedition**
(Richard II was putting down a rebellion in Ireland when Bolingbroke returned to
England from exile)   **151 intercepted** interrupted

HOTSPUR   But, soft,° I pray you, did King Richard then   155
    Proclaim my brother° Edmund Mortimer
    Heir to the crown?
NORTHUMBERLAND   He did; myself did hear it.
HOTSPUR   Nay, then I cannot blame his cousin° king,
    That wished him on the barren mountains starve.
    But shall it be that you that set the crown   160
    Upon the head of this forgetful man,
    And for his sake wear the detested blot
    Of murderous subornation°—shall it be
    That you a world of curses undergo,
    Being the agents, or base second means,°   165
    The cords, the ladder, or the hangman rather?
    Oh, pardon me that I descend so low
    To show the line and the predicament°
    Wherein you range° under this subtle king!
    Shall it for shame be spoken in these days,   170
    Or fill up chronicles in time to come,
    That men of your nobility and power
    Did gage them° both in an unjust behalf,
    As both of you—God pardon it!—have done,
    To put down Richard, that sweet lovely rose,   175
    And plant this thorn, this canker,° Bolingbroke?
    And shall it in more shame be further spoken
    That you are fooled, discarded, and shook off
    By him for whom these shames ye underwent?
    No! Yet° time serves wherein you may redeem   180
    Your banished honors and restore yourselves
    Into the good thoughts of the world again;
    Revenge° the jeering and disdained° contempt
    Of this proud king, who studies day and night
    To answer° all the debt he owes to you   185

---

155 **soft** wait a minute   156 **brother** brother-in-law   158 **cousin** (with a pun on cozen, "cheat")   163 **murderous subornation** the suborning of, or inciting to, murder   165 **second means** agents   168 **To . . . predicament** to show the direction things are moving and the danger to you   169 **range** (1) are ranked; (2) stray   173 **gage them** engage, pledge themselves   176 **canker** (1) canker rose or dog rose, wild and unfragrant (2) ulcer   180 **Yet** still   183 **Revenge** and wherein you may revenge yourself against | **disdained** disdainful   185 **answer** satisfy, discharge

Even with the bloody payment of your deaths.
Therefore, I say—
WORCESTER   Peace, cousin,° say no more.
And now I will unclasp a secret book,
And to your quick-conceiving° discontents
I'll read you matter deep and dangerous,   190
As full of peril and adventurous spirit
As to o'erwalk a current roaring loud
On the unsteadfast footing of a spear.°
HOTSPUR If he fall in, good night, or sink or swim!°
Send danger from the east unto the west,   195
So° honor cross it from the north to south,
And let them grapple. Oh, the blood more stirs
To rouse a lion than to start a hare!
NORTHUMBERLAND [to Worcester]
Imagination of some great exploit
Drives him beyond the bounds of patience.   200
HOTSPUR By heaven, methinks it were an easy leap
To pluck bright honor from the pale-faced moon,
Or dive into the bottom of the deep,
Where fathom line° could never touch the ground,
And pluck up drownèd honor by the locks,   205
So he that doth redeem her thence might wear
Without corrival° all her dignities;
But out upon this half-faced fellowship!°
WORCESTER [to Northumberland]
He apprehends° a world of figures° here,
But not the form° of what he should attend.°—   210
Good cousin, give me audience for a while.
HOTSPUR I cry you mercy.°
WORCESTER   Those same noble Scots
That are your prisoners—

187 cousin nephew   189 quick-conceiving comprehending quickly   193 spear spear
laid across a stream as a narrow bridge   194 If . . . swim anyone daring such a thing
will face a life-or-death challenge (Hotspur's imagination is fired by the thought of
risking everything on such an attempt)   196 So provided that (also at l. 206)
204 fathom line a weighted line marked at fathom intervals (six feet), used for
measuring the depth of water   207 corrival rival, competitor   208 out . . . fellowship!
down with this paltry business of sharing glory with others   209 apprehends snatches
at | figures figures of the imagination, or figures of speech   210 form essential nature |
attend give attention to   212 cry you mercy beg your pardon

HOTSPUR   I'll keep them all.
By God, he shall not have a Scot of them,
No, if a scot° would save his soul, he shall not!   215
I'll keep them, by this hand.
WORCESTER   You start away
And lend no ear unto my purposes.
Those prisoners you shall keep.
HOTSPUR   Nay, I will, that's flat.°
He said he would not ransom Mortimer,
Forbade my tongue to speak of Mortimer,   220
But I will find him when he lies asleep,
And in his ear I'll holler "Mortimer!"
Nay, I'll have a starling shall be taught to speak
Nothing but "Mortimer," and give it him
To keep his anger still° in motion.   225
WORCESTER   Hear you, cousin, a word.
HOTSPUR   All studies° here I solemnly defy,°
Save how to gall and pinch this Bolingbroke,
And that same sword-and-buckler° Prince of Wales.
But that I think his father loves him not   230
And would be glad he met with some mischance,
I would have him poisoned with a pot of ale.
WORCESTER   Farewell, kinsman. I'll talk to you
When you are better tempered to attend.
NORTHUMBERLAND [*to Hotspur*]
Why, what a wasp-stung and impatient fool   235
Art thou to break into this woman's mood,
Tying thine ear to no tongue but thine own!
HOTSPUR
Why, look you, I am whipped and scourged with rods,
Nettled° and stung with pismires,° when I hear
Of this vile politician,° Bolingbroke.   240
In Richard's time—what do you call the place?—
A plague upon it, it is in Gloucestershire;
'Twas where the madcap duke his uncle kept,°

214–15 Scot . . . scot Scotsman . . . trifling amount   **218 that's flat** that's for sure
225 still continually   **227 studies** pursuits | **defy** renounce   **229 sword-and-
buckler** swashbuckling (gentlemen generally preferred to wear the rapier and the
dagger)   **239 Nettled** stung with nettles | **pismires** ants (from the urinous smell of
an anthill)   **240 politician** deceitful schemer   **243 kept** dwelled

His uncle York; where I first bowed my knee
Unto this king of smiles, this Bolingbroke—   245
'Sblood, when you and he came back from Ravenspurgh.°
NORTHUMBERLAND   At Berkeley Castle.°
HOTSPUR   You say true.
Why, what a candy° deal of courtesy
This fawning greyhound then did proffer me!   250
"Look when° his infant fortune came to age,"
And "gentle Harry Percy," and "kind cousin"—
Oh, the devil take such cozeners!°—God forgive me!
Good uncle, tell your tale; I have done.
WORCESTER   Nay, if you have not, to it again;   255
We will stay° your leisure.
HOTSPUR   I have done, i'faith.
WORCESTER   Then once more to your Scottish prisoners.
Deliver them up° without their ransom straight,
And make the Douglas' son° your only mean°
For powers° in Scotland, which, for divers reasons   260
Which I shall send you written, be assured
Will easily be granted. [*To Northumberland*] You, my lord,
Your son in Scotland being thus employed,
Shall secretly into the bosom creep°
Of that same noble prelate well beloved,   265
The Archbishop.
HOTSPUR   Of York, is it not?
WORCESTER   True, who bears hard°
His brother's death at Bristol, the Lord Scroop.
I speak not this in estimation,°   270
As what I think might be, but what I know
Is ruminated, plotted, and set down,
And only stays but to behold the face
Of that occasion that shall bring it on.

---

246 Ravenspurgh on the Yorkshire coast, at the mouth of the Humber River, where Bolingbroke landed on his return from exile (*Richard II*, 2.1.296)   **247 Berkeley Castle** castle near Bristol   **249 candy** sugared, flattering   **251 Look when** when, as soon as   **253 cozeners** cheats (with pun on *cousins*)   **256 stay** await   **258 Deliver them up** free them   **259 the Douglas' son** Mordake (see 1.1.71 and note) | **mean** agent   **260 For powers** for raising an army   **264 secretly . . . creep** win the confidence   **268 bears hard** resents   **270 estimation** guesswork

HOTSPUR   I smell it. Upon my life, it will do well.   275
NORTHUMBERLAND   Before the game is afoot thou still let'st slip.°
HOTSPUR   Why, it cannot choose but be° a noble plot.
    And then the power° of Scotland and of York
    To join with Mortimer, ha?
WORCESTER   And so they shall.
HOTSPUR   In faith, it is exceedingly well aimed.°   280
WORCESTER   And 'tis no little reason bids us speed,
    To save our heads by raising of a head;°
    For, bear ourselves as even° as we can,
    The King will always think him° in our debt,
    And think we think ourselves unsatisfied   285
    Till he hath found a time to pay us home.°
    And see already how he doth begin
    To make us strangers to his looks of love.
HOTSPUR   He does, he does. We'll be revenged on him.
WORCESTER   Cousin, farewell. No further go in this   290
    Than I by letters shall direct your course.
    When time is ripe, which will be suddenly,°
    I'll steal to Glendower and Lord Mortimer,
    Where you and Douglas and our powers at once,°
    As I will fashion it, shall happily° meet   295
    To bear our fortunes in our own strong arms,°
    Which now we hold at much uncertainty.
NORTHUMBERLAND
    Farewell, good brother. We shall thrive, I trust.
HOTSPUR
    Uncle, adieu. Oh, let the hours be short
    Till fields° and blows and groans applaud our sport!   300
                        Exeunt [in separate groups]

276 **still let'st slip** always let loose the dogs   277 **cannot choose but be** cannot help being   278 **power** army   280 **aimed** designed   282 **head** army   283 **even** carefully 284 **him** himself   286 **home** (1) fully (2) with a thrust to the heart   292 **suddenly** soon   294 **at once** all together   295 **happily** fortunately   296 **arms** (1) limbs (2) military might   300 **fields** battlefields

ACT 2
SCENE 1

Enter a Carrier° with a lantern in his hand

FIRST CARRIER   Heigh-ho! An° it be not four by the day,° I'll be
hanged. Charles's Wain° is over the new chimney, and yet
our horse° not packed. What, ostler!°

OSTLER [*within*]   Anon,° anon.

FIRST CARRIER   I prithee, Tom, beat° Cut's saddle,° put a few   5
flocks° in the point.° Poor jade° is wrung in the withers° out
of all cess.°

Enter another Carrier

SECOND CARRIER   Peas and beans° are as dank here as a dog,°
and that is the next° way to give poor jades the bots.° This
house° is turned upside down since Robin Ostler died.   10

FIRST CARRIER   Poor fellow never joyed since the price of oats
rose. It was the death of him.

SECOND CARRIER   I think this be the most villainous house in all
London road for fleas. I am stung like a tench.°

FIRST CARRIER   Like a tench? By the Mass, there is ne'er a king   15
Christian° could be better bit than I have been since the first
cock.°

SECOND CARRIER   Why, they will allow us ne'er a jordan,° and
then we leak in your chimney,° and your chamber-lye° breeds
fleas like a loach.°   20

2.1. Location: An innyard on the London-Canterbury road. **Summary:** Two carriers
are suspicious of Gadshill's attempt to pry information, and a lantern, from them.
Gadshill gloats with the snooping Chamberlain, who helps plan the robbery, about
the lofty status of his co-conspirators.
0.1 *Carrier* one whose trade was conveying goods, usually by pack-horses   **1 An** if |
by the day in the morning   **2 Charles's Wain** Charlemagne's wagon; the constellation
Ursa Major (the Big Dipper)   **3 horse** horses | **ostler** stable groom   **4 Anon** right
away, coming   **5 beat** soften | **Cut's saddle** packsaddle of the horse named *Cut*,
meaning "bobtailed"   **6 flocks** tufts of wool | **point** pommel of the saddle | **jade**
nag | **wrung . . . withers** chafed (by his saddle) on the ridge between his shoulder-
blades   **7 cess** measure, estimate   **8 Peas and beans** horse fodder | **dank . . . dog**
damp as can be   **9 next** nearest, quickest | **bots** intestinal maggots   **10 house** inn
14 tench a spotted fish, whose spots may have been likened to flea bites   **15–16**
king Christian Christian king, accustomed to have the best of everything
16–17 first cock midnight   **18 jordan** chamberpot   **19 chimney** fireplace |
chamber-lye urine   **20 loach** a small freshwater fish, thought to harbor parasites

FIRST CARRIER [*calling*] What, Ostler! Come away° and be hanged! Come away.

SECOND CARRIER I have a gammon of bacon° and two races° of ginger, to be delivered as far as Charing Cross.°

FIRST CARRIER God's body, the turkeys in my pannier° are quite 25
starved. What, ostler! A plague on thee! Hast thou never an eye in thy head? Canst not hear? An° 'twere not as good deed as drink to break the pate on thee, I am a very villain. Come, and be hanged!° Hast no faith° in thee?

Enter Gadshill

GADSHILL Good morrow, carriers. What's o'clock? 30

FIRST CARRIER I think it be two o'clock.°

GADSHILL I prithee, lend me thy lantern to see my gelding° in the stable.

FIRST CARRIER Nay, by God, soft,° I know a trick worth two of that, i'faith. 35

GADSHILL [*to the Second Carrier*] I pray thee, lend me thine.

SECOND CARRIER Ay, when, canst tell?° Lend me thy lantern, quoth° he! Marry, I'll see thee hanged first.

GADSHILL Sirrah carrier, what time do you mean to come to London? 40

SECOND CARRIER Time enough to go to bed with a candle,° I warrant thee.—Come, neighbor Mugs, we'll call up the gentlemen. They will along with company, for they have great charge.°   *Exeunt* [*Carriers*]

GADSHILL What, ho! Chamberlain!° 45

Enter Chamberlain

CHAMBERLAIN At hand, quoth pickpurse.°

21 Come away come along **23 gammon of bacon** ham | **races** roots **24 Charing Cross** a market town lying between London and Westminster **25 pannier** basket **27 An** if **27–9 An . . . hanged!** I'll be hanged if it wouldn't be a good idea to smack you on the head; come along, damn you! **29 faith** trustworthiness **31 two o'clock** (an evasive answer; the First Carrier knows that it is at least four o'clock; see l. 1) **32 gelding** castrated male horse **34 soft** wait a minute **37 Ay . . . tell?** you must be joking **38 quoth he** forsooth, indeed **41 Time . . . candle** soon enough (another evasive answer) **43–4 They . . . charge** they wish to travel in company, because they have lots of valuable cargo **45 Chamberlain** (male equivalent of a chambermaid; his entrance in the Quarto at l. 44 may suggest that he is visible before Gadshill calls for him, giving point to his remark about being "at hand") **46 At . . . pickpurse** I am right beside you, as the pickpurse said

GADSHILL That's even as fair° as—at hand, quoth the
chamberlain; for thou variest no more from picking of
purses than giving direction doth from laboring; thou layest
the plot how.°   50

CHAMBERLAIN Good morrow, Master Gadshill. It holds current
that° I told you yesternight: there's a franklin° in the Weald°
of Kent hath brought three hundred marks° with him in
gold. I heard him tell it to one of his company last night at
supper—a kind of auditor, one that hath abundance of   55
charge too, God knows what. They are up already, and call
for eggs and butter. They will away presently.°

GADSHILL Sirrah, if they meet not with Saint Nicholas' clerks,°
I'll give thee this neck.

CHAMBERLAIN No, I'll none° of it. I pray thee, keep that for the   60
hangman, for I know thou worshipest Saint Nicholas as
truly as a man of falsehood may.

GADSHILL What° talkest thou to me of the hangman? If I hang,
I'll make a fat pair of gallows; for if I hang, old Sir John
hangs with me, and thou knowest he is no starveling. Tut,   65
there are other Trojans° that thou dream'st not of, the which
for sport sake are content to do the profession° some grace,°
that would, if matters should be looked into, for their own
credit sake make all whole.° I am joined with no foot-
landrakers,° no long-staff sixpenny strikers,° none of these   70
mad mustachio purple-hued malt-worms,° but with nobility
and tranquillity,° burgomasters and great oneyers,° such as
can hold in,° such as will strike sooner than speak, and
speak sooner than drink, and drink sooner than pray. And

47 **fair** good, apt   49–50 **thou variest . . . how** you don't actually do the stealing,
but you give directions, like a master workman to his apprentices   51–2 **holds
current that** holds true what   52 **a franklin** a yeoman owning his own land |
Weald wooded region   53 **marks** coins of the value of thirteen shillings four pence
57 **presently** immediately   58 **Saint Nicholas' clerks** highwaymen (Saint Nicholas
was popularly supposed the patron of thieves)   60 **I'll none** I want none   63 **What**
why   66 **Trojans** jolly fellows, roisterers   67 **profession** robbery | **grace** credit,
favor   68–9 **for . . . whole** for the sake of their own reputation will make sure that
all goes well (Gadshill hints that they may be joined by some persons of social
importance, such as the Prince)   69–70 **foot-landrakers** thieves who travel on foot
70 **long-staff sixpenny strikers** robbers with long staves who would knock down
their victims for sixpence   71 **mustachio . . . malt-worms** purple-faced drunkards
with huge mustaches   72 **tranquillity** those who lead easy lives | **oneyers** ones,
persons (?)   73 **hold in** keep a secret; hold fast

yet, zounds, I lie, for they pray continually to their saint, the   75
commonwealth, or rather not pray to her but prey on her,
for they ride up and down on her and make her their boots.°

CHAMBERLAIN   What, the commonwealth their boots? Will she
hold out water in foul way?°

GADSHILL   She will, she will. Justice hath liquored° her. We steal   80
as in a castle,° cocksure. We have the receipt° of fern seed;°
we walk invisible.

CHAMBERLAIN   Nay, by my faith, I think you are more
beholding° to the night than to fern seed for your walking
invisible.   85

GADSHILL   Give me thy hand. Thou shalt have a share in our
purchase,° as I am a true man.

CHAMBERLAIN   Nay, rather let me have it as you are a false thief.

GADSHILL   Go to;° *homo* is a common name to all men.° Bid
the ostler bring my gelding out of the stable. Farewell, you   90
muddy° knave.   [*Exeunt separately*]

ACT 2
SCENE 2

Enter Prince, Poins, Peto, and [Bardolph]

POINS   Come, shelter, shelter! I have removed Falstaff's horse,
and he frets° like a gummed velvet.

PRINCE   Stand close.°   [*They step aside*]

Enter Falstaff

77 boots booty (with pun on *boots*, "shoes")   **78–9 Will . . . way?** will she let you go dry in muddy roads? will she protect you in tight places?   **80 liquored** (1) made waterproof by oiling (2) bribed (3) made drunk   **81 as in a castle** in complete security | **receipt** recipe, formula | **of fern seed** of becoming invisible (since fern seed, almost invisible itself, was popularly supposed to render its possessor invisible)   **84 beholding** beholden   **87 purchase** booty   **89 Go to** (an expression of impatience) ***homo* . . . men** the Latin name for man applies to all types; the phrase "true man" applies to me as well as the next man   **91 muddy** stupid

2.2. Location: The highway, near Gad's Hill. **Summary:** A gasping Falstaff knows his horse has been hidden by Poins, but still manages with his companions to triumph over the terrified travelers. His swaggering is cut short by the disguised Hal and Poins, who rob him in turn.

2 frets (1) is vexed (2) rubs and frays like *gummed velvet*, velvet made glossy with a stiffening gum   **3 close** concealed

FALSTAFF Poins! Poins, and be hanged! Poins!

PRINCE [*coming forward*] Peace, ye fat-kidneyed rascal! What 5
a brawling dost thou keep!°

FALSTAFF Where's Poins, Hal?

PRINCE He is walked up to the top of the hill. I'll go seek him.

[*He steps aside*]

FALSTAFF I am accursed to rob in that thief's company. The
rascal hath removed my horse and tied him I know not 10
where. If I travel but four foot by the square° further afoot,
I shall break my wind.° Well, I doubt not but to die a fair°
death for all° this, if I scape hanging for killing that rogue. I
have forsworn his company hourly any time this two-and-
twenty years, and yet I am bewitched with the rogue's 15
company. If the rascal have not given me medicines° to
make me love him, I'll be hanged; it could not be else—I
have drunk medicines. Poins! Hal! A plague upon you both!
Bardolph! Peto! I'll starve ere I'll rob a foot further. An
'twere not as good a deed as drink to turn true man and to 20
leave these rogues, I am the veriest varlet that ever chewed
with a tooth.° Eight yards of uneven ground is three-score-
and-ten miles afoot with me, and the stony-hearted villains
know it well enough. A plague upon it when thieves cannot
be true one to another! (*They whistle.*) Whew!° A plague 25
upon you all! Give me my horse, you rogues, give me my
horse, and be hanged!

PRINCE [*coming forward*] Peace, ye fat-guts! Lie down. Lay
thine ear close to the ground and list° if thou canst hear the
tread of travelers. 30

FALSTAFF Have you any levers to lift me up again, being down?
'Sblood, I'll not bear mine own flesh so far afoot again for
all the coin in thy father's Exchequer.° What a plague mean
ye to colt° me thus?

PRINCE Thou liest. Thou art not colted, thou art uncolted. 35

---

6 **keep** keep up   11 **square** a measuring tool   12 **break my wind** gasp for air (a
secondary sense of "expel gas" is possible) | **fair** exemplary   13 **for all** despite all
16 **medicines** love potions   19–22 **An . . . tooth** if it don't think it's a good idea to
reform and turn informer, I'm the damnedest scoundrel that ever lived (cf. 2.1.27–9
and n)   25 **Whew** (perhaps Falstaff tries to answer the whistling he hears or mocks
it)   29 **list** listen   33 **Exchequer** royal treasury   34 **colt** trick, cheat (in l. 35, Prince
Hal puns on the common meaning)

FALSTAFF   I prithee, good Prince Hal, help me to my horse,° good king's son.

PRINCE   Out, ye rogue! Shall I be your ostler?

FALSTAFF   Go hang thyself in thine own heir-apparent garters! If I be ta'en, I'll peach° for this. An I have not ballads made on   40 you all and sung to filthy tunes, let a cup of sack be my poison. When a jest is so forward,° and afoot° too! I hate it.

Enter Gadshill

GADSHILL   Stand!°

FALSTAFF   So I do, against my will.

POINS [*coming forward with Bardolph and Peto*]   Oh, 'tis our   45 setter.° I know his voice.

BARDOLPH   What news?

GADSHILL   Case ye,° case ye, on with your vizards! There's money of the King's coming down the hill; 'tis going to the King's Exchequer.   50

FALSTAFF   You lie, ye rogue, 'tis going to the King's Tavern.

GADSHILL   There's enough to make us° all.

FALSTAFF   To be hanged.

PRINCE   Sirs, you four shall front° them in the narrow lane; Ned Poins and I will walk lower.° If they scape from your   55 encounter, then they light on us.

PETO   How many be there of them?

GADSHILL   Some eight or ten.

FALSTAFF   Zounds, will they not rob us?

PRINCE   What, a coward, Sir John Paunch?   60

FALSTAFF   Indeed, I am not John of Gaunt,° your grandfather, but yet no coward, Hal.

PRINCE   Well, we leave that to the proof.°

---

36 help . . . horse help me to find my horse (but in l. 38, the Prince comically retorts as though having been asked to hold the stirrup while Falstaff mounted, as an ostler would do)   **40 peach** inform on you   **42 so forward** so far advanced | **afoot** (1) in progress (2) on foot, not on horseback   **43 Stand!** don't move (but Falstaff answers in the sense of "stand on one's feet")   **46 setter** arranger of the robbery (see 1.2.95 and n)   **48 Case ye** put on your masks   **52 make us all** make our fortunes (or, as Falstaff sees it, make us be hanged)   **54 front** confront   **55 lower** further downhill   **61 John of Gaunt** Henry IV's father, born at Ghent (and hence giving Falstaff a chance to pun on *gaunt* as the opposite of his fatness)   **63 proof** test

POINS   Sirrah Jack, thy horse stands behind the hedge. When thou need'st him, there thou shalt find him. Farewell, and   65 stand fast.

FALSTAFF   Now cannot I strike him, if I should be hanged.°

PRINCE   [to Poins]   Ned, where are our disguises?

POINS   [to Prince]   Here, hard by. Stand close.

                                [Exeunt Prince and Poins]

FALSTAFF   Now, my masters, happy man be his dole,° say I.   70 Every man to his business.   *[They stand aside]*

                            Enter the Travelers

FIRST TRAVELER   Come, neighbor. The boy shall lead our horses down the hill; we'll walk afoot awhile, and ease our legs.

THIEVES   [coming forward]   Stand!

TRAVELERS   Jesus bless us!   75

FALSTAFF   Strike! Down with them! Cut the villains' throats! Ah, whoreson caterpillars, bacon-fed knaves!° They hate us youth. Down with them, fleece them!

TRAVELERS   Oh, we are undone, both we and ours forever!

FALSTAFF   Hang ye, gorbellied° knaves, are ye undone? No, ye   80 fat chuffs;° I would your store° were here. On, bacons,° on! What, ye knaves, young men must live. You are grandjurors,° are ye? We'll jure ye, 'faith.

        Here they rob them and bind them. Exeunt

      Enter the Prince and Poins [in buckram]

PRINCE   The thieves have bound the true men. Now could thou and I rob the thieves and go merrily to London, it would be   85 argument° for a week, laughter for a month, and a good jest forever.

POINS   Stand close. I hear them coming.

                            [They stand aside]

                         Enter the thieves again

---

67 **Now . . . hanged** (Falstaff wishes he could hit Poins, who is too quick for him) 70 **happy . . . dole** may happiness be every man's portion or lot   77 **Ah . . . knaves!** ah, you abominable parasites, you over-fed rascals!   80 **gorbellied** big-bellied 81 **chuffs** churls, rich but miserly | **store** total wealth | **bacons** fat men 82 **grandjurors** men of wealth, able to serve on juries   86 **argument** a subject for conversation

FALSTAFF Come, my masters,° let us share, and then to horse
before day. An the Prince and Poins be not two arrant°   90
cowards, there's no equity° stirring. There's no more valor
in that Poins than in a wild duck.
                    [*The thieves begin to share the booty*]
PRINCE Your money!
POINS Villains!
          As they are sharing, the Prince and Poins set upon them.
          They all run away, and Falstaff, after a blow or two, runs
                    away too, leaving the booty behind them
PRINCE Got with much ease. Now merrily to horse.   95
The thieves are all scattered and possessed with fear
So strongly that they dare not meet each other;
Each takes his fellow for an officer.
Away, good Ned. Falstaff sweats to death
And lards° the lean earth as he walks along.   100
Were't not for laughing, I should pity him.
POINS How the fat rogue roared!   *Exeunt*

ACT 2
SCENE 3

Enter Hotspur, solus,° reading a letter

HOTSPUR "But, for mine own part, my lord, I could be well
contented to be there, in respect of the love I bear your
house."° He could be contented; why is he not, then? In
respect of the love he bears our house! He shows in this he
loves his own barn better than he loves our house. Let me see   5
some more. "The purpose you undertake is dangerous"—
why, that's certain. 'Tis dangerous to take a cold, to sleep, to
drink; but I tell you, my lord fool, out of this nettle, danger,

89 **masters** good sirs 90 **arrant** notorious, unmitigated 91 **equity** judgment,
discernment 100 **lards** drips fat on, bastes

2.3. Location: Hotspur's estate (identified historically as **Warkworth Castle** in
Northumberland). Summary: Hotspur reads and angrily comments on a letter from
an unnamed "lord fool" who refuses to join the Percy revolt. Hotspur's wife, Kate
(Lady Percy), asks what has so preoccupied him of late, and despite some spirited
teasing between them, he refuses to confide in her.
0.1 *solus* alone 3 **house** family (but Hotspur replies derisively in ll. 3–5 as though
to the literal sense of a building that one might compare to a barn)

we pluck this flower, safety. "The purpose you undertake is
dangerous, the friends you have named uncertain, the time   10
itself unsorted,° and your whole plot too light for the
counterpoise of° so great an opposition." Say you so, say
you so? I say unto you again, you are a shallow, cowardly
hind,° and you lie. What a lack-brain is this! By the Lord,
our plot is a good plot as ever was laid, our friends true and   15
constant; a good plot, good friends, and full of expectation;°
an excellent plot, very good friends. What a frosty-spirited
rogue is this! Why, my lord of York° commends the plot and
the general course of the action. Zounds, an I were now by
this rascal,° I could brain him with his lady's fan.° Is there   20
not my father, my uncle, and myself? Lord Edmund
Mortimer, my lord of York, and Owen Glendower? Is there
not besides the Douglas? Have I not all their letters to meet
me in arms by the ninth of the next month, and are they not
some of them set forward already? What a pagan° rascal is   25
this, an infidel! Ha, you shall see now in very sincerity of fear
and cold heart will he to the King and lay open all our
proceedings. Oh, I could divide myself and go to buffets° for
moving° such a dish of skim milk with so honorable an
action! Hang him, let him tell the King, we are prepared. I   30
will set forward tonight.

                                        Enter his Lady

How now, Kate? I must leave you within these two hours.
LADY PERCY   Oh, my good lord, why are you thus alone?
For what offense have I this fortnight been
A banished woman from my Harry's bed?   35
Tell me, sweet lord, what is't that takes from thee
Thy stomach,° pleasure, and thy golden sleep?
Why dost thou bend thine eyes upon the earth
And start so often when thou sit'st alone?
Why hast thou lost the fresh blood in thy cheeks   40

---

11 unsorted unsuitable   **11–12 for . . . of** to counterbalance   **14 hind** menial,
peasant   **16 expectation** promise   **18 lord of York** Archbishop Scroop (also in
l. 22)   **19–20 an . . . rascal** if I were face to face with this rascal, instead of reading
his letter   **20 his lady's fan** his wife's fan—a suitable light weapon with which to
chastise such a milktoast   **25 pagan** unbelieving   **28 divide . . . buffets** fight with
myself   **29 moving** urging   **37 stomach** appetite

And given my treasures and my rights of thee°
To thick-eyed° musing and curst° melancholy?
In thy faint° slumbers I by thee have watched°
And heard thee murmur tales of iron wars,
Speak terms of manage° to thy bounding steed,   45
Cry, "Courage! To the field!" And thou hast talked
Of sallies and retires,° of trenches, tents,
Of palisadoes, frontiers, parapets,
Of basilisks, of cannon, culverin,°
Of prisoners' ransom, and of soldiers slain,   50
And all the currents of a heady° fight.
Thy spirit within thee hath been so at war,
And thus hath so bestirred thee in thy sleep,
That beads of sweat have stood upon thy brow
Like bubbles in a late-disturbèd° stream,   55
And in thy face strange motions have appeared,
Such as we see when men restrain their breath
On some great sudden hest.° Oh, what portents are these?
Some heavy business hath my lord in hand,
And I must know it, else he loves me not.   60

HOTSPUR [*calling*]
    What, ho!

                                    [*Enter a Servant*]

            Is Gilliams with the packet° gone?
SERVANT   He is, my lord, an hour ago.
HOTSPUR   Hath Butler brought those horses from the sheriff?°
SERVANT   One horse, my lord, he brought even° now.
HOTSPUR   What horse? A roan,° a crop-ear, is it not?   65
SERVANT   It is, my lord.
HOTSPUR   That roan shall be my throne.
    Well, I will back° him straight. Oh, *Esperance!*°
    Bid Butler lead him forth into the park.

                                    [*Exit Servant*]

41 **And . . . thee** and given the precious right I have as wife to share your thoughts (and marital pleasures [RL]) 42 **thick-eyed** dull-sighted, vacant, abstracted | **curst** ill-tempered 43 **faint** restless | **watched** lain awake 45 **manage** horsemanship 47 **retires** retreats 48–9 **Of . . . culverin** of stakes set in the ground for defense, of ramparts, protective walls, of large and smaller cannon 51 **heady** headlong 55 **late-disturbèd** recently stirred up 58 **hest** command; endeavor 61 **packet** parcel of letters [RL] 63 **sheriff** bailiff 64 **even** just 65 **roan** roan-colored, with white or grey interspersed in the overall color of the coat 67 **back** mount *Esperance* Hope (the motto of the Percy family)

LADY PERCY   But hear you, my lord.

HOTSPUR   What say'st thou, my lady?   70

LADY PERCY   What is it carries you away?°

HOTSPUR   Why, my horse, my love, my horse.

LADY PERCY   Out,° you mad-headed ape!
   A weasel hath not such a deal of spleen°
   As you are tossed° with. In faith,   75
   I'll know your business, Harry, that I will.
   I fear my brother Mortimer doth stir
   About his title,° and hath sent for you
   To line° his enterprise; but if you go—

HOTSPUR   So far afoot, I shall be weary, love.   80

LADY PERCY   Come, come, you paraquito,° answer me
   Directly unto this question that I ask.
   In faith, I'll break thy little finger, Harry,
   An if° thou wilt not tell me all things true.

HOTSPUR   Away,   85
   Away, you trifler! Love? I love thee not;
   I care not for thee, Kate. This is no world
   To play with mammets° and to tilt with lips.°
   We must have bloody noses and cracked crowns,°
   And pass them current too. Gods° me, my horse!   90
   What say'st thou, Kate? What wouldst thou have with me?

LADY PERCY   Do you not love me? Do you not, indeed?
   Well, do not, then, for since you love me not
   I will not love myself. Do you not love me?
   Nay, tell me if you speak in jest or no.   95

HOTSPUR   Come, wilt thou see me ride?
   And when I am a-horseback I will swear
   I love thee infinitely. But hark you, Kate,
   I must not have you henceforth question me

---

71 carries you away carries you beyond the bounds of reason and judgment (but Hotspur puns on the literal meaning)   **73 Out** (an expression of impatience)   **74 spleen** (the spleen was thought to be the source of impulsive and irritable behavior)   **75 tossed** tossed about, agitated   **78 title** claim to the throne   **79 line** strengthen   **81 paraquito** little parrot (a term of endearment)   **84 An if** if   **88 mammets** dolls (with a quibble on the Latin *mamma* meaning "breast") | **tilt with lips** compete by exchanging kisses [RL]   **89 crowns** (1) heads (2) coins worth five shillings (cracked coins would not "pass current," as Hotspur jokes in the next line)   **90 Gods me** God save me

Whither I go, nor reason whereabout.°   100
Whither I must, I must; and, to conclude,
This evening must I leave you, gentle Kate.
I know you wise, but yet no farther wise
Than Harry Percy's wife; constant you are,
But yet a woman; and for secrecy,   105
No lady closer,° for I well believe
Thou wilt not utter what thou dost not know,
And so far will I trust thee, gentle Kate.
LADY PERCY   How, so far?
HOTSPUR   Not an inch further. But hark you, Kate: 110
Whither I go, thither shall you go too.
Today will I set forth, tomorrow you.
Will this content you, Kate?
LADY PERCY   It must, of force.°   *Exeunt*

ACT 2
SCENE 4

Enter Prince and Poins

PRINCE   Ned, prithee, come out of that fat° room, and lend me
thy hand to laugh a little.
POINS   Where hast been, Hal?
PRINCE   With three or four loggerheads° amongst three or four
score hogsheads.° I have sounded the very bass° string of   5
humility. Sirrah, I am sworn brother to a leash of drawers,°

---

100 reason whereabout ask about what   **106 closer** more close-mouthed   **114 of
force** perforce, of necessity

2.4. Location: A tavern in Eastcheap, London, usually identified as the Boar's Head.
Some tavern furniture, including stools, is provided onstage. **Summary:** Hal and
Poins await Falstaff's appearance, and the Prince passes the time by learning tavern
slang and playing a cruel, unexplained game with Francis the tapster. Falstaff enters
in high performative mode. Exposed by Hal's revelation that he and Poins have
robbed him, he rebounds with inventive pomposity and the call for an improvised
play. Upon learning that Hal must meet with his father the next day, Falstaff and the
Prince rehearse that confrontation. The arrival of a sheriff investigating the robbery
of 2.2 sends Falstaff into hiding behind an arras, where he promptly falls asleep.

1 fat stuffy, or, a vat room   **4 loggerheads** blockheads   **5 hogsheads** wine barrels |
bass (with a pun on *base*)   **6 leash of drawers** three waiters (*leash* is often used in
sporting language for a set of three animals—hounds, hawks, deer, etc. [RL])

and can call them all by their Christian names, as Tom, Dick, and Francis.° They take it already upon their salvation° that, though I be but Prince of Wales, yet I am the king of courtesy, and tell me flatly I am no proud Jack° like   10 Falstaff, but a Corinthian,° a lad of mettle, a good boy—by the Lord, so they call me!—and when I am King of England I shall command all the good lads in Eastcheap. They call drinking deep "dyeing scarlet";° and when you breathe in your watering° they cry "hem!" and bid you "play it off."°   15 To conclude, I am so good a proficient in one quarter of an hour that I can drink with any tinker in his own language during my life. I tell thee, Ned, thou hast lost much honor that thou wert not with me in this action. But, sweet Ned— to sweeten which name of Ned, I give thee this pennyworth   20 underskinker,° one that never spake other English in his life than "Eight shillings and sixpence," and "You are welcome," with this shrill addition, "Anon, anon, sir! Score a pint of bastard in the Half-Moon,"° or so. But, Ned, to drive away the time till Falstaff come, I prithee do thou   25 stand in some by-room° while I question my puny drawer° to what end he gave me the sugar; and do thou never leave calling "Francis," that his tale to me may be nothing but "Anon." Step aside, and I'll show thee a precedent.°

[Exit Poins]   30

POINS [*within*]   Francis!

PRINCE   Thou art perfect.

POINS [*within*]   Francis!

Enter [Francis, a] drawer

7–8 Tom, Dick, and Francis (some editors and critics believe the names play on the expression "any Tom, Dick, and Harry," despite sketchy evidence of this expression before the 19th c.; if so, the replacement of "Harry" with "Francis" implies an analogy between the reluctant royal "apprentice" and the inkeeper's apprentice) [RL]   **8–9 take . . . salvation** already maintain it as they hope to be saved   **10 Jack** (1) Jack Falstaff (2) fellow   **11 Corinthian** gay blade, good sport (Corinth was reputed to be licentious)   **13–14 They . . . scarlet** (either because excessive drinking causes a red complexion or because urine, produced by *drinking deep*, was sometimes used for fixing dyes)   **14–15 breathe . . . watering** pause for breath in your drinking   **15 play it off** drink it up   **21 sugar** (used to sweeten wine)   **22 underskinker** assistant to a waiter or bartender   **24–5 Anon . . . Half-Moon** coming, sir!—charge a pint of a sweet Spanish wine to the customers in the room of the inn called "the Half-Moon"   **27 by-room** side-room | **puny drawer** inexperienced tapster or bartender   **30 precedent** example

FRANCIS Anon, anon, sir.—Look down into the Pomgarnet,° Ralph.   35

PRINCE Come hither, Francis.

FRANCIS My lord?

PRINCE How long hast thou to serve,° Francis?

FRANCIS Forsooth, five years, and as much as to—

POINS [*within*] Francis!   40

FRANCIS [*calling*] Anon, anon, sir.

PRINCE Five year! By'r Lady,° a long lease for the clinking of pewter. But Francis, darest thou be so valiant as to play the coward with thy indenture° and show it a fair pair of heels and run from it?   45

FRANCIS Oh, Lord, sir, I'll be sworn upon all the books° in England, I could find in my heart—

POINS [*within*] Francis!

FRANCIS [*calling*] Anon, sir.

PRINCE How old art thou, Francis?   50

FRANCIS Let me see, about Michaelmas° next I shall be—

POINS [*within*] Francis!

FRANCIS [*calling*] Anon, sir. Pray, stay a little, my lord.

PRINCE Nay, but hark you, Francis: for the sugar thou gavest me, 'twas a pennyworth, was 't not?   55

FRANCIS Oh, Lord, I would it had been two!

PRINCE I will give thee for it a thousand pound. Ask me when thou wilt, and thou shalt have it.

POINS [*within*] Francis!

FRANCIS [*calling*] Anon, anon.   60

PRINCE Anon,° Francis? No, Francis; but tomorrow, Francis, or, Francis, o'Thursday, or indeed, Francis, when thou wilt. But, Francis—

FRANCIS My lord?

PRINCE Wilt thou rob this leathern-jerkin, crystal-button, 65 not-pated, agate-ring, puke-stocking, caddis-garter, smooth-tongue, Spanish-pouch—°

---

34 Pomgarnet Pomegranate (another room in the inn) **38 serve** serve out your apprenticeship **42 By'r Lady** By Our Lady **44 indenture** contract of apprenticeship **46 books** Bibles **51 Michaelmas** September 29 **61 Anon** (strictly speaking, "Anon" means "immediately") [RL] **65–7 Wilt . . . Spanish-pouch** will you rob your master of your services by running away, this man with his leather jacket, transparent buttons, cropped hair, a ring with small figures in an agate stone for a seal, dark woolen stockings, worsted garters, an ingratiating flattering manner of speech, wallet of Spanish leather

FRANCIS   Oh, Lord, sir, who do you mean?

PRINCE   Why, then, your brown bastard is your only drink; for
look you, Francis, your white canvas doublet will sully. In   70
Barbary, sir, it° cannot come to so much.°

FRANCIS   What, sir?

POINS [*within*]   Francis!

PRINCE   Away, you rogue! Dost thou not hear them call?

> *Here they both call him; the drawer stands*
> *amazed, not knowing which way to go*

> *Enter Vintner*°

VINTNER   What° stand'st thou still and hear'st such a calling?   75
Look to the guests within. [*Exit Francis*] My lord, old Sir
John, with half a dozen more, are at the door. Shall I let
them in?

PRINCE   Let them alone awhile, and then open the door.

> [*Exit Vintner*]

[*Calling*]   Poins!   80

> *Enter Poins*

POINS   Anon, anon, sir.

PRINCE   Sirrah, Falstaff and the rest of the thieves are at the
door. Shall we be merry?

POINS   As merry as crickets, my lad. But hark ye, what cunning
match° have you made with this jest of the drawer? Come,   85
what's the issue?°

PRINCE   I am now of all humors that have showed themselves
humors since the old days of Goodman° Adam to the pupil°
age of this present twelve o'clock at midnight.°

> [*Enter Francis, hurrying across the stage with wine*]

What's o'clock, Francis?   90

FRANCIS   Anon, anon, sir.   [*Exit*]

PRINCE   That ever this fellow should have fewer words than a
parrot, and yet the son of a woman! His industry is upstairs
and downstairs, his eloquence the parcel of a reckoning.° I

69–71 Why . . . much (the Prince talks seeming nonsense in order to bewilder Francis,
but he also implies that Francis should stick to his trade, since he will not cut much
of a figure in the world)   **71 it** sugar   **74.3 *Vintner*** Innkeeper   **75 What** why
85 match game, contest   **86 issue** outcome, point   **87–9 I . . . midnight** I'm now in a
mood for anything that has happened in the whole history of the world   **88 Goodman**
(title for a yeoman) | **pupil** youthful   **94 parcel . . . reckoning** items of a bill

am not yet of Percy's mind, the Hotspur of the north, he that   95
kills me° some six or seven dozen of Scots at a breakfast,
washes his hands, and says to his wife, "Fie upon this quiet
life! I want work." "Oh, my sweet Harry," says she, "how
many hast thou killed today?" "Give my roan horse a
drench,"° says he,° and answers, "Some fourteen," an hour   100
after, "a trifle, a trifle." I prithee, call in Falstaff. I'll play
Percy, and that damned brawn° shall play Dame Mortimer
his wife. "Rivo!"° says the drunkard. Call in ribs,° call in
tallow.°

Enter Falstaff, [Gadshill, Bardolph, and
Peto; Francis following with wine]

POINS   Welcome, Jack. Where hast thou been?   105

FALSTAFF   A plague of° all cowards, I say, and a vengeance too!
Marry and amen! Give me a cup of sack, boy. Ere I lead this
life long, I'll sew nether-stocks,° and mend them and foot°
them too. A plague of all cowards! Give me a cup of sack,
rogue. Is there no virtue extant?   *He drinketh*   110

PRINCE   Didst thou never see Titan° kiss a dish of butter,
pitiful-hearted Titan, that° melted at the sweet tale of the
sun's? If thou didst, then behold that compound.°

FALSTAFF   You rogue, here's lime in this sack° too. There is
nothing but roguery to be found in villainous man, yet a   115
coward is worse than a cup of sack with lime in it. A
villainous coward! Go thy ways, old Jack, die when thou
wilt. If manhood, good manhood, be not forgot upon the
face of the earth, then am I a shotten herring.° There lives
not three good men unhanged in England, and one of them   120
is fat and grows old, God help the while!° A bad world, I
say. I would I were a weaver;° I could sing psalms or
anything. A plague of all cowards, I say still.

96 kills me kills (*me* is used colloquially)   **100 drench** draft (sometimes of medicine) |
says he he tells a servant   **102 brawn** fat boar   **103 Rivo** (an exclamation of
uncertain meaning, but related to drinking) | **ribs** rib roast   **104 tallow** fat
drippings   **106 of** on   **108 netherstocks** stockings (the sewing or mending of which
is a menial occupation) | **foot** make a new foot for   **111 Titan** the sun   **112 that**
the butter   **113 compound** melting butter, Falstaff   **114 lime in this sack** lime
added to make the wine sparkle   **119 a shotten herring** a herring that has cast its
roe and is consequently thin   **121 the while** in these bad times   **122 weaver** (many
psalm-singing Protestant immigrants from the Low Countries were weavers)

PRINCE   How now, woolsack,° what mutter you?

FALSTAFF   A king's son! If I do not beat thee out of thy kingdom   125
with a dagger of lath,° and drive all thy subjects afore thee
like a flock of wild geese, I'll never wear hair on my face
more. You, Prince of Wales!

PRINCE   Why, you whoreson round man, what's the matter?

FALSTAFF   Are not you a coward? Answer me to that. And Poins   130
there?

POINS   Zounds, ye fat paunch, an ye call me coward, by the
Lord, I'll stab thee.

FALSTAFF   I call thee coward? I'll see thee damned ere I call thee
coward, but I would give a thousand pound I could run as   135
fast as thou canst. You are straight enough in the shoulders;
you care not who sees your back. Call you that backing of
your friends? A plague upon such backing! Give me them
that will face me. Give me a cup of sack. I am a rogue if I
drunk today.   140

PRINCE   Oh, villain, thy lips are scarce wiped since thou
drunk'st last.

FALSTAFF   All is one for that.° (*He drinketh.*) A plague of all
cowards, still say I.

PRINCE   What's the matter?   145

FALSTAFF   What's the matter? There be four of us here have
ta'en a thousand pound this day morning.°

PRINCE   Where is it, Jack, where is it?

FALSTAFF   Where is it? Taken from us it is. A hundred upon
poor four of us.   150

PRINCE   What, a hundred, man?

FALSTAFF   I am a rogue if I were not at half-sword° with a dozen
of them two hours together. I have scaped° by miracle. I am
eight times thrust through the doublet,° four through the
hose,° my buckler° cut through and through, my sword   155
hacked like a handsaw—*ecce signum!*° I never dealt better
since I was a man. All would not do.° A plague of all

---

124 woolsack bale of wool   **126 dagger of lath** (the Vice, a stock comic figure in
morality plays, was so armed)   **143 All . . . that** no matter   **147 this day morning**
this morning   **152 at half-sword** fighting at close quarters   **153 scaped** escaped
154 doublet Elizabethan upper garment like a jacket   **155 hose** close-fitting
breeches | **buckler** shield   **156 *ecce signum*** behold the proof (familiar words from
the Mass)   **157 All . . . do** all that I did was of no use

cowards! Let them speak. If they speak more or less than truth, they are villains and the sons of darkness.

PRINCE Speak, sirs, how was it? 160

GADSHILL We four set upon some dozen—

FALSTAFF Sixteen at least, my lord.

GADSHILL And bound them.

PETO No, no, they were not bound.

FALSTAFF You rogue, they were bound, every man of them, or I 165
am a Jew else, an Hebrew Jew.°

GADSHILL As we were sharing, some six or seven fresh men set
upon us—

FALSTAFF And unbound the rest, and then come in the other.°

PRINCE What, fought you with them all? 170

FALSTAFF All? I know not what you call all, but if I fought not
with fifty of them, I am a bunch of radish. If there were not
two- or three-and-fifty upon poor old Jack, then am I no
two-legged creature.

PRINCE Pray God you have not murdered some of them. 175

FALSTAFF Nay, that's past praying for. I have peppered two of
them. Two I am sure I have paid, two rogues in buckram
suits.° I tell thee what, Hal, if I tell thee a lie, spit in my face,
call me horse. Thou knowest my old ward.° Here I lay,° and
thus I bore my point. [*He demonstrates his stance*] Four 180
rogues in buckram let drive at me—

PRINCE What, four? Thou said'st but two even° now.

FALSTAFF Four, Hal, I told thee four.

POINS Ay, ay, he said four.

FALSTAFF These four came all afront,° and mainly° thrust at 185
me. I made me° no more ado but took all their seven points
in my target,° thus.

PRINCE Seven? Why, there were but four even now.

FALSTAFF In buckram?

POINS Ay, four, in buckram suits. 190

FALSTAFF Seven, by these hilts,° or I am a villain else.

PRINCE [*aside to Poins*] Prithee, let him alone. We shall have
more anon.

---

166 Jew . . . Hebrew Jew (an instance of Elizabethan antisemitism) [RL] **169 other**
others **177–8 buckram suits** (see 1.2.160) [RL] **179 ward** defensive stance, parry |
lay stood **182 even** just **185 afront** abreast | **mainly** powerfully **186 made me** made
(*me* is used colloquially) **187 target** shield **191 by these hilts** by my sword hilt

FALSTAFF   Dost thou hear me, Hal?

PRINCE   Ay, and mark° thee too, Jack.   195

FALSTAFF   Do so, for it is worth the listening to. These nine in
buckram that I told thee of—

PRINCE   So, two more already.

FALSTAFF   Their points° being broken—

POINS   Down fell their hose.   200

FALSTAFF   Began to give me ground; but I followed me° close,
came in foot and hand; and with a thought° seven of the
eleven I paid.

PRINCE   Oh, monstrous! Eleven buckram men grown out of two!

FALSTAFF   But, as the devil would have it, three misbegotten   205
knaves in Kendal° green came at my back and let drive at me;
for it was so dark, Hal, that thou couldst not see thy hand.

PRINCE   These lies are like their father° that begets them, gross
as a mountain, open, palpable. Why, thou claybrained guts,
thou knotty-pated° fool, thou whoreson, obscene, greasy   210
tallow-keech—°

FALSTAFF   What, art thou mad? Art thou mad? Is not the truth
the truth?

PRINCE   Why, how couldst thou know these men in Kendal
green when it was so dark thou couldst not see thy hand?   215
Come, tell us your reason. What sayest thou to this?

POINS   Come, your reason, Jack, your reason.

FALSTAFF   What, upon compulsion? Zounds, an I were at the
strappado,° or all the racks in the world, I would not tell
you on compulsion. Give you a reason on compulsion? If   220
reasons were as plentiful as blackberries,° I would give no
man a reason upon compulsion, I.

PRINCE   I'll be no longer guilty of this sin. This sanguine°
coward, this bed-presser, this horse-backbreaker, this huge
hill of flesh—   225

---

195 mark (1) pay heed (2) keep count   **199 points** sword points (but Poins puns on
the sense of laces, by which the hose were attached to the doublet)   **201 followed
me** followed   **202 with a thought** quick as a thought   **206 Kendal** a town known
for its textiles   **208 their father** (1) Falstaff (2) the devil, proverbially the father
of lies   **210 knotty-pated** thickheaded   **211 tallow-keech** lump of tallow
219 strappado a kind of torture   **221 reasons . . . blackberries** (Falstaff puns on
raisins, pronounced nearly like *reasons*)   **223 sanguine** ruddy

FALSTAFF 'Sblood, you starveling, you eel-skin, you dried
neat's° tongue, you bull's pizzle,° you stockfish!° Oh, for
breath to utter what is like thee! You tailor's yard,° you
sheath, you bowcase, you vile standing tuck°—

PRINCE Well, breathe awhile, and then to it again, and when 230
thou hast tired thyself in base comparisons, hear me speak
but this.

POINS Mark, Jack.

PRINCE We two saw you four set on four and bound them, and
were masters of their wealth. Mark now how a plain tale 235
shall put you down. Then did we two set on you four, and,
with a word,° outfaced° you from your prize, and have it,
yea, and can show it you here in the house. And, Falstaff,
you carried your guts away as nimbly, with as quick
dexterity, and roared for mercy, and still run and roared, as 240
ever I heard bull calf. What a slave art thou, to hack thy
sword as thou hast done, and then say it was in fight! What
trick, what device, what starting-hole° canst thou now find
out to hide thee from this open and apparent shame?

POINS Come, let's hear, Jack. What trick hast thou now? 245

FALSTAFF By the Lord, I knew ye as well as he that made ye.
Why, hear you, my masters, was it for me to kill the heir
apparent? Should I turn upon the true prince? Why, thou
knowest I am as valiant as Hercules, but beware instinct.
The lion will not touch the true prince. Instinct is a great 250
matter; I was now a coward on instinct. I shall think the
better of myself and thee during my life—I for a valiant lion,
and thou for a true prince. But by the Lord, lads, I am glad
you have the money. Hostess, clap to the doors! Watch°
tonight, pray° tomorrow. Gallants, lads, boys, hearts of 255
gold, all the titles of good fellowship come to you! What,
shall we be merry? Shall we have a play extempore?°

PRINCE Content; and the argument° shall be thy running away.

FALSTAFF Ah, no more of that, Hal, an thou lovest me!

Enter Hostess

227 **neat's** ox's | **pizzle** penis | **stockfish** dried cod   228 **yard** yardstick   229 **standing
tuck** rapier standing on its point, or no longer pliant   237 **with a word** (1) in a
word (2) with a minimum of speech | **outfaced** frightened   243 **starting-hole** point
of shelter (like a rabbit's hole)   254 **Watch** (1) keep watchful vigil (see Matthew
26.41) (2) carouse   255 **pray** (1) pray to God (2) prey   257 **play** **extempore**
improvised role playing [RL]   258 **argument** plot of the play

HOSTESS   Oh, Jesu, my lord the Prince!   260

PRINCE   How now, my lady the hostess, what say'st thou to me?

HOSTESS   Marry, my lord, there is a nobleman of the court at
door would speak with you. He says he comes from your
father.

PRINCE   Give him as much as will make him a royal man,° and   265
send him back again to my mother.

FALSTAFF   What manner of man is he?

HOSTESS   An old man.

FALSTAFF   What doth° Gravity out of his bed at midnight? Shall
I give him his answer?   270

PRINCE   Prithee, do, Jack.

FALSTAFF   Faith, and I'll send him packing.   *Exit*

PRINCE   Now, sirs. By'r Lady, you fought fair; so did you, Peto;
so did you, Bardolph. You are lions too, you ran away upon
instinct, you will not touch the true prince; no, fie!   275

BARDOLPH   Faith, I ran when I saw others run.

PRINCE   Faith, tell me now in earnest, how came Falstaff's
sword so hacked?

PETO   Why, he hacked it with his dagger, and said he would
swear truth out of England but he would° make you believe   280
it was done in fight, and persuaded us to do the like.

BARDOLPH   Yea, and to tickle our noses with spear grass to
make them bleed, and then to beslubber° our garments with
it and swear it was the blood of true men. I did that° I did
not this seven year before: I blushed to hear his monstrous   285
devices.

PRINCE   Oh, villain, thou stolest a cup of sack eighteen years ago
and wert taken with the manner,° and ever since thou hast
blushed extempore.° Thou hadst fire° and sword on thy side,
and yet thou ran'st away. What instinct hadst thou for it?   290

BARDOLPH   My lord, do you see these meteors?° Do you behold
these exhalations?°   [*Pointing to his own face*]

PRINCE   I do.

---

265 **Give . . . man** (Prince Hal puns on the value of coins: a *noble* was worth six shillings
eight pence; a *royal* was worth ten shillings)   269 **What doth** why is   280 **swear . . .
would** swear oaths until they go out of fashion if he did not   283 **beslubber**
smear, cover   284 **that** something   288 **taken . . . manner** caught with the goods
289 **extempore** without needing any occasion (Bardolph is red-faced whether he blushes
or not) | **fire** a red nose and complexion caused by heavy drinking   291, 292 **meteors,
exhalations** the red blotches on Bardolph's face

BARDOLPH   What think you they portend?°
PRINCE   Hot livers and cold purses.°   295
BARDOLPH   Choler,° my lord, if rightly taken.°
PRINCE   No, if rightly taken, halter.°

Enter Falstaff°

Here comes lean Jack, here comes bare-bone.—How now,
my sweet creature of bombast?° How long is't ago, Jack,
since thou sawest thine own knee?   300
FALSTAFF   My own knee? When I was about thy years, Hal, I
was not an eagle's talon in the waist; I could have crept into
any alderman's thumb ring. A plague of sighing and grief! It
blows a man up like a bladder. There's villainous news
abroad. Here was Sir John Bracy from your father. You   305
must to the court in the morning. That same mad fellow of
the north, Percy, and he of Wales that gave Amamon° the
bastinado° and made Lucifer cuckold° and swore the devil
his true liegeman° upon the cross of a Welsh hook°—what a
plague call you him?   310
POINS   Owen Glendower.
FALSTAFF   Owen, Owen, the same; and his son-in-law Mortimer,
and old Northumberland, and that sprightly Scot of Scots,
Douglas, that runs a-horseback up a hill perpendicular—
PRINCE   He that rides at high speed, and with his pistol kills a   315
sparrow flying.
FALSTAFF   You have hit it.°
PRINCE   So did he never the sparrow.

---

294 portend signify (meteors, comets, and other meteorological phenomena were
widely regarded as omens of disaster)   **295 Hot . . . purses** livers inflamed by drink
and purses made empty by spending   **296 Choler** a choleric or combative
temperament | **taken** understood (but the Prince, in his next speech, uses the word
to mean "arrested")   **297 halter** hangman's noose (the Prince plays on Bardolph's
choler, which he takes as *collar*)   **297.1** (Falstaff's entry in the Quarto after l. 296
suggests he is visible to the audience while the Prince talks of a hangman's halter)
299 bombast (1) cotton padding (2) fustian speech   **307 Amamon** (the name of a
demon)   **308 bastinado** beating on the soles of the feet | **made . . . cuckold** gave
Lucifer his horns, the sign of cuckoldry   **308–9 and swore . . . liegeman** and made
the devil take an oath of allegiance as a true subject   **309 Welsh hook** curved-
bladed pike lacking the cross shape of the sword on which such oaths were usually
sworn   **317 hit it** described it exactly (but the Prince takes *hit* literally in the
next line)

FALSTAFF   Well, that rascal hath good mettle in him; he will
not run.°   320

PRINCE   Why, what a rascal art thou then to praise him so for
running!

FALSTAFF   A-horseback, ye cuckoo; but afoot he will not budge
a foot.

PRINCE   Yes, Jack, upon instinct.   325

FALSTAFF   I grant ye, upon instinct. Well, he is there too, and
one Mordake, and a thousand blue-caps° more. Worcester is
stolen away tonight. Thy father's beard is turned white with
the news. You may buy land now as cheap as stinking
mackerel.   330

PRINCE   Why, then, it is like,° if there come a hot June and this
civil buffeting hold,° we shall buy maidenheads as they buy
hobnails, by the hundreds.

FALSTAFF   By the mass, lad, thou sayest true; it is like we shall
have good trading that way. But tell me, Hal, art not thou   335
horrible afeard? Thou being heir apparent, could the world
pick thee out three such enemies again as that fiend
Douglas, that spirit Percy, and that devil Glendower? Art
thou not horribly afraid? Doth not thy blood thrill at it?

PRINCE   Not a whit, i'faith. I lack some of thy instinct.   340

FALSTAFF   Well, thou wilt be horribly chid° tomorrow when thou
comest to thy father. If thou love me, practice an answer.

PRINCE   Do thou stand for my father, and examine me upon the
particulars of my life.

FALSTAFF   Shall I? Content. This chair shall be my state,° this   345
dagger my scepter, and this cushion my crown.
                    [*Falstaff establishes himself on his "throne"*]

PRINCE   Thy state is taken for a joint stool,° thy golden scepter
for a leaden° dagger, and thy precious rich crown for a
pitiful bald crown.

FALSTAFF   Well, an the fire of grace be not quite out of thee,   350
now shalt thou be moved. Give me a cup of sack to make my

---

320 run flee (but the Prince answers punningly in the sense of "ride at high speed")
327 blue-caps Scottish soldiers   **331 like** likely   **332 hold** continues   **341 chid**
chided   **345 state** chair of state, throne   **347 joint stool** a stool made by a joiner or
furniture maker   **348 leaden** of soft metal, hence inferior

eyes look red, that it may be thought I have wept; for I must
speak in passion, and I will do it in King Cambyses' vein.°

PRINCE Well, here is my leg.   [*He bows*]

FALSTAFF And here is my speech. Stand aside, nobility.   355

HOSTESS Oh, Jesu, this is excellent sport, i'faith!

FALSTAFF Weep not, sweet queen, for trickling tears are vain.

HOSTESS Oh, the Father,° how he holds his countenance!°

FALSTAFF For God's sake, lords, convey° my tristful° queen,
For tears do stop° the floodgates of her eyes.   360

HOSTESS Oh, Jesu, he doth it as like one of these harlotry°
players° as ever I see!

FALSTAFF Peace, good pint pot; peace, good tickle-brain.°—
Harry, I do not only marvel where thou spendest thy time,
but also how thou art accompanied; for though the   365
camomile, the more it is trodden on the faster it grows, yet
youth, the more it is wasted the sooner it wears.° That thou
art my son I have partly thy mother's word, partly my own
opinion, but chiefly a villainous trick° of thine eye and a
foolish hanging of thy nether lip that doth warrant° me. If   370
then thou be son to me, here lies the point: why, being son to
me, art thou so pointed at? Shall the blessed sun of heaven
prove a micher° and eat blackberries? A question not to be
asked. Shall the son of England prove a thief and take purses?
A question to be asked. There is a thing, Harry, which thou   375
hast often heard of, and it is known to many in our land by
the name of pitch. This pitch,° as ancient writers do report,
doth defile;° so doth the company thou keepest. For, Harry,
now I do not speak to thee in drink but in tears, not in
pleasure but in passion,° not in words only but in woes also.   380

---

353 in . . . vein in the ranting and (by Shakespeare's time) old-fashioned style of
Thomas Preston's *Cambyses*, an early Elizabethan tragedy **358 the Father** in God's
name | **holds his countenance** keeps a straight face **359 convey** escort away |
tristful sorrowing **360 stop** fill **361 harlotry** scurvy, vagabond **362 players**
actors **363 tickle-brain** (a slang term for strong liquor, here applied as a nickname
for the tavern hostess) **365–7 for though . . . wears** (Falstaff parodies the style of
John Lyly's *Euphues*, with its elaborate balanced antitheses, alliterative effects, and
illustrations drawn from fanciful natural history; *camomile* is an aromatic creeping
herb whose flowers and leaves are used medicinally) **369 trick** trait **370 warrant**
assure **373 micher** truant **377–8 This . . . defile** (an allusion to the familiar
proverb from Ecclesiasticus 13.1 about the defilement of touching pitch) **377 pitch**
a sticky, black residue from the distillation of tar, used to seal wood from moisture
380 passion sorrow

And yet there is a virtuous man whom I have often noted in
thy company, but I know not his name.

PRINCE What manner of man, an it like° Your Majesty?

FALSTAFF A goodly portly° man, i'faith, and a corpulent; of a
cheerful look, a pleasing eye, and a most noble carriage;   385
and, as I think, his age some fifty, or, by'r Lady, inclining to
threescore; and now I remember me, his name is Falstaff. If
that man should be lewdly° given, he deceiveth me; for,
Harry, I see virtue in his looks. If then the tree may be known
by the fruit,° as the fruit by the tree, then peremptorily° I   390
speak it, there is virtue in that Falstaff. Him keep with, the
rest banish. And tell me now, thou naughty varlet, tell me,
where hast thou been this month?

PRINCE Dost thou speak like a king? Do thou stand for me,
and I'll play my father.   395

FALSTAFF Depose me? If thou dost it half so gravely, so
majestically, both in word and matter, hang me up by the
heels for a rabbit-sucker° or a poulter's° hare.

[*Hal takes Falstaff's place on the "throne"*]

PRINCE Well, here I am set.°

FALSTAFF And here I stand. Judge, my masters.   400

PRINCE Now, Harry, whence come you?

FALSTAFF My noble lord, from Eastcheap.

PRINCE The complaints I hear of thee are grievous.

FALSTAFF 'Sblood,° my lord, they are false.—Nay, I'll tickle ye
for° a young prince, i'faith.   405

PRINCE Swearest thou, ungracious boy? Henceforth ne'er
look on me. Thou art violently carried away from grace.
There is a devil haunts thee in the likeness of an old fat
man; a tun° of man is thy companion. Why dost thou
converse° with that trunk of humors,° that bolting-hutch°   410
of beastliness, that swollen parcel of dropsies,° that huge
bombard° of sack, that stuffed cloak-bag° of guts, that

383 **an it like** if it please   384 **portly** (1) stately (2) corpulent   388 **lewdly** wickedly
389–90 **If . . . by the fruit** (see Matthew 12.33)   390 **peremptorily** decisively
398 **rabbit-sucker** unweaned rabbit | **poulter's** poulterer's   399 **set** seated
404 **'Sblood** by Christ's blood   404–5 **tickle ye for** amuse you in the role of   409 **tun**
(1) large barrel (2) ton   410 **converse** associate | **humors** body fluids, diseases |
bolting-hutch large bin   411 **dropsies** accumulations of fluids causing swelling
412 **bombard** leathern drinking vessel | **cloak-bag** portmanteau

roasted Manningtree ox° with the pudding° in his belly,
that reverend Vice,° that gray Iniquity,° that father ruffian,
that vanity° in years? Wherein is he good but to taste sack   415
and drink it? Wherein neat and cleanly° but to carve a capon°
and eat it? Wherein cunning° but in craft? Wherein crafty
but in villainy? Wherein villainous but in all things?
Wherein worthy but in nothing?

FALSTAFF   I would Your Grace would take me with you.°   420
Whom means Your Grace?

PRINCE   That villainous abominable misleader of youth, Falstaff,
that old white-bearded Satan.

FALSTAFF   My lord, the man I know.

PRINCE   I know thou dost.   425

FALSTAFF   But to say I know more harm in him than in myself
were to say more than I know. That he is old, the more the
pity, his white hairs do witness it; but that he is, saving your
reverence,° a whoremaster, that I utterly deny. If sack and
sugar be a fault, God help the wicked! If to be old and merry   430
be a sin, then many an old host° that I know is damned. If to
be fat be to be hated, then Pharaoh's lean kine° are to be
loved. No, my good lord, banish Peto, banish Bardolph,
banish Poins; but for sweet Jack Falstaff, kind Jack Falstaff,
true Jack Falstaff, valiant Jack Falstaff, and therefore more   435
valiant being as he is old Jack Falstaff, banish not him thy
Harry's company, banish not him thy Harry's company—
banish plump Jack, and banish all the world.

PRINCE   I do, I will.   [*A knocking.*
                    Exeunt Hostess, Francis, and Bardolph]
                                      Enter Bardolph, running

BARDOLPH   Oh, my lord, my lord! The sheriff with a most   440
monstrous watch° is at the door.

---

413 **Manningtree ox** (Manningtree, a town in Essex, had noted fairs where, no
doubt, oxen were roasted whole) | **pudding** sausage-like entrails   414 **Vice,
Iniquity** (allegorical names for the chief comic character and tempter in morality
plays)   415 **vanity** person given to worldly desires   416 **cleanly** (1) pure (2) deft |
a capon a castrated rooster for the table   417 **cunning** (1) skillful (2) crafty   420 **take
me with you** let me catch up with your meaning   428–9 **saving your reverence** with
my apology for using offensive language   431 **host** innkeeper   432 **Pharaoh's lean
kine** (see Genesis 41, where Pharaoh's dream of seven well-fattened cattle being
devoured by seven lean ones is interpreted by Joseph as a prophecy of seven years'
famine to come)   441 **watch** posse of constables

FALSTAFF   Out, ye rogue! Play out the play. I have much to say
in the behalf of that Falstaff.

Enter the Hostess

HOSTESS   Oh, Jesu, my lord, my lord!
PRINCE   Heigh, heigh! The devil rides upon a fiddle-stick.° What's   445
the matter?
HOSTESS   The sheriff and all the watch are at the door. They are
come to search the house. Shall I let them in?
FALSTAFF   Dost thou hear, Hal? Never call a true piece of gold a
counterfeit. Thou art essentially made without seeming so.°   450
PRINCE   And thou a natural coward without instinct.
FALSTAFF   I deny your major.° If you will deny° the sheriff, so; if
not, let him enter. If I become° not a cart° as well as another
man, a plague on my bringing up!° I hope I shall as soon be
strangled with a halter as another.   455
PRINCE   Go hide thee behind the arras.° The rest walk up above.°
Now, my masters, for a true face and good conscience.
FALSTAFF   Both which I have had, but their date is out,° and
therefore I'll hide me.   [*He hides behind the arras*]
PRINCE   Call in the sheriff.   460

[*Exeunt all except the Prince and Peto*]

Enter Sheriff and the Carrier

Now, Master Sheriff, what is your will with me?
SHERIFF   First, pardon me, my lord. A hue and cry°
Hath followed certain men unto this house.
PRINCE   What men?
SHERIFF   One of them is well known, my gracious lord,   465
A gross, fat man.
CARRIER   As fat as butter.
PRINCE   The man, I do assure you, is not here,
For I myself at this time have employed him.

---

445 The . . . fiddlestick here's much ado about nothing   449–50 Dost . . . seeming
so (in this difficult passage, Falstaff seems to suggest that he is true gold, not counterfeit, and so should not be betrayed to the watch by the Prince, who, he hopes, is not
merely playacting at the tavern but is truly one of its madcap members)   452 deny
your major reject your major premise | deny refuse entrance to   453 become befit,
adorn | cart hangman's cart   454 bringing up (1) upbringing (2) being brought
before the authorities to be hanged   456 arras wall hanging or tapestry   456 up
above upstairs   458 date is out lease has run out   462 hue and cry outcry calling
for the pursuit of a felon

And, Sheriff, I will engage° my word to thee
That I will, by tomorrow dinnertime,°   470
Send him to answer thee, or any man,
For anything he shall be charged withal;
And so let me entreat you leave the house.
SHERIFF I will, my lord. There are two gentlemen
Have in this robbery lost three hundred marks.   475
PRINCE It may be so. If he have robbed these men,
He shall be answerable; and so farewell.
SHERIFF Good night, my noble lord.
PRINCE I think it is good morrow,° is it not?
SHERIFF Indeed, my lord, I think it be two o'clock.   480
                                        Exit [with Carrier]
PRINCE This oily rascal is known as well as Paul's.° Go call
him forth.
PETO [*discovering Falstaff*] Falstaff—Fast asleep behind the
arras, and snorting like a horse.
PRINCE Hark, how hard he fetches breath. Search his pockets. 485
(*He searcheth his pockets, and findeth certain papers.*) What
hast thou found?
PETO Nothing but papers, my lord.
PRINCE Let's see what they be. Read them.
PETO [*reads*]
Item, A capon, ...2s. 2d.   490
Item, Sauce, ...4d.
Item, Sack, two gallons, ...5s. 8d.
Item, Anchovies and sack after supper, ...2s. 6d.
Item, Bread, ...ob.°
PRINCE Oh, monstrous! But one halfpennyworth of bread to   495
this intolerable deal of sack? What there is else, keep close;°
we'll read it at more advantage.° There let him sleep till day.
I'll to the court in the morning. We must all to the wars, and
thy place shall be honorable. I'll procure this fat rogue a
charge of foot,° and I know his death will be a march of   500
twelve score.° The money shall be paid back again with

---

469 **engage** pledge   470 **dinnertime** about noon   479 **morrow** morning   481 **Paul's**
Saint Paul's Cathedral   494 **ob.** obolus, halfpenny   496 **close** hidden   497 **advantage**
favorable opportunity   500 **charge of foot** command of a company of infantry
501 **twelve score** two hundred and forty yards

advantage.° Be with me betimes° in the morning; and so,
good morrow, Peto.

PETO   Good morrow, good my lord.

                     Exeunt [separately. Falstaff is concealed
                            once more behind the arras°]

ACT 3
SCENE 1

Enter Hotspur, Worcester, Lord Mortimer,
[and] Owen Glendower

MORTIMER   These promises are fair, the parties sure,
And our induction° full of prosperous hope.°

HOTSPUR   Lord Mortimer, and cousin Glendower,
Will you sit down? And uncle Worcester—
A plague upon it, I have forgot the map.   5

GLENDOWER *[producing a map]*
No, here it is. Sit, cousin Percy,
Sit, good cousin Hotspur—for by that name
As oft as Lancaster° doth speak of you
His cheek looks pale, and with a rising sigh
He wisheth you in heaven.

HOTSPUR   And you in hell,   10
As oft as he hears Owen Glendower spoke of.

GLENDOWER   I cannot blame him. At my nativity
The front° of heaven was full of fiery shapes,
Of burning cressets,° and at my birth

---

502 **advantage** interest | **betimes** early   504.1–2 *Exeunt . . . arras* (onstage, the
arras is evidently arranged so that Falstaff can exit behind it once the scene is over)

3.1. Location: Wales. Glendower's residence. (Holinshed places a meeting of the
rebel deputies at Bangor in the Archdeacon's house, but in this present
"unhistorical" scene, as invented by Shakespeare, Glendower is host throughout.)
Seats are provided onstage. Summary: Hotspur angers his ally Glendower by
satirizing his mythology and by caviling about his share of a divided kingdom. He
is chastized by his brother-in-law Mortimer and his uncle Worcester. The scene
ends more tenderly with the leave-taking of Hotspur's and Mortimer's wives, but
with Hotspur's exuberant humor intact.

2 **induction** beginning | **prosperous hope** hope of prospering   8 **Lancaster** King
Henry, here demoted to Duke of Lancaster   13 **front** brow, face (as also at l. 36)
14 **cressets** lights burning in metal baskets suspended from the ends of long poles or
ceilings; hence, meteors

The frame and huge foundation of the earth　　　　　　15
Shaked like a coward.
HOTSPUR　　　　　　　　　Why, so it would have done
　At the same season, if your mother's cat
　Had but kittened, though yourself had never been born.
GLENDOWER　I say the earth did shake when I was born.
HOTSPUR　And I say the earth was not of my mind,　　　20
　If you suppose as fearing you it shook.
GLENDOWER
　The heavens were all on fire; the earth did tremble.
HOTSPUR　Oh, then the earth shook to see the heavens on fire,
　And not in fear of your nativity.
　Diseasèd nature oftentimes breaks forth　　　　　　25
　In strange eruptions; oft the teeming earth
　Is with a kind of colic pinched and vexed
　By the imprisoning of unruly wind
　Within her womb, which, for enlargement° striving,
　Shakes the old beldam° earth and topples down　　　30
　Steeples and moss-grown towers. At your birth
　Our grandam earth, having this distemp'rature,°
　In passion° shook.
GLENDOWER　　　　　　Cousin, of° many men
　I do not bear these crossings.° Give me leave
　To tell you once again that at my birth　　　　　　35
　The front of heaven was full of fiery shapes,
　The goats ran from the mountains, and the herds
　Were strangely clamorous to the frighted fields.
　These signs have marked me extraordinary,
　And all the courses of my life do show　　　　　　40
　I am not in the roll of common men.
　Where is he living, clipped in with the sea
　That chides the banks of England, Scotland, Wales,
　Which calls me pupil or hath read to me?°

---

29 **enlargement** release　30 **beldam** grandmother　32 **distemp'rature** disorder
33 **passion** suffering | **of** from　34 **crossings** contradictions　42–4 **Where . . . to
me?** where is there anyone in all of sea-walled Great Britain who can claim to have
been my instructor?

And bring him out that is but woman's son   45
Can trace me in the tedious ways of art
And hold me pace in deep experiments.°
HOTSPUR   I think there's no man speaks better Welsh.°
I'll to dinner.
MORTIMER   Peace, cousin Percy; you will make him mad.   50
GLENDOWER   I can call° spirits from the vasty deep.°
HOTSPUR   Why, so can I, or so can any man;
But will they come when you do call for them?
GLENDOWER
Why, I can teach you, cousin, to command the devil.
HOTSPUR   And I can teach thee, coz, to shame the devil   55
By telling truth. Tell truth and shame the devil.
If thou have power to raise him, bring him hither,
And I'll be sworn I have power to shame him hence.
Oh, while you live, tell truth and shame the devil!
MORTIMER   Come, come, no more of this unprofitable chat.   60
GLENDOWER   Three times hath Henry Bolingbroke made head°
Against my power;° thrice from the banks of Wye
And sandy-bottomed Severn have I sent him
Bootless° home and weather-beaten back.
HOTSPUR   Home without boots, and in foul weather too!   65
How scapes he agues,° in the devil's name?
GLENDOWER   Come, here is the map. Shall we divide our right
According to our threefold order ta'en?°
MORTIMER   The Archdeacon° hath divided it
Into three limits° very equally: 70
England, from Trent and Severn hitherto,°
By south and east is to my part assigned;
All westward, Wales beyond the Severn shore,

45–7 And . . . experiments and I challenge you to produce a single human being who can follow my tracks in the arcane craft of magic or keep up with me in occult experiments   **48 speaks better Welsh** (Hotspur hides an insult behind the literal meaning, since "to speak Welsh" meant colloquially both "to boast" and "to speak nonsense")   **51 call** summon (but Hotspur sardonically replies in the sense of "call out to," whether or not there is any response) | **vasty deep** lower world   **61 made head** raised a force   **62 power** army   **64 Bootless** without advantage (but Hotspur quibbles on the sense of "barefoot")   **66 agues** fevers   **68 order ta'en** arrangements made   **69 Archdeacon** the Archdeacon of Bangor, in whose house, according to Holinshed, a meeting took place between deputies of the rebel leaders   **70 limits** regions   **71 hitherto** to this point

And all the fertile land within that bound,
To Owen Glendower; and, dear coz,° to you   75
The remnant northward, lying off from Trent.
And our indentures tripartite° are drawn,°
Which being sealèd interchangeably—
A business that this night may execute°—
Tomorrow, cousin Percy, you and I   80
And my good lord of Worcester will set forth
To meet your father and the Scottish power,
As is appointed us, at Shrewsbury.
My father° Glendower is not ready yet,
Nor shall we need his help these fourteen days.   85
[*To Glendower*]
Within that space you may° have drawn together
Your tenants, friends, and neighboring gentlemen.
GLENDOWER   A shorter time shall send me to you, lords;
And in my conduct° shall your ladies come,
From whom you now must steal and take no leave,   90
For there will be a world of water shed
Upon the parting of your wives and you.
HOTSPUR [*consulting the map*]
Methinks my moiety,° north from Burton here,
In quantity equals not one of yours.
See how this river comes me cranking in°   95
And cuts me from the best of all my land
A huge half-moon, a monstrous cantle,° out.
I'll have the current in this place dammed up,
And here the smug° and silver Trent shall run
In a new channel, fair and evenly.   100
It shall not wind with such a deep indent
To rob me of so rich a bottom° here.

---

75 **coz** cousin, brother-in-law   77 **tripartite** drawn up in triplicate, each document *sealèd interchangeably* (l. 78) with the seal of all signatories | **drawn** drawn up   79 **this night may execute** may be carried out tonight   84 **father** father-in-law   86 **may** will be able to   89 **conduct** escort   93 **moiety** share   95 **comes me cranking in** comes bending in on my share (the Trent, by turning northward to the North Sea instead of continuing eastward into the Wash, cuts Hotspur off from rich land in Lincolnshire and its vicinity)   97 **cantle** piece   99 **smug** smooth   102 **bottom** valley

GLENDOWER   Not wind? It shall, it must. You see it doth.

MORTIMER
Yea, but mark how he bears his course and runs me° up
With like advantage on the other side,   105
Gelding the opposèd continent° as much
As on the other side it takes from you.

WORCESTER   Yea, but a little charge° will trench° him here
And on this north side win this cape of land;
And then he runs straight and even.   110

HOTSPUR   I'll have it so. A little charge will do it.

GLENDOWER   I'll not have it altered.

HOTSPUR   Will not you?

GLENDOWER   No, nor you shall not.

HOTSPUR   Who shall say me nay?   115

GLENDOWER   Why, that will I.

HOTSPUR   Let me not understand you, then; speak it in Welsh.

GLENDOWER   I can speak English, lord, as well as you;
For I was trained up in the English court,
Where, being but young, I framèd to the harp°   120
Many an English ditty lovely well,
And gave the tongue a helpful ornament°—
A virtue that was never seen in you.

HOTSPUR   Marry, and I am glad of it with all my heart!
I had rather be a kitten and cry "mew"   125
Than one of these same meter balladmongers.
I had rather hear a brazen can'stick turned°
Or a dry wheel grate on the axletree,°
And that would set my teeth nothing° on edge,
Nothing so much as mincing poetry.   130
'Tis like the forced gait of a shuffling° nag.

GLENDOWER   Come, you shall have Trent turned.

---

104 runs me runs (*me* is used colloquially)   **106 Gelding . . . continent** cutting off from the land which it bounds on the opposite side (the Trent's southerly loop from Stoke to Burton deprives Mortimer of a piece of land, just as its later northerly course deprives Hotspur)   **108 charge** expenditure | **trench** provide a new channel   **120 framèd to the harp** set to harp accompaniment   **122 gave . . . ornament** added to the words a pleasing ornament of music; also, gave to the English tongue the ornament of music and poetry   **127 can'stick turned** candlestick turned on a lathe   **128 axletree** axle   **129 nothing** not at all   **131 shuffling** hobbled

HOTSPUR   I do not care. I'll give thrice so much land
  To any well-deserving friend;
  But in the way of bargain, mark ye me,   135
  I'll cavil on the ninth part of a hair.°
  Are the indentures drawn?° Shall we be gone?
GLENDOWER   The moon shines fair; you may away by night.
  I'll haste the writer° and withal°
  Break with° your wives of your departure hence.   140
  I am afraid my daughter will run mad,
  So much she doteth on her Mortimer.   *Exit*
MORTIMER   Fie, cousin Percy, how you cross my father!
HOTSPUR   I cannot choose. Sometimes he angers me
  With telling me of the moldwarp° and the ant,   145
  Of the dreamer Merlin° and his prophecies,
  And of a dragon and a finless fish,
  A clip-winged griffin° and a moulten° raven,
  A couching° lion and a ramping° cat,
  And such a deal of skimble-skamble° stuff   150
  As puts me from my faith.° I tell you what:
  He held me last night at least nine hours
  In reckoning up the several° devils' names
  That were his lackeys. I cried "Hum," and "Well, go to,"°
  But marked him not a word. Oh, he is as tedious   155
  As a tirèd horse, a railing wife,
  Worse than a smoky house. I had rather live
  With cheese and garlic in a windmill, far,
  Than feed on cates° and have him talk to me
  In any summer house in Christendom.   160
MORTIMER   In faith, he is a worthy gentleman,
  Exceedingly well read, and profited°

136 cavil . . . hair argue about the most trivial detail   **137 drawn** drawn up   **139 writer** scrivener who would be drawing the indentures | **withal** also   **140 Break with** inform   **145 moldwarp** mole (Holinshed tells us that the division was arranged because of a prophecy that represented King Henry as the mole and the others as the dragon, the lion, and the wolf, who should divide the land among them)   **146 Merlin** the bard, prophet, and magician of Arthurian story, Welsh in origin   **148 griffin** a fabulous beast, half lion, half eagle | **moulten** having molted   **149 couching** couchant, crouching (Heraldic term) | **ramping** rampant, advancing on its hind legs (Hotspur is ridiculing the heraldic emblems that Glendower holds so dear)   **150 skimble-skamble** foolish, nonsensical   **151 puts . . . faith** drives me from my (Christian) faith   **153 several** various   **154 go to** you don't say   **159 cates** delicacies   **162 profited** proficient

In strange concealments,° valiant as a lion
And wondrous affable, and as bountiful
As mines of India. Shall I tell you, cousin?   165
He holds your temper° in a high respect
And curbs himself even of his natural scope°
When you come 'cross° his humor. Faith, he does.
I warrant you that man is not alive
Might° so have tempted him as you have done   170
Without the taste of danger and reproof.
But do not use it oft, let me entreat you.

WORCESTER [*to Hotspur*]
In faith, my lord, you are too willful-blame,°
And since your coming hither have done enough
To put him quite besides° his patience.   175
You must needs learn, lord, to amend this fault.
Though sometimes it show greatness, courage, blood°—
And that's the dearest grace° it renders you—
Yet oftentimes it doth present° harsh rage,
Defect of manners, want of government,°   180
Pride, haughtiness, opinion,° and disdain,
The least of which haunting a nobleman
Loseth men's hearts and leaves behind a stain
Upon the beauty of all parts besides,°
Beguiling° them of commendation.   185

HOTSPUR
Well, I am schooled. Good manners be your speed!°
Here come our wives, and let us take our leave.

Enter Glendower with the ladies

MORTIMER   This is the deadly spite° that angers me:
My wife can speak no English, I no Welsh.

GLENDOWER   My daughter weeps she'll not part with you;   190
She'll be a soldier too, she'll to the wars.

---

163 **concealments** occult practices   166 **temper** temperament   167 **scope** freedom of speech   168 **come 'cross** contradict   170 **Might** who could   173 **too willful-blame** blameworthy for too much self-will   175 **besides** out of   177 **blood** spirit   178 **dearest grace** best (and costliest) credit   179 **present** represent   180 **want of government** lack of self-control   181 **opinion** vanity, arrogance   184 **all parts besides** all other abilities   185 **Beguiling** depriving   186 **Good . . . speed!** may these good manners you praise so bring you success! (said wryly; Hotspur doubts that good manners count for much in a time of war)   188 **spite** vexation

MORTIMER   Good father, tell her that she and my aunt° Percy
  Shall follow in your conduct° speedily.
Glendower speaks to her in Welsh,
and she answers him in the same

GLENDOWER   She is desperate here;° a peevish self-willed harlotry,°
  One that no persuasion can do good upon.   195
The lady speaks in Welsh

MORTIMER [*to her*]   I understand thy looks. That pretty Welsh°
  Which thou pourest down from these swelling heavens°
  I am too perfect° in; and, but for shame,
  In such a parley° should I answer thee.
The lady again in Welsh

  I understand thy kisses and thou mine,   200
  And that's a feeling disputation.°
  But I will never be a truant, love,
  Till I have learned thy language; for thy tongue
  Makes Welsh as sweet as ditties highly penned,°
  Sung by a fair queen in a summer's bower,   205
  With ravishing division,° to her lute.

GLENDOWER   Nay, if you melt,° then will she run mad.
The lady speaks again in Welsh

MORTIMER   Oh, I am ignorance itself in this!

GLENDOWER   She bids you on the wanton rushes° lay you down
  And rest your gentle head upon her lap,   210
  And she will sing the song that pleaseth you
  And on your eyelids crown the god of sleep,°
  Charming your blood with pleasing heaviness,°
  Making such difference° twixt wake and sleep
  As is the difference betwixt day and night   215

---

192 aunt (Percy's wife, here called Kate, was aunt of Edmund Mortimer, the fifth Earl of March, but was sister-in-law to the Sir Edward Mortimer who married Glendower's daughter) **193 conduct** safe-conduct, escort **194 desperate here** adamant on this point (her decision to accompany Mortimer) | **peevish self-willed harlotry** childish, willful, silly wench **196 That pretty Welsh** your eloquent tears **197 heavens** eyes **198 perfect** proficient **199 such a parley** the same language (of weeping) **201 disputation** conversation, debate **204 highly penned** eloquently composed, in high style **206 division** variation, passage in which rapid short notes vary a theme **207 melt** weep **209 wanton rushes** soft floor covering **212 crown . . . sleep** make sleep supreme ruler **213 heaviness** drowsiness **214 difference** nearly indistinguishable difference

The hour before the heavenly-harnessed team°
Begins his golden progress in the east.
MORTIMER   With all my heart I'll sit and hear her sing.
By that time will our book,° I think, be drawn.
GLENDOWER   Do so;   220
And those musicians that shall play to you
Hang in the air a thousand leagues from hence,
And straight they shall be here. Sit, and attend.
                    [*Mortimer reclines with his head in his wife's lap*]
HOTSPUR   Come, Kate, thou art perfect in lying down; come,
quick, quick, that I may lay my head in thy lap.   225
LADY PERCY   Go, ye giddy goose.
          [*Hotspur lies with his head in Kate's lap*] *The music plays*
HOTSPUR   Now I perceive the devil understands Welsh;
And 'tis no marvel he is so humorous.°
By'r Lady, he is a good musician.
LADY PERCY   Then should you be nothing but musical, for you 230
are altogether governed by humors. Lie still, ye thief,° and
hear the lady sing in Welsh.
HOTSPUR   I had rather hear Lady, my brach,° howl in Irish.
LADY PERCY   Wouldst thou have thy head broken?°
HOTSPUR   No.   235
LADY PERCY   Then be still.
HOTSPUR   Neither, 'tis a woman's fault.°
LADY PERCY   Now God help° thee!
HOTSPUR   To the Welsh lady's bed.
LADY PERCY   What's that?   240
HOTSPUR   Peace, she sings.
                    Here the lady sings a Welsh song
HOTSPUR   Come, Kate, I'll have your song too.
LADY PERCY   Not mine, in good sooth.
HOTSPUR   Not yours, in good sooth! Heart,° you swear like a
comfit maker's° wife. "Not you, in good sooth," and "as true 245
as I live," and "as God shall mend me,"and "as sure as day,"

216 **the heavenly-harnessed team** the team of horses drawing the chariot of the
sun 219 **book** document, indentures 228 **humorous** whimsical, capricious
231 **thief** rascal 233 **brach** bitch hound 234 **broken** struck so as to break the skin
237 **Neither . . . fault** I won't do that either; it's womanish to be submissive 238 **help**
amend (but Hotspur answers in the sense of "assist with an amour") 244 **Heart** by
Christ's heart 245 **comfit maker's** confectioner's

And givest such sarcenet° surety for thy oaths
As if thou never walk'st further than Finsbury.°
Swear me, Kate, like a lady as thou art,
A good mouth-filling oath, and leave "in sooth,"   250
And such protest of pepper-gingerbread,°
To velvet-guards° and Sunday citizens.
Come, sing.

LADY PERCY I will not sing.

HOTSPUR 'Tis the next way to turn tailor, or be redbreast 255
teacher.° An the indentures be drawn, I'll away within these
two hours; and so, come in when ye will.   *Exit*

GLENDOWER Come, come, Lord Mortimer. You are as slow
As hot Lord Percy is on fire to go.
By this° our book is drawn; we'll but° seal,   260
And then to horse immediately.

MORTIMER With all my heart.   *Exeunt*

ACT 3
SCENE 2

Enter the King, Prince of Wales, and others

KING Lords, give us leave. The Prince of Wales and I
Must have some private conference; but be near at hand,
For we shall presently have need of you.
                                        Exeunt Lords

I know not whether God will have it so
For some displeasing service I have done,   5
That in his secret doom° out of my blood°

---

247 **sarcenet** soft, flimsy (from the soft silken material known as *sarcenet*)
248 **Finsbury** a field just outside London frequented by the London citizenry (Hotspur jokes with Kate as though she were a citizen's wife, using the pious and modest oaths of such people) 251 **protest . . . gingerbread** mealy-mouthed protestations 252 **velvet-guards** wives who wear velvet trimming 255–6 **'Tis . . . teacher** the only use one might put singing to is to become a tailor (since tailors were noted for effeminacy and singing at their work) or an instructor to caged songbirds before they are sold (Hotspur airily dismisses singing, as he does poetry) 260 **By this** by this time | **but** just

3.2. Location: The royal court (historically, Westminster). **Summary:** Hal meets with his father, whose bitter reproaches prompt solemn vows to redeem himself by defeating Hotspur and the rebel forces.
6 **doom** judgment | **blood** offspring

He'll breed revengement and a scourge for me;
But thou dost in thy passages° of life
Make me believe that thou art only marked
For the hot vengeance and the rod of heaven   10
To punish my mistreadings.° Tell me else,°
Could such inordinate° and low desires,
Such poor, such bare, such lewd,° such mean attempts,°
Such barren pleasures, rude society,
As thou art matched withal° and grafted to,   15
Accompany the greatness of thy blood
And hold their level° with thy princely heart?

PRINCE So please Your Majesty, I would I could
 Quit° all offenses with as clear excuse
 As well as I am doubtless° I can purge   20
 Myself of many I am charged withal.
 Yet such extenuation let me beg
 As, in reproof° of many tales devised,
 Which oft the ear of greatness needs must hear
 By smiling pickthanks and base newsmongers,°   25
 I may, for some things true, wherein my youth
 Hath faulty wandered and irregular,
 Find pardon on my true submission.

KING God pardon thee! Yet let me wonder, Harry,
 At thy affections,° which do hold a wing°   30
 Quite from° the flight of all thy ancestors.
 Thy place in Council thou hast rudely° lost,
 Which by thy younger brother is supplied,
 And art almost an alien to the hearts
 Of all the court and princes of my blood.   35
 The hope and expectation of thy time°

---

8 **passages** course, conduct **9–11 thou . . . mistreadings** (1) you are marked as the means of heaven's vengeance against me, or (2) you are marked to suffer heaven's vengeance because of my sins **11 else** how otherwise **12 inordinate** (1) immoderate (2) unworthy of your rank **13 lewd** low, base | **attempts** undertakings **15 withal** with **17 hold their level** claim equality **19 Quit** acquit myself of **20 doubtless** certain **23 in reproof** upon disproof **25 By . . . newsmongers** from smiling flatterers and ignoble talebearers **30 affections** inclinations | **hold a wing** fly a course **31 from** at variance with **32 rudely** by violence (according to an apocryphal story, Prince Hal boxed the ears of the Lord Chief Justice and was sent to prison for it; see *2 Henry IV*, 1.2.49–50, 177, and 5.2.70–1) **36 The hope . . . time** the hopes that people had for you

Is ruined, and the soul of every man
Prophetically do forethink thy fall.
Had I so lavish of my presence been,
So common-hackneyed° in the eyes of men,   40
So stale and cheap to vulgar company,
Opinion,° that did help me to the crown,
Had still kept loyal to possession°
And left me in reputeless banishment,
A fellow of no mark nor likelihood.°   45
By being seldom seen, I could not stir
But like a comet I was wondered at,
That men would tell their children, "This is he!"
Others would say, "Where, which is Bolingbroke?"
And then I stole all courtesy from heaven,°   50
And dressed myself in such humility
That I did pluck allegiance from men's hearts,
Loud shouts and salutations from their mouths,
Even in the presence of the crownèd King.
Thus did I keep my person fresh and new,   55
My presence, like a robe pontifical,°
Ne'er seen but wondered at; and so my state,
Seldom but sumptuous, showed like a feast
And won by rareness such solemnity.°
The skipping King, he ambled up and down   60
With shallow jesters and rash bavin° wits,
Soon kindled and soon burnt; carded his state,°
Mingled his royalty with cap'ring fools,
Had his great name profanèd with their scorns,°
And gave his countenance, against his name,   65
To laugh at gibing boys and stand the push
Of every beardless vain comparative;°

40 **common-hackneyed** cheapened, vulgarized   42 **Opinion** public opinion   43 **to possession** to Richard II's sovereignty   45 **mark nor likelihood** importance or likeliness to succeed   50 **I . . . heaven** I assumed a bearing of the utmost meekness   56 **pontifical** like that of a pope or archbishop   57–9 **and so . . . solemnity** and so my magnificence on public occasions, infrequent but always sumptuous, looked festive and achieved by this rarity a suitable formal impressiveness   61 **bavin** brushwood, soon burnt out   62 **carded his state** debased his royal dignity (to *card* is to stir or mix, hence to adulterate)   64 **with their scorns** by his favorites' scornful and contemptuous behavior   65–7 **And gave . . . comparative** and lent his authority, to the detriment of his royal dignity and reputation, to find amusement in young scoffers and submit himself to the insolence of every frivolous witcracker

Grew a companion to the common streets,
Enfeoffed himself° to popularity,
That, being daily swallowed by men's eyes,   70
They surfeited with honey and began
To loathe the taste of sweetness, whereof a little
More than a little is by much too much.
So when he had occasion to be seen,
He was but as the cuckoo is in June,   75
Heard, not regarded—seen, but with such eyes
As, sick and blunted with community,°
Afford no extraordinary gaze,
Such as is bent on sunlike majesty
When it shines seldom in admiring eyes;   80
But rather drowsed and hung their eyelids down,
Slept in his face, and rendered such aspect
As cloudy men use to their adversaries,°
Being with his presence glutted, gorged, and full.
And in that very line,° Harry, standest thou;   85
For thou hast lost thy princely privilege
With vile participation.° Not an eye
But is aweary of thy common sight,
Save mine, which hath desired to see thee more—
Which now doth that° I would not have it do,   90
Make blind itself with foolish tenderness.°
PRINCE   I shall hereafter, my thrice gracious lord,
    Be more myself.
KING   For all the world°
    As thou art to this hour was Richard then
    When I from France set foot at Ravenspurgh,   95
    And even as I was then is Percy now.
    Now, by my scepter, and my soul to boot,°
    He hath more worthy interest to the state
    Than thou the shadow of succession.°

---

69 **Enfeoffed himself** gave himself up   77 **community** commonness   82–3 **Slept . . .
adversaries** dozed off right before his eyes, and looked at the King in the way sullen
men look at their adversaries   85 **line** degree, category   87 **vile participation** base
association or companionship   90 **that** that which   91 **tenderness** tears   93 **For all
the world** in every way   97 **to boot** in addition   98–9 **He . . . succession** this rebel
Hotspur has a better claim to the throne than your merely hereditary claim
unsupported by deeds

For of no right, nor color like to right,°   100
He doth fill fields with harness° in the realm,
Turns head° against the lion's° armèd jaws,
And, being no more in debt to years than thou,°
Leads ancient lords and reverend bishops on
To bloody battles and to bruising arms.   105
What never-dying honor hath he got
Against renownèd Douglas! Whose° high deeds,
Whose hot incursions and great name in arms
Holds from all soldiers chief majority°
And military title capital°   110
Through all the kingdoms that acknowledge Christ.
Thrice hath this Hotspur, Mars in swaddling clothes,
This infant warrior, in his enterprises
Discomfited° great Douglas, ta'en him once,
Enlargèd° him and made a friend of him,   115
To fill the mouth of deep defiance up°
And shake the peace and safety of our throne.
And what say you to this? Percy, Northumberland,
The Archbishop's Grace° of York, Douglas, Mortimer,
Capitulate° against us and are up.°   120
But wherefore do I tell these news to thee?
Why, Harry, do I tell thee of my foes,
Which art my nearest and dearest° enemy?
Thou that art like° enough, through vassal° fear,
Base inclination, and the start of spleen,°   125
To fight against me under Percy's pay,
To dog his heels and curtsy at his frowns,
To show how much thou art degenerate.
PRINCE Do not think so. You shall not find it so.
And God forgive them that so much have swayed   130

___

100 of . . . to right having no rightful claim or even the pretext of one   101 harness
armor, men in armor   102 Turns head leads an armed insurrection | lion's King's
103 being . . . thou being no older than you (though historically Hotspur was 23
years older than the prince)   107 Whose Hotspur's   109 majority preeminence
110 capital chief, principal   114 Discomfited defeated   115 Enlargèd freed
116 To . . . up to swell the roar of deep defiance   119 The Archbishop's Grace His
Grace the Archbishop   120 Capitulate form a league, draw up articles | up up in
arms   123 dearest (1) most precious (2) direst   124 like likely | vassal slavish
125 Base . . . spleen inclination for baseness, and sudden bursts of capricious
irascibility

Your Majesty's good thoughts away from me!
I will redeem all this on Percy's head
And in the closing of some glorious day
Be bold to tell you that I am your son,
When I will wear a garment all of blood   135
And stain my favors° in a bloody mask,
Which, washed away, shall scour my shame with it.
And that shall be the day, whene'er it lights,°
That this same child of honor and renown,
This gallant Hotspur, this all-praisèd knight,   140
And your unthought-of° Harry chance to meet.
For° every honor sitting on his helm,
Would they were multitudes, and on my head
My shames redoubled! For the time will come
That I shall make this northern youth exchange   145
His glorious deeds for my indignities.
Percy is but my factor,° good my lord,
To engross up° glorious deeds on my behalf;
And I will call him to so strict account
That he shall render every glory up,   150
Yea, even the slightest worship of his time,°
Or I will tear the reckoning from his heart.
This in the name of God I promise here,
The which if He be pleased I shall perform,
I do beseech Your Majesty may salve°   155
The long-grown wounds of my intemperance.°
If not, the end of life cancels all bonds,
And I will die a hundred thousand deaths
Ere break the smallest parcel of this vow.
KING   A hundred thousand rebels die in this!   160
    Thou shalt have charge° and sovereign trust herein.

                                            Enter Blunt

How now, good Blunt? Thy looks are full of speed.

---

136 **favors** features 138 **lights** dawns 141 **unthought-of** lightly valued, disregarded 142 **For** as for 147 **factor** agent 148 **engross up** amass, buy up 151 **even . . . time** every smallest honor he has ever won 155 **salve** soothe, heal 156 **intemperance** dissolute living 161 **charge** command (of troops)

BLUNT   So hath the business that I come to speak of.
 Lord Mortimer of Scotland° hath sent word
 That Douglas and the English rebels met   165
 The eleventh of this month at Shrewsbury.
 A mighty and a fearful head° they are,
 If promises be kept on every hand,
 As ever offered foul play in a state.
KING   The Earl of Westmorland set forth today,   170
 With him my son, Lord John of Lancaster;
 For this advertisement° is five days old.
 On Wednesday next, Harry, you shall set forward;
 On Thursday we ourselves will march. Our meeting°
 Is Bridgnorth.° And, Harry, you shall march   175
 Through Gloucestershire; by which account,
 Our business valuèd,° some twelve days hence
 Our general forces at Bridgnorth shall meet.
 Our hands are full of business. Let's away!
 Advantage feeds him° fat° while men delay. *Exeunt* 180

ACT 3
SCENE 3

Enter Falstaff and Bardolph

FALSTAFF   Bardolph, am I not fallen away° vilely since this last
 action?° Do I not bate?° Do I not dwindle? Why, my skin
 hangs about me like an old lady's loose gown; I am withered
 like an old applejohn.° Well, I'll repent, and that suddenly,

---

164 **Lord Mortimer of Scotland** (a Scottish nobleman, unrelated to Glendower's son-in-law)   167 **head** armed force   172 **advertisement** tidings, news   174 **meeting** place of rendezvous   175 **Bridgnorth** a town near Shrewsbury   177 **Our business valuèd** estimating how long our business will take   180 **Advantage . . . fat** opportunity (for rebellion) prospers | **him** himself

3.3. Location: A tavern in Eastcheap, as in 2.4. Summary: Falstaff's exchanges with Bardolph and Mistress Quickly are virtuoso displays of mockery, self-pity, and larceny; Hal's entry gives him a more challenging sparring partner. After a surprisingly flippant remark about his reconciliation with his father, Hal makes military arrangements, which include putting Falstaff in charge of a company of foot soldiers.

1 **fallen away** shrunk   2 **action** the robbery at Gad's Hill | **bate** lose weight   4 **applejohn** a kind of apple still in good eating condition when shriveled

while I am in some liking.° I shall be out of heart° shortly,   5
and then I shall have no strength to repent. An I have not
forgotten what the inside of a church is made of, I am a
peppercorn,° a brewer's horse.° The inside of a church!
Company, villainous company, hath been the spoil of me.

BARDOLPH   Sir John, you are so fretful° you cannot live long.   10

FALSTAFF   Why, there is it. Come sing me a bawdy song; make
me merry. I was as virtuously given° as a gentleman need to
be, virtuous enough: swore little, diced not above seven
times—a week, went to a bawdy house not above once in a
quarter—of an hour, paid money that I borrowed—three or   15
four times, lived well and in good compass;° and now I live
out of all order, out of all compass.

BARDOLPH   Why, you are so fat, Sir John, that you must needs be
out of all compass, out of all reasonable compass, Sir John.

FALSTAFF   Do thou amend thy face, and I'll amend my life.   20
Thou art our admiral,° thou bearest the lantern° in the
poop, but 'tis in the nose of thee. Thou art the Knight of the
Burning Lamp.°

BARDOLPH   Why, Sir John, my face does you no harm.

FALSTAFF   No, I'll be sworn, I make as good use of it as many a   25
man doth of a death's-head or a *memento mori.*° I never see
thy face but I think upon hellfire and Dives° that lived in
purple; for there he is in his robes, burning, burning. If thou
wert any way given to virtue, I would swear by thy face; my
oath should be "By this fire, that's God's angel."° But thou   30
art altogether given over,° and wert indeed, but for the light
in thy face, the son of utter darkness. When thou ran'st up
Gad's Hill in the night to catch my horse, if I did not think

---

5 **liking** (1) good bodily condition (2) inclination | **out of heart** (1) disinclined, disheartened (2) out of condition   8 **peppercorn** unground dried pepper berry | **brewer's horse** one that is old, withered, and decrepit   10 **fretful** (1) anxious (2) fretted, frayed   12 **given** inclined   16 **good compass** reasonable limits; also, in Bardolph's speech, girth, circumference   21 **admiral** flagship | **lantern** a light for the rest of the fleet to follow; here applied to Bardolph's inflamed nose, red from overdrinking   22–3 **Knight . . . Lamp** Falstaff parodies the names of heroes in popular chivalric romances   26 *memento mori* reminder of death, such as a death's-head or a skull engraved on a seal ring   27 **Dives** the rich man who went to hell, referred to in Luke 16.19–31   30 "**By . . . angel**" (Psalms 104.4, Hebrews 1.7, and Exodus 3.2 describe angels that appear in flames of fire)   31 **given over** abandoned to wickedness

thou hadst been an *ignis fatuus*° or a ball of wildfire,° there's
no purchase in money. Oh, thou art a perpetual triumph,°   35
an everlasting bonfire light! Thou hast saved me a thousand
marks in links° and torches, walking with thee in the night
betwixt tavern and tavern; but the sack that thou hast drunk
me would have bought me lights as good cheap° at the
dearest chandler's° in Europe. I have maintained that   40
salamander° of yours with fire any time this two-and-thirty
years. God reward me for it!

BARDOLPH   'Sblood, I would my face were in your belly!°

FALSTAFF   God-a-mercy! So should I be sure to be heartburned.

Enter Hostess

How now, Dame Partlet° the hen? Have you inquired yet   45
who picked my pocket?

HOSTESS   Why, Sir John, what do you think, Sir John? Do you
think I keep thieves in my house? I have searched, I have
inquired, so has my husband, man by man, boy by boy,
servant by servant. The tithe° of a hair was never lost in my   50
house before.

FALSTAFF   Ye lie, hostess. Bardolph was shaved° and lost many
a hair;° and I'll be sworn my pocket was picked. Go to, you
are a woman, go.

HOSTESS   Who, I? No, I defy thee! God's light,° I was never   55
called so in mine own house before.

FALSTAFF   Go to, I know you well enough.

HOSTESS   No, Sir John, you do not know me, Sir John. I know
you, Sir John. You owe me money, Sir John, and now you
pick a quarrel to beguile me of it. I bought you a dozen of   60
shirts to your back.

FALSTAFF   Dowlas,° filthy dowlas. I have given them away to
bakers' wives; they have made bolters° of them.

34 *ignis fatuus* will-o'-the-wisp | **wildfire** fireworks; lightning; will-o'-the-wisp
35 **triumph** procession led by torches   37 **links** torches, flares   39 **good cheap**
cheap   40 **dearest chandler's** most expensive candle maker's   41 **salamander** lizard
reputed to be able to live in fire   43 **I . . . belly** (a colloquial way of objecting to an
insult; Falstaff responds in the literal sense: a face like yours would give me massive
indigestion)   45 **Partlet** (traditional name of a hen)   50 **tithe** tenth part   52 **was
shaved** (1) had his beard cut (2) was cheated and robbed   52–3 **lost many a hair** (1) was
shaved (2) was made bald by syphilis   55 **God's light** (a mild oath)   62 **Dowlas** a
coarse kind of linen   63 **bolters** cloths for sifting flour

HOSTESS   Now, as I am a true woman, holland° of eight
shillings an ell.° You owe money here besides, Sir John, for   65
your diet° and by-drinkings,° and money lent you, four-and-
twenty pound.

FALSTAFF   He° had his part of it. Let him pay.

HOSTESS   He? Alas, he is poor, he hath nothing.

FALSTAFF   How, poor? Look upon his face. What call you rich?   70
Let them coin his nose, let them coin his cheeks. I'll not pay
a denier.° What, will you make a younker° of me? Shall I not
take mine ease in mine inn but I shall have my pocket
picked? I have lost a seal ring of my grandfather's worth
forty mark.   75

HOSTESS   Oh, Jesu, I have heard the Prince tell him, I know not
how oft, that that ring was copper.

FALSTAFF   How? The Prince is a Jack,° a sneak-up.° 'Sblood, an
he were here, I would cudgel him like a dog if he would say so.

> *Enter the Prince [with Peto], marching, and Falstaff*
> *meets him playing upon his truncheon° like a fife*

How now, lad, is the wind in that door,° i'faith? Must we all   80
march?

BARDOLPH   Yea, two and two, Newgate° fashion.

HOSTESS   My lord, I pray you, hear me.

PRINCE   What say'st thou, Mistress Quickly? How doth thy
husband? I love him well; he is an honest man.   85

HOSTESS   Good my lord, hear me.

FALSTAFF   Prithee, let her alone and list to me.

PRINCE   What say'st thou, Jack?

FALSTAFF   The other night I fell asleep here behind the arras°
and had my pocket picked. This house is turned bawdy house;   90
they pick pockets.

PRINCE   What didst thou lose, Jack?

FALSTAFF   Wilt thou believe me, Hal? Three or four bonds of
forty pound apiece and a seal ring of my grandfather's.

---

64 holland fine linen   **65 an ell** a measure of forty-five inches   **66 diet** meals | **by-**
drinkings drinks between meals   **68 He** Bardolph   **72 denier** one-twelfth of a
French sou; type of very small coin | **younker** greenhorn   **78 Jack** knave, rascal |
sneak-up sneak   **79.2 *truncheon*** officer's staff   **80 is . . . door** is that the way the
wind is blowing   **82 Newgate** a famous city prison in London (prisoners marched
two by two)   **89 arras** curtain

PRINCE   A trifle, some eightpenny matter.   95

HOSTESS   So I told him, my lord, and I said I heard Your Grace
say so; and, my lord, he speaks most vilely of you, like a
foulmouthed man as he is, and said he would cudgel you.

PRINCE   What, he did not!

HOSTESS   There's neither faith, truth, nor womanhood in me else.   100

FALSTAFF   There's no more faith in thee than in a stewed prune,°
nor no more truth in thee than in a drawn fox;° and for
womanhood, Maid Marian may be the deputy's wife of the
ward to thee.° Go, you thing, go.

HOSTESS   Say, what thing, what thing?   105

FALSTAFF   What thing? Why, a thing to thank God on.

HOSTESS   I am no thing° to thank God on, I would thou
shouldst know it! I am an honest man's wife, and, setting
thy knighthood aside,° thou art a knave to call me so.

FALSTAFF   Setting thy womanhood aside, thou art a beast to say   110
otherwise.

HOSTESS   Say, what beast, thou knave, thou?

FALSTAFF   What beast? Why, an otter.

PRINCE   An otter, Sir John! Why an otter?

FALSTAFF   Why? She's neither fish nor flesh; a man knows not   115
where to have° her.

HOSTESS   Thou art an unjust man in saying so. Thou or any
man knows where to have me, thou knave, thou.

PRINCE   Thou sayst true, hostess, and he slanders thee most
grossly.   120

HOSTESS   So he doth you, my lord, and said this other day you
owed him a thousand pound.

PRINCE   Sirrah, do I owe you a thousand pound?

FALSTAFF   A thousand pound, Hal? A million. Thy love is
worth a million; thou owest me thy love.   125

---

101 stewed prune (customarily associated with bawdy houses)   **102 drawn fox** fox
driven from cover and wily in getting back   **103–4 Maid . . . thee** Maid Marian, a
disreputable woman in Robin Hood ballads, morris dances, and the like, was a
model of respectability compared with you   **106–7 What thing . . . no thing** (with
sexual quibbles)   **108–9 setting . . . aside** (Mistress Quickly means, "without
wishing to offend your rank of knighthood," but Falstaff replies in l. 110 with the
meaning, "setting aside your womanhood as of no value or pertinence")   **116 have**
understand (with a sly suggestion of sexual possession—a meaning that eludes
Mistress Quickly)

HOSTESS Nay, my lord, he called you Jack and said he would cudgel you.

FALSTAFF Did I, Bardolph?

BARDOLPH Indeed, Sir John, you said so.

FALSTAFF Yea, if he said my ring was copper.   130

PRINCE I say 'tis copper. Darest thou be as good as thy word now?

FALSTAFF Why, Hal, thou knowest, as thou art but man, I dare; but as thou art prince, I fear thee as I fear the roaring of the lion's whelp.°   135

PRINCE And why not as the lion?

FALSTAFF The King himself is to be feared as the lion. Dost thou think I'll fear thee as I fear thy father? Nay, an I do, I pray God my girdle break.

PRINCE Oh, if it should, how would thy guts fall about thy 140 knees! But, sirrah, there's no room for faith, truth, nor honesty in this bosom of thine; it is all filled up with guts and midriff. Charge an honest woman with picking thy pocket? Why, thou whoreson, impudent, embossed° rascal,° if there were anything in thy pocket but tavern reckonings, 145 memorandums° of bawdy houses, and one poor penny-worth of sugar candy to make thee long-winded, if thy pocket were enriched with any other injuries° but these, I am a villain. And yet you will stand to it;° you will not pocket up° wrong! Art thou not ashamed?   150

FALSTAFF Dost thou hear, Hal? Thou knowest in the state of innocency Adam fell; and what should poor Jack Falstaff do in the days of villainy? Thou see'st I have more flesh than another man, and therefore more frailty. You confess then you picked my pocket.   155

PRINCE It appears so by the story.

FALSTAFF Hostess, I forgive thee. Go make ready breakfast. Love thy husband, look to thy servants, cherish thy guests. Thou shalt find me tractable to any honest reason; thou see'st I am pacified still.° Nay, prithee, begone.   *Exit Hostess* 160

---

135 whelp cub **144 embossed** (1) swollen with fat (2) foaming at the mouth and exhausted, like a hunted animal | **rascal** (1) scoundrel (2) immature and inferior deer **146 memorandums** souvenirs **148 injuries** those things you claim to have lost, thereby suffering harm **149 stand to it** make a stand, insist on your supposed rights **150 pocket up** endure silently **160 still** always

Now, Hal, to the news at court: for the robbery, lad, how is
that answered?

PRINCE   Oh, my sweet beef, I must still be good angel to thee.
The money is paid back again.

FALSTAFF   Oh, I do not like that paying back. 'Tis a double   165
labor.°

PRINCE   I am good friends with my father and may do
anything.

FALSTAFF   Rob me the exchequer the first thing thou dost, and
do it with unwashed hands° too.   170

BARDOLPH   Do, my lord.

PRINCE   I have procured thee, Jack, a charge of foot.°

FALSTAFF   I would it had been of horse. Where shall I find one°
that can steal well? Oh, for a fine thief, of the age of two-
and-twenty or thereabouts! I am heinously unprovided.°   175
Well, God be thanked for these rebels; they offend none but
the virtuous.° I laud them, I praise them.

PRINCE   Bardolph!

BARDOLPH   My lord?

PRINCE [*giving letters*]

Go bear this letter to Lord John of Lancaster,   180
To my brother John; this to my lord of Westmorland.
                                        [*Exit Bardolph*]
Go, Peto, to horse, to horse, for thou and I
Have thirty miles to ride yet ere dinnertime.
                                             [*Exit Peto*]
Jack, meet me tomorrow in the Temple Hall°
At two o'clock in the afternoon.   185
There shalt thou know thy charge, and there receive
Money and order for their furniture.°
The land is burning. Percy stands on high,
And either we or they must lower lie.   [*Exit*]

---

166 **double labor** the taking and the returning   170 **with unwashed hands** without
further ado   172 **charge of foot** command of a company of infantry   173 **one** a
companion in thievery (Falstaff sees war as the opportunity for stealing and
conning)   175 **unprovided** ill-equipped   176–7 **they . . . virtuous** the rebels, by
providing the occasion of war, give dishonest men a chance to profiteer and hence
offend only those who are honest   184 **Temple Hall** at the Inner Temple, one of the
Inns of Court   187 **furniture** equipment, furnishing

FALSTAFF

Rare words! Brave° world! Hostess, my breakfast, come!   190
Oh, I could wish this tavern were my drum!°   [*Exit*]

ACT 4
SCENE 1

[Enter Hotspur, Worcester, and Douglas]

HOTSPUR Well said, my noble Scot. If speaking truth
In this fine age were not thought flattery,
Such attribution° should the Douglas have
As not a soldier of this season's stamp
Should go so general current through the world.°   5
By God, I cannot flatter; I do defy°
The tongues of soothers!° But a braver° place
In my heart's love hath no man than yourself.
Nay, task me to my word;° approve° me, lord.
DOUGLAS Thou art the king of honor.   10
No man so potent breathes upon the ground
But I will beard him.°

Enter one [a Messenger] with letters

HOTSPUR   Do so, and 'tis well.—
What letters hast thou there?—I can but thank you.°
MESSENGER These letters come from your father.
HOTSPUR Letters from him? Why comes he not himself?   15

---

190 **Brave** splendid   191 **drum** (possibly Falstaff means that he wishes he could
continue to enjoy this tavern instead of risking his life in battle; he may also be
punning on *tavern/taborn*, *taborin*, a kind of drum)

4.1. Location: The rebel camp near Shrewsbury. Summary: The scene begins and ends
with bad news for the rebels as they prepare for battle: Northumberland is apparently
ill and Glendower is delayed. Worcester and Douglas are concerned while Hotspur,
at first troubled, is eager for a confrontation with a magnificently armed Hal, as
described by Vernon, and glorious battle with the King's formidable army.

3 **attribution** praise, tribute   4–5 **As . . . world** that no one coined as a soldier in this
current campaign should enjoy such a current reputation (to *go . . . current* is to be
put into circulation, continuing the image of coining in l. 4)   6 **defy** proclaim
against   7 **soothers** flatterers | **braver** better, dearer   9 **task . . . word** challenge me
to make good my word | **approve** test   11–12 **No . . . him** I am ready to defy
anyone alive   13 **I can . . . you** (said to Douglas)

MESSENGER   He cannot come, my lord. He is grievous sick.

HOTSPUR   Zounds, how has he the leisure to be sick
In such a jostling° time? Who leads his power?
Under whose government° come they along?

MESSENGER   His letters bears his mind, not I, my lord.   20

> [*Hotspur reads the letter*]

WORCESTER   I prithee, tell me, doth he keep° his bed?

MESSENGER   He did, my lord, four days ere I set forth,
And at the time of my departure thence
He was much feared° by his physicians.

WORCESTER   I would the state of time° had first been whole   25
Ere he by sickness had been visited.
His health was never better worth than now.

HOTSPUR   Sick now? Droop now? This sickness doth infect
The very life-blood of our enterprise;
'Tis catching hither, even to our camp.   30
He writes me here that inward sickness—
And that his friends by deputation
Could not so soon be drawn,° nor did he think it meet°
To lay so dangerous and dear a trust
On any soul removed but on his own.°   35
Yet doth he give us bold advertisement°
That with our small conjunction° we should on,°
To see how fortune is disposed to us;
For, as he writes, there is no quailing° now,
Because the King is certainly possessed°   40
Of all our purposes. What say you to it?

WORCESTER   Your father's sickness is a maim° to us.

HOTSPUR   A perilous gash, a very limb lopped off.
And yet, in faith, it is not! His present want°
Seems more° than we shall find it. Were it good   45
To set the exact wealth of all our states°
All at one cast?° To set so rich a main°

---

18 **jostling** contending, clashing   19 **government** command   21 **keep** keep to
24 **feared** feared for   25 **time** the times   32–3 **And that . . . drawn** and that his allies
could not so soon be assembled by anyone other than himself, any deputy   33 **meet**
appropriate   35 **On . . . own** on anyone other than himself   36 **advertisement**
counsel, advice   37 **conjunction** joint force | **on** go on   39 **quailing** losing heart
40 **possessed** informed   42 **maim** injury   44 **want** absence   45 **more** more serious
46 **To . . . states** to stake the absolute total of our resources   47 **cast** throw of the
dice | **main** stake in gambling; also, an army

On the nice° hazard° of one doubtful hour?
It were not good, for therein should we read
The very bottom and the soul of hope,°   50
The very list,° the very utmost bound
Of all our fortunes.

DOUGLAS   Faith, and so we should;
Where now remains a sweet reversion,°
We may boldly spend upon the hope
Of what is to come in.   55
A comfort of retirement° lives in this.

HOTSPUR   A rendezvous, a home to fly unto,
If that the devil and mischance look big°
Upon the maidenhead° of our affairs.

WORCESTER   But yet I would your father had been here.   60
The quality and hair° of our attempt
Brooks° no division. It will be thought
By some that know not why he is away
That wisdom, loyalty,° and mere dislike
Of our proceedings kept the Earl from hence.   65
And think how such an apprehension°
May turn the tide of fearful faction°
And breed a kind of question in our cause.
For well you know we of the off'ring side°
Must keep aloof from strict arbitrament,°   70
And stop all sight-holes,° every loop from whence
The eye of reason may pry in upon us.
This absence of your father's draws° a curtain
That shows the ignorant a kind of fear
Before not dreamt of.

HOTSPUR   You strain too far.°   75
I rather of his absence make this use:

---

48 nice precarious, delicate | **hazard** (1) game at dice (2) venture   **49–50 should . . . hope** we should discover the utmost foundation and basis of our hopes, the most we could rely on   **51 list** limit   **53 Where . . . reversion** since as things stand we can expect reinforcements (a *reversion* is literally part of an estate yet to be inherited)   **56 retirement** something to fall back on   **58 big** threatening   **59 maidenhead** commencement   **61 hair** kind, nature   **62 Brooks** tolerates   **64 loyalty** to the crown   **66 apprehension** (1) perception (2) apprehensiveness   **67 fearful faction** timid support   **69 off'ring side** side that attacks   **70 strict arbitrament** just inquiry or investigation   **71 sight-holes** peep-holes (*loop* or *loophole* has the same meaning)   **73 draws** draws aside, opens   **75 strain too far** exaggerate

It lends a luster and more great opinion,°
A larger dare° to our great enterprise,
Than if the Earl were here; for men must think,
If we without his help can make a head°   80
To push against a kingdom, with his help
We shall o'erturn it topsy-turvy down.
Yet° all goes well, yet all our joints° are whole.
DOUGLAS   As heart can think. There is not such a word
Spoke of in Scotland as this term of fear.   85

Enter Sir Richard Vernon

HOTSPUR   My cousin Vernon, welcome, by my soul.
VERNON   Pray God my news be worth a welcome, lord.
The Earl of Westmorland, seven thousand strong,
Is marching hitherwards; with him Prince John.
HOTSPUR   No harm. What more?
VERNON   And further I have learned   90
The King himself in person is set forth,
Or hitherwards intended° speedily,
With strong and mighty preparation.
HOTSPUR   He shall be welcome too. Where is his son,
The nimble-footed madcap Prince of Wales,   95
And his comrades, that doffed the world aside
And bid it pass?°
VERNON   All furnished,° all in arms
All plumed like estridges, that with the wind
Bated like eagles having lately bathed,°
Glittering in golden coats,° like images,°   100
As full of spirit as the month of May
And gorgeous as the sun at midsummer,
Wanton° as youthful goats, wild as young bulls.
I saw young Harry, with his beaver° on,

---

77 **opinion** renown   78 **dare** daring   80 **make a head** raise an armed force   83 **Yet** still | **joints** limbs   92 **intended** on the verge of departure   96–7 **that doffed . . . pass?** that thumbed their noses at responsibilities, telling the world to mind its own business?   97 **furnished** equipped   98–9 **All . . . bathed** all plumed with ostrich feathers, fluttering their wings in the wind like eagles having just bathed (the text may be defective)   100 **coats** (1) coats of mail (2) heraldic coats of arms | **images** gilded statues   103 **Wanton** sportive, frolicsome   104 **beaver** visor; hence, helmet

His cuisses° on his thighs, gallantly armed,   105
Rise from the ground like feathered Mercury,
And vaulted with such ease into his seat°
As if an angel dropped down from the clouds
To turn and wind° a fiery Pegasus°
And witch° the world with noble horsemanship.   110
HOTSPUR   No more, no more! Worse than the sun in March
This praise doth nourish agues.° Let them come.
They come like sacrifices° in their trim,°
And to the fire-eyed maid° of smoky war
All hot and bleeding will we offer them.   115
The mailèd° Mars shall on his altar sit
Up to the ears in blood. I am on fire
To hear this rich reprisal° is so nigh,
And yet not ours. Come, let me taste° my horse,
Who is to bear me like a thunderbolt   120
Against the bosom of the Prince of Wales.
Harry to Harry shall, hot horse to horse,
Meet and ne'er part till one drop down a corse.°
Oh, that Glendower were come!
VERNON   There is more news:
I learned in Worcester, as I rode along,   125
He cannot draw his power° this fourteen days.
DOUGLAS   That's the worst tidings that I hear of yet.
WORCESTER   Ay, by my faith, that bears a frosty sound.
HOTSPUR   What may the King's whole battle° reach unto?
VERNON   To thirty thousand.
HOTSPUR   Forty let it be!   130
My father and Glendower being both away,
The powers of us° may serve so great a day.
Come, let us take a muster speedily.
Doomsday is near; die all, die merrily.

---

105 cuisses armor for the thighs   **107 seat** saddle   **109 wind** wheel about |
Pegasus winged horse of Greek mythology   **110 witch** bewitch   **111–12 Worse . . .
agues** (the spring sun was believed to give impetus to chills and fevers, by drawing
up vapors; Vernon's speech, says Hotspur, gives one the shudders)   **113 sacrifices**
beasts for sacrifice | **trim** fine apparel, trappings   **114 maid** Bellona, goddess of war
116 mailèd dressed in mail, armor   **118 reprisal** prize   **119 taste** try, feel under
me   **123 corse** corpse   **126 draw his power** muster his army   **129 battle** army
132 The . . . us our forces

DOUGLAS Talk not of dying. I am out of° fear   135
Of death or death's hand for this one half year.

Exeunt

ACT 4
SCENE 2

Enter Falstaff, [and] Bardolph

FALSTAFF Bardolph, get thee before to Coventry; fill me a bottle
of sack. Our soldiers shall march through; we'll to Sutton
Coldfield° tonight.

BARDOLPH Will you give me money, Captain?

FALSTAFF Lay out,° lay out.   5

BARDOLPH This bottle makes an angel.°

FALSTAFF An if it do, take it for thy labor; an if it make twenty,
take them all; I'll answer the coinage.° Bid my lieutenant
Peto meet me at town's end.

BARDOLPH I will, Captain. Farewell.   *Exit*   10

FALSTAFF If I be not ashamed of my soldiers, I am a soused
gurnet.° I have misused the King's press° damnably. I have
got, in exchange of a hundred and fifty soldiers, three
hundred and odd pounds. I press me° none but good°
householders, yeomen's° sons, inquire me out contracted°   15
bachelors, such as had been asked twice on the banns°—
such a commodity of warm° slaves as had as lief° hear the

---

135 **out of** free from

4.2. Location: A public road near Coventry. Summary: Falstaff's prose soliloquy
reveals that he has taken bribes to release able-bodied men from his company,
instead forcing into service 150 poor, ragged indigents and prisoners. Hal and
Westmoreland, urging speed, are surprised by his pathetic troops, but Falstaff
dismisses their concerns.

2–3 Sutton Coldfield (in Warwickshire near Coventry) **5 Lay out** pay for it yourself
6 makes an angel makes ten shillings I've spent for you (but Falstaff answers as
though *makes* means "produces," implying that Bardolph can profit from the
transaction) **8 I'll . . . coinage** I'll take responsibility for any proceeds **11–12 soused
gurnet** a kind of pickled fish **12 King's press** royal warrant for the impressment of
troops **14 press me** draft, conscript | **good** wealthy **15 yeomen's** small
freeholders' | **contracted** engaged to be married **16 banns** public announcements,
declared on three Sundays in succession, of an intent to marry **17 warm** loving
their comfort | **lief** willingly

devil as a drum, such as fear the report of a caliver° worse
than a struck° fowl or a hurt wild duck. I pressed me none
but such toasts-and-butter,° with hearts in their bellies no   20
bigger than pins' heads, and they have bought out their
services;° and now my whole charge° consists of ancients,°
corporals, lieutenants, gentlemen of companies°—slaves as
ragged as Lazarus in the painted cloth,° where the glutton's
dogs licked his sores, and such as indeed were never   25
soldiers, but discarded unjust° servingmen, younger sons to
younger brothers,° revolted° tapsters, and hostlers trade-
fallen,° the cankers° of a calm world and a long peace, ten
times more dishonorable-ragged than an old feazed
ancient.° And such have I, to fill up the rooms of them as   30
have bought out their services, that you would think that I
had a hundred and fifty tattered prodigals° lately come from
swine keeping, from eating draff° and husks. A mad° fellow
met me on the way and told me I had unloaded all the
gibbets° and pressed the dead bodies. No eye hath seen such   35
scarecrows. I'll not march through Coventry with them,
that's flat.° Nay, and the villains march wide betwixt the legs
as if they had gyves° on, for indeed I had the most of them
out of prison. There's not a shirt and a half in all my
company, and the half shirt is two napkins tacked together   40
and thrown over the shoulders like a herald's coat without
sleeves; and the shirt, to say the truth, stolen from my host°
at Saint Albans,° or the red-nose innkeeper of Daventry.°
But that's all one;° they'll find linen enough on every hedge.°

Enter the Prince [and the] Lord of Westmorland

18 **caliver** musket   19 **struck** wounded   20 **toasts-and-butter** weaklings   21–2 **bought
. . . services** paid, bribed, to be released from military duty   22 **charge** company,
troop | **ancients** ensigns, standard-bearers (by appointing a disproportionate
number of junior officers, Falstaff has made it possible to collect for himself their
more substantial pay)   23 **gentlemen of companies** a kind of junior officer
24 **painted cloth** cheap hangings for a room (for the story of Lazarus the beggar and
Dives the rich man, see Luke 16.19–31)   26 **unjust** dishonest   26–7 **younger . . .
brothers** (with no possibility of inheritance)   27 **revolted** runaway   27–8 **trade-fallen**
whose business has fallen away   28 **cankers** cankerworms that destroy leaves and buds
(used figuratively)   29–30 **feazed ancient** frayed flag   32 **prodigals** spendthrifts (see
Luke 15.15–16)   33 **draff** hogwash | **mad** madcap   35 **gibbets** gallows   37 **that's
flat** that's for sure   38 **gyves** fetters   42 **my host** the innkeeper   43 **Saint Albans,
Daventry** (towns north and west of London, on the road to Coventry)   44 **that's all one**
no matter   47 **hedge** (where wet linen was spread out to dry and could be easily stolen)

PRINCE How now, blown° Jack? How now, quilt?°   45

FALSTAFF What, Hal? How now, mad wag? What a devil dost thou in Warwickshire?—My good lord of Westmorland, I cry you mercy.° I thought Your Honor had already been at Shrewsbury.

WESTMORLAND Faith, Sir John, 'tis more than time that I were   50 there, and you too; but my powers° are there already. The King, I can tell you, looks for us all. We must away° all night.

FALSTAFF Tut, never fear° me. I am as vigilant as a cat to steal cream.   55

PRINCE I think, to steal cream indeed, for thy theft hath already made thee butter.° But tell me, Jack, whose fellows are these that come after?

FALSTAFF Mine, Hal, mine.

PRINCE I did never see such pitiful rascals.   60

FALSTAFF Tut, tut, good enough to toss;° food for powder,° food for powder. They'll fill a pit as well as better. Tush, man, mortal men, mortal men.

WESTMORLAND Ay, but, Sir John, methinks they are exceeding poor and bare,° too beggarly.   65

FALSTAFF Faith, for° their poverty, I know not where they had that, and for their bareness, I am sure they never learned that of me.

PRINCE No, I'll be sworn, unless you call three fingers in the ribs° bare. But, sirrah, make haste. Percy is already in the field.   70

Exit

FALSTAFF What, is the King encamped?

WESTMORLAND He is, Sir John. I fear we shall stay too long.

[Exit]

FALSTAFF Well,

To the latter end of a fray and the beginning of a feast

Fits a dull fighter and a keen guest.°   *Exit*   75

45 **blown** swollen, inflated; also, short of wind | **quilt** thickly padded   48 **cry you mercy** beg your pardon   51 **powers** soldiers   52 **must away** must march   54 **fear** worry about   56–7 **thy . . . butter** all the cream (rich things) you have stolen has been churned into butterfat in your barrel-like belly   61 **toss** toss on a pike | **food for powder** cannon fodder   65 **poor and bare** inferior and threadbare (but Falstaff puns on the sense of "financially strapped and lean")   66 **for** as for   69 **three . . . ribs** Falstaff's fat-covered ribs (a *finger* was a measure of three-fourths of an inch)   75–6 **To . . . guest** better to be late to a battle and early to a feast (*keen* means "with keen appetite")

❖

ACT 4
SCENE 3

Enter Hotspur, Worcester, Douglas, [and] Vernon

HOTSPUR We'll fight with him tonight.

WORCESTER   It may not be.

DOUGLAS You give him then° advantage.

VERNON   Not a whit.

HOTSPUR Why say you so? Looks he not for supply?°

VERNON So do we.

HOTSPUR   His is certain; ours is doubtful.

WORCESTER Good cousin, be advised, stir not tonight.   5

VERNON Do not, my lord.

DOUGLAS   You do not counsel well.
    You speak it out of fear and cold heart.

VERNON Do me no slander, Douglas. By my life,
    And I dare well maintain it with my life,
    If well-respected° honor bid me on,   10
    I hold as little counsel° with weak fear
    As you, my lord, or any Scot that this day lives.
    Let it be seen tomorrow in the battle
    Which of us fears.

DOUGLAS Yea, or tonight.   15

VERNON Content.

HOTSPUR Tonight, say I.

VERNON Come, come, it may not be. I wonder much,
    Being men of such great leading° as you are,
    That you foresee not what impediments   20
    Drag back our expedition.° Certain horse°
    Of my cousin Vernon's are not yet come up.

4.3. Location: The rebel camp near Shrewsbury. Summary: Hotspur presses for immediate combat even though his forces are not yet ready. Sir Walter Blunt arrives from the King with an offer of pardon if they will submit their grievances for consideration. Hotspur replies with an angry review of recent events, but relents and sends his uncle Worcester to negotiate.

2 then if you wait (addressed to Worcester, not Hotspur)   **3 supply** reinforcements
10 well-respected well weighed or considered   **11 I hold . . . counsel** I have as little
to do   **19 leading** leadership   **21 expedition** speedy progress | **horse** cavalry (as
also at l. 23)

Your uncle Worcester's horse came but today,
And now their pride and mettle° is asleep,
Their courage with hard labor tame and dull,   25
That not a horse is half the half of himself.
HOTSPUR   So are the horses of the enemy
In general journey-bated° and brought low.
The better part of ours are full of rest.
WORCESTER   The number of the King exceedeth our.   30
For God's sake, cousin, stay till all come in.
                    The trumpet sounds a parley°

                    Enter Sir Walter Blunt

BLUNT   I come with gracious offers from the King,
If you vouchsafe me hearing and respect.°
HOTSPUR   Welcome, Sir Walter Blunt; and would to God
You were of our determination!°   35
Some of us love you well; and even those some°
Envy your great deservings and good name
Because° you are not of our quality°
But stand against us like an enemy.
BLUNT   And God defend° but still° I should stand so,   40
So long as out of limit° and true rule
You stand against anointed majesty.
But to my charge.° The King hath sent to know
The nature of your griefs° and whereupon
You conjure from the breast of civil peace   45
Such bold hostility, teaching his duteous land
Audacious cruelty. If that° the King
Have any way your good deserts forgot,
Which he confesseth to be manifold,
He bids you name your griefs, and with all speed   50
You shall have your desires with interest
And pardon absolute for yourself and these
Herein misled by your suggestion.°

---

24 pride and mettle spirit   **28 journey-bated** tired from the journey   **31.1** *parley* trumpet summons to a conference   **33 respect** attention   **35 determination** persuasion (in the fight)   **36 even those some** those same persons   **38 Because** only because | **quality** party   **40 defend** forbid | **still** always   **41 limit** bounds of allegiance   **43 charge** commission   **44 griefs** grievances   **47 If that** if   **53 suggestion** instigation

HOTSPUR   The King is kind; and well we know the King
  Knows at what time to promise, when to pay.   55
  My father and my uncle and myself
  Did give him that same royalty he wears,
  And when he was not six-and-twenty strong,
  Sick in the world's regard, wretched and low,
  A poor unminded° outlaw sneaking home,   60
  My father gave him welcome to the shore;
  And when he heard him swear and vow to God
  He came but to be Duke of Lancaster,
  To sue his livery and beg his peace°
  With tears of innocency and terms of zeal,   65
  My father, in kind heart and pity moved,
  Swore him assistance, and performed it too.
  Now when the lords and barons of the realm
  Perceived Northumberland did lean to him,
  The more and less came in with cap and knee,°   70
  Met him in boroughs, cities, villages,
  Attended° him on bridges, stood in lanes,°
  Laid gifts before him, proffered him their oaths,
  Gave him their heirs as pages,° followed him
  Even at the heels in golden° multitudes.   75
  He presently, as greatness knows itself,°
  Steps me° a little higher than his vow°
  Made to my father while his blood was poor°
  Upon the naked shore at Ravenspurgh,
  And now, forsooth, takes on him to reform   80
  Some certain edicts and some strait° decrees
  That lie too heavy on the commonwealth,
  Cries out upon abuses, seems to weep
  Over his country's wrongs; and by this face,°

---

60 unminded disregarded   **64 To sue . . . peace** to petition to take possession of his
rightful inheritance and be reconciled with King Richard II   **70 The more . . . knee**
persons of all ranks came to him with cap in hand and with bended knee
72 Attended waited for | **stood in lanes** stood row-deep along the roads   **74 Gave . . .
pages** brought him their heirs to serve as pages and also as hostages to the fathers'
loyalty   **75 golden** (1) auspicious, celebrating (2) majestically attired   **76 knows
itself** perceives its own strength   **77 Steps me** steps (*me* is used colloquially) | **vow**
Bolingbroke's vow to seek no more than his inheritance   **78 while . . . poor** while
Bolingbroke's spirits were still humbled and his dynastic claim in question   **81 strait**
strict   **84 face** show, pretense

This seeming brow of justice, did he win   85
The hearts of all that he did angle for;
Proceeded further—cut me° off the heads
Of all the favorites that the absent King
In deputation left behind him here
When he was personal° in the Irish war.   90

BLUNT   Tut, I came not to hear this.

HOTSPUR   Then to the point.
In short time after, he deposed the King,
Soon after that, deprived him of his life,
And in the neck of that° tasked° the whole state;
To make that worse, suffered his kinsman March—   95
Who is, if every owner were well placed,°
Indeed his king—to be engaged° in Wales,
There without ransom to lie forfeited;°
Disgraced me° in my happy° victories,
Sought to entrap me by intelligence;°   100
Rated° mine uncle from the Council board;
In rage dismissed my father from the court;
Broke oath on oath, committed wrong on wrong,
And in conclusion drove us to seek out
This head of safety,° and withal° to pry   105
Into his title, the which we find
Too indirect for long continuance.

BLUNT   Shall I return this answer to the King?

HOTSPUR   Not so, Sir Walter. We'll withdraw awhile.
Go to the King; and let there be impawned°   110
Some surety for a safe return again,
And in the morning early shall mine uncle
Bring him our purposes.° And so farewell.

BLUNT   I would you would accept of grace and love.

HOTSPUR   And maybe so we shall.

BLUNT   Pray God you do. [*Exeunt*]   115

---

87 cut me cut   **90 personal** in person   **94 in . . . that** next, immediately after | **tasked** laid taxes upon   **96 if . . . placed** if every claimant were given his proper place   **97 engaged** held as hostage   **98 lie forfeited** remain prisoner, unreclaimed   **99 Disgraced me** (by demanding the prisoners; see 1.3.23 ff) | **happy** fortunate   **100 intelligence** secret information, from spies   **101 Rated** scolded   **105 head of safety** armed force for our protection | **withal** also   **110 impawned** pledged   **113 purposes** proposals.

❖

ACT 4
SCENE 4

Enter [the] Archbishop of York, [and] Sir Michael

ARCHBISHOP [*giving letters*]
    Hie, good Sir Michael, bear this sealèd brief°
    With wingèd haste to the Lord Marshal,°
    This to my cousin Scroop,° and all the rest
    To whom they are directed. If you knew
    How much they do import, you would make haste.   5
SIR MICHAEL   My good lord, I guess their tenor.
ARCHBISHOP   Like° enough you do.
    Tomorrow, good Sir Michael, is a day
    Wherein the fortune of ten thousand men
    Must bide the touch;° for, sir, at Shrewsbury,   10
    As I am truly given to understand,
    The King with mighty and quick-raisèd power
    Meets with Lord Harry. And I fear, Sir Michael,
    What with the sickness of Northumberland,
    Whose power was in the first proportion,°   15
    And what with Owen Glendower's absence thence,
    Who with them was a rated sinew° too
    And comes not in, o'erruled by prophecies,
    I fear the power of Percy is too weak
    To wage an instant° trial with the King.   20
SIR MICHAEL   Why, my good lord, you need not fear;
    There is Douglas and Lord Mortimer.
ARCHBISHOP   No, Mortimer is not there.

4.4. Location: York. The Archbishop's palace. **Summary:** Despite Sir Michael's assurances, the Archbishop, a rebellious church leader mentioned in 1.3, is pessimistic about the rebel's chances. He hopes to shore up his defenses should his fears prove true.
1 brief letter, dispatch   **2 Lord Marshal** Thomas Mowbray, son of the Duke of Norfolk who is exiled in *Richard II*, and a longtime enemy of the new King   **3 Scroop** perhaps Sir Stephen Scroop of *Richard II*, 3.2.91–218, or Lord Scroop of Masham of *Henry V*, 2.2   **7 Like** likely   **10 bide the touch** be put to the test (like gold) **15 in . . . proportion** of the largest size   **17 rated sinew** main strength or support reckoned upon   **20 instant** immediate

SIR MICHAEL   But there is Mordake, Vernon, Lord Harry Percy,
    And there is my lord of Worcester, and a head°   25
    Of gallant warriors, noble gentlemen.
ARCHBISHOP   And so there is. But yet the King hath drawn
    The special head° of all the land together:
    The Prince of Wales, Lord John of Lancaster,
    The noble Westmorland, and warlike Blunt,   30
    And many more corrivals° and dear men
    Of estimation° and command in arms.
SIR MICHAEL   Doubt not, my lord, they shall be well opposed.
ARCHBISHOP   I hope no less, yet needful 'tis to fear;
    And, to prevent the worst, Sir Michael, speed.   35
    For if Lord Percy thrive not, ere the King
    Dismiss his power he° means to visit us,
    For he hath heard of our confederacy,
    And 'tis but wisdom to make strong against him.
    Therefore make haste. I must go write again   40
    To other friends; and so farewell, Sir Michael.

                          Exeunt [separately]

ACT 5
SCENE 1

Enter the King, Prince of Wales, Lord John
of Lancaster, Sir Walter Blunt, [and] Falstaff

KING   How bloodily the sun begins to peer
    Above yon bosky° hill! The day looks pale
    At his distemperature.°
PRINCE   The southern wind
    Doth play the trumpet° to his° purposes,

25 **head** troop 28 **special head** notable leaders 31 **corrivals** partners in the
enterprise 32 **estimation** reputation, importance 37 **he** the King

5.1. Location: The King's camp near Shrewsbury. **Summary:** Worcester and the
King's bitter exchange is halted by Prince Hal's chivalric proposal to meet Hotspur
in single combat. Though the King refuses, he does make an offer of pardon. The
scene ends with Falstaff alone on stage, raising skeptical questions about the nature
of honor.

2 **bosky** bushy 3 **his distemperature** the sun's unhealthy appearance 4 **trumpet**
trumpeter | **his** its, the sun's

And by his hollow whistling in the leaves   5
Foretells a tempest and a blust'ring day.
KING   Then with the losers let it sympathize,
For nothing can seem foul to those that win.

The trumpet sounds

Enter Worcester [and Vernon]

How now, my lord of Worcester? 'Tis not well
That you and I should meet upon such terms   10
As now we meet. You have deceived our trust
And made us doff our easy° robes of peace
To crush our old limbs in ungentle steel.
This is not well, my lord, this is not well.
What say you to it? Will you again unknit   15
This churlish knot of all-abhorrèd war
And move in that obedient orb° again
Where you did give a fair and natural light,
And be no more an exhaled meteor,°
A prodigy of fear,° and a portent   20
Of broachèd° mischief to the unborn times?
WORCESTER   Hear me, my liege:
For mine own part, I could be well content
To entertain° the lag end of my life
With quiet hours, for I protest   25
I have not sought the day of this dislike.°
KING   You have not sought it? How comes it, then?
FALSTAFF   Rebellion lay in his way, and he found it.
PRINCE   Peace, chewet,° peace!
WORCESTER   It pleased Your Majesty to turn your looks   30
Of favor from myself and all our house;
And yet I must remember° you, my lord,
We were the first and dearest of your friends.
For you my staff of office did I break

---

12 **easy** comfortable   17 **orb** orbit, sphere of action (the King's subjects, like planets and stars in the Ptolemaic cosmos, were supposed to revolve around the kingly center, comparable to the earth, in fixed courses)   19 **exhaled meteor** (meteors were believed to be vapors drawn up or *exhaled* by the sun and visible as streaks of light; they were regarded as ill omens)   20 **prodigy of fear** fearful omen   21 **broachèd** set flowing, already begun   24 **entertain** occupy   26 **the . . . dislike** this time of discord   29 **chewet** chough, jackdaw (here, a chatterer)   32 **remember** remind

In Richard's time, and posted° day and night   35
To meet you on the way, and kiss your hand,
When yet you were in place and in account
Nothing° so strong and fortunate as I.
It was myself, my brother, and his son
That brought you home° and boldly did outdare   40
The dangers of the time. You swore to us,
And you did swear that oath at Doncaster,
That you did nothing purpose 'gainst the state,
Nor claim no further than your new-fall'n° right,
The seat of Gaunt, dukedom of Lancaster.   45
To this we swore our aid. But in short space
It rained down fortune show'ring on your head,
And such a flood of greatness fell on you—
What with our help, what with the absent King,
What with the injuries° of a wanton° time,   50
The seeming sufferances° that you had borne,
And the contrarious winds that held the King
So long in his unlucky Irish wars
That all in England did repute him dead—
And from this swarm of fair advantages   55
You took occasion° to be quickly wooed
To grip the general sway into your hand;
Forgot your oath to us at Doncaster;
And being fed by us, you used us so
As that ungentle gull, the cuckoo's bird,°   60
Useth the sparrow; did oppress our nest,
Grew by our feeding to so great a bulk
That even our love° durst not come near your sight
For fear of swallowing; but with nimble wing
We were enforced, for safety sake, to fly   65
Out of your sight and raise this present head,°
Whereby we stand opposèd by such means°
As you yourself have forged against yourself

35 **posted** rode swiftly   38 **Nothing** not at all   40 **home** back to England from exile   44 **new-fall'n** recently inherited (by the death of John of Gaunt)   50 **injuries** abuses | **wanton** ill-managed   51 **sufferances** suffering, distress   56 **occasion** the opportunity   60 **ungentle . . . bird** rude nestling, the cuckoo's young offspring (the cuckoo lays its eggs in other birds' nests)   63 **our love** we who loved you   66 **head** armed force   67 **opposèd . . . means** goaded into opposition by such factors

By unkind usage, dangerous countenance,°
And violation of all faith and troth   70
Sworn to us in your younger enterprise.
KING   These things indeed you have articulate,°
Proclaimed at market crosses,° read in churches,
To face° the garment of rebellion
With some fine color° that may please the eye   75
Of fickle changelings° and poor discontents,
Which gape and rub the elbow° at the news
Of hurly-burly innovation.°
And never yet did insurrection want°
Such water-colors° to impaint his° cause,   80
Nor moody° beggars, starving for a time
Of pell-mell havoc° and confusion.
PRINCE   In both your° armies there is many a soul
Shall pay full dearly for this encounter,
If once they join in trial. Tell your nephew   85
The Prince of Wales doth join with all the world
In praise of Henry Percy. By my hopes°—
This present enterprise set off his head°—
I do not think a braver gentleman,
More active-valiant or more valiant-young,   90
More daring or more bold, is now alive
To grace this latter age with noble deeds.
For my part, I may speak it to my shame,
I have a truant been to chivalry;
And so I hear he doth account me too.   95
Yet this before my father's majesty:
I am content that he shall take the odds
Of his great name and estimation,°
And will, to save the blood on either side,
Try fortune with him in a single fight.   100

---

69 dangerous countenance threatening behavior   **72 articulate** set forth, specified   **73 market crosses** (Christian crosses were often erected in the centers of market-places—a good place for public announcements)   **74 face** trim, adorn   **75 color** (1) hue (2) specious appearance   **76 changelings** turncoats   **77 rub the elbow** hug themselves with delight   **78 innovation** rebellion   **79 want** lack   **80 water-colors** thin excuses (see *color*, l. 75) | **his** its   **81 moody** sullen, angry   **82 havoc** plundering   **83 both your** your and our   **87 hopes** hopes of salvation   **88 This . . . head** if this present rebellion is taken from his account, not held against him   **98 estimation** reputation

KING   And, Prince of Wales, so dare we venture° thee,
    Albeit° considerations infinite
    Do make against it.—No, good Worcester, no.
    We love our people well; even those we love
    That are misled upon your cousin's° part;   105
    And, will they° take the offer of our grace,°
    Both he and they and you, yea, every man
    Shall be my friend again, and I'll be his.
    So tell your cousin, and bring me word
    What he will do. But if he will not yield,   110
    Rebuke and dread correction wait on us,°
    And they shall do their office. So, begone.
    We will not now be troubled with reply.
    We offer fair; take it advisedly.
                                    Exit Worcester [with Vernon]
PRINCE   It will not be accepted, on my life.   115
    The Douglas and the Hotspur both together
    Are confident against the world in arms.
KING   Hence, therefore, every leader to his charge;
    For on their answer will we set on them,
    And God befriend us as our cause is just!   120
                                    Exeunt. Manent° Prince, Falstaff
FALSTAFF   Hal, if thou see me down in the battle and bestride°
    me, so;° 'tis a point of friendship.
PRINCE   Nothing but a colossus can do thee that friendship.
    Say thy prayers, and farewell.
FALSTAFF   I would 'twere bedtime, Hal, and all well.   125
PRINCE   Why, thou owest God a death.°   [*Exit*]
FALSTAFF   'Tis not due yet; I would be loath to pay him before
    his day. What need I be so forward with him that calls not
    on me? Well, 'tis no matter; honor pricks° me on. Yea, but
    how if honor prick me off° when I come on? How then?   130
    Can honor set to° a leg? No. Or an arm? No. Or take away
    the grief° of a wound? No. Honor hath no skill in surgery,

---

101 venture hazard, risk   **102 Albeit** although it be that (the subjunctive has the
force of "were it not that")   **105 cousin's** nephew's   **106 will they** if they will |
grace pardon   **111 wait on us** are awaiting my royal command   **120.1 *Manent*** they
remain onstage   **121 bestride** stand over in order to defend   **122 so** well and good
126 thou . . . death (proverbial, with a pun on *debt*)   **129 pricks** spurs   **130 prick
me off** mark me off (as one dead)   **131 set to** rejoin or set   **132 grief** pain

then? No. What is honor? A word. What is in that word
"honor"? What is that "honor"? Air. A trim reckoning!
Who hath it? He that died o' Wednesday. Doth he feel it? 135
No. Doth he hear it? No. 'Tis insensible, then? Yea, to the
dead. But will it not live with the living? No. Why?
Detraction° will not suffer° it. Therefore I'll none of it.
Honor is a mere scutcheon.° And so ends my catechism.°

Exit

ACT 5
SCENE 2

Enter Worcester [and] Sir Richard Vernon

WORCESTER Oh, no, my nephew must not know, Sir Richard,
  The liberal and kind offer of the King.
VERNON 'Twere best he did.
WORCESTER   Then are we all undone.
  It is not possible, it cannot be,
  The King should keep his word in loving us;   5
  He will suspect us still and find a time
  To punish this offense in other faults.°
  Suspicion all our lives shall be stuck full of eyes;°
  For treason is but trusted like the fox,
  Who, never so° tame, so cherished, and locked up,   10
  Will have a wild trick° of his ancestors.
  Look how we can, or sad° or merrily,
  Interpretation will misquote our looks,
  And we shall feed like oxen at a stall,
  The better cherished still the nearer death.   15

---

138 **Detraction** slander | **suffer** allow   139 **scutcheon** heraldic emblem carried in
funerals, displayed on coaches, etc.; it was the lowest form of symbol, having no
pennon or other insignia | **catechism** the principles of faith given in the form of
question and answer

5.2. **Location:** Near the rebel camp. **Summary:** Worcester's lie to Hotspur, that the
King rejected their just demands, together with glowing reports of Hal's noble
demeanor, bring Hotspur to a fever pitch for battle.
7 **To . . . faults** to find other faults in us to punish (as a way of getting back at us for
defying him militarily)   8 **stuck . . . eyes** provided with many eyes, suspiciously
inquisitive   10 **never so** be he never so   11 **trick** trait   12 **or sad** either sad

My nephew's trespass may be well forgot;
It hath the excuse of youth and heat of blood,
And an adopted name of privilege°—
A harebrained Hotspur, governed by a spleen.°
All his offenses live upon my head   20
And on his father's. We did train° him on,
And, his corruption being ta'en from us,°
We as the spring° of all shall pay for all.
Therefore, good cousin, let not Harry know
In any case the offer of the King.   25

Enter Hotspur [and Douglas, with soldiers]

VERNON Deliver° what you will; I'll say 'tis so.
  Here comes your cousin.
HOTSPUR   My uncle is returned.
  Deliver up° my lord of Westmorland.
  Uncle, what news?
WORCESTER The King will bid you battle presently.   30
DOUGLAS Defy him by° the lord of Westmorland.
HOTSPUR Lord Douglas, go you and tell him so.
DOUGLAS Marry, and shall, and very willingly. *Exit Douglas*
WORCESTER There is no seeming mercy in the King.
HOTSPUR Did you beg any? God forbid!   35
WORCESTER I told him gently of our grievances,
  Of his oathbreaking, which he mended thus,
  By now forswearing that he is forsworn.
  He calls us rebels, traitors, and will scourge
  With haughty arms this hateful name in us.   40

Enter Douglas

DOUGLAS Arm, gentlemen, to arms! For I have thrown
  A brave° defiance in King Henry's teeth,
  And Westmorland, that was engaged,° did bear it;
  Which cannot choose but bring him quickly on.

---

18 an adopted . . . privilege a nickname, "Hotspur," to justify his rashness **19 spleen** intemperate impulse **21 train** incite, draw **22 his . . . us** since his guilt originated in us **23 spring** source **26 Deliver** report **28 Deliver up** release (as hostage; see 4.3.110–11) **31 Defy him by** send back your defiance with **42 brave** proud **43 engaged** held as hostage

WORCESTER   The Prince of Wales stepped forth before the King,   45
   And, nephew, challenged you to single fight.
HOTSPUR   Oh, would the quarrel lay upon our heads,
   And that no man might draw short breath today
   But I and Harry Monmouth!° Tell me, tell me,
   How showed his tasking?° Seemed it in contempt?   50
VERNON   No, by my soul. I never in my life
   Did hear a challenge urged° more modestly,
   Unless a brother should a brother dare
   To gentle° exercise and proof of arms.°
   He gave you all the duties° of a man,   55
   Trimmed up your praises° with a princely tongue,
   Spoke your deservings like a chronicle,
   Making you ever better than his praise
   By still dispraising praise valued with you;°
   And, which became him like a prince indeed,   60
   He made a blushing cital° of himself,
   And chid his truant youth with such a grace
   As if he mastered there a double spirit
   Of teaching and of learning instantly.°
   There did he pause. But let me tell the world,   65
   If he outlive the envy° of this day,
   England did never owe° so sweet a hope,
   So much misconstrued in his wantonness.°
HOTSPUR   Cousin, I think thou art enamorèd
   On his follies. Never did I hear   70
   Of any prince so wild a liberty.°
   But be he as he will, yet once ere night
   I will embrace him with a soldier's arm,
   That he shall shrink under my courtesy.°
   Arm, arm with speed! And, fellows, soldiers, friends,   75
   Better consider what you have to do

---

49 Monmouth (a name for the Prince, taken from the Welsh town where he was born)
50 showed his tasking appeared his giving the challenge   **52 urged** put forward
54 gentle befitting noble birth | **proof of arms** test of martial skill   **55 duties** due
merits   **56 Trimmed . . . praises** adorned his praise of you   **59 By . . . you** by
consistently disparaging praise itself as not sufficient to measure your true worth
61 cital account, recital   **64 instantly** simultaneously   **66 envy** hostility   **67 owe**
own   **68 wantonness** playful sportiveness   **71 liberty** licentiousness   **74 shrink under
my courtesy** (1) be daunted by my greater courtesy (2) fall back before my attack

Than I, that have not well the gift of tongue,
Can lift your blood up with persuasion.

Enter a Messenger

FIRST MESSENGER   My lord, here are letters for you.
HOTSPUR   I cannot read them now.   80
Oh, gentlemen, the time of life is short!
To spend that shortness basely were too long
If life did ride upon a dial's point,
Still ending at the arrival of an hour.°
An if we live, we live to tread on kings;   85
If die, brave° death, when princes die with us!
Now, for° our consciences, the arms are fair°
When the intent of bearing them is just.

Enter another [Messenger]

SECOND MESSENGER
My lord, prepare. The King comes on apace.
HOTSPUR   I thank him that he cuts me from my tale,   90
For I profess not talking.° Only this—
Let each man do his best. And here draw I
A sword, whose temper I intend to stain
With the best blood that I can meet withal
In the adventure of this perilous day.   95
Now, *Esperance*!° Percy! And set on.
Sound all the lofty instruments of war,
And by that music let us all embrace;
For, heaven to earth,° some of us never shall
A second time do such a courtesy.   100
Here they embrace. The trumpets sound. [Exeunt]

82–4 To . . . hour life is too short to spend it basely, even if life were to last only the
time needed for the dial (or sundial) to advance a single hour, ending when that
hour is up   86 brave glorious   87 for as for | fair just   91 I . . . talking I have no
calling as an orator   96 *Esperance* (the motto of the Percy family)   99 heaven to
earth I'll wager heaven against earth

ACT 5
SCENE 3

The King enters with his power° [and passes over the stage]. Alarum° to the battle. Then enter Douglas, and Sir Walter Blunt [dressed like King Henry]

BLUNT   What is thy name, that in the battle thus
Thou crossest me? What honor dost thou seek
Upon my head?

DOUGLAS   Know then my name is Douglas,
And I do haunt thee in the battle thus
Because some tell me that thou art a king.   5

BLUNT   They tell thee true.

DOUGLAS   The lord of Stafford dear° today hath bought
Thy likeness,° for instead of thee, King Harry,
This sword hath ended him. So shall it thee,
Unless thou yield thee as my prisoner.   10

BLUNT   I was not born a yielder, thou proud Scot,
And thou shalt find a king that will revenge
Lord Stafford's death.   *They fight. Douglas kills Blunt*

Then enter Hotspur

HOTSPUR   Oh, Douglas, hadst thou fought at Holmedon thus,
I never had triumphed upon a Scot.   15

DOUGLAS   All's done, all's won; here breathless° lies the King.

HOTSPUR   Where?

DOUGLAS   Here.

HOTSPUR   This, Douglas? No. I know this face full well.
A gallant knight he was; his name was Blunt,   20
Semblably furnished° like the King himself.

DOUGLAS   A fool go with thy soul,° whither it goes!
A borrowed title hast thou bought too dear.
Why didst thou tell me that thou wert a king?

5.3. Location: Shrewsbury field. The scene is virtually continuous. Summary: The King strategically sends many into battle dressed like him. Blunt is one, and is killed by Douglas. Moralizing briefly over Blunt's body, Falstaff reveals that he has led nearly all of his ragamuffins to their deaths. Hal asks Falstaff to lend him a weapon, and is angered by his old companion's ill-timed joke.
0.1 *power* army   **0.2** *Alarum* trumpet signal to advance   **7 dear** dearly   **7–8 bought Thy likeness** paid for his resemblance to you   **16 breathless** dead   **21 Semblably furnished** similarly accoutered   **22 A . . . soul** may the stigma of "fool" accompany your soul (for having dressed as a decoy of King Henry)

HOTSPUR The King hath many marching in his coats.° 25
DOUGLAS Now, by my sword, I will kill all his coats!
I'll murder all his wardrobe, piece by piece,
Until I meet the King.
HOTSPUR   Up, and away!
Our soldiers stand full fairly for the day.°   [*Exeunt*]

Alarum. Enter Falstaff, solus

FALSTAFF Though I could scape shot-free° at London, I fear 30
the shot here; here's no scoring° but upon the pate. Soft,
who are you? Sir Walter Blunt. There's honor for you.
Here's no vanity!° I am as hot as molten lead, and as heavy
too. God keep lead out of me! I need no more weight than
mine own bowels. I have led my ragamuffins where they are 35
peppered. There's not three of my hundred and fifty left
alive, and they are for the town's end,° to beg during life.
But who comes here?

Enter the Prince

PRINCE What, stands thou idle here? Lend me thy sword.
Many a nobleman lies stark and stiff 40
Under the hoofs of vaunting enemies,
Whose deaths are yet unrevenged. I prithee,
Lend me thy sword.
FALSTAFF Oh, Hal, I prithee, give me leave to breathe awhile.
Turk Gregory° never did such deeds in arms as I have done 45
this day. I have paid Percy, I have made him sure.°
PRINCE He is, indeed, and living to kill thee.
I prithee, lend me thy sword.

---

25 coats vests worn over armor embroidered with a coat of arms **29 stand . . . day**
seem in an auspicious position, likely to win the victory **30 shot-free** without
paying the tavern bill **31 scoring** (1) cutting (2) marking up of charges, by notches
on a stick or on the inn door **33 Here's no vanity!** (ironically) if this doesn't show
what I was saying about honor, then nothing does! **37 town's end** city gate,
frequented by beggars **45 Turk Gregory** (*Turk* is an abusive term signifying a
tyrant, and Gregory refers probably to Pope Gregory XIII, who was assumed to
have encouraged the Massacre of Saint Bartholomew [1572], in which many
French Protestants were slain, and to have encouraged plots against Elizabeth)
46 made him sure made sure of him (but Prince Hal takes *sure* in a different sense,
meaning "safe")

FALSTAFF   Nay, before God, Hal, if Percy be alive, thou gets not
my sword; but take my pistol, if thou wilt.   50
PRINCE   Give it me. What, is it in the case?
FALSTAFF   Ay, Hal, 'tis hot, 'tis hot.° There's that will sack a city.
The Prince draws it out and finds it to be a bottle of sack
PRINCE   What, is it a time to jest and dally now?
He throws the bottle at him. Exit
FALSTAFF   Well, if Percy be alive, I'll pierce° him. If he do come
in my way, so;° if he do not, if I come in his willingly, let him   55
make a carbonado° of me. I like not in such grinning honor
as Sir Walter hath. Give me life, which if I can save, so; if
not, honor comes unlooked for, and there's an end.°   [*Exit*]

ACT 5
SCENE 4

*Alarum. Excursions.° Enter the King, the Prince, Lord
John of Lancaster, [and the] Earl of Westmorland*

KING   I prithee,
Harry, withdraw thyself; thou bleedest too much.
Lord John of Lancaster, go you with him.
LANCASTER   Not I, my lord, unless I did bleed too.
PRINCE   I beseech Your Majesty, make up,°   5
Lest your retirement° do amaze° your friends.

---

52 **hot** (Falstaff implies he has been firing at the enemy)   54 **Percy . . . pierce**
(Elizabethan pronunciation rendered the pun more obvious than it is now)   55 **so**
well and good   56 **carbonado** meat scored across for broiling   58 **there's an end**
(1) that concludes the subject of my catechism (see 5.1.129–39) (2) thus life ends.

5.4. Location: Scene continues at Shrewsbury field. **Summary:** Despite a serious
wound, Hal refuses to leave the field and saves his father's life by driving off
Douglas. Hotspur's entry finally brings the two youths together, but their
confrontation shares the stage with Falstaff's combat with Douglas. Falstaff feigns
death as Hal kills Hotspur, and the Prince bids farewell to what he believes are two
dead men. Once he leaves, Falstaff revives, stabs Hotspur's thigh, and when the
Prince returns, concocts a heroic tale about having killed him. Hal lets him have his
way, and Falstaff, carrying Hotspur's body off stage, imagines himself growing
great and mending his ways.

0.1 *Excursions* sorties (the fallen body of Blunt may be removed at some point or
may be onstage still at 5.4.77 when Hal kills Hotspur)   5 **make up** go forward
6 **retirement** retreat | **amaze** alarm

KING   I will do so. My lord of Westmorland,
   Lead him to his tent.
WESTMORLAND   Come, my lord, I'll lead you to your tent.
PRINCE   Lead me, my lord? I do not need your help.   10
   And God forbid a shallow scratch should drive
   The Prince of Wales from such a field as this,
   Where stained nobility lies trodden on
   And rebels' arms triumph in massacres!
LANCASTER   We breathe° too long. Come, cousin Westmorland,   15
   Our duty this way lies. For God's sake, come.
                    [*Exeunt Prince John and Westmorland*]
PRINCE   By God, thou hast deceived me, Lancaster!
   I did not think thee lord of such a spirit.
   Before, I loved thee as a brother, John,
   But now I do respect thee as my soul.   20
KING   I saw him hold Lord Percy at the point°
   With lustier maintenance° than I did look for
   Of such an ungrown warrior.
PRINCE   Oh, this boy lends mettle to us all!   *Exit*

                    [*Enter Douglas*]

DOUGLAS   Another king? They grow like Hydra's heads.°   25
   I am the Douglas, fatal to all those
   That wear those colors° on them. What art thou
   That counterfeit'st the person of a king?
KING   The King himself, who, Douglas, grieves at heart
   So many of his shadows° thou hast met   30
   And not the very King. I have two boys
   Seek° Percy and thyself about the field;
   But, seeing thou fall'st on me so luckily,
   I will assay thee;° and defend thyself.
DOUGLAS   I fear thou art another counterfeit;   35
   And yet, in faith, thou bearest thee like a king.
   But mine I am sure thou art, whoe'er thou be,
   And thus I win thee.

15 **breathe** rest, pause for breath (as also at l. 47)   21 **at the point** at sword's point
22 **lustier maintenance** more vigorous bearing   25 **Hydra's heads** (the heads of the
Lernaean Hydra grew again as fast as they were cut off)   27 **colors** the colors of the
King's insignia   30 **shadows** having form without substance   32 **Seek** who seek
34 **assay thee** put you to the test

They fight; the King being in danger, enter Prince of Wales
PRINCE   Hold up thy head, vile Scot, or thou art like°
    Never to hold it up again! The spirits   40
    Of valiant Shirley, Stafford, Blunt, are in my arms.
    It is the Prince of Wales that threatens thee,
    Who never promiseth but he means to pay.°
                         They fight. Douglas flieth
    Cheerly, my lord. How fares Your Grace?
    Sir Nicholas Gawsey hath for succor sent,   45
    And so hath Clifton. I'll to Clifton straight.
KING   Stay and breathe awhile.
    Thou hast redeemed thy lost opinion,°
    And showed thou mak'st some tender of° my life
    In this fair rescue thou hast brought to me.   50
PRINCE   Oh, God, they did me too much injury
    That ever said I hearkened° for your death.
    If it were so, I might have let alone
    The insulting° hand of Douglas over you,
    Which would have been as speedy in your end   55
    As all the poisonous potions in the world,
    And saved the treacherous labor of your son.
KING   Make up° to Clifton; I'll to Sir Nicholas Gawsey.
                             Exit King

                        Enter Hotspur

HOTSPUR   If I mistake not, thou art Harry Monmouth.
PRINCE   Thou speak'st as if I would deny my name.   60
HOTSPUR   My name is Harry Percy.
PRINCE   Why then, I see
    A very valiant rebel of the name.
    I am the Prince of Wales; and think not, Percy,
    To share with me in glory any more.
    Two stars keep not their motion in one sphere,   65
    Nor can one England brook° a double reign
    Of Harry Percy and the Prince of Wales.

---

39 like likely   **43 pay** (1) settle a debt (2) kill   **48 opinion** reputation   **49 thou . . . of** you have some care for   **52 hearkened** listened (as for welcome news)   **54 insulting** exulting   **58 Make up** advance   **66 brook** endure

HOTSPUR   Nor shall it, Harry, for the hour is come
   To end the one of us; and would to God
   Thy name in arms were now as great as mine!   70
PRINCE   I'll make it greater ere I part from thee,
   And all the budding honors on thy crest
   I'll crop° to make a garland for my head.
HOTSPUR   I can no longer brook thy vanities.°   *They fight*

Enter Falstaff

FALSTAFF   Well said,° Hal! To it, Hal! Nay, you shall find no boy's   75
play here, I can tell you.

*Enter Douglas. He fighteth with Falstaff, who
falls down as if he were dead. [Exit Douglas]
The Prince killeth° Percy*

HOTSPUR   Oh, Harry, thou hast robbed me of my youth!
   I better brook the loss of brittle life
   Than those proud titles thou hast won of me;
   They wound my thoughts worse than thy sword my flesh.   80
   But thoughts, the slaves of life, and life, time's fool,°
   And time, that takes survey of all the world,
   Must have a stop. Oh, I could prophesy,
   But that the earthy and cold hand of death
   Lies on my tongue. No, Percy, thou art dust,   85
   And food for—   *[He dies]*
PRINCE   For worms, brave Percy. Fare thee well, great heart.
   Ill-weaved ambition, how much art thou shrunk!
   When that this body did contain a spirit,
   A kingdom for it was too small a bound;   90
   But now two paces of the vilest earth
   Is room enough. This earth that bears thee dead
   Bears not alive so stout° a gentleman.
   If thou wert sensible of courtesy,°
   I should not make so dear° a show of zeal;°   95
   But let my favors° hide thy mangled face,

---

73 **crop** pluck   74 **vanities** empty boasts   75 **Well said** well done   76.3 ***killeth***
mortally wounds   81 **thoughts . . . fool** our mental consciousness, which is
dependent on physical existence, and our life itself, which is subject to time   93 **stout**
valiant   94 **sensible of courtesy** able to hear my praise   95 **dear** handsome,
heartfelt | **zeal** admiration   96 **favors** plume, scarf, glove, or similar article

And, even in thy behalf, I'll thank myself
For doing these fair rites of tenderness.
>   [*He covers Hotspur's face with a scarf or other favor*]
Adieu, and take thy praise with thee to heaven!
Thy ignominy sleep with thee in the grave,   100
But not remembered in thy epitaph!
>   *He spieth Falstaff on the ground*
What, old acquaintance, could not all this flesh
Keep in a little life? Poor Jack, farewell!
I could have better spared a better man.
Oh, I should have a heavy° miss of thee   105
If I were much in love with vanity.°
Death hath not struck so fat a deer today,
Though many dearer, in this bloody fray.
Emboweled° will I see thee by and by.
Till then in blood by noble Percy lie.   *Exit*   110
>   *Falstaff riseth up*

FALSTAFF Emboweled? If thou embowel me today, I'll give you
leave to powder° me and eat me too tomorrow. 'Sblood,
'twas time to counterfeit, or that hot termagant° Scot had
paid° me, scot and lot° too. Counterfeit? I lie, I am no counterfeit. To die is to be a counterfeit, for he is but the counterfeit of   115
a man who hath not the life of a man; but to counterfeit
dying, when a man thereby liveth, is to be no counterfeit but
the true and perfect image of life indeed. The better part° of
valor is discretion, in the which better part I have saved my
life. Zounds, I am afraid of this gunpowder Percy, though he   120
be dead. How if he should counterfeit too and rise? By my
faith, I am afraid he would prove the better counterfeit.
Therefore I'll make him sure; yea, and I'll swear I killed him.
Why may not he rise as well as I? Nothing confutes me but
eyes,° and nobody sees me. Therefore, sirrah [*stabbing him*],   125
with a new wound in your thigh, come you along with me.
>   *He takes up Hotspur on his back*

---

105 heavy (1) serious (2) corpulent **106 vanity** frivolity **109 Emboweled**
disemboweled, for embalming and burial **112 powder** salt **113 termagant** violent
and blustering, like the heathen god of the Saracens in medieval and Renaissance
lore **114 paid** killed | **scot and lot** in full (originally the phrase was the term for a
parish tax) **118 part** constituent part, quality, role **124–5 Nothing . . . eyes**
nothing can contradict me but an eyewitness

Enter Prince [and] John of Lancaster

PRINCE   Come, brother John; full bravely hast thou fleshed°
Thy maiden sword.

LANCASTER   But soft, whom have we here?
Did you not tell me this fat man was dead?

PRINCE   I did; I saw him dead,   130
Breathless and bleeding on the ground.—Art thou alive?
Or is it fantasy that plays upon our eyesight?
I prithee, speak. We will not trust our eyes
Without our ears. Thou art not what thou seem'st.

FALSTAFF   No, that's certain, I am not a double man;° but if I   135
be not Jack Falstaff, then am I a Jack.° There is Percy
[*throwing the body down*]. If your father will do me any
honor, so; if not, let him kill the next Percy himself. I look to
be either earl or duke, I can assure you.

PRINCE   Why, Percy I killed myself and saw thee dead.   140

FALSTAFF   Didst thou? Lord, Lord, how this world is given to
lying! I grant you I was down and out of breath, and so was
he; but we rose both at an instant° and fought a long hour
by Shrewsbury clock. If I may be believed, so; if not, let
them that should reward valor bear the sin upon their own   145
heads. I'll take it upon my death° I gave him this wound in
the thigh. If the man were alive and would deny it, zounds, I
would make him eat a piece of my sword.

LANCASTER   This is the strangest tale that ever I heard.

PRINCE   This is the strangest fellow, brother John.—   150
Come, bring your luggage nobly on your back.
For my part, if a lie° may do thee grace,°
I'll gild it with the happiest° terms I have.

                                        A retreat is sounded

The trumpet sounds retreat; the day is our.
Come, brother, let us to the highest° of the field,   155
To see what friends are living, who are dead.

                            Exeunt [Prince of Wales and Lancaster]

---

127 **fleshed** initiated (in battle)   135 **double man** (1) specter (2) two men   136 **Jack**
knave   143 **at an instant** simultaneously   146 **take . . . death** swear with my
eternal soul at risk   152 **a lie** this lie of yours | **grace** credit   153 **happiest** most
felicitous   155 **highest** highest vantage point

FALSTAFF   I'll follow, as they say, for reward. He that rewards
me, God reward him! If I do grow great, I'll grow less; for
I'll purge,° and leave sack, and live cleanly as a nobleman
should do.   160

Exit [bearing off the body]

ACT 5
SCENE 5

*The trumpets sound. Enter the King, Prince of Wales,
Lord John of Lancaster, Earl of Westmorland, with
Worcester and Vernon prisoners*

KING   Thus ever did rebellion find rebuke.
Ill-spirited Worcester! Did not we send grace,
Pardon, and terms of love to all of you?
And wouldst thou turn our offers contrary?
Misuse the tenor of thy kinsman's trust?°   5
Three knights upon our party slain today,
A noble earl, and many a creature else
Had been alive this hour,
If like a Christian thou hadst truly borne
Betwixt our armies true intelligence.°   10
WORCESTER   What I have done my safety urged me to;
And I embrace this fortune patiently,
Since not to be avoided it falls on me.
KING   Bear Worcester to the death, and Vernon too.
Other offenders we will pause upon.   15
              [Exeunt Worcester and Vernon, guarded]
How goes the field?

---

159 purge (1) reduce in weight, using laxatives (2) repent

5.5. Location: The battlefield. Summary: King Henry declares the battle won and
reproaches Worcester before sending him and Vernon to their deaths. Hal, however,
frees their Scottish ally Douglas for his noble deeds, and the King plans complete
victory.

5 Misuse . . . trust? would you abuse Hotspur's confidence in you (by concealing the
generosity of my offer, in your role as emissary)?   **10 intelligence** information,
report

PRINCE   The noble Scot, Lord Douglas, when he saw
    The fortune of the day quite turned from him,
    The noble Percy slain, and all his men
    Upon the foot of fear,° fled with the rest;   20
    And falling from a hill, he was so bruised
    That the pursuers took him. At my tent
    The Douglas is; and I beseech Your Grace
    I may dispose of him.
KING   With all my heart.
PRINCE   Then, brother John of Lancaster,   25
    To you this honorable bounty° shall belong.
    Go to the Douglas, and deliver him
    Up to his pleasure, ransomless and free.
    His valors shown upon our crests° today
    Have taught us how to cherish such high deeds   30
    Even in the bosom of our adversaries.
LANCASTER   I thank Your Grace for this high courtesy,
    Which I shall give away° immediately.
KING   Then this remains, that we divide our power.
    You, son John, and my cousin Westmorland   35
    Towards York shall bend you° with your dearest° speed
    To meet Northumberland and the prelate Scroop,
    Who, as we hear, are busily in arms.
    Myself and you, son Harry, will towards Wales,
    To fight with Glendower and the Earl of March.   40
    Rebellion in this land shall lose his° sway,
    Meeting the check of such another day;°
    And since this business so fair° is done,
    Let us not leave° till all our own be won.   *Exeunt*

20 Upon . . . fear fleeing in panic   26 this honorable bounty the honor of this
bounteous act   29 crests helmets   33 give away pass along, confer on Douglas
36 bend you direct your course | dearest most urgent   41 his its   42 Meeting . . .
day when the rebellion is entirely repulsed at one more battlefield   43 fair
successfully   44 leave leave off

The Second Part of
KING HENRY
THE FOURTH

by William Shakespeare

The Second Part of
KING HENRY
THE FOURTH

The Actor's Names

RUMOR, *the Presenter*

KING HENRY THE FOURTH

PRINCE HENRY, *afterwards crowned* KING HENRY THE FIFTH

PRINCE JOHN OF LANCASTER

HUMPHREY [DUKE] OF GLOUCESTER } *sons to Henry IV and brethren to Henry V*

THOMAS [DUKE] OF CLARENCE

[EARL OF] NORTHUMBERLAND

[SCROOP,] THE ARCHBISHOP OF YORK

[LORD] MOWBRAY

[LORD] HASTING

LORD BARDOLPH } *opposites against King Henry IV*

TRAVERS

MORTON

[SIR JOHN] COLEVILLE

[EARL OF] WARWICK

[EARL OF] WESTMORLAND

[EARL OF] SURREY } *of the King's party*

GOWER

HARCOURT

[BLUNT]
LORD CHIEF JUSTICE } *of the King's party*
[*His* SERVANT]

POINS
[SIR JOHN] FALSTAFF
BARDOLPH
PISTOL } *irregular humorists*
PETO
[FALSTAFF'S] PAGE

SHALLOW
SILENCE } *both country justices*
DAVY, *servant to Shallow*
FANG *and* SNARE, *two sergeants*
MOLDY, SHADOW, WART, FEEBLE, [*and*]
  BULLCALF, *country soldiers*
[FRANCIS, *a drawer*]

NORTHUMBERLAND'S WIFE
PERCY'S WIDOW [LADY PERCY]
HOSTESS QUICKLY
DOLL TEARSHEET
DRAWERS
BEADLES
GROOMS
[PORTER]

EPILOGUE

[*Lords, Attendants, Messengers, Pages, Musicians, Officers, etc.*]

        SCENE: England

INDUCTION

Enter Rumor, painted full of tongues

RUMOR   Open your ears, for which of you will stop
    The vent of hearing when loud Rumor speaks?

Induction. Location: Although the allegory of Rumor, based ultimately on Virgil's depiction of Fama as full of eyes, ears, and tongues in the *Aeneid* (4.179–90), is

I, from the orient to the drooping west,
Making the wind my post-horse,° still° unfold
The acts commencèd on this ball of earth.   5
Upon my tongues continual slanders ride,
The which in every language I pronounce,
Stuffing the ears of men with false reports.
I speak of peace while covert enmity,
Under the smile of safety, wounds the world.   10
And who but Rumor, who but only I,
Make fearful musters° and prepared defense,
Whiles the big° year, swoll'n with some other grief,
Is thought with child by the stern tyrant War,
And no such matter?° Rumor is a pipe°   15
Blown by surmises, jealousies,° conjectures,
And of so easy and so plain a stop°
That the blunt° monster with uncounted° heads,
The still-discordant wav'ring multitude,
Can play upon it. But what° need I thus   20
My well-known body to anatomize°
Among my household?° Why is Rumor here?
I run before King Harry's victory,
Who in a bloody field by Shrewsbury
Hath beaten down young Hotspur and his troops,   25
Quenching the flame of bold rebellion
Even with the rebels' blood. But what mean I
To speak so true at first? My office is
To noise abroad that Harry Monmouth° fell

---

timeless, Rumor is here represented as standing in front of Northumberland's
castle, Warkworth. The play is supposed to open immediately after the battle of
Shrewsbury, in which Henry Percy, or Hotspur, and the Scottish Earl of Douglas
have been overthrown. We are concerned first of all with the news of the battle with
which *1 Henry IV* ended. Summary: Rumor proclaims his dishonesty, as well as his
familiarity with the playhouse. His reversed report of the rebels' victory includes the
success of Hotspur over Prince Hal.
4 post-horse horse kept at an inn or post-house for the use of travelers | **still**
continually **12 musters** assemblies of soldiers **13 big** swollen, pregnant with
disaster **15 And no such matter** and yet there is no substance in such rumors |
pipe recorder (a wind instrument) **16 jealousies** suspicions **17 of . . . stop** whose
stops or openings are so easily played on **18 blunt** stupid, dull-witted | **uncounted**
countless **20 what** why **21 anatomize** lay open minutely, explain **22 household**
retinue, the audience **29 Harry Monmouth** Prince Hal (who was born at
Monmouth in Wales)

Under the wrath of noble Hotspur's sword,   30
And that the King before the Douglas' rage
Stooped his anointed head as low as death.
This have I rumored through the peasant° towns
Between that royal field of Shrewsbury
And this worm-eaten hold° of ragged stone,   35
Where Hotspur's father, old Northumberland,
Lies crafty-sick.° The posts come tiring on,°
And not a man of them brings other news
Than they have learned of me. From Rumor's tongues
They bring smooth comforts false, worse than true wrongs.°   40

                                   Exit Rumor

ACT 1
SCENE 1

Enter the Lord Bardolph° at one door

LORD BARDOLPH
Who keeps° the gate here, ho?

                               [Enter the Porter]

                     Where is the Earl?

PORTER   What shall I say you are?

LORD BARDOLPH   Tell thou the Earl
That the Lord Bardolph doth attend° him here.

PORTER
His Lordship is walked forth into the orchard.
Please it Your Honor knock but at the gate,   5

---

33 peasant rural, provincial   **35 hold** stronghold, fortress   **37 crafty-sick** feigning sickness | **The . . . on** the messengers gallop hard, exhausting their horses   **40 smooth . . . wrongs** false good news that is ultimately worse than hurtful truth

1.1. Location: Warkworth. Before Northumberland's castle. Summary: Lord Bardolph (not the tavern denizen) unknowingly conveys a false account of the battle at Shrewsbury to Northumberland, but he is contradicted by Travers and Morton's painful news. Northumberland, called "crafty sick" by Rumor, thunders in despair until he is counseled by Morton that support by the Archbishop of York (see *1 Henry IV*, 4.4) brings new hope to their cause.
0.1 Lord Bardolph (an ally of the Percies; not to be confused with Bardolph, Falstaff's red-faced companion)   **1 keeps** guards   **3 attend** await

And he himself will answer.

Enter the Earl [of] Northumberland [in a
nightcap, supporting himself with a crutch]

LORD BARDOLPH   Here comes the Earl
                                  [Exit Porter]

NORTHUMBERLAND

What news, Lord Bardolph? Every minute now
Should be the father of some stratagem.°
The times are wild. Contention, like a horse
Full of high feeding,° madly hath broke loose   10
And bears down all before him.

LORD BARDOLPH   Noble Earl,
I bring you certain news from Shrewsbury.

NORTHUMBERLAND

Good, an° God will!

LORD BARDOLPH   As good as heart can wish.
The King is almost wounded to the death,
And, in the fortune of my lord your son,   15
Prince Harry slain outright; and both the Blunts
Killed by the hand of Douglas. Young Prince John
And Westmorland and Stafford fled the field,
And Harry Monmouth's brawn,° the hulk Sir John,
Is prisoner to your son. Oh, such a day,   20
So fought, so followed,° and so fairly won,
Came not till now to dignify the times
Since Caesar's fortunes!°

NORTHUMBERLAND   How is this derived?°
Saw you the field? Came you from Shrewsbury?

LORD BARDOLPH

I spake with one, my lord, that came from thence,   25
A gentleman well bred and of good name,
That freely rendered me these news for true.

Enter Travers

---

8 stratagem violent deed   **10 high feeding** too-rich fodder   **13 an** if   **19 brawn** fat boar   **21 followed** carried through   **23 Since Caesar's fortunes** since Julius Caesar defeated Pharnaces at Zela in 47 B.C., proclaiming *Veni, vidi, vici* ("I came, I saw, I overcame"); the alliteration in l. 21 (*fought, followed, fairly*) recalls that famous message | **derived** learned, obtained

NORTHUMBERLAND   Here comes my servant Travers, who I sent
  On Tuesday last to listen after news.
LORD BARDOLPH   My lord, I overrode° him on the way,   30
  And he is furnished with no certainties
  More than he haply° may retail° from me.
NORTHUMBERLAND
  Now, Travers, what good tidings comes with you?
TRAVERS   My lord, Sir John Umfrevill° turned me back
  With joyful tidings and, being better horsed,   35
  Outrode me. After him came spurring hard
  A gentleman almost forspent° with speed
  That stopped by me to breathe° his bloodied° horse.
  He asked the way to Chester, and of him
  I did demand° what news from Shrewsbury.   40
  He told me that rebellion had bad luck
  And that young Harry Percy's spur was cold.
  With that, he gave his able horse the head,°
  And bending forward struck his armèd heels
  Against the panting sides of his poor jade°   45
  Up to the rowel head,° and starting° so
  He seemed in running to devour the way,
  Staying° no longer question.
NORTHUMBERLAND   Ha? Again:
  Said he young Harry Percy's spur was cold?
  Of Hotspur, Coldspur? That rebellion   50
  Had met ill luck?
LORD BARDOLPH   My lord, I'll tell you what:
  If my young lord your son have not the day,°
  Upon mine honor, for a silken point°
  I'll give my barony. Never talk of it.
NORTHUMBERLAND
  Why should that gentleman that rode by Travers   55
  Give then such instances of loss?
LORD BARDOLPH   Who, he?

30 overrode overtook   **32 haply** perhaps | **retail** relate   **34 Sir John Umfrevill** perhaps the *gentleman* mentioned in l. 26   **37 forspent** exhausted   **38 breathe** rest | **bloodied** with spurring   **40 demand** ask   **43 gave . . . head** loosened the reins with which he had reined in his powerful horse   **45 jade** nag   **46 rowel head** the end of the spur, in which the barbed wheel turns | **starting** springing forward   **48 Staying** waiting for   **52 day** victory   **53 point** tag for fastening clothes (something of very small value)

He was some hilding° fellow that had stol'n
The horse he rode on and, upon my life,
Spoke at a venture.° Look, here comes more news.

Enter Morton

NORTHUMBERLAND   Yea, this man's brow, like to a title leaf,°   60
Foretells the nature of a tragic volume.
So looks the strand whereon the imperious flood
Hath left a witnessed usurpation.°
Say, Morton, didst thou come from Shrewsbury?
MORTON   I ran from Shrewsbury, my noble lord,   65
Where hateful death put on his ugliest mask
To fright our party.
NORTHUMBERLAND   How doth my son and brother?
Thou tremblest, and the whiteness in thy cheek
Is apter than thy tongue to tell thy errand.
Even such a man, so faint, so spiritless,   70
So dull, so dead in look, so woebegone,
Drew Priam's curtain° in the dead of night
And would have told him half his Troy was burnt;
But Priam found the fire ere he his tongue,°
And I my Percy's death ere thou report'st it.   75
This thou wouldst say, "Your son did thus and thus;
Your brother thus; so fought the noble Douglas"—
Stopping° my greedy ear with their bold deeds.
But in the end, to stop my ear indeed,°
Thou hast a sigh to blow away this praise,   80
Ending with "Brother, son, and all are dead."
MORTON   Douglas is living, and your brother, yet;
But for my lord your son—
NORTHUMBERLAND   Why, he is dead.
See what a ready tongue suspicion hath!
He° that but fears the thing he would not know   85
Hath by instinct knowledge from others' eyes
That what he feared is chancèd.° Yet speak, Morton.

57 **hilding** good-for-nothing   59 **at a venture** at random, recklessly   60 **title leaf**
title page   62–3 **So . . . usurpation** so looks the shore whereon the invading ocean
has left behind the evidence of its encroachment; (Morton's brow is furrowed like
wrinkled sand)   72 **Priam's curtain** the bedcurtains of Priam, King of Troy   74 **ere . . .
tongue** before the messenger had time to speak   78 **Stopping** filling   79 **stop . . .
indeed** prevent my ever hearing again   85 **He** the person   87 **is chancèd** has occurred

Tell thou an earl his divination° lies,
And I will take it as a sweet disgrace
And make thee rich for doing me such wrong.   90
MORTON   You are too great to be by me gainsaid.°
Your spirit° is too true, your fears too certain.
NORTHUMBERLAND   Yet, for° all this, say not that Percy's dead.
I see a strange confession in thine eye.
Thou shak'st thy head and hold'st it fear or sin   95
To speak a truth. If he be slain, say so.
The tongue offends not that reports his death;
And he doth sin that doth belie° the dead,
Not he which says the dead is not alive.
Yet the first bringer of unwelcome news   100
Hath but a losing office,° and his tongue
Sounds ever after as a sullen° bell
Remembered tolling° a departing friend.
LORD BARDOLPH   I cannot think, my lord, your son is dead.
MORTON   I am sorry I should force you to believe   105
That which I would to God I had not seen;
But these mine eyes saw him in bloody state,
Rend'ring faint quittance,° wearied and outbreathed,°
To Harry Monmouth, whose swift wrath beat down
The never-daunted Percy to the earth,   110
From whence with life he never more sprung up.
In few,° his death, whose spirit lent a fire
Even to the dullest peasant in his camp,
Being bruited° once, took fire and heat away
From the best-tempered° courage in his troops;   115
For from his metal° was his party steeled,
Which once in him abated,° all the rest
Turned on themselves,° like dull and heavy lead.
And as the thing that's heavy in itself

88 **divination** prophecy   91 **gainsaid** contradicted   92 **spirit** intuition, powers of perception   93 **for** in spite of   98 **belie** slander, misreport   101 **losing office** thankless task   102 **sullen** mournful   103 **tolling** ringing the funeral bell for   108 **quittance** requital, resistance | **outbreathed** out of breath   112 **In few** in few words   114 **bruited** rumored, reported   115 **best-tempered** like the highest quality steel   116 **metal** (1) steel, continuing the metaphor of l. 115 (2) mettle, courage   117 **abated** (1) blunted (2) slackened   118 **Turned on themselves** (1) bent backwards (2) turned and ran

Upon enforcement° flies with greatest speed,   120
So did our men, heavy in Hotspur's loss,
Lend to this weight such lightness with their fear
That arrows fled not swifter toward their aim
Than did our soldiers, aiming at their safety,
Fly from the field. Then was that noble Worcester   125
Too soon ta'en prisoner; and that furious Scot,
The bloody Douglas, whose well-laboring sword
Had three times slain th'appearance of the King,°
'Gan vail his stomach° and did grace° the shame
Of those that turned their backs, and in his flight,   130
Stumbling in fear, was took. The sum of all
Is that the King hath won and hath sent out
A speedy power° to encounter you, my lord,
Under the conduct° of young Lancaster
And Westmorland. This is the news at full.   135

NORTHUMBERLAND   For this I shall have time enough to mourn.
In poison there is physic;° and these news,
Having been well, that would have made me sick,°
Being sick, have° in some measure made me well.
And as the wretch whose fever-weakened joints   140
Like strengthless hinges buckle under life,°
Impatient of his fit,° breaks like a fire
Out of his keeper's° arms, even so my limbs,
Weakened with grief, being now enraged with grief,°
Are thrice themselves. Hence, therefore, thou nice° crutch!   145
                    [*He throws away his crutch*]
A scaly gauntlet° now with joints of steel
Must glove this hand. And hence, thou sickly coif!°
                    [*He takes off his nightcap*]
Thou art a guard too wanton° for the head

120 **Upon enforcement** when set forcibly in motion   128 **th'appearance of the King**
warriors dressed like the King (see *1 Henry IV*, 5.3 and 5.4.25–38)   129 **'Gan . . .
stomach** began to abate or lower his courage | **grace** sanction (by his own running
away)   133 **power** armed force   134 **conduct** command   137 **physic** medicine
138 **Having . . . sick** that would have made me sick if I had been well   139 **Being sick,
have** I being sick, this same news has   141 **buckle under life** bend under the weight of
the living man   142 **fit** attack of illness   143 **keeper's** nurse's   144 **grief . . . grief**
pain and sickness . . . sorrow   145 **nice** delicate, effeminate   146 **scaly gauntlet**
armored glove   147 **sickly coif** close-fitting cap worn by an invalid   148 **wanton**
effeminate, luxurious

Which princes, fleshed° with conquest, aim to hit.
Now bind my brows with iron, and approach°   150
The ragged'st° hour that time and spite dare bring
To frown upon th'enragèd Northumberland!
Let heaven kiss earth! Now let not Nature's hand
Keep the wild flood° confined! Let order die,
And let this world no longer be a stage   155
To feed contention in a ling'ring act;°
But let one spirit of the firstborn Cain°
Reign in all bosoms, that,° each heart being set
On bloody courses, the rude scene° may end,
And darkness be the burier of the dead!   160

LORD BARDOLPH
    This strainèd° passion doth you wrong, my lord.
MORTON   Sweet Earl, divorce not wisdom from your honor.
    The lives of all your loving complices°
    Lean on your health, the which, if you give o'er
    To stormy passion, must perforce° decay.   165
    You cast th'event° of war, my noble lord,
    And summed the account of chance,° before you said
    "Let us make head."° It was your presurmise°
    That in the dole° of blows your son might drop.
    You knew he walked o'er perils, on an edge,   170
    More likely to fall in than to get o'er;
    You were advised° his flesh was capable
    Of° wounds and scars, and that his forward° spirit
    Would lift him where most trade° of danger ranged.
    Yet did you say, "Go forth." And none of this,   175
    Though strongly apprehended, could restrain
    The stiff-borne action.° What hath then befall'n,

149 **fleshed** inflamed by the taste of blood and success   150 **approach** let approach
151 **ragged'st** roughest   154 **flood** river, ocean   156 **in . . . act** in a drawn-out act
(as of a play) (Northumberland wishes for an end to the lingering dissolution of a
world in conflict)   157 **of . . . Cain** of murder   158 **that** so that   159 **rude scene**
(1) violent action (2) crude play (see l. 156 and n.)   161 **strainèd** excessive   163 **complices** allies   165 **perforce** necessarily   166 **cast th'event** calculated the outcome
167 **summed . . . chance** summed up and weighed the risks   168 **make head** raise an
army | **presurmise** presupposition   169 **dole** dealing out, distribution (with a possible
punning suggestion of "grief, sorrow")   172 **advised** aware   173 **Of** of receiving |
forward eager, ardent   174 **trade** trafficking   175–7 **And none . . . action** and yet
none of these potential dangers, though strongly understood to be possible, could hold
back a military action that was resolutely carried out

Or what hath this bold enterprise brought forth,
More than that being which was like to be?°
LORD BARDOLPH   We all that are engagèd to° this loss   180
Knew that we ventured on such dangerous seas
That if we wrought out life 'twas ten to one.°
And yet we ventured, for the gain proposed
Choked the respect° of likely peril feared;
And since we are o'erset,° venture again.   185
Come, we will all put forth,° body and goods.
MORTON   'Tis more than time. And, my most noble lord,
I hear for certain, and dare speak the truth,
The gentle Archbishop of York is up
With well-appointed powers.° He is a man   190
Who with a double surety° binds his followers.
My lord your son had only° but the corpse,°
But° shadows and the shows of men, to fight.°
For that same word "rebellion" did divide
The action of their bodies from their souls,   195
And they did fight with queasiness, constrained,
As men drink potions,° that their weapons only
Seemed on our side; but, for° their spirits and souls,
This word "rebellion," it had froze them up
As fish are in a pond. But now the Bishop   200
Turns insurrection to religion.°
Supposed° sincere and holy in his thoughts,
He's followed both with body and with mind,
And doth enlarge his rising with the blood
Of fair King Richard, scraped from Pomfret stones;°   205
Derives from heaven his quarrel and his cause;

179 **that . . . be** what was likely to occur   180 **engagèd to** involved in   182 **if . . . one** if we came out alive, we survived ten-to-one odds   184 **Choked the respect** suppressed the consideration   185 **o'erset** defeated, overthrown   186 **all put forth** (1) all set out, as though putting out to sea (2) stake everything   189–90 **The gentle . . . powers** the nobly born Archbishop Scroop is ready with well-equipped troops   191 **a double surety** both temporal and spiritual authority   192 **only** but only | **corpse** the bodies without the souls   193 **But** only | **to fight** to use for fighting   197 **As . . . potions** the way people drink distasteful medicines, queasily   198 **for** as for   201 **to religion** into a sacred cause   202 **Supposed** rightly thought to be (*supposed*, however, also means *believed erroneously* or *uncertainly* [RL])   204–5 **And doth . . . stones** and attracts new supporters and allies to the cause of rebellion by sanctifying as a holy relic the blood of Richard II, scraped from the stones of Pontefract Castle where the King was murdered

Tells them he doth bestride° a bleeding land
Gasping for life under great Bolingbroke;°
And more and less° do flock to follow him.

NORTHUMBERLAND   I knew of this before, but, to speak truth,   210
This present grief had wiped it from my mind.
Go in with me, and counsel every man°
The aptest way for safety and revenge.
Get posts° and letters, and make° friends with speed—
Never so few, and never yet more need.   *Exeunt*   215

ACT 1
SCENE 2

*Enter Sir John [Falstaff] alone, with his
Page bearing his sword and buckler°*

FALSTAFF   Sirrah,° you giant, what says the doctor to my water?°

PAGE   He said, sir, the water itself was a good healthy water,
but, for the party that owed° it, he might have more diseases
than he knew for.°

FALSTAFF   Men of all sorts take a pride to gird° at me. The brain   5
of this foolish-compounded° clay, man, is not able to invent
anything that tends to laughter more than I invent or is
invented on me. I am not only witty in myself, but the cause
that wit is in other men. I do here walk before thee like a
sow that hath overwhelmed all her litter but one. If the   10
Prince put thee into my service for any other reason than to
set me off,° why then I have no judgment. Thou whoreson°

---

207 **bestride** stand over to protect   208 **Bolingbroke** King Henry IV, here deprived
of his title by the Archbishop   209 **more and less** all classes   212 **counsel every
man** let every man give advice as to   214 **posts** messengers | **make** collect

1.2. Location: London. A street. Summary: Falstaff, witty and more self-important
than ever, suffers from physical and financial decline. The Chief Justice reminds him
of the Gadshill robbery, but Falstaff's reported military service puts him out of
harm's way for the present. After the Chief Justice refuses to lend him 1,000 pounds,
Falstaff begins scheming for other means of support.

0.2 *buckler* shield   1 **Sirrah** (form of address to a social inferior) | **to my water** about
my urine sample   3 **owed** owned   4 **knew for** was aware of   5 **gird** jeer   6 **foolish-
compounded** composed of folly   12 **set me off** be a foil to me, show me to the best
advantage | **whoreson** (a generalized term of abuse meaning "vile" or "detestable")

mandrake,° thou art fitter to be worn in my cap° than to wait at my heels.° I was never manned with an agate° till now; but I will inset you neither in gold nor silver, but in vile apparel, and send you back again to your master for a jewel—the juvenal,° the Prince your master, whose chin is not yet fledge.° I will sooner have a beard grow in the palm of my hand than he shall get one of his cheek, and yet he will not stick° to say his face is a face royal.° God may finish it when he will; 'tis not a hair° amiss yet. He may keep it still at° a face royal, for a barber shall never earn sixpence out of it; and yet he'll be crowing as if he had writ man° ever since his father was a bachelor. He may keep his own grace,° but he's almost out of mine, I can assure him. What said Master Dommelton about the satin for my short cloak and my slops?°

PAGE   He said, sir, you should procure him better assurance° than Bardolph.° He would not take his bond and yours; he liked not the security.

FALSTAFF   Let him be damned, like the glutton!° Pray God his tongue be hotter!° A whoreson Achitophel,° a rascally yea-forsooth knave,° to bear a gentleman in hand° and then stand upon security!° The whoreson smoothy-pates° do now wear nothing but high shoes and bunches of keys° at their girdles; and if a man is through with them in honest taking up,° then they must stand upon security. I had as lief°

---

13 **mandrake** plant with a forked, man-shaped root | **fitter . . . cap** as small and decorous as a brooch worn in my hat   14 **wait at my heels** wait in attendance on me, follow me about | **manned . . . agate** provided with a servant as small as the little figures cut in agate stone for jewelry and seal rings   17 **juvenal** youth   18 **fledge** covered with down   20 **stick** hesitate | **face royal** (punning on the *royal*, a coin with the King's face stamped on it)   21 **a hair** (1) a single hair of the beard (2) a jot   22 **at** at the value of   23–4 **writ man** called himself man   25 **grace** (1) title suited to his royal rank (2) favor   27 **slops** loose breeches   28 **assurance** guarantee   29 **Bardolph** (one of Falstaff's followers, not the Lord Bardolph of scene 1)   31 **the glutton** (a reference to the parable of Dives the rich man, who, sent to hell for his covetousness, cried out imploringly that Lazarus, the poor leper, might dip his finger in water to cool Dives's burning tongue, Luke 16.19–31)   32 **hotter** than Dives's tongue in hell | **Achitophel** abettor of Absalom's treason against David (2 Samuel 15–17)   32–3 **yea-forsooth knave** Puritan tradesman who uses mild oaths but is a rascal for all that | **bear . . . in hand** delude a gentleman with false hopes   34 **stand upon security** insist upon guarantee of payment (as also at l. 37) | **smoothy-pates** (alludes to the short hair of Puritan tradesmen)   35 **high shoes . . . keys** (indications of their financial prosperity and putting on airs)   36–7 **is . . . taking up** has agreed with them straightforwardly on credit terms   37 **lief** willingly

they would put ratsbane° in my mouth as offer to stop it
with security. I looked 'a° should have sent me two-and-
twenty yards of satin, as I am a true knight, and he sends me   40
"security"! Well, he may sleep in security,° for he hath the
horn of abundance,° and the lightness° of his wife shines
through it. And yet cannot he see,° though he have his own
lantern° to light him. Where's Bardolph?

PAGE He's gone into Smithfield° to buy Your Worship a horse.   45

FALSTAFF I bought him in Paul's,° and he'll buy me a horse in
Smithfield. An° I could get me but a wife in the stews,° I
were manned, horsed, and wived.°

> *Enter [the] Lord Chief Justice [and his Servant]*

PAGE Sir, here comes the nobleman that committed° the Prince
for striking him about Bardolph.   50

FALSTAFF Wait close;° I will not see him.

> *[He tries to slip away]*

CHIEF JUSTICE What's he that goes there?

SERVANT Falstaff, an't please Your Lordship.

CHIEF JUSTICE He that was in question° for the robbery?

SERVANT He, my lord. But he hath since done good service at   55
Shrewsbury, and, as I hear, is now going with some charge°
to the Lord John of Lancaster.

CHIEF JUSTICE What, to York? Call him back again.

SERVANT Sir John Falstaff!

FALSTAFF Boy, tell him I am deaf.   60

PAGE You must speak louder; my master is deaf.

---

38 ratsbane rat poison   **39 looked 'a** expected that he   **41 in security** in a false and
complacent sense of security   **42 horn of abundance** (1) cornucopia (2) cuckold's
horn, a sign of his wife's infidelity | **lightness** (1) wantonness (2) light showing
through a lantern (which would have windows of *horn*, thereby giving the cuckold
a lantern in his own forehead)   **43 cannot he see** he cannot see his own wife's
infidelity   **44 lantern** (the Quarto spelling "lanthorne" preserves Falstaff's
continued joke about cuckold's horns)   **45 Smithfield** district near Saint Paul's
Cathedral, famous as a livestock market   **46 Paul's** Saint Paul's Cathedral nave,
resort of servingmen seeking employment   **47 An** if | **stews** brothels   **47–8 I . . .
wived** (proverbially, to be thus provided with a servant, a horse, and a wife at Saint
Paul's, Smithfield, and Westminster, respectively, was to be taken for a sucker)
49 committed to prison (according to an apocryphal story, Prince Hal boxed the
ears of the Lord Chief Justice; see *1 Henry IV*, 3.2.32 and n., and *2 Henry IV*,
5.2.70–1)   **51 close** concealed   **54 in question** under judicial examination   **56 charge**
command of soldiers

CHIEF JUSTICE   I am sure he is, to the hearing of anything good.—Go pluck him by the elbow; I must speak with him.

SERVANT   Sir John!

FALSTAFF   What, a young knave, and begging? Is there not wars? 65
Is there not employment? Doth not the King lack subjects?
Do not the rebels need soldiers? Though it be a shame to be
on any side but one, it is worse shame to beg than to be on
the worst side, were it worse than the name of rebellion can
tell how to make it.° 70

SERVANT   You mistake me, sir.

FALSTAFF   Why, sir, did I say you were an honest man? Setting
my knighthood and my soldiership aside, I had lied in my
throat if I had said so.°

SERVANT   I pray you, sir, then set your knighthood and your 75
soldiership aside, and give me leave° to tell you you lie in
your throat if you say I am any other than an honest man.

FALSTAFF   I give thee leave to tell me so? I lay aside that which
grows to° me? If thou get'st any leave of me, hang me; if
thou tak'st leave, thou wert better be hanged. You hunt 80
counter.° Hence! Avaunt!

SERVANT   Sir, my lord would speak with you.

CHIEF JUSTICE   Sir John Falstaff, a word with you.

FALSTAFF   My good lord! God give Your Lordship good time of
day. I am glad to see Your Lordship abroad.° I heard say 85
Your Lordship was sick. I hope Your Lordship goes abroad
by advice.° Your Lordship, though not clean past your
youth, have yet some smack of age in you, some relish of the
saltness° of time in you, and I most humbly beseech Your
Lordship to have a reverent care of your health. 90

CHIEF JUSTICE   Sir John, I sent for you before your expedition to
Shrewsbury.

FALSTAFF   An't please Your Lordship, I hear His Majesty is
returned with some discomfort from Wales.

69–70 were it . . . make it even if that side were worse than the hated name of
"rebellion" it can teach us to understand what it is   **72–4 Setting . . . so** granted
that true knights and soldiers do not tell lies, I would have lied outrageously if I had
called you an honest man   **76 leave** permission   **79 grows to** is an integral part of
80–1 hunt counter run the wrong way on the trail (a hunting term)   **85 abroad** out
of doors   **87 by advice** by medical advice   **89 saltness** flavor, relish

CHIEF JUSTICE   I talk not of His Majesty. You would not come   95
   when I sent for you.

FALSTAFF   And I hear, moreover, His Highness is fallen into this
   same whoreson apoplexy.

CHIEF JUSTICE   Well, God mend him! I pray you, let me speak
   with you.   100

FALSTAFF   This apoplexy, as I take it, is a kind of lethargy, an't
   please Your Lordship, a kind of sleeping in the blood, a
   whoreson tingling.

CHIEF JUSTICE   What° tell you me of it? Be it as it is.

FALSTAFF   It hath it original° from much grief, from study, and   105
   perturbation of the brain. I have read the cause of his°
   effects in Galen.° It is a kind of deafness.

CHIEF JUSTICE   I think you are fallen into the disease, for you
   hear not what I say to you.

FALSTAFF   Very well, my lord, very well. Rather, an't please you,   110
   it is the disease of not listening, the malady of not marking,
   that I am troubled withal.

CHIEF JUSTICE   To punish you by the heels° would amend the
   attention of your ears, and I care not if I do become your
   physician.   115

FALSTAFF   I am as poor as Job,° my lord, but not so patient.
   Your Lordship may minister the potion of imprisonment to
   me in respect of poverty;° but how I should be your patient
   to follow your prescriptions, the wise may make some dram
   of a scruple,° or indeed a scruple itself.   120

CHIEF JUSTICE   I sent for you, when there were matters against
   you for your life,° to come speak with me.

FALSTAFF   As I was then advised by my learned counsel in the
   laws of this land service,° I did not come.

CHIEF JUSTICE   Well, the truth is, Sir John, you live in great infamy.   125

FALSTAFF   He that buckles himself in my belt cannot live in less.

104 What why   **105 it original** its origin   **106 his** its   **107 Galen** the famous
Greek authority on medicine   **113 punish . . . heels** set you in the stocks or fetters
116 Job the long-suffering protagonist of the Book of Job   **118 in . . . poverty** by
reason of my being too poor to pay a fine   **119–20 make . . . scruple** entertain some
small portion of doubt (*dram* and *scruple* are small apothecaries' weights)   **122 for
your life** carrying the death penalty   **124 land service** military service (with a pun
on avoiding the "service" of a legal summons and also on Falstaff's *land service* at
Gad's Hill; Falstaff points to his sword and shield as his *learned counsel*, his legal
counsel)

CHIEF JUSTICE   Your means° are very slender, and your waste is great.

FALSTAFF   I would it were otherwise; I would my means were greater, and my waist slenderer.   130

CHIEF JUSTICE   You have misled the youthful Prince.

FALSTAFF   The young Prince hath misled me. I am the fellow with the great belly, and he my dog.°

CHIEF JUSTICE   Well, I am loath to gall a new-healed wound. Your day's service at Shrewsbury hath a little gilded over   135 your night's exploit° on Gad's Hill. You may thank th'unquiet time for your quiet o'erposting° that action.

FALSTAFF   My lord?

CHIEF JUSTICE   But since all is well, keep it so. Wake not a sleeping wolf.   140

FALSTAFF   To wake a wolf is as bad as smell a fox.°

CHIEF JUSTICE   What, you are as a candle, the better part burnt out.

FALSTAFF   A wassail candle,° my lord, all tallow.° If I did say of wax,° my growth would approve the truth.°   145

CHIEF JUSTICE   There is not a white hair on your face but should have his effect of gravity.°

FALSTAFF   His effect of gravy,° gravy, gravy.

CHIEF JUSTICE   You follow the young Prince up and down, like his ill angel.°   150

FALSTAFF   Not so, my lord. Your ill angel is light,° but I hope he that looks upon me will take me without weighing.° And yet in some respects I grant I cannot go.° I cannot tell.° Virtue is

127 means financial resources   **132–3 I am . . . dog** (Falstaff seems to compare himself to the man in the moon with his dog; the *great belly* is the full moon)   **136 exploit** the famous robbery in *1 Henry IV*, 2.2   **137 o'erposting** escaping the consequences of **141 smell a fox** suspect something (compare with "smell a rat"; Falstaff implies that the Justice is not to be trusted)   **144 wassail candle** large candle lighted up at a feast | **tallow** a mixture of animal fats (as contrasted with bees' wax)   **145 wax** beeswax (with a pun on "growth") | **approve the truth** confirm the statement   **146–7 but . . . gravity** but should testify to the gravity and wisdom of age   **148 gravy** grease, sweat; Falstaff jests that the huge bulk of his advanced years produces not gravity but sweat, which was thought to be an exuding of fat from the body   **150 ill angel** evil attendant spirit (but Falstaff quibbles on the meaning "a clipped angel," a coin worth six shillings eight pence)   **151 light** underweight (because the coin is "clipped"; refers also to Satan, "an angel of light," 2 Corinthians 11.14)   **152 take . . . weighing** accept me at face value without putting me on the scales or considering the matter further   **153 go** (1) walk (2) pass current | **cannot tell** (1) don't know what to think (2) don't count as good money

of so little regard in these costermongers'° times that true
valor is turned bearward;° pregnancy° is made a tapster, and   155
his quick wit wasted in giving reckonings.° All the other
gifts appurtenant° to man, as the malice of this age shapes
them, are not worth a gooseberry. You that are old consider
not the capacities of us that are young; you do measure the
heat of our livers with the bitterness of your galls.° And we   160
that are in the vaward° of our youth, I must confess, are
wags° too.

CHIEF JUSTICE   Do you set down your name in the scroll of
youth, that are written down old with all the characters° of
age? Have you not a moist eye, a dry hand, a yellow cheek,   165
a white beard, a decreasing leg, an increasing belly? Is not
your voice broken, your wind short, your chin double, your
wit single,° and every part about you blasted° with
antiquity? And will you yet call yourself young? Fie, fie, fie,
Sir John!   170

FALSTAFF   My lord, I was born about three of the clock in the
afternoon, with a white head and something a° round belly.
For° my voice, I have lost it with halloing° and singing of
anthems. To approve° my youth further, I will not. The truth
is, I am only old in judgment and understanding; and he that   175
will caper with me° for a thousand marks,° let him lend me
the money, and have at him!° For the box of the ear° that
the Prince gave you, he gave it like a rude prince, and you
took it like a sensible° lord. I have checked° him for it, and
the young lion repents—[*aside*] marry,° not in ashes and   180
sackcloth,° but in new silk and old sack.°

154 **costermongers'** materialistic (a costermonger is a hawker of fruits or vegetables)
155 **bearward** one who handles tame bears | **pregnancy** quickness (of wit),
intellectual capacity   156 **reckonings** tavern bills   157 **appurtenant** belonging
160 **heat . . . galls** (the liver was thought to be the source of passion and to be active
in youth; the gall was thought to be the seat of melancholy and rancor, and to
become prevalent with age)   161 **vaward** vanguard leading into middle age   162 **wags**
high-spirited youths   164 **characters** (1) characteristics (2) letters   168 **single** feeble |
blasted withered, blighted   172 **something a** a somewhat   173 **For** for (also in
l. 177) | **halloing** shouting to hounds   174 **approve** prove   176 **caper with me**
compete with me in dancing | **marks** coins worth thirteen shillings four pence
177 **have at him!** I challenge him to dance more nimbly than I! | **box of the ear** (see
l. 49 and n.)   179 **sensible** (1) intelligent (2) capable of receiving physical sensations |
checked rebuked   180 **marry** indeed (literally, "by the Virgin Mary")   180-1 **ashes
and sackcloth** penitent's garb   181 **sack** a white Spanish wine

CHIEF JUSTICE   Well, God send the Prince a better companion!

FALSTAFF   God send the companion a better prince! I cannot rid my hands of him.

CHIEF JUSTICE   Well, the King hath severed you and Prince Harry. 185
I hear you are going with Lord John of Lancaster against the Archbishop and the Earl of Northumberland.

FALSTAFF   Yea, I thank your pretty sweet wit for it. But look° you pray, all you that kiss my lady Peace at home, that our armies join not in a hot day; for, by the Lord, I take but two 190 shirts out with me, and I mean not to sweat extraordinarily. If it be a hot day, and I brandish anything but a bottle, I would I might never spit white° again. There is not a dangerous action can peep out his° head but I am thrust upon it. Well, I cannot last ever. But it was alway yet° the 195 trick° of our English nation, if they have a good thing, to make it too common. If ye will needs say I am an old man, you should give me rest. I would to God my name were not so terrible to the enemy as it is. I were better to be eaten to death with a rust than to be scoured to nothing with 200 perpetual motion.

CHIEF JUSTICE   Well, be honest, be honest; and God bless your expedition!

FALSTAFF   Will Your Lordship lend me a thousand pound to furnish° me forth? 205

CHIEF JUSTICE   Not a penny, not a penny. You are too impatient to bear crosses.° Fare you well. Commend me to my cousin Westmorland.

[Exeunt Chief Justice and his Servant]

FALSTAFF   If I do, fillip° me with a three-man beetle.° A man can no more separate age and covetousness than 'a can part 210 young limbs and lechery; but the gout galls the one, and the pox pinches the other, and so both the degrees prevent my curses.° Boy!

---

188 look be sure, take care that   **193 spit white** from thirst   **194 his** its, the dangerous military action   **195 alway yet** always   **196 trick** habit   **205 furnish** equip   **207 crosses** (1) afflictions (2) silver coins stamped with the figure of the cross   **208 fillip** knock | **three-man beetle** a huge pile-driving mallet requiring three men to wield it   **212–13 both . . . curses** both age and youth, the one afflicted with gout and the other with *pox*, or syphilis, have their own curses which anticipate mine

PAGE   Sir?

FALSTAFF   What money is in my purse?   215

PAGE   Seven groats° and two pence.

FALSTAFF   I can get no remedy against this consumption of the purse; borrowing only lingers° and lingers it out, but the disease is incurable. [*He gives letters.*] Go bear this letter to my lord of Lancaster, this to the Prince, this to the Earl of   220 Westmorland, and this to old Mistress Ursula,° whom I have weekly sworn to marry since I perceived the first white hair of my chin. About it. You know where to find me.   [*Exit Page*] A pox of this gout! Or, a gout of this pox! For the one or the other plays the rogue with my great toe. 'Tis no matter if I   225 do halt;° I have the wars for my color,° and my pension shall seem the more reasonable. A good wit will make use of anything. I will turn diseases to commodity.°   [*Exit*]

ACT 1
SCENE 3

*Enter the Archbishop [of York], Thomas Mowbray°
(Earl Marshal), the Lord Hastings, and [Lord] Bardolph*

ARCHBISHOP

Thus have you heard our cause and known our means;
And, my most noble friends, I pray you all,
Speak plainly your opinions of our hopes.
And first, Lord Marshal, what say you to it?

MOWBRAY   I well allow the occasion of our arms,°   5

But gladly would be better satisfied
How in° our means we should advance ourselves

---

216 groats coins worth four pence   **218 lingers** prolongs, draws   **221 Ursula** (Mistress Quickly's first name? or else another woman to whom Falstaff has made empty promises)   **226 halt** limp | **color** excuse   **228 commodity** profit

1.3. Location: York. The Archbishop's palace. **Summary:** Rebel leaders try to gauge their chances. Lord Bardolph mistrusts Northumberland, despite the latter's outburst and resolve in 1.1. The rebels base their hopes on the King's divided forces and the people's fickleness.

0.1 *Thomas Mowbray* son of Thomas Mowbray, Duke of Norfolk, who was banished by Richard II   **5 allow . . . arms** concede the justice of our arming   **7 in** with

To look with forehead° bold and big enough
Upon the power and puissance° of the King.
HASTINGS   Our present musters grow upon the file°   10
To five-and-twenty thousand men of choice;°
And our supplies live largely in the hope°
Of great Northumberland; whose bosom burns
With an incensèd fire of injuries.

LORD BARDOLPH
The question then, Lord Hastings, standeth thus: 15
Whether our present five-and-twenty thousand
May hold up head° without Northumberland?
HASTINGS   With him, we may.
LORD BARDOLPH   Yea, marry, there's the point.
But if without him we be thought too feeble,
My judgment is we should not step too far   20
Till we had his assistance by the hand;
For in a theme° so bloody-faced as this
Conjecture, expectation, and surmise
Of aids incertain should not be admitted.
ARCHBISHOP   'Tis very true, Lord Bardolph, for indeed   25
It was young Hotspur's case at Shrewsbury.

LORD BARDOLPH
It was, my lord; who lined° himself with hope,
Eating the air on promise of supply,°
Flatt'ring himself with project of a power°
Much smaller° than the smallest of his thoughts,   30
And so, with great imagination
Proper to° madmen, led his powers to death
And winking° leapt into destruction.
HASTINGS   But, by your leave, it never yet did hurt
To lay down likelihoods and forms of hope.   35
LORD BARDOLPH   Yes, if this present quality of war—
Indeed the instant action, a cause on foot—

---

8 **forehead** assurance, defiant gaze   9 **puissance** strength   10 **upon the file** according to our records   11 **men of choice** choice men   12 **And . . . hope** and our chance of getting reinforcements depends largely on our hopes   17 **hold up head** be a sufficient military power   22 **theme** business   27 **lined** fortified   28 **Eating . . . supply** living in false hopes of reinforcement   29 **project . . . power** anticipation of the arrival of an armed force   30 **Much smaller** that proved in fact to be much smaller   32 **Proper to** characteristic of   33 **winking** shutting his eyes

Lives so in hope, as in an early spring
We see th'appearing buds, which to prove fruit
Hope gives not so much warrant as despair   40
That frosts will bite them.° When we mean to build,
We first survey the plot, then draw the model;°
And when we see the figure° of the house,
Then must we rate° the cost of the erection,
Which if we find outweighs ability,°   45
What do we then but draw anew the model
In fewer offices,° or at least° desist
To build at all? Much more, in this great work,
Which is almost to pluck a kingdom down
And set another up, should we survey   50
The plot of situation and the model,
Consent° upon a sure foundation,
Question surveyors,° know our own estate,°
How able such a work to undergo,
To weigh against his opposite;° or else   55
We fortify in paper° and in figures,
Using the names of men instead of men,
Like one that draws the model of an house
Beyond his power to build it, who, half through,
Gives o'er and leaves his part-created cost°   60
A naked subject° to the weeping clouds
And waste for churlish winter's tyranny.
HASTINGS   Grant that our hopes, yet° likely of fair birth,
Should be stillborn, and that we now possessed
The utmost man of expectation,°   65
I think we are a body strong enough,
Even as we are, to equal with the King.

36–41 **Yes . . . them** yes, it's all right to hope, so long as we bear in mind that our hopes, given the present situation of war already on foot, may turn out to be like hopes for the first-appearing buds of spring—buds that too often are frost-bitten (the text may be corrupt here)   42 **model** plan   43 **figure** design   44 **rate** estimate   45 **ability** ability to pay   47 **offices** rooms | **at least** at the worst   52 **Consent** agree   53 **surveyors** architects | **estate** wealth   55 **his opposite** adverse conditions   56 **in paper** merely on paper   60 **part-created cost** partly finished splendor   61 **naked subject** exposed (helpless) victim   63 **yet** still   65 **The . . . expectation** all the men that we might hope to have

LORD BARDOLPH
  What, is the King but five-and-twenty thousand?
HASTINGS   To us no more, nay, not so much, Lord Bardolph.
  For his divisions, as the times do brawl,°   70
  Are in three heads:° one power against the French,
  And one against Glendower; perforce° a third
  Must take up° us. So is the unfirm King
  In three divided, and his coffers sound°
  With hollow poverty and emptiness.   75
ARCHBISHOP
  That he should draw his several strengths° together
  And come against us in full puissance
  Need not be dreaded.
HASTINGS   If he should do so,
  To French and Welsh he leaves his back unarmed,
  They baying° him at the heels. Never fear that.   80
LORD BARDOLPH   Who is it like should° lead his forces hither?
HASTINGS   The Duke of Lancaster and Westmorland;
  Against the Welsh, himself and Harry Monmouth.
  But who is substituted° 'gainst the French,
  I have no certain notice.
ARCHBISHOP   Let us on,   85
  And publish the occasion of our arms.°
  The commonwealth is sick of their own choice;
  Their overgreedy love hath surfeited.
  An habitation giddy and unsure
  Hath he that buildeth on the vulgar heart.°   90
  O thou fond many,° with what loud applause
  Didst thou beat heaven° with blessing Bolingbroke,
  Before he was what thou wouldst have him be!
  And being now trimmed in° thine own desires,
  Thou, beastly feeder, art so full of him   95

---

70 **as . . . brawl** in accordance with the discordant necessity of the time   71 **heads** armies   72 **perforce** necessarily   73 **take up** encounter, oppose   74 **sound** resound, echo   76 **several strengths** various armies   80 **baying** pursuing (like hunting dogs)   81 **Who . . . should** who is likely to   84 **substituted** delegated   86 **And . . . arms** and proclaim the reason for our taking up arms   89–90 **An . . . heart** anyone who pins his hopes on the affection of the multitude has built his house on shaky foundations   91 **fond many** foolish multitude   92 **beat heaven** rattle the skies   94 **trimmed in** furnished with, dressed in

That thou provok'st thyself to cast him up.°
So, so, thou common dog, didst thou disgorge°
Thy glutton bosom of the royal Richard;
And now thou wouldst eat thy dead vomit up,
And howl'st to find it. What trust is in these times?   100
They that, when Richard lived, would have him die,
Are now become enamored on his grave.
Thou, that threw'st dust upon his goodly head
When through proud London he came sighing on
After th'admirèd heels of Bolingbroke,   105
Criest now, "O earth, yield us that king again,
And take thou this!" Oh, thoughts of men accurst!
Past and to come seems best; things present, worst.
MOWBRAY   Shall we go draw our numbers° and set on?°
HASTINGS   We are time's subjects, and time bids begone.   110

Exeunt

ACT 2
SCENE 1

*Enter Hostess [Quickly] of the tavern and
two officers: [Fang, followed by Snare]*

HOSTESS   Master Fang, have you entered the action?°
FANG   It is entered.
HOSTESS   Where's your yeoman? Is't a lusty yeoman?° Will 'a
stand to't?°
FANG [*looking around him*]   Sirrah—where's Snare?   5
HOSTESS   Oh, Lord, ay, good Master Snare.
SNARE [*from behind them*]   Here, here.
FANG   Snare, we must arrest Sir John Falstaff.
HOSTESS   Yea, good Master Snare, I have entered° him and all.

96 **cast him up** vomit him, discard him   97 **disgorge** vomit   109 **draw our numbers**
assemble or muster our forces | **set on** march
2.1. **Location: London. A street. Summary:** Mistress Quickly attempts to have
Falstaff imprisoned for debt. Resisting arrest, he persuades her to drop the charges
and to lend him more money. The Chief Justice, who entered to investigate the
ruckus, receives the latest military reports.
1 **entered the action** recorded the lawsuit   3 **yeoman** sheriff's man   3–4 **Will . . .
to't?** will he fight boldly?   9 **entered** brought action against in court

SNARE It may chance° cost some of us our lives, for he will   10
stab.

HOSTESS Alas the day, take heed of him! He stabbed me in
mine own house, most beastly, in good faith. 'A cares not
what mischief he does; if his weapon be out, he will foin°
like any devil; he will spare neither man, woman, nor child.   15

FANG If I can close° with him, I care not for his thrust.

HOSTESS No, nor I neither. I'll be at your elbow.

FANG An I but fist° him once, and 'a come but within my
vice°—

HOSTESS I am undone by his going,° I warrant you; he's an   20
infinitive° thing upon my score.° Good Master Fang, hold
him sure. Good Master Snare, let him not scape. 'A comes
continuantly° to Pie Corner°—saving your manhoods°—to
buy a saddle; and he is indited° to dinner to the Lubber's
Head° in Lumbert° street, to Master Smooth's the silkman. I   25
pray you, since my exion° is entered and my case so openly
known to the world, let him be brought in to his answer. A
hundred mark° is a long one° for a poor lone woman to
bear; and I have borne, and borne, and borne, and have
been fubbed off,° and fubbed off, and fubbed off, from this   30
day to that day, that it is a shame to be thought on. There is
no honesty in such dealing, unless a woman should be made
an ass and a beast, to bear every knave's wrong. Yonder he
comes, and that arrant malmsey-nose° knave, Bardolph,

---

10 **chance** possibly   14 **foin** thrust in fencing; with unintended sexual double meaning, as also in *stabbed* (12), *weapon* (14), *thrust* (16), *undone* (20), *thing* (21), *saddle* (suggesting a prostitute, 24), *entered* (26), *case* (female genitals, 26), *openly known to the world* (26–7), *brought in* (27), *a long one* (28), etc.   16 **close** grapple   18 **fist** seize   19 **vice** vise, grip   20 **going** going without paying   21 **infinitive** (Hostess Quickly's malapropism for "infinite," endless) | **score** accounts   23 **continuantly** (perhaps a mixup of "continually" and "incontinently," immediately) | **Pie Corner** a corner in the Smithfield district of London, known for its cooks' shops | **saving your manhoods** with apologies for mentioning anything so indelicate   24 **indited** (for "invited")   24–5 **Lubber's Head** Libbard's Head, Leopard's Head Inn   25 **Lumbert** Lombard   26 **exion** action, lawsuit   28 **mark** (worth thirteen shillings four pence) | **long one** huge reckoning (with unconscious sexual suggestion)   30 **fubbed off** put off with excuses (probably with unintended sexual meaning, continued from *borne, and borne* and then carried forward in *bear* [33], *do me* [36], *stand to me* [55–6], etc.)   34 **malmsey-nose** red-nosed (from drinking malmsey, a sweet red wine)

with him. Do your offices, do your offices. Master Fang and 35
Master Snare, do me,° do me, do me your offices.

Enter Sir John [Falstaff], and Bardolph, and the Boy [Page]

FALSTAFF How now, whose mare's dead?° What's the matter?

FANG Sir John, I arrest you at the suit of Mistress Quickly.

FALSTAFF Away, varlets!—Draw, Bardolph. Cut me off the
villain's head. Throw the quean° in the channel.° 40

[They draw]

HOSTESS Throw me in the channel? I'll throw thee in the
channel. Wilt thou? Wilt thou? Thou bastardly rogue!
Murder, murder! Ah, thou honeysuckle° villain! Wilt thou
kill God's officers and the King's? Ah, thou honeyseed°
rogue! Thou art a honeyseed, a man-queller,° and a 45
woman-queller.°

FALSTAFF Keep them off, Bardolph.

OFFICERS A rescue!° A rescue!

HOSTESS Good people, bring a rescue or two. Thou woo't,
woo't thou?° Thou woo't, woo't ta?° Do, do, thou rogue! 50
Do, thou hempseed!°

PAGE Away, you scullion,° you rampallian,° you fustilarian!°
I'll tickle your catastrophe.°

Enter [the] Lord Chief Justice and his men

CHIEF JUSTICE What is the matter? Keep the peace here, ho!

HOSTESS Good my lord, be good to me. I beseech you, stand 55
to° me.

CHIEF JUSTICE

How now, Sir John? What° are you brawling here?
Doth this become your place, your time, and business?
You should have been well on your way to York.—

---

36 do me do your duty for me (with unintended sexual suggestion) **37 whose
mare's dead?** what's all the fuss about? **40 quean** slut, hussy | **channel** street
gutter **43 honeysuckle** (for "homicidal") **44 honeyseed** (for "homicide") **45 man-
queller** murderer **46 woman-queller** destroyer of women (but with suggestion also
of "seducer") **48 A rescue!** come help the officers in their rescue of the hostess!
(said to anyone within earshot) **50 woo't thou** wilt thou | **ta** thou **51 hempseed**
(alludes perhaps to the Page and his diminutive size; Hangman's rope was made of
hemp; Mistress Quickly may mean "homicide"; cf. *honeyseed* in l. 44) **52 scullion**
kitchen wench | **rampallian** scoundrel, ruffian | **fustilarian** fat, frowsy woman
53 catastrophe backside **55–6 stand to** stand by (with bawdy suggestion) **57 What**
why

Stand from him, fellow. Wherefore hang'st thou upon him?   60

HOSTESS   Oh, my most worshipful lord, an't please Your
Grace, I am a poor widow of Eastcheap, and he is arrested
at my suit.

CHIEF JUSTICE   For what sum?

HOSTESS   It is more than for some, my lord, it is for all, all I   65
have. He hath eaten me out of house and home; he hath
put all my substance into that fat belly of his. But I will
have some of it out again, or I will ride thee o'nights° like
the mare.°

FALSTAFF   I think I am as like to ride the mare, if I have any   70
vantage of ground° to get up.°

CHIEF JUSTICE   How comes this, Sir John? Fie, what man of
good temper would endure this tempest of exclamation?°
Are you not ashamed to enforce a poor widow to so rough a
course to come by her own?°   75

FALSTAFF   What is the gross sum that I owe thee?

HOSTESS   Marry, if thou wert an honest man, thyself and the
money too. Thou didst swear to me upon a parcel-gilt°
goblet, sitting in my Dolphin chamber,° at the round table,
by a seacoal° fire, upon Wednesday in Wheeson° week,   80
when the Prince broke° thy head for liking° his father to a
singing-man° of Windsor, thou didst swear to me then, as I
was washing thy wound, to marry me and make me my lady
thy wife. Canst thou deny it? Did not goodwife° Keech,° the
butcher's wife, come in then and call me gossip° Quickly?   85
Coming in to borrow a mess° of vinegar, telling us she had a
good dish of prawns,° whereby° thou didst desire to eat
some, whereby I told thee they were ill for a green° wound?
And didst thou not, when she was gone downstairs, desire

---

68 **o'nights** by night   69 **mare** nightmare   71 **vantage of ground** superior position |
get up mount (with intended sexual suggestion, continued from *ride the mare* in
l. 70)   72–3 **what . . . exclamation?** what man of good disposition would have
behaved so as to invite such vituperation?   75 **come by her own** get what is hers
78 **parcel-gilt** partly gilded   79 **Dolphin chamber** (the name of a room in her inn)
80 **seacoal** bituminous coal, brought in by sea | **Wheeson** Whitsun (Pentecost)
81 **broke** hit, made a cut on | **liking** comparing   82 **singing-man** chorister
84 **goodwife** (title of a married woman) | **Keech** (literally, "a lump of tallow")
85 **gossip** (literally, a fellow godparent; hence, a female friend)   86 **mess** small
quantity   87 **prawns** shrimps | **whereby** whereupon   88 **green** fresh, raw

me to be no more so familiarity° with such poor people, 90
saying that ere long they should call me madam? And didst
thou not kiss me and bid me fetch thee thirty shillings? I put
thee now to thy book oath.° Deny it if thou canst.

FALSTAFF My lord, this is a poor mad soul, and she says up and
down the town that her eldest son is like you. She hath been 95
in good case,° and the truth is, poverty hath distracted her.°
But for° these foolish officers, I beseech you I may have
redress against them.

CHIEF JUSTICE Sir John, Sir John, I am well acquainted with
your manner of wrenching the true case the false way. It is 100
not a confident brow, nor the throng of words that come
with such more than impudent sauciness from you, can
thrust me from a level° consideration. You have, as it
appears to me, practiced upon the easy-yielding spirit of
this woman and made her serve your uses° both in purse 105
and in person.

HOSTESS Yea, in truth, my lord.

CHIEF JUSTICE Pray thee, peace.—Pay her the debt you owe
her, and unpay the villainy you have done her. The one you
may do with sterling money, and the other with current° 110
repentance.

FALSTAFF My lord, I will not undergo this sneap° without reply.
You call honorable boldness impudent sauciness. If a man
will make curtsy° and say nothing, he is virtuous. No, my
lord, my humble duty remembered,° I will not be your suitor. 115
I say to you, I do desire deliverance from these officers, being
upon hasty employment in the King's affairs.

CHIEF JUSTICE You speak as having power to do wrong.° But
answer in th'effect of your reputation,° and satisfy the poor
woman. 120

FALSTAFF Come hither, hostess.   *[He takes her aside]*

Enter a messenger [Gower]

---

90 familiarity (the Hostess's word for "familiar")   **93 book oath** oath on a Bible   **96 in good case** well-to-do (perhaps with bawdy suggestion) | **distracted her** driven her mad   **97 for** as for   **103 level** fair-minded, evenhanded   **105 serve your uses** (with erotic suggestion)   **110 current** genuine (with an allusion to current, or lawful, coin, the *sterling* of l. 110)   **112 sneap** reproof   **114 curtsy** bow   **115 my . . . remembered** with all due consideration of the respect I owe to your position   **118 as . . . wrong** as if you had the license to do whatever wrong you wish to do   **119 in . . . reputation** in a manner becoming a man of your reputation

CHIEF JUSTICE   Now, Master Gower, what news?

GOWER   The King, my lord, and Harry Prince of Wales
Are near at hand. The rest the paper tells.
                    [*He gives a letter. The Chief Justice reads*]

FALSTAFF [*to Mistress Quickly*]   As I am a gentleman.   125

HOSTESS   Faith, you said so before.

FALSTAFF   As I am a gentleman. Come, no more words of it.

HOSTESS   By this heavenly ground I tread on, I must be fain° to
pawn both my plate° and the tapestry of my dining chambers.

FALSTAFF   Glasses, glasses, is the only drinking.° And for thy   130
walls, a pretty slight drollery,° or the story of the Prodigal,°
or the German hunting in water work,° is worth a thousand
of these bed-hangers° and these fly-bitten tapestries. Let it be
ten pound, if thou canst. Come, an 'twere° not for thy
humors,° there's not a better wench in England. Go wash   135
thy face, and draw° the action. Come, thou must not be in
this humor with me. Dost not know me? Come, come, I
know thou wast set on to this.

HOSTESS   Pray thee, Sir John, let it be but twenty nobles.°
I'faith, I am loath to pawn my plate, so God save me, la!   140

FALSTAFF   Let it alone; I'll make other shift.° You'll be a fool
still.

HOSTESS   Well, you shall have it, though I pawn my gown. I
hope you'll come to supper. You'll pay me all together?

FALSTAFF   Will I live?° [*To Bardolph*] Go with her, with her;   145
hook on,° hook on.

HOSTESS   Will you have Doll Tearsheet meet you at supper?

FALSTAFF   No more words. Let's have her.
        Exeunt Hostess and Sergeant [Fang, Bardolph, and others]

CHIEF JUSTICE [*to Gower*]   I have heard better news.

FALSTAFF   What's the news, my lord?   150

---

128 fain obliged, content   **129 plate** platters, etc., of silver or gold plate
130 Glasses . . . drinking glasses are all the fashion now for drinking, instead of
metal tankards   **131 drollery** e.g., a Dutch comic genre painting | **the Prodigal** the
Prodigal Son (see Luke 15.11–32)   **132 German . . . work** hunting scene painted by
a German or Dutch artist as imitation tapestry **133 bed-hangers** (Falstaff implies
that the Hostess's tapestries are only good enough to serve as curtains around a
four-poster bed)   **134 an 'twere** if it were   **135 humors** whims, vagaries   **136 draw**
withdraw   **139 nobles** coins current at six shillings eight pence   **141 shift**
expedient   **145 Will I live?** as sure as I live   **146 hook on** follow her

CHIEF JUSTICE [*to Gower*] Where lay the King tonight?°
GOWER At Basingstoke,° my lord.
FALSTAFF I hope, my lord, all's well. What is the news, my lord?
CHIEF JUSTICE [*to Gower*] Come all his forces back?
GOWER No, fifteen hundred foot,° five hundred horse° 155
  Are marched up to° my lord of Lancaster,
  Against Northumberland and the Archbishop.
FALSTAFF Comes the King back from Wales, my noble lord?
CHIEF JUSTICE [*to Gower*]
  You shall have letters of me presently.°
  Come, go along with me, good Master Gower. 160
                                            [*They start to go*]
FALSTAFF My lord!
CHIEF JUSTICE What's the matter?
FALSTAFF Master Gower, shall I entreat you with me to dinner?°
GOWER I must wait upon° my good lord here, I thank you, 165
  good Sir John.
CHIEF JUSTICE Sir John, you loiter here too long, being you are
  to take soldiers up° in counties as you go.
FALSTAFF Will you sup° with me, Master Gower?
CHIEF JUSTICE What foolish master taught you these manners, 170
  Sir John?
FALSTAFF Master Gower, if they become me not, he was a fool
  that taught them me.—This is the right fencing grace,° my
  lord: tap for tap, and so part fair.°
CHIEF JUSTICE Now the Lord lighten° thee! Thou art a great 175
  fool.   [*Exeunt separately*]

151 tonight this past night   152 Basingstoke a town in Hampshire   155 foot foot
soldiers | horse cavalry troops   156 to to be led by   159 presently immediately
164 dinner midday meal   165 wait upon accompany   167–8 being . . . up seeing
that you are to levy soldiers   169 sup come to supper   173 grace form, style
(Falstaff is saying that, by refusing to answer the Chief Justice's questions in ll.
162 ff., Falstaff is only paying him back tit for tat for ignoring Falstaff's questions,
ll. 150–60)   174 fair on good terms   175 lighten (1) enlighten (2) reduce in
weight

ACT 2
SCENE 2

Enter the Prince [Henry, and] Poins

PRINCE Before God, I am exceeding weary.

POINS Is't come to that? I had thought weariness durst not have attached° one of so high blood.

PRINCE Faith, it does me, though it discolors the complexion of my greatness° to acknowledge it. Doth it not show° vilely   5
in me to desire small beer?°

POINS Why, a prince should not be so loosely studied° as to remember so weak a composition.°

PRINCE Belike° then my appetite was not princely got,° for, by my troth, I do now remember the poor creature, small beer.   10
But indeed these humble considerations make me out of love with my greatness. What a disgrace is it to me to remember thy name! Or to know thy face tomorrow! Or to take note how many pair of silk stockings thou hast, viz.,° these, and those that were thy peach-colored ones! Or to bear° the   15
inventory of thy shirts, as, one for superfluity° and another for use! But that the tennis-court keeper knows better than I; for it is a low ebb of linen with thee when thou keepest not racket there, as thou hast not done a great while, because the rest of the low countries have made a shift to eat   20
up thy holland.° And God knows whether those that bawl

2.2. Location: London. Prince Henry's dwelling. Summary: Hal confides to Poins about the awkwardness of his situation, and the two exchange pointedly ironic views of each other. After Bardolph delivers a grandiose, self-serving letter from Falstaff, they plan to disguise themselves as tapsters to spy on him and his companions.
3 attached seized   **4–5 discolors . . . greatness** puts a blush on the cheek of my high rank   **5 show** appear   **6 small beer** weak kind of beer, hence inferior   **7 studied** versed, inclined   **8 so . . . composition** weak beer, trifles   **9 Belike** probably | **got** begotten   **14 viz.** namely (an abbreviation of the Latin *videlicet*)   **15 bear** bear in mind   **16 for superfluity** in reserve as a clean change (of shirt)   **17–21 But . . . holland** the keeper of the tennis court knows that your inventory of shirts is at a low ebb and that you do not have a clean shirt to shift into, because you have not been seen at the tennis court lately, the reason being that you have sold or pawned your best shirt to pay for your visits to brothels (with wordplay on *rest* as meaning "repose" and "remainder," on *the low countries* as meaning "the Netherlands" and "the lower members, the sexual organs," on *shift* as meaning "contrivance" and "change of clothes," and on *holland* as meaning "fine linen from Holland" and "the Netherlands," as before)

out the ruins of thy linen° shall inherit His kingdom.° But
the midwives say the children are not in the fault,°
whereupon the world increases and kindreds° are mightily
strengthened.   25

POINS   How ill it follows, after you have labored so hard, you
should talk so idly!° Tell me, how many good young princes
would do so, their fathers being so sick as yours at this time is?

PRINCE   Shall I tell thee one thing, Poins?

POINS   Yes, faith, and let it be an excellent good thing.   30

PRINCE   It shall serve among wits of no higher breeding than
thine.

POINS   Go to.° I stand the push° of your one thing that you
will tell.

PRINCE   Marry, I tell thee it is not meet that I should be sad,°   35
now my father is sick. Albeit I could tell to thee, as to one it
pleases me, for fault of a better, to call my friend, I could be
sad, and sad indeed too.

POINS   Very hardly° upon such a subject.

PRINCE   By this hand, thou thinkest me as far in the devil's   40
book as thou and Falstaff for obduracy and persistency. Let
the end try the man. But I tell thee, my heart bleeds
inwardly that my father is so sick. And keeping such vile
company as thou art hath in reason taken from me all
ostentation° of sorrow.   45

POINS   The reason?

PRINCE   What wouldst thou think of me if I should weep?

POINS   I would think thee a most princely hypocrite.

PRINCE   It would be every man's thought, and thou art a
blessed fellow to think as every man thinks. Never a man's   50
thought in the world keeps the roadway° better than thine.
Every man would think me an hypocrite indeed. And what
accites° your most worshipful thought to think so?

21–2 those . . . linen your bastards, who cry out from your cast-off shirts made into
swaddling clothes   22 inherit His kingdom go to heaven (see Matthew 5.10, 25.34,
or 19.14: "Suffer the little children . . . to come to me, for of such is the kingdom of
heaven")   23 in the fault to be blamed (for being illegitimate)   24 kindreds
families   27 talk so idly manage to say so little   33 Go to (an expression of
impatience) | push attack, thrust   35 it is . . . sad it would seem very inappropriate
if I were to appear sad (given my reputation as a prodigal son)   39 Very hardly not
very likely   45 ostentation outward manifestation   51 keeps the roadway follows
the common way of thinking   53 accites induces (with a quibble on "summons")

POINS   Why, because you have been so lewd° and so much
engraffed° to Falstaff.   55

PRINCE   And to thee.

POINS   By this light, I am well spoke on; I can hear it with mine
own ears. The worst that they can say of me is that I am a
second brother° and that I am a proper fellow of my hands,°
and those two things I confess I cannot help. By the Mass,   60
here comes Bardolph.

Enter Bardolph and Boy [Page]

PRINCE   And the boy that I gave Falstaff. 'A had him from me
Christian, and look if the fat villain have not transformed
him ape.°

BARDOLPH   God save Your Grace!   65

PRINCE   And yours, most noble Bardolph!

POINS [*to Bardolph*]   Come, you virtuous ass, you bashful fool,
must you be blushing?° Wherefore° blush you now? What a
maidenly man-at-arms are you become! Is't such a matter to
get a pottle pot's maidenhead?°   70

PAGE   'A calls me e'en now,° my lord, through a red lattice,°
and I could discern° no part of his face from the window. At
last I spied his eyes, and methought he had made two holes
in the alewife's petticoat° and so peeped through.

PRINCE [*to Poins*]   Has not the boy profited?   75

BARDOLPH   Away, you whoreson upright° rabbit, away!

PAGE   Away, you rascally Althaea's dream,° away!

PRINCE   Instruct us, boy. What dream, boy?

PAGE   Marry, my lord, Althaea dreamt she was delivered of a
firebrand, and therefore I call him her dream.   80

PRINCE   A crown's° worth of good interpretation. There 'tis, boy.
[*He gives money*]

---

54 **lewd** base   55 **engraffed** closely attached   59 **second brother** a younger son,
without inheritance | **proper . . . hands** good fighter   63–4 **have . . . ape** has not
dressed him fantastically   68 **blushing** red-faced (from drink) | **Wherefore** why
70 **get . . . maidenhead** knock off a two-quart tankard of ale   71 **e'en now** just now,
a moment ago | **red lattice** (red lattices identified taverns)   72 **discern** distinguish
74 **petticoat** red petticoat—a sign of disreputability   76 **upright** standing on two
legs   77 **Althaea's dream** (Althaea dreamed that her newborn son would live only
so long as a brand on the fire lasted; the Page mistakenly relates Hecuba's dream:
when pregnant with Paris, Hecuba dreamed she would be delivered of a firebrand
that would destroy Troy)   81 **A crown's** five shillings'

POINS   Oh, that this blossom could be kept from cankers!° Well, there is sixpence to preserve thee.°

[*He gives money*]

BARDOLPH   An° you do not make him be hanged among you, the gallows shall have wrong.   85

PRINCE   And how doth thy master, Bardolph?

BARDOLPH   Well, my lord. He heard of Your Grace's coming to town. There's a letter for you.

[*He gives a letter*]

POINS   Delivered with good respect.° And how doth the martlemas,° your master?   90

BARDOLPH   In bodily health, sir.

POINS   Marry, the immortal part needs a physician, but that moves not him. Though that be sick, it dies not.

PRINCE   I do allow this wen° to be as familiar with me as my dog, and he holds his place,° for look you how he writes.   95

[*He shows the letter to Poins*]

POINS [*reading the superscription*]   "John Falstaff, knight."— Every man must know that,° as oft as he has occasion to name himself, even like those that are kin to the King, for they never prick their finger but they say, "There's some of the King's blood spilt." "How comes that?" says he that   100 takes upon him not to conceive.° The answer is as ready as a borrower's cap:° "I am the King's poor cousin, sir."

PRINCE   Nay, they will be kin to us, or they will fetch it from Japheth.° But the letter. [*He reads.*] "Sir John Falstaff knight, to the son of the King nearest his father, Harry   105 Prince of Wales, greeting."

POINS   Why, this is a certificate.°

---

82 cankers cankerworms, worms that destroy buds and leaves   **83 to preserve thee** (allusion to the cross on the sixpence)   **84 An** if   **89 good respect** proper ceremony (said ironically)   **90 martlemas** martinmas beef, beef slaughtered on November 11 (and fattened beforehand)   **94 wen** swelling   **95 holds his place** keeps up his familiarity with me   **97 Every . . . that** Falstaff wants to make sure that everyone is aware of his knightly rank   **101 takes . . . conceive** pretends not to understand   **101–2 as ready . . . cap** as quick in coming forth as a cap is doffed by one seeking aid   **103–4 Nay . . . Japheth** such petitioners insistently claim that they are connected to us of the royal family, if not in fact able to trace their ancestry all the way back to Japheth, the third son of Noah and the ancestor of all gentiles, hence of all Europeans (Genesis 10.2–5)   **107 certificate** (by putting his own name before that of the Prince as addressee, Falstaff has misappropriated a style normally reserved for sovereigns addressing subjects)

PRINCE   Peace! [*He reads*] "I will imitate the honorable Romans in brevity."

POINS   Sure he means brevity in breath, short-winded.   110

PRINCE [*reads*]   "I commend me to thee, I commend thee, and I leave thee.° Be not too familiar with Poins, for he misuses thy favors so much that he swears thou art to marry his sister Nell. Repent at idle times as thou mayst, and so farewell.   115

"Thine, by yea and no,° which is as much as to say, as thou usest him, Jack Falstaff with my familiars,° John with my brothers and sisters, and Sir John with all Europe."

POINS   My lord, I'll steep° this letter in sack and make him   120
eat it.

PRINCE   That's to make him eat twenty° of his words. But do you use me thus, Ned? Must I marry your sister?

POINS   God send the wench no worse fortune! But I never said so.   125

PRINCE   Well, thus we play the fools with the time, and the spirits of the wise sit in the clouds and mock us.—Is your master here in London?

BARDOLPH   Yea, my lord.

PRINCE   Where sups he? Doth the old boar feed in the old frank?°   130

BARDOLPH   At the old place, my lord, in Eastcheap.

PRINCE   What company?

PAGE   Ephesians, my lord, of the old church.°

PRINCE   Sup any women with him?

PAGE   None, my lord, but old Mistress Quickly and Mistress   135
Doll Tearsheet.

PRINCE   What pagan° may that be?

PAGE   A proper gentlewoman, sir, and a kinswoman of my master's.

PRINCE   Even such kin as the parish heifers are to the town   140
bull.° Shall we steal upon them, Ned, at supper?

111–12 **I commend . . . leave thee** (Falstaff self-importantly adopts the brief style of Julius Caesar's famous *veni, vidi, vici*; see 1.1.23 and n.)   116 **by yea and no** (a mild Puritan oath)   117 **familiars** intimate friends   120 **steep** soak   122 **twenty** a considerable number   130 **frank** sty, pen (often thought to refer to the Boar's Head Tavern)   133 **Ephesians . . . church** good fellows of the usual, disreputable fellowship   137 **pagan** harlot   140–1 **town bull** a communally owned bull that local farmers could mate with their heifers

POINS   I am your shadow, my lord; I'll follow you.

PRINCE   Sirrah, you boy, and Bardolph, no word to your
master that I am yet come to town. There's for your silence.

[He gives money]

BARDOLPH   I have no tongue, sir.   145

PAGE   And for mine, sir, I will govern it.

PRINCE   Fare you well; go. *[Exeunt Bardolph and Page]* This
Doll Tearsheet should° be some road.°

POINS   I warrant you, as common as the way between Saint
Albans and London.   150

PRINCE   How might we see Falstaff bestow° himself tonight in
his true colors, and not ourselves be seen?

POINS   Put on two leathern jerkins° and aprons, and wait upon
him at his table as drawers.°

PRINCE   From a God to a bull? A heavy descension!° It was   155
Jove's case.° From a prince to a prentice? A low
transformation! That shall be mine, for in everything the
purpose must weigh with° the folly. Follow me, Ned.

Exeunt

ACT 2
SCENE 3

Enter Northumberland, his wife [Lady Northumberland],
and the wife to Harry Percy [Lady Percy]

NORTHUMBERLAND

I pray thee, loving wife and gentle daughter,°
Give even way unto my rough affairs.°
Put not you on the visage of the times°

---

148 should must | **road** common whore   **151 bestow** behave   **153 jerkins** jackets
154 drawers tapsters, tavern waiters   **155 heavy descension** grievous descent or
degradation   **156 Jove's case** (Jupiter, for the love of Europa, transformed himself
into a bull)   **158 weigh with** match; counterbalance

2.3. Location: Warkworth. Before Northumberland's castle. Summary: Northumberland's wife and daughter-in-law plead with him not to go into battle.
Hotspur's widow, Lady Percy, offers an idealized portrait of her late husband, and
the two women convince Northumberland to delay entering the fray, as Lord
Bardolph feared in 1.3.
1 daughter daughter-in-law   **2 Give . . . affairs** make things as easy for me as you can
at this difficult time   **3 Put . . . times** don't look as bleak or troubled as are the times

And be like them to Percy° troublesome.

LADY NORTHUMBERLAND   I have given over; I will speak no more.   5
Do what you will; your wisdom be your guide.

NORTHUMBERLAND   Alas, sweet wife, my honor is at pawn,
And, but° my going, nothing can redeem it.

LADY PERCY   Oh, yet, for God's sake, go not to these wars!
The time was, father, that you broke your word,   10
When you were more endeared° to it than now,
When your own Percy, when my heart's dear Harry,
Threw many a northward look to see his father
Bring up his powers; but he did long in vain.
Who then persuaded you to stay at home?   15
There were two honors lost, yours and your son's.
For° yours, the God of heaven brighten it!
For his, it stuck upon him as the sun
In the gray° vault of heaven, and by his light
Did all the chivalry° of England move   20
To do brave acts. He was indeed the glass°
Wherein the noble youth did dress themselves.
He had no legs that practiced not his gait;°
And speaking thick,° which nature made his blemish,
Became the accents of the valiant,   25
For those that could speak low and tardily
Would turn their own perfection to abuse
To seem like him.° So that in speech, in gait,
In diet, in affections of delight,°
In military rules, humors of blood,°   30
He was the mark° and glass, copy and book,
That fashioned others. And him—oh, wondrous him!—
Oh, miracle of men!—him did you leave,
Second to none, unseconded° by you,°
To look upon the hideous god of war   35
In disadvantage,° to abide a field°

---

4 to Percy to me   **8 but** except for   **11 endeared** pledged, bound by affection   **17 For** as for (also in l. 18)   **19 gray** sky-blue   **20 chivalry** men-at-arms   **21 glass** mirror   **23 He . . . gait** there was no man alive and able to walk who did not imitate Hotspur's stride   **24 thick** impulsively, impetuously   **27–8 turn . . . him** debase their own manner of speech and adopt his   **29 affections of delight** tastes for pleasure   **30 humors of blood** temperament   **31 mark** mark to aim at   **34 Second . . . you** this man who was second to none | **unseconded** unsupported   **36 In disadvantage** outnumbered | **abide a field** face a battle

Where nothing but the sound of Hotspur's name
Did seem defensible.° So you left him.
Never, oh, never do his ghost the wrong
To hold your honor more precise and nice°   40
With others than with him! Let them alone.
The Marshal and the Archbishop are strong.
Had my sweet Harry had but half their numbers,
Today might I, hanging on Hotspur's neck,
Have talked of Monmouth's° grave.

NORTHUMBERLAND   Beshrew your heart,°   45
Fair daughter, you do draw my spirits from me
With new lamenting° ancient oversights.
But I must go and meet with danger there,
Or it will seek me in another place
And find me worse provided.°

LADY NORTHUMBERLAND   Oh, fly to Scotland,   50
Till that the nobles and the armèd commons
Have of their puissance made a little taste.°

LADY PERCY If they get ground and vantage of° the King,
Then join you with them like a rib of steel,
To make strength stronger; but, for all our loves,   55
First let them try themselves. So did your son;
He was so suffered.° So came° I a widow,
And never shall have length of life enough
To rain upon remembrance with mine eyes,°
That it may grow and sprout as high as heaven   60
For recordation° to my noble husband.

NORTHUMBERLAND
Come, come, go in with me. 'Tis with my mind
As with the tide swelled up unto his height,
That makes a still-stand,° running neither way.
Fain° would I go to meet the Archbishop,   65
But many thousand reasons hold me back.

---

38 defensible able to make defense **40 To . . . nice** to be more punctilious in
honoring your commitments **45 Monmouth's** Prince Hal's (since he was born at
Monmouth) | **Beshrew your heart** (a reproachful oath) **47 new lamenting**
lamenting anew **50 provided** prepared **52 Have . . . taste** have put their strength
to some test **53 get . . . of** achieve a military advantage over **57 suffered** allowed
to proceed | **came** became **59 To rain . . . eyes** to water remembrance with my
tears, as though it were a plant like rosemary **61 recordation** remembrance,
memorial **64 still-stand** point of balance, standstill **65 Fain** Gladly

I will resolve for° Scotland. There am I,
Till time and vantage° crave my company.   *Exeunt*

ACT 2
SCENE 4

Enter a Drawer, [Francis, and another]

FRANCIS   What the devil hast thou brought there? Applejohns?°
Thou knowest Sir John cannot endure an applejohn.

SECOND DRAWER   Mass,° thou sayst true. The Prince once set a
dish of applejohns before him, and told him there were five
more Sir Johns, and, putting off his hat, said, "I will now   5
take my leave of these six dry, round, old, withered knights."
It angered him to the heart. But he hath forgot that.

FRANCIS   Why, then, cover,° and set them down. And see if
thou canst find out Sneak's noise;° Mistress Tearsheet would
fain hear some music.   10

Enter Will [a third Drawer]

THIRD DRAWER   Dispatch!° The room where they supped is too
hot; they'll come in straight.°

FRANCIS   Sirrah, here will be the Prince and Master Poins anon,
and they will put on two of our jerkins and aprons, and Sir
John must not know of it. Bardolph hath brought word.   15

THIRD DRAWER   By the Mass, here will be old utas.° It will be an
excellent stratagem.

SECOND DRAWER   I'll see if I can find out Sneak.   *Exit°*

Enter Mistress Quickly [the Hostess] and Doll Tearsheet

---

67 **resolve for** decide to go to   68 **vantage** opportunity

2.4. Location: London. A tavern in Eastcheap, usually identified as the Boar's Head.
Some tavern furniture is provided. **Summary:** Falstaff passes time at the tavern with
Mistress Quickly and prostitute Doll Tearsheet. When Doll quarrels with a
boisterous Pistol, Falstaff drives him out. Hal and Poins, disguised as tapsters, catch
Falstaff disparaging them, forcing him to invent more lies. Peto interrupts with
serious news about preparations for war.

1 **Applejohns** a kind of apple eaten when shriveled and withered   3 **Mass** by the
Mass   8 **cover** spread the cloth, set the table   9 **noise** band of musicians
11 **Dispatch** hurry up   12 **straight** very soon   16 **old utas** rare fun   18 **s.d.** *Exit*
(Will may exit too, and perhaps Francis exits at 30; the *drawers* or tapsters
presumably come and go, serving the customers)

HOSTESS I'faith, sweetheart, methinks now you are in an
excellent good temperality.° Your pulsidge° beats as   20
extraordinarily° as heart would desire, and your color, I
warrant you, is as red as any rose, in good truth, la! But,
i'faith, you have drunk too much canaries,° and that's a
marvelous searching° wine, and it perfumes° the blood ere
one can say, "What's this?" How do you now?   25

DOLL Better than I was. Hem!

HOSTESS Why, that's well said. A good heart's worth gold. Lo,
here comes Sir John.

Enter Sir John [Falstaff]

FALSTAFF [*singing*] "When Arthur first in court"°—
Empty the jordan.°   [*Exit a Drawer*]   30
[*Singing*] "And was a worthy king"—
How now, Mistress Doll?

HOSTESS Sick of a calm,° yea, good faith.

FALSTAFF So is all her sect.° An they be once in a calm, they
are sick.   35

DOLL A pox damn you, you muddy rascal, is that all the
comfort you give me?

FALSTAFF You make fat rascals,° Mistress Doll.

DOLL I make them? Gluttony and diseases make them; I make
them not.   40

FALSTAFF If the cook help to make the gluttony, you help to
make the diseases, Doll. We catch of you, Doll, we catch of
you. Grant that, my poor virtue, grant that.

DOLL Yea, joy, our chains and our jewels.°

FALSTAFF "Your brooches, pearls, and ouches."° For to serve   45
bravely is to come halting off, you know; to come off the
breach with his pike bent bravely, and to surgery bravely; to
venture upon the charged chambers° bravely—

DOLL Hang yourself, you muddy conger, hang yourself!

20 **temperality** temper | **pulsidge** pulse **21 extraordinarily** ordinarily, regularly
23 canaries canary (a light, sweet wine from the Canary Islands) **24 searching**
penetrating | **perfumes** permeates **29 "When . . . court"** (a fragment from the
ballad "Sir Launcelot du Lake") **30 jordan** chamber pot **33 calm** qualm **34 sect**
sex **38 rascals** (1) lean deer (2) good-for-nothings **44 Yea . . . jewels** yes, indeed,
you *catch* or steal our valuables **45 "Your brooches . . . ouches"** (a line from a
ballad, but also referring to venereal scabs and sores) **48 charged chambers** small
cannon; with bawdy double meaning, as in *breach* and *pike* (47), *surgery* (venereal
treatment, 47), *conger* (eel, with sexual connotation, 49), *bear* (56) etc.

HOSTESS   By my troth, this is the old fashion. You two never   50
  meet but you fall to some discord. You are both, i' good
  truth, as rheumatic° as two dry toasts; you cannot one bear
  with another's confirmities.° What the goodyear!° One must
  bear,° and that [*to Doll*] must be you. You are the weaker
  vessel, as they say, the emptier vessel.   55

DOLL   Can a weak empty vessel bear such a huge full
  hogshead?° There's a whole merchant's venture° of
  Bordeaux stuff° in him; you have not seen a hulk° better
  stuffed in the hold. Come, I'll be friends with thee, Jack.
  Thou art going to the wars, and whether I shall ever see thee   60
  again or no there is nobody cares.

Enter Drawer°

DRAWER   Sir, Ancient° Pistol's below, and would speak with you.

DOLL   Hang him, swaggering rascal! Let him not come hither.
  It is the foul-mouthed'st rogue in England.

HOSTESS   If he swagger, let him not come here. No, by my faith,   65
  I must live among my neighbors. I'll no° swaggerers. I am in
  good name and fame° with the very best. Shut the door;
  there comes no swaggerers here. I have not lived all this
  while to have swaggering now. Shut the door, I pray you.

FALSTAFF   Dost thou hear, Hostess?   70

HOSTESS   Pray ye, pacify yourself, Sir John. There comes no
  swaggerers here.

FALSTAFF   Dost thou hear? It is mine ancient.

HOSTESS   Tilly-fally,° Sir John, ne'er tell me. And your ancient
  swaggerer comes not in my doors. I was before Master   75
  Tisick,° the debuty,° t'other day, and, as he said to me, 'twas
  no longer ago than Wednesday last, i'good faith, "Neighbor
  Quickly," says he—Master Dumbe, our minister, was by
  then—"Neighbor Quickly," says he, "receive those that are
  civil, for," said he, "you are in an ill name."° Now 'a said   80

---

52 rheumatic (blunder for "choleric" or "splenetic"?)   **53 confirmities** (for
"infirmities") | **What the goodyear!** (an expletive, meaning something like "what
the devil")   **54 bear** (1) put up with another's infirmities (2) bear the weight of a
lover (3) bear children   **57 hogshead** large cask | **venture** cargo   **58 Bordeaux
stuff** wine | **hulk** large, unwieldy cargo ship   **61.1 *Drawer*** (perhaps Francis)
62 Ancient ensign, standard-bearer   **66 I'll no** I'll have no   **67 fame** reputation
74 Tilly-fally Fiddlesticks   **76 Tisick** (literally, phthisic, a cough or consump-
tion) | **debuty** deputy, deputy alderman   **80 are . . . name** have a bad reputation

so, I can tell whereupon.° "For," says he, "you are an honest
woman, and well thought on; therefore take heed what
guests you receive. Receive," says he, "no swaggering
companions."° There comes none here. You would bless
you° to hear what he said. No, I'll no swaggerers. 85

FALSTAFF He's no swaggerer, hostess; a tame cheater,° i'faith;
you may stroke him as gently as a puppy greyhound. He'll
not swagger with a Barbary hen,° if her feathers turn back in
any show of resistance.— Call him up, drawer.

[Exit Drawer]

HOSTESS Cheater,° call you him? I will bar no honest man my 90
house, nor no cheater, but I do not love swaggering, by my
troth. I am the worse when one says "swagger." Feel,
masters, how I shake; look you, I warrant you.

DOLL So you do, hostess.

HOSTESS Do I? Yea, in very truth, do I, an 'twere° an aspen 95
leaf. I cannot abide swaggerers.

Enter Ancient Pistol, [Bardolph,] and Boy [Page]

PISTOL God save you, Sir John!

FALSTAFF Welcome, Ancient Pistol. Here, Pistol, I charge° you
with a cup of sack. Do you discharge upon° mine hostess.

PISTOL I will discharge upon her, Sir John, with two bullets. 100

FALSTAFF She is pistol-proof°, sir; you shall not hardly° offend
her.°

HOSTESS Come, I'll drink no proofs nor no bullets. I'll drink no
more than will do me good, for no man's pleasure, I.

PISTOL Then to you, Mistress Dorothy; I will charge you. 105

DOLL Charge me? I scorn you, scurvy companion. What, you
poor, base, rascally, cheating, lack-linen° mate?° Away, you
moldy rogue, away! I am meat° for your master.

81 whereupon upon what grounds   **84 companions** fellows   **84–5 You . . . bless
you** you'd be surprised   **86 tame cheater** harmless card sharper   **88 Barbary hen**
guinea hen (slang term for a prostitute)   **90 Cheater** (Mistress Quickly may
understand the word as *escheator*, "an officer of the King's exchequer")   **95 an
'twere** as if I were   **98 charge** (1) pledge, drink to (2) load (as in loading a pistol)
99 discharge upon toast; with bawdy double meaning; see also *charge, Pistol, bullets*
(testicles), *meat* (slang for "whore"), etc.   **101 pistol-proof** (1) invulnerable to the
charms of Pistol (2) sexually impregnable to the *discharge of bullets* (testicles) |
shall not hardly shall scarcely (a colloquial expression)   **101–2 offend her** do her
any harm (with sexual suggestion)   **107 lack-linen** without a shirt to your name |
mate low fellow   **108 meat** (with a pun on "mate"; pronounced alike)

PISTOL   I know you, Mistress Dorothy.

DOLL   Away, you cutpurse rascal! You filthy bung,° away! By   110
this wine, I'll thrust my knife in your moldy chops° an you
play the saucy cuttle° with me. Away, you bottle-ale rascal!
You basket-hilt stale juggler,° you! Since when,° I pray you,
sir? God's light, with two points° on your shoulder? Much!°

PISTOL   God let me not live, but I will murder your ruff° for   115
this.

FALSTAFF   No more, Pistol, I would not have you go off here.
Discharge yourself of our company, Pistol.

HOSTESS   No, good Captain Pistol, not here, sweet Captain.

DOLL   Captain? Thou abominable damned cheater, art thou   120
not ashamed to be called captain? An captains were of my
mind, they would truncheon you out° for taking their names
upon you before you have earned them. You a captain? You
slave, for what? For tearing a poor whore's ruff in a bawdy
house? He a captain? Hang him, rogue! He lives upon   125
moldy stewed prunes° and dried cakes. A captain? God's
light, these villains will make the word as odious as the
word "occupy,°" which was an excellent good word before
it was ill sorted.° Therefore captains had need° look to't.

BARDOLPH   Pray thee, go down,° good Ancient.   130

FALSTAFF   Hark thee hither, Mistress Doll.

PISTOL   Not I. I tell thee what, Corporal Bardolph, I could tear
her. I'll be revenged of her.

PAGE   Pray thee, go down.

PISTOL   I'll see her damned first, to Pluto's damned lake,° by   135
this hand, to th'infernal deep,
With Erebus° and tortures vile also.

---

110 bung (1) pickpocket (2) something that fills a hole   **111 chops** jaws   **111–2 an
. . . cuttle** if you try any of your tricks (*cuttle* was a slang term for a pickpocket's
cutting knife)   **113 You basket-hilt . . . juggler** (doll compares Pistol to a cheap
entertainer who shows off his prowess in fencing with cudgels that are equipped
with basketwork hilts) | **Since when** since when do you claim to be so brave and
military?   **114 points** lace tags, probably used here to hold together Pistol's tattered
linen | **Much!** (an exclamation of scornful incredulity)   **115 murder your ruff** tear
your pleated, starched collar (such as prostitutes wore)   **122 truncheon you out**
cudgel you out of here   **126 stewed prunes** (associated with brothels)   **128 occupy**
fornicate   **129 ill sorted** corrupted, put in such bad company | **had need** would do
well to   **130 go down** calm down, or, go downstairs and leave   **135 Pluto's
damned lake** a river of the underworld   **137 Erebus** the underworld

Hold hook and line, say I.
Down, down, dogs! Down, faitors!°
Have we not Hiren° here?   140
HOSTESS   Good Captain Peesel, be quiet; 'tis very late, i'faith. I
beseek° you now, aggravate° your choler.
PISTOL   These be good humors,° indeed! Shall packhorses
And hollow pampered jades of Asia,
Which cannot go but thirty mile a day,   145
Compare with Caesars, and with cannibals,°
And Troiant° Greeks?° Nay, rather damn them with
King Cerberus,° and let the welkin° roar.
Shall we fall foul for toys?°
HOSTESS   By my troth, Captain, these are very bitter words.   150
BARDOLPH   Begone, good Ancient. This will grow to a brawl
anon.
PISTOL   Die men like dogs! Give crowns like pins!° Have we not
Hiren here?
HOSTESS   O' my word, Captain, there's none such here.° What   155
the goodyear, do you think I would deny her?° For God's
sake, be quiet.
PISTOL   Then feed and be fat, my fair Calipolis.°
Come, give's some sack.
Si fortune me tormente, sperato me contento.°   160

---

139 faitors imposters, cheats   **140 Hiren** Pistol's fanciful name for his sword, with
a seeming allusion to a lost play by Peele, *The Turkish Mahomet and Hiren the Fair
Greek. Hiren* means "Irene," "Peace" (throughout, Pistol's colorful speech is full of
echoes of the contemporary theater)   **142 beseek** beseech | **aggravate** (for
"moderate")   **143 good humors** fine goings-on   **143–7 Shall . . . Greeks**
(misquotation from Marlowe's *2 Tamburlaine*, 4.4.1–2)   **146 cannibals** (the
association here with Caesar would seem to suggest "Hannibals," but *cannibals*
appears in the apparent source for this passage, John Eliot's *Orthoepia Gallica*,
1593; Pistol is ready to take on cannibals, Trojan Greeks, or anybody)
147 Troiant Trojan   **148 Cerberus** three-headed dog guarding the entrance to
Hades | **welkin** heavens   **149 fall . . . toys** fall out over trifles   **153 Give crowns
like pins!** pass out kingdoms as if they were of the value of a pin! (as Tamburlaine
does to his followers)   **155 there's none such here** (the hostess seems to think that
Pistol is asking after Hiren or Irene as though she were a whore living in the
tavern)   **156 deny her** keep her from you; deny that she was here, if she were
158 Then . . . Calipolis (garbled version of a line in Peele's *The Battle of Alcazar*,
2.3.70)   **160 Si . . . contento** if fortune torments me, hope contents me (an
ignorant medley of Spanish and Italian)

Fear we broadsides?° No, let the fiend give fire.°
Give me some sack, and, sweetheart, lie thou there.
                                    [*He lays down his sword*]
Come we to full points° here, and are etceteras nothings?°
FALSTAFF   Pistol, I would be quiet.
PISTOL   Sweet knight, I kiss thy neaf.°   165
What, we have seen the seven stars.°
DOLL   For God's sake, thrust him downstairs. I cannot endure
such a fustian° rascal.
PISTOL
"Thrust him downstairs?" Know we not Galloway nags?°
FALSTAFF   Quoit° him down, Bardolph, like a shovegroat shilling.°   170
Nay, an 'a do nothing but speak nothing, 'a shall be nothing
here.°
BARDOLPH   Come, get you downstairs.
PISTOL [*snatching up his sword*]
What, shall we have incision?° Shall we imbrue?°
Then death rock me asleep,° abridge my doleful days!   175
Why then, let grievous, ghastly, gaping wounds
Untwine the Sisters Three.° Come, Atropos, I say!
HOSTESS   Here's goodly stuff toward!°
FALSTAFF   Give me my rapier, boy.
DOLL   I pray thee, Jack, I pray thee, do not draw.   180
FALSTAFF [*to Pistol*]   Get you downstairs.   [*They fight*]
HOSTESS   Here's a goodly tumult! I'll forswear keeping house
afore I'll be in these tirrits° and frights. So, murder, I
warrant now. Alas, alas, put up your naked weapons, put up
your naked weapons.   185
                              [*Exit Bardolph, driving Pistol out*]

---

161 broadsides volleys fired from one side of a ship | **give fire** shoot   **163 full
points** full stops, periods; also, swords' points | **etceteras nothings** (both words
suggest the female sexual anatomy)   **165 neaf** fist   **166 the seven stars** the Pleiades,
or Big Dipper (Pistol means they have shared many night adventures)   **168 fustian**
bombastic, worthless   **169 Galloway nags** an Irish breed of small but swift horses
(here used abusively to mean "harlots")   **170 Quoit** throw | **shove-groat shilling**
an Edward VI shilling used in shove-groat, a game in which the coins were shoved
toward a mark   **171–2 an 'a . . . here** if he spouts nonsense he must get out of here
174 incision bloodshed | **imbrue** dye with blood   **175 death . . . asleep** (quotation
from a poem written by Anne Boleyn or her brother as they awaited execution)
177 the Sisters Three the three Fates: Clotho (who spun or *untwined* the thread of
life), Lachesis (who unwound it), and Atropos (who severed it)   **178 toward** about
to happen   **183 tirrits** agitations, fits

DOLL I pray thee, Jack, be quiet; the rascal's gone. Ah, you whoreson little valiant villain, you!

HOSTESS Are you not hurt i'th' groin? Methought 'a made a shrewd° thrust at your belly.

[Enter Bardolph]

FALSTAFF Have you turned him out o'doors?   190

BARDOLPH Yea, sir. The rascal's drunk. You have hurt him, sir, i'th' shoulder.

FALSTAFF A rascal! To brave° me?

DOLL Ah, you sweet little rogue, you! Alas, poor ape, how thou sweat'st! Come, let me wipe thy face. Come on, you 195 whoreson chops.° Ah, rogue, i'faith, I love thee. Thou art as valorous as Hector of Troy,° worth five of Agamemnon,° and ten times better than the Nine Worthies.° Ah, villain!

FALSTAFF A rascally slave! I will toss the rogue in a blanket.°

DOLL Do, an thou dar'st for thy heart.° An thou dost, I'll 200 canvass thee between a pair of sheets.°

Enter Music°

PAGE The music is come, sir.

FALSTAFF Let them play. Play, sirs. Sit on my knee, Doll. A rascal bragging slave! The rogue fled from me like quicksilver.   205

DOLL *[sitting on his knee]* I'faith, and thou followed'st him like a church.° Thou whoreson little tidy° Bartholomew boar-pig,° when wilt thou leave fighting o'days and foining° o'nights, and begin to patch up thine old body for heaven?

Enter [behind] Prince and Poins [disguised as drawers]

189 shrewd vicious   193 brave defy   196 chops fat cheeks   197 Hector of Troy leader of the Trojans; the type of valor | Agamemnon leader of the Greeks at Troy 198 Nine Worthies Hector, Alexander, Julius Caesar; Joshua, David, Judas Maccabaeus; Arthur, Charlemagne, Godfrey of Boulogne   199 toss . . . blanket (a humiliating punishment for cowards and rascals)   200 an . . . heart if your heart tells you to   201 canvass . . . sheets (doll's more sexual version of tossing in a blanket)   201.1 *Music* musicians   207 like a church (implying perhaps that Falstaff has borne down on Pistol with his impressive bulk) | tidy plump, tender 207–8 Bartholomew boar-pig (allusion to the serving of roast pig at Bartholomew Fair, August 24, in Smithfield)   208 foining thrusting, fornicating

FALSTAFF   Peace, good Doll, do not speak like a death's-head;° 210
do not bid me remember mine end.

DOLL   Sirrah, what humor's the Prince of?°

FALSTAFF   A good shallow young fellow. 'A would have made a
good pantler,° 'a would ha' chipped bread° well.

DOLL   They say Poins has a good wit.   215

FALSTAFF   He a good wit? Hang him, baboon! His wit's as thick
as Tewkesbury mustard.° There's no more conceit° in him
than is in a mallet.°

DOLL   Why does the Prince love him so, then?

FALSTAFF   Because their legs are both of a bigness,° and 'a plays 220
at quoits° well, and eats conger and fennel,° and drinks off
candles' ends for flapdragons,° and rides the wild mare°
with the boys, and jumps upon joint stools,° and swears
with a good grace, and wears his boots very smooth° like
unto the sign of the Leg,° and breeds no bate with telling of 225
discreet stories;° and such other gambol° faculties 'a has
that show a weak mind and an able body, for the which the
Prince admits him. For the Prince himself is such another;
the weight of a hair will turn the scales between their
avoirdupois.°   230

PRINCE [*to Poins*]   Would not this nave° of a wheel have his
ears cut off?°

POINS   Let's beat him before° his whore.

PRINCE   Look whe'er the withered elder° hath not his poll
clawed like a parrot.°   235

---

210 **death's-head** skull, used emblematically as a reminder of the inevitability of
death   212 **what . . . of?** what is the Prince's disposition, temperament, mood?
214 **pantler** pantry worker | **chipped bread** cut off the hard bread crusts
217 **Tewkesbury mustard** (Tewkesbury in Gloucestershire was famous for mustard)
217 **conceit** wit   218 **mallet** wooden hammer, heavy and not at all sharp   220 **of a
bigness** of equal size   221 **quoits** a throwing game played across a net like badminton,
but with a flat ring that is caught and thrown back | **conger and fennel** conger eel
seasoned with a yellow-flowered herb (rich fare, likely to dull the wits)   221–2 **drinks
. . . flapdragons** drinks liquor with a lighted candle floating in it, or extinguishes the
candle with his mouth (a tavern sport)   222 **wild mare** leapfrog, or a game in which
boys pile on top of one another until the *mare* collapses   223 **joint stools** stools made
by a joiner or craftsman   224 **smooth** well-fitting   225 **sign . . . Leg** sign over a
bootmaker's shop   225–6 **breeds . . . stories** creates no ill will by tattling secrets
226 **gambol** sportive   230 **avoirdupois** weight   231 **nave** hub (refers to Falstaff's
rotundity; with a pun on "knave")   231–2 **have . . . off** as the punishment for
slandering royalty   233 **before** in front of   234 **elder** (1) elder tree (2) old man
234–5 **poll . . . parrot** (Doll is probably rumpling the hair on Falstaff's head, his *poll*)

POINS   Is it not strange that desire should so many years outlive
performance?

FALSTAFF   Kiss me, Doll.

PRINCE [*to Poins*]   Saturn and Venus this year in conjunction?°
What says th'almanac to that?   240

POINS   And look whether the fiery Trigon,° his man, be not
lisping to his master's old tables,° his notebook,° his counsel
keeper.

FALSTAFF [*to Doll*]   Thou dost give me flattering busses.°

DOLL   By my troth, I kiss thee with a most constant heart.   245

FALSTAFF   I am old, I am old.

DOLL   I love thee better than I love e'er a scurvy young boy of
them all.

FALSTAFF   What stuff° wilt have a kirtle° of? I shall receive
money o' Thursday; shalt have a cap tomorrow. A merry   250
song. Come, it grows late; we'll to bed. Thou'lt forget me
when I am gone.

DOLL   By my troth, thou'lt set me a-weeping an thou say'st so.
Prove that ever I dress myself handsome till thy return—
well, hearken a'th'end.°   255

FALSTAFF   Some sack, Francis.

PRINCE, POINS [*coming forward*]   Anon, anon,° sir.

FALSTAFF   Ha? A bastard son of the King's? And art not thou
Poins his brother?

PRINCE   Why, thou globe of sinful continents,° what a life dost   260
thou lead!

FALSTAFF   A better than thou. I am a gentleman; thou art a
drawer.

---

239 Saturn . . . conjunction will the planets that govern saturnine old age and love
be near one another in the heavens?   **241 fiery Trigon** (the twelve signs of the
zodiac were divided into four *trigons* or triangles, one of which, consisting of Aries,
Leo, and Sagittarius, was characterized as fiery; these three form a triangle because
they are not contiguous on the circle of the zodiac but occur at points equivalent
roughly to April, August, and December, at 120-degree intervals; the other three
trigons were characterized as watery, airy, and earthy; the joke here is directed
against Bardolph's fiery face)   **242 lisping . . . notebook** whispering lovingly to
Falstaff's old confidante, Mistress Quickly | **tables** notebook (for assignations)
244 busses kisses   **249 stuff** material | **kirtle** skirt   **255 hearken a'th'end** wait and
see   **257 Anon, anon** (the cry of the drawer, or tapster, in answering his customers'
demands for service, as in *1 Henry IV*, 2.4.24 ff)   **260 globe . . . continents** (1) spherical
person made up entirely of sinful contents (2) terrestrial globe of continents in
which sin is omnipresent

PRINCE   Very true, sir, and I come to draw you out by the ears.°

HOSTESS   Oh, the Lord preserve Thy Grace! By my troth, 265
welcome to London. Now, the Lord bless that sweet face of
thine! Oh, Jesu, are you come from Wales?

FALSTAFF   Thou whoreson mad compound° of majesty, by this
light flesh and corrupt blood,° thou art welcome.

DOLL   How, you fat fool! I scorn you. 270

POINS   My lord, he will drive you out of your revenge and turn
all to a merriment, if you take not the heat.°

PRINCE   You whoreson candle-mine° you, how vilely did you
speak of me even now before this honest, virtuous, civil
gentlewoman! 275

HOSTESS   God's blessing of your good heart! And so she is, by
my troth.

FALSTAFF   Didst thou hear me?

PRINCE   Yea, and you knew me, as you did when you ran away
by Gad's Hill.° You knew I was at your back, and spoke it 280
on purpose to try my patience.

FALSTAFF   No, no, no, not so, I did not think thou wast within
hearing.

PRINCE   I shall drive you then to confess the willful abuse,° and
then I know how to handle you. 285

FALSTAFF   No abuse, Hal, o' mine honor, no abuse.

PRINCE   Not? To dispraise me, and call me pantler and bread-
chipper and I know not what?

FALSTAFF   No abuse, Hal.

POINS   No abuse? 290

FALSTAFF   No abuse, Ned, i'th' world, honest Ned, none. I
dispraised him before the wicked, that the wicked might not
fall in love with thee [*to Hal*]; in which doing, I have done
the part of a careful friend and a true subject, and thy father
is to give me thanks for it. No abuse, Hal. None, Ned, none. 295
No, faith, boys, none.

---

264 **draw . . . ears** (as one might grab by the ears a naughty child caught in some
mischief)   268 **compound** lump, mass   268–9 **by . . . blood** (an extension of the
oath, "by this light," here reworded to apply to Doll)   272 **if . . . heat** if you don't
strike while the iron is hot   273 **candle-mine** magazine or storehouse of tallow
279–80 **Yea . . . Gad's Hill** (see *1 Henry IV*, 2.4)   284 **to confess . . . abuse** to
confess that you slandered me intentionally

PRINCE   See now whether pure fear and entire° cowardice doth
not make thee wrong this virtuous gentlewoman to close
with° us. Is she° of the wicked? Is thine hostess here of the
wicked? Or is thy boy of the wicked? Or honest Bardolph,   300
whose zeal burns in his nose, of the wicked?

POINS   Answer, thou dead elm, answer.

FALSTAFF   The fiend hath pricked down° Bardolph irrecoverable,
and his face is Lucifer's privy° kitchen, where he doth nothing
but roast maltworms.° For° the boy, there is a good angel   305
about him, but the devil blinds° him too.

PRINCE   For the women?

FALSTAFF   For one of them, she's in hell already and burns°
poor souls. For th'other, I owe her money, and whether she
be damned° for that I know not.   310

HOSTESS   No, I warrant you.

FALSTAFF   No, I think thou art not; I think thou art quit for
that.° Marry, there is another indictment upon thee, for
suffering flesh to be eaten° in thy house, contrary to the law,
for the which I think thou wilt howl.°   315

HOSTESS   All victuallers° do so. What's a joint of mutton or two
in a whole Lent?

PRINCE   You, gentlewoman—

DOLL   What says Your Grace?

FALSTAFF   His Grace says that which his flesh rebels against.°   320

Peto knocks at door

HOSTESS   Who knocks so loud at door? Look to th' door there,
Francis.

[*Francis goes to the door. Enter Peto*]

PRINCE   Peto, how now, what news?

---

297 **entire** sheer   298–9 **to close with** in order to appease and come to terms with |
she Doll   303 **pricked down** marked, or designated   304 **privy** private   305 **malt-
worms** topers, drunkards | **for** as for (also in ll. 307 and 308)   306 **blinds** (so that
he cannot see his Good Angel)   308 **burns** infects with venereal disease   310 **damned**
(since usury was condemned by the church as well as the state)   312–3 **quit for
that** (1) acquitted of that charge (2) repaid (as much as you are ever likely to be)
314 **flesh to be eaten** (allusion to enactments to prevent the sale of meat in Lent; with
sexual double entendre on *mutton*, "whore")   315 **howl** (in hell)   316 **victuallers**
innkeepers   320 **His . . . against** (Falstaff wryly observes that sexual arousal and
feelings of revulsion are often linked; with wordplay on *Grace* as both an honorific
form of address for a prince and a spiritual quality)

PETO The King your father is at Westminster,
    And there are twenty weak and wearied posts°   325
    Come from the north. And as I came along
    I met and overtook a dozen captains,
    Bareheaded, sweating, knocking at the taverns,
    And asking everyone for Sir John Falstaff.
PRINCE By heaven, Poins, I feel me much to blame,   330
    So idly to profane the precious time
    When tempest of commotion,° like the south°
    Borne° with black vapor, doth begin to melt
    And drop upon our bare unarmèd heads.
    Give me my sword and cloak. Falstaff, good night.   335
                      Exeunt Prince and Poins, [and Peto]
FALSTAFF Now comes in the sweetest morsel of the night, and
    we must hence and leave it unpicked.
        [Knocking within. Bardolph goes to the door]
    More knocking at the door!

                          [Bardolph returns]

    How now, what's the matter?
BARDOLPH You must away to court, sir, presently.°   340
    A dozen captains stay at door for you.
FALSTAFF *[to the Page]* Pay the musicians, sirrah. Farewell,
    hostess; farewell, Doll. You see, my good wenches, how men
    of merit are sought after. The undeserver may sleep, when
    the man of action is called on. Farewell, good wenches. If I 345
    be not sent away post,° I will see you again ere I go.
DOLL I cannot speak. If my heart be not ready to burst—well,
    sweet Jack, have a care of thyself.
FALSTAFF Farewell, farewell.
                        Exit [with Bardolph and Page]
HOSTESS Well, fare thee well. I have known thee these twenty- 350
    nine years come peascod time,° but an honester and truer-
    hearted man—well, fare thee well.
BARDOLPH *[at the door]* Mistress Tearsheet!
HOSTESS What's the matter?

---

325 posts messengers   **332 commotion** insurrection | **south** south wind (regarded
as a breeder of tempests)   **333 Borne** laden   **340 presently** immediately   **346 post**
immediately   **351 peascod time** early summer, when peas are still unripe

BARDOLPH   Bid Mistress Tearsheet come to my master.   355
HOSTESS   Oh, run, Doll, run; run, good Doll. Come.— She
  comes blubbered.°—Yea, will you come, Doll?

                                                        Exeunt

ACT 3
SCENE 1

Enter the King in his nightgown,° alone [with a Page]

KING   Go call the Earls of Surrey and of Warwick;
  But ere they come, bid them o'erread° these letters
  And well consider of them. Make good speed.
                        [*He gives letters. Exit Page*]
  How many thousand of my poorest subjects
  Are at this hour asleep! O sleep, O gentle sleep,   5
  Nature's soft nurse, how have I frighted thee,
  That thou no more wilt weigh my eyelids down
  And steep my senses in forgetfulness?
  Why rather, sleep, liest thou in smoky cribs,°
  Upon uneasy° pallets stretching thee,°   10
  And hushed with buzzing night-flies to thy slumber,
  Than in the perfumed chambers of the great,
  Under the canopies of costly state,°
  And lulled with sound of sweetest melody?
  O thou dull° god, why liest thou with the vile°   15
  In loathsome beds, and leavest the kingly couch
  A watch-case° or a common 'larum bell?
  Wilt thou upon the high and giddy mast
  Seal up the shipboy's eyes, and rock his brains
  In cradle of the rude° imperious surge   20

---

357 **blubbered** disfigured with weeping

3.1. Location: Westminster. The royal court. Summary: The King laments the woes of kingship, tormented with insomnia and the flux of events that renders all alliances and friendships untrustworthy. Warwick renews his sense of purpose.

0.1 *nightgown* dressing gown   2 o'erread read over   9 cribs hovels   10 uneasy uncomfortable | thee thyself   13 state magnificence   15 dull drowsy | vile low in rank   17 watch-case sentry box, or a space in which the occupant is restlessly aware of the passage of time   20 rude turbulent

And in the visitation° of the winds,
Who° take the ruffian billows by the top,
Curling their monstrous heads and hanging them
With deafing° clamor in the slippery° clouds,
That,° with the hurly,° death itself awakes?   25
Canst thou, O partial sleep, give thy repose
To the wet sea-boy in an hour so rude,
And, in the calmest and most stillest night,
With all appliances° and means to boot,°
Deny it to a king? Then happy low,° lie down!   30
Uneasy lies the head that wears a crown.

Enter Warwick, Surrey, and Sir John Blunt°

WARWICK Many good morrows to Your Majesty!
KING Is it good morrow, lords?
WARWICK 'Tis one o'clock, and past.
KING Why, then, good morrow to you all, my lords.   35
Have you read o'er the letters that I sent you?
WARWICK We have, my liege.
KING Then you perceive the body of our kingdom,
How foul it is, what rank° diseases grow,
And with what danger near the heart of it.   40
WARWICK It is but as a body yet distempered,°
Which to his° former strength may be restored
With good advice and little° medicine.
My Lord Northumberland will soon be cooled.
KING O God, that one might read the book of fate,   45
And see the revolution of the times°
Make mountains level, and the continent,°
Weary of solid firmness, melt itself
Into the sea, and other times to see
The beachy girdle of the ocean   50

---

21 **visitation** violent onset   22 **Who** which, the winds   24 **deafing** deafening |
slippery quickly slipping by   25 **That** so that | **hurly** tumult   29 **appliances** aids
to induce sleep | **to boot** as well, besides   30 **low** humble persons   31.1 *Sir John
Blunt* (since he says nothing and is omitted from the Folio, his presence may be
unnecessary, but see l. 35, "to you all")   39 **rank** festering   41 **distempered** sick
42 **his** its   43 **little** a little   46 **revolution of the times** changes brought by the
passage of time   47 **continent** dry land

Too wide for Neptune's hips,° how chance's mocks°
And changes fill the cup of alteration
With divers liquors! Oh, if this were seen,
The happiest youth, viewing his progress through,°
What perils past, what crosses° to ensue,   55
Would shut the book and sit him down and die.
'Tis not ten years gone
Since Richard and Northumberland, great friends,
Did feast together, and in two years after
Were they at wars. It is but eight years since   60
This Percy° was the man nearest my soul,
Who like a brother toiled in my affairs
And laid his love and life under my foot,°
Yea, for my sake, even to the eyes of° Richard
Gave him defiance. But which of you was by—   65
[*To Warwick*] You, cousin Nevil,° as I may remember—
When Richard, with his eye brimful of tears,
Then checked and rated° by Northumberland,
Did speak these words, now proved a prophecy:
"Northumberland, thou ladder by the which   70
My cousin Bolingbroke ascends my throne"?—
Though then, God knows, I had no such intent,
But that necessity so bowed the state
That I and greatness were compelled to kiss—
"The time shall come," thus did he follow it,   75
"The time will come, that foul sin, gathering head,
Shall break into corruption"°—so went on,
Foretelling this same° time's condition
And the division of our amity.
WARWICK   There is a history in all men's lives,   80
Figuring° the nature of the times deceased,°
The which observed, a man may prophesy,

50–1 **The beachy . . . hips** (the King compares the sea to a girdle around the waist of the sea god Neptune, *too wide* because the sea has receded, leaving a dry strand)
51 **chance's mocks** the mockeries of Fortune   54 **progress through** life's progress from beginning to end   55 **crosses** afflictions   61 **This Percy** Northumberland
63 **under my foot** at my service   64 **to the eyes of** face to face with   66 **Nevil** (an error; this Earl of Warwick's surname is Beauchamp)   68 **checked and rated** rebuked   70–7 **Northumberland . . . corruption** (See *Richard II*, 5.1.55 ff)
78 **same** present   81 **Figuring** depicting, reproducing | **deceased** past

With a near aim, of the main chance° of things
As yet not come to life, who° in their seeds
And weak beginnings lie intreasurèd.°   85
Such things become the hatch and brood° of time,
And by the necessary form° of this
King Richard might create a perfect guess
That great Northumberland, then false to him,
Would of that seed grow to a greater falseness,   90
Which should not find a ground to root upon
Unless on you.

KING   Are these things then necessities?
Then let us meet them like necessities;
And that same word even now cries out on us.°
They say the Bishop and Northumberland   95
Are fifty thousand strong.

WARWICK   It cannot be, my lord.
Rumor doth double, like the voice and echo,
The numbers of the feared. Please it Your Grace
To go to bed. Upon my soul, my lord,
The powers that you already have sent forth   100
Shall bring this prize in very easily.
To comfort you the more, I have received
A certain instance° that Glendower is dead.
Your Majesty hath been this fortnight ill,
And these unseasoned° hours perforce must add   105
Unto your sickness.

KING   I will take your counsel.
And were these inward° wars once out of hand,°
We would, dear lords, unto the Holy Land.°   *Exeunt*

83 **main chance** probable outcome   84 **who** which   85 **intreasurèd** stored up
86 **hatch and brood** offspring, consequence   87 **necessary form** inevitable pattern
94 **cries . . . us** calls us to action; reproves us for inaction   103 **certain instance**
unquestionable proof   105 **unseasoned** unseasonable, late   107 **inward** civil |
out of hand done with   108 **We . . . Land** (compare the last four lines of *Richard
II* and *1 Henry IV*, 1.1.18–27)

ACT 3
SCENE 2

Enter Justice Shallow and Justice Silence

SHALLOW   Come on, come on, come on, give me your hand, sir,
give me your hand, sir. An early stirrer, by the rood!° And
how doth my good cousin° Silence?

SILENCE   Good morrow, good cousin Shallow.

SHALLOW   And how doth my cousin your bedfellow? And your   5
fairest daughter and mine, my goddaughter Ellen?

SILENCE   Alas, a black ouzel,° cousin Shallow!

SHALLOW   By yea and no, sir. I dare say my cousin William is
become a good scholar. He is at Oxford still, is he not?

SILENCE   Indeed, sir, to my cost.   10

SHALLOW   'A must then to the Inns o' Court° shortly. I was
once of Clement's Inn,° where I think they will talk of mad
Shallow yet.

SILENCE   You were called "lusty° Shallow" then, cousin.

SHALLOW   By the Mass, I was called anything, and I would   15
have done anything indeed too, and roundly° too. There
was I, and Little John Doit of Staffordshire, and black
George Barnes, and Francis Pickbone, and Will Squele, a
Cotswold° man. You had not four such swinge-bucklers° in
all the Inns o' Court again. And I may say to you, we knew   20
where the bona-robas° were and had the best of them all at
commandment.° Then was Jack Falstaff, now Sir John, a
boy, and page to Thomas Mowbray,° Duke of Norfolk.

SILENCE   This Sir John, cousin, that comes hither anon about
soldiers?   25

3.2. Location: Gloucestershire. **Before Justice Shallow's house. A table and chairs
must be provided onstage. Summary:** Falstaff visits Silence and Shallow, an old
schoolmate given to exaggerating his wild youth but also grown shrewd and
prosperous. As in *1 Henry IV* (4.2), Falstaff's choice of recruits is purely self-
interested. Noting Shallow's success, he plans to make him a mark.
2 rood cross   **3 cousin** kinsman (as also at ll. 4, 5, and 8)   **7 ouzel** blackbird
(Ellen is dark-complexioned, not fair)   **11 Inns o' Court** legal societies of London
12 Clement's Inn one of the Inns of Chancery; in Shallow's time, these institutions
prepared one for the Inns of Court   **14 lusty** merry, lascivious   **16 roundly**
robustly, without ceremony   **19 Cotswold** from the Cotswold Hills in
Gloucestershire | **swinge-bucklers** swashbucklers, roisterers   **21 bona-robas** good-
looking wenches, smart-looking prostitutes   **22–3 at commandment** at our beck
and call   **23 Thomas Mowbray** (rival to Bolingbroke in *Richard II*)

SHALLOW   The same Sir John, the very same. I see° him break
   Scoggin's° head at the court gate, when 'a was a crack° not
   thus high. And the very same day did I fight with one
   Sampson Stockfish, a fruiterer, behind Gray's Inn.° Jesu,
   Jesu, the mad days that I have spent! And to see how many   30
   of my old acquaintance are dead!

SILENCE   We shall all follow, cousin.

SHALLOW   Certain, 'tis certain, very sure, very sure. Death, as
   the Psalmist saith, is certain to all, all shall die.° How° a
   good yoke of bullocks at Stamford fair?   35

SILENCE   By my troth, I was not there.

SHALLOW   Death is certain. Is old Double of your town living
   yet?

SILENCE   Dead, sir.

SHALLOW   Jesu, Jesu, dead! 'A drew a good bow; and dead? 'A   40
   shot a fine shoot. John o' Gaunt° loved him well, and betted
   much money on his head. Dead? 'A would have clapped i'th'
   clout at twelve score,° and carried you a forehand shaft a
   fourteen and fourteen and a half,° that it would have done a
   man's heart good to see. How a score of ewes now?   45

SILENCE   Thereafter as they be;° a score of good ewes may be
   worth ten pounds.

SHALLOW   And is old Double dead?

SILENCE   Here come two of Sir John Falstaff's men, as I think.

Enter Bardolph and one with him

SHALLOW   Good morrow, honest gentlemen.   50

BARDOLPH   I beseech you, which is Justice Shallow?

SHALLOW   I am Robert Shallow, sir, a poor esquire° of this
   county, and one of the King's justices of the peace. What is
   your good pleasure with me?

---

26 see saw   27 Scoggin's (perhaps John Scogan, court jester to Edward IV and
protagonist of an Elizabethan jestbook known as "Scogan's Jests") | crack pert
little boy   29 Gray's Inn one of the Inns of Court   33–4 Death . . . die (See Psalm
89.48)   34 How how much (is the asking price for)   41 John o' Gaunt (father of
Henry IV)   42–3 clapped . . . score hit the bull's-eye at 240 yards   43–4 carried . . .
half could shoot a heavy arrow in a straight line rather than in a curved trajectory
for a distance of 280 to 290 yards (*you* is used colloquially)   46 Thereafter . . . be
according to their quality   52 esquire (a social rank between gentleman and knight)

BARDOLPH   My captain, sir, commends him° to you, my   55
captain, Sir John Falstaff, a tall° gentleman, by heaven, and
a most gallant leader.

SHALLOW   He greets me well, sir. I knew him a good
backsword° man. How doth the good knight? May I ask
how my lady his wife doth?   60

BARDOLPH   Sir, pardon; a soldier is better accommodated° than
with a wife.

SHALLOW   It is well said, in faith, sir, and it is well said indeed
too. "Better accommodated"! It is good, yea, indeed is it.
Good phrases are surely, and ever were, very commendable.   65
"Accommodated"! It comes of "*accommodo.*" Very good, a
good phrase.

BARDOLPH   Pardon sir, I have heard the word. "Phrase" call
you it? By this day, I know not the phrase. But I will
maintain the word with my sword to be a soldierlike word,   70
and a word of exceeding good command,° by heaven.
"Accommodated"; that is, when a man is, as they say,
accommodated; or when a man is being whereby 'a may be
thought to be accommodated, which is an excellent thing.

Enter Falstaff

SHALLOW   It is very just.°—Look, here comes good Sir John.—   75
Give me your good hand, give me Your Worship's good
hand. By my troth, you like well° and bear your years very
well. Welcome, good Sir John.

FALSTAFF   I am glad to see you well, good Master Robert
Shallow.—Master Surecard, as I think?   80

SHALLOW   No, Sir John, it is my cousin Silence, in commission
with me.°

FALSTAFF   Good Master Silence, it well befits you should be of
the peace.°

SILENCE   Your good Worship is welcome.   85

---

55 commends him sends his respects   **56 tall** valiant   **59 backsword** cudgel with a
basket hilt used for fencing practice (see the note for 2.4.113)   **61 accommodated**
furnished, equipped (a bit of fine language on Bardolph's part, perhaps with sexual
innuendo)   **71 a word . . . command** a perfectly good military term   **75 just** true
77 like well are in good condition, thrive   **81–2 in . . . me** serving as a fellow justice
of the peace   **83–4 of the peace** a magistrate (with a play on the name *Silence,*
"peace")

FALSTAFF   Fie, this is hot weather, gentlemen. Have you provided me here half a dozen sufficient° men?

SHALLOW   Marry, have we, sir. Will you sit?

[*They sit at a table*]

FALSTAFF   Let me see them, I beseech you.

SHALLOW   Where's the roll? Where's the roll? Where's the roll?   90
Let me see, let me see, let me see. So, so, so, so, so, so, so;
yea, marry, sir. Ralph Moldy! Let them appear as I call; let
them do so, let them do so. Let me see, where is Moldy?

[*Enter Moldy°*]

MOLDY   Here, an't° please you.

SHALLOW   What think you, Sir John? A good-limbed fellow,   95
young, strong, and of good friends.°

FALSTAFF   Is thy name Moldy?

MOLDY   Yea, an't please you.

FALSTAFF   'Tis the more time thou wert used.

SHALLOW   Ha, ha, ha! Most excellent, i'faith! Things that are   100
moldy lack use. Very singular good, in faith, well said, Sir
John, very well said.

FALSTAFF   Prick him.° [*Shallow writes on the muster roll*]

MOLDY   I was pricked° well enough before, an you could have
let me alone. My old dame° will be undone now for one to   105
do her husbandry° and her drudgery. You need not to have
pricked me. There are other men fitter to go out than I.

FALSTAFF   Go to. Peace, Moldy, you shall go, Moldy, it is time
you were spent.°

MOLDY   Spent?   110

SHALLOW   Peace, fellow, peace. Stand aside. Know you where
you are? For th'other,° Sir John, let me see: Simon Shadow!

[*Enter Shadow*]

---

87 sufficient fit for service   **93.1 *Enter Moldy*** (the recruits may be brought on all at once)   **94 an't** if it (also in l. 98)   **96 of good friends** well connected by family   **103 Prick him** mark him down on the list   **104 pricked** (1) vexed, grieved (2) turning sour or moldy (with sexual suggestion also, continued in *undone, husbandry, drudgery,* and *spent*, "sexually used up")   **105 dame** wife (rather than "mother," in view of the sexual punning)   **106 husbandry** farm work (but see the note at l. 104)   **109 spent** used up (but see the note at l. 104)   **112 other** others

FALSTAFF Yea, marry, let me have him to sit under. He's like° to be a cold° soldier.

SHALLOW Where's Shadow?   115

SHADOW Here, sir.

FALSTAFF Shadow, whose son art thou?

SHADOW My mother's son, sir.

FALSTAFF Thy mother's son!° Like enough, and thy father's shadow.° So the son of the female is the shadow of the male. 120 It is often so, indeed; but much of the father's substance.

SHALLOW Do you like him, Sir John?

FALSTAFF Shadow will serve° for summer.° Prick him [*aside*], for we have a number of shadows° fill° up the muster book.

SHALLOW Thomas Wart!   125

[*Enter Wart*]

FALSTAFF Where's he?

WART Here, sir.

FALSTAFF Is thy name Wart?

WART Yea, sir.

FALSTAFF Thou art a very ragged wart.   130

SHALLOW Shall I prick him, Sir John?

FALSTAFF It were superfluous, for his apparel is built upon his back and the whole frame stands upon pins.° Prick him no more.

SHALLOW Ha, ha, ha! You can do it, sir, you can do it.° I 135 commend you well.—Francis Feeble!

[*Enter Feeble*]

FEEBLE Here, sir.

SHALLOW What trade art thou, Feeble?

FEEBLE A woman's tailor, sir.

---

113 **like** likely 114 **cold** (1) cool, deliberate (2) cowardly 119 **son** (with play on "sun," continuing in the following lines) 120 **shadow** image and namesake (but, Falstaff jests, the father is only uncertainly copied in his son, since no man can ever be sure of his paternity the way a mother is sure that a child is truly hers; yet the child consumes much of the father's *substance*) 123 **serve** (1) suffice (2) be inducted | **for summer** (when shade is desirable) 124 **shadows** fictitious names for which the officer in charge receives pay | **fill** to fill 133 **the whole . . . pins** he's pinned together, badly made physically, and therefore needs no more pinpricks (in a carpentry metaphor, the *pins* are also pegs for joining timber) 135 **can do it** know how to make a joke

SHALLOW   Shall I prick him, sir?   140

FALSTAFF   You may. But if he had been a man's tailor, he'd a'
   pricked° you.—Wilt thou make as many holes in an enemy's
   battle° as thou hast done in a woman's petticoat?

FEEBLE   I will do my good will, sir. You can have no more.

FALSTAFF   Well said, good woman's tailor! Well said, courageous   145
   Feeble! Thou wilt be as valiant as the wrathful dove or most
   magnanimous° mouse. Prick the woman's tailor. Well,
   Master Shallow, deep, Master Shallow.

FEEBLE   I would Wart might have gone, sir.

FALSTAFF   I would thou wert a man's tailor, that thou mightst   150
   mend him and make him fit to go. I cannot put him to° a
   private soldier that is the leader of so many thousands.° Let
   that suffice, most forcible Feeble.

FEEBLE   It shall suffice, sir.

FALSTAFF   I am bound° to thee, reverend Feeble. Who is next?   155

SHALLOW   Peter Bullcalf o'th' green!

                                                [Enter Bullcalf]

FALSTAFF   Yea, marry, let's see Bullcalf.

BULLCALF   Here, sir.

FALSTAFF   'Fore God, a likely° fellow! Come, prick me Bullcalf
   till he roar again.   160

BULLCALF   Oh, Lord! Good my lord Captain—

FALSTAFF   What, dost thou roar before thou art pricked?

BULLCALF   Oh, Lord, sir! I am a diseased man.

FALSTAFF   What disease hast thou?

BULLCALF   A whoreson cold, sir, a cough, sir, which I caught   165
   with ringing in the King's affairs upon his coronation day,°
   sir.

FALSTAFF   Come, thou shalt go to the wars in a gown.° We will
   have away° thy cold, and I will take such order° that thy
   friends shall ring for thee.°—Is here all?   170

141–2 a' pricked (1) have attired (2) have thrust you through (with suggestion of
male sexual penetration of the male; tailors were often considered effeminate)
143 battle army   **147 magnanimous** stouthearted   **151 put him to** enlist him as
152 thousands of vermin, lice   **155 bound** obliged   **159 likely** able-bodied
166 ringing . . . day ringing the church bells to celebrate the anniversary of the
King's coronation   **168 gown** dressing gown   **169 have away** do away with | **take
such order** provide   **170 for thee** (1) in your place (2) at your death

SHALLOW   Here is two more called than your number; you
must have but four here, sir. And so, I pray you, go in with
me to dinner.

FALSTAFF   Come, I will go drink with you, but I cannot tarry°
dinner. I am glad to see you, by my troth, Master Shallow.   175

SHALLOW   Oh, Sir John, do you remember since° we lay all
night in the Windmill° in Saint George's Field?°

FALSTAFF   No more of that, good Master Shallow, no more of
that.

SHALLOW   Ha! 'Twas a merry night. And is Jane Nightwork   180
alive?

FALSTAFF   She lives, Master Shallow.

SHALLOW   She never could away with° me.

FALSTAFF   Never, never; she would always say she could not
abide Master Shallow.   185

SHALLOW   By the Mass, I could anger her to the heart. She was
then a bona-roba. Doth she hold her own well?

FALSTAFF   Old, old, Master Shallow.

SHALLOW   Nay, she must be old. She cannot choose but be old.
Certain she's old, and had Robin Nightwork by old   190
Nightwork before I came to Clement's Inn.

SILENCE   That's fifty-five year ago.

SHALLOW   Ha, cousin Silence, that thou hadst seen that that
this knight and I have seen! Ha, Sir John, said I well?

FALSTAFF   We have heard the chimes at midnight, Master   195
Shallow.

SHALLOW   That we have, that we have, in faith, Sir John, we
have. Our watchword was "Hem, boys!"° Come, let's to
dinner, come, let's to dinner. Jesus, the days that we have
seen! Come, come.   200

Exeunt [*Falstaff and the Justices*]

BULLCALF   Good Master Corporate° Bardolph, stand° my
friend, and here's four Harry ten shillings° in French crowns

174 **tarry** spare the time for   176 **since** when   177 **the Windmill** a brothel, or an
inn in a brothel district | **Saint George's Field** a popular place of resort on the south
bank of the Thames   183 **away with** tolerate   198 **Hem, boys!** down the hatch!
201 **Corporate** (for "Corporal") | **stand** be, act as   202 **Harry ten shillings** money
coined in the reign of Henry VII, current in late Elizabethan times at half the face
value (the reference is anachronistic; four such coins would be worth twenty
shillings, or one pound; Bullcalf gives his bribe in *French crowns*, worth four
shillings each; presumably he gives five such coins)

for you. [*He gives money*] In very truth, sir, I had as lief° be hanged, sir, as go. And yet for mine own part, sir, I do not care, but rather because I am unwilling, and for mine own 205 part have a desire to stay with my friends. Else, sir, I did not care, for mine own part, so much.

BARDOLPH Go to, stand aside.

MOLDY And, good Master Corporal Captain, for my old dame's sake, stand my friend. She has nobody to do anything° about 210 her when I am gone, and she is old and cannot help herself. [*He gives money*] You shall have forty,° sir.

BARDOLPH Go to, stand aside.

FEEBLE By my troth, I care not. A man can die but once. We owe God a death. I'll ne'er bear a base mind. An't be my 215 destiny, so; an't be not, so. No man's too good to serve 's prince. And let it go which way it will, he that dies this year is quit° for the next.

BARDOLPH Well said. Thou'rt a good fellow.

FEEBLE Faith, I'll bear° no base mind. 220

Enter Falstaff and the Justices

FALSTAFF Come, sir, which men shall I have?

SHALLOW Four of which you please.

BARDOLPH [*to Falstaff*] Sir, a word with you. [*Aside*] I have three pound to free Moldy and Bullcalf.

FALSTAFF Go to, well.° 225

SHALLOW Come, Sir John, which four will you have?

FALSTAFF Do you choose for me.

SHALLOW Marry, then, Moldy, Bullcalf, Feeble, and Shadow.

FALSTAFF Moldy and Bullcalf: for° you, Moldy, stay at home till you are past service;° and for your part, Bullcalf, grow 230 till you come unto it.° I will none of you.

SHALLOW Sir John, Sir John, do not yourself wrong. They are your likeliest men, and I would have you served with the best.

---

203 **lief** willingly   209–10 **old dame's . . . do anything** (with a sexually equivocal suggestion of mother or wife; see similar innuendo at l. 105)   212 **forty** forty shillings   218 **quit** free, clear   220 **bear** have   225 **Go to, well** all right, fine, say no more   229 **for** as for   230 **past service** (1) too old to serve militarily (2) too old for sexual functioning   231 **come unto it** (1) are a man old enough to fight (2) have arrived at sexual maturity

FALSTAFF Will you tell me, Master Shallow, how to choose a 235
man? Care I for the limb, the thews,° the stature, bulk, and
big assemblance° of a man? Give me the spirit, Master
Shallow. Here's Wart; you see what a ragged appearance it
is. 'A shall charge you and discharge you° with the motion
of a pewterer's hammer,° come off and on swifter than he 240
that gibbets on the brewer's bucket.° And this same half-
faced° fellow, Shadow; give me this man. He presents no
mark to the enemy; the foeman may with as great aim°
level° at the edge of a penknife. And for a retreat, how
swiftly will this Feeble the woman's tailor run off! Oh, give 245
me the spare men, and spare me the great ones.—Put me a
caliver° into Wart's hand, Bardolph.
BARDOLPH [*giving Wart a musket*] Hold, Wart, traverse.° Thus,
thus, thus.
FALSTAFF Come, manage me your caliver. So. [*Wart performs* 250
maneuvers with the musket.] Very well. Go to. Very good,
exceeding good. Oh, give me always a little, lean, old,
chapped, bald shot.° Well said,° i'faith, Wart, thou'rt a good
scab.° Hold, there's a tester° for thee.
                                              [*He gives sixpence*]
SHALLOW He is not his craft's master; he doth not do it right. I 255
remember at Mile End Green,° when I lay° at Clement's
Inn—I was then Sir Dagonet in Arthur's show°—there was a
little quiver° fellow, and 'a would manage you his piece°
thus [*Shallow demonstrates*], and 'a would about and
about, and come you in and come you in.° "Ra-ta-ta!" 260

236 **thews** strength 237 **assemblance** appearance, frame 239 **charge . . . discharge you** load and fire 239–40 **motion . . . hammer** precise, quick motion
240–1 **come . . . bucket** raise and lower his musket quicker than a brewer's man
raises and lowers the beam (*bucket*) of the brewer's yoke across his shoulders
241–2 **half-faced** thin-faced (alludes to the profile portraits on coins) 243 **as great
aim** as much likelihood of hitting the target 244 **level** aim 247 **caliver** light
musket 248 **traverse** march, or, perhaps, perform the manual of arms, an exercise
drill with a musket 253 **shot** marksman | **Well said** well done 254 **scab** rascal
(punning on the name *Wart*) | **tester** sixpence 256 **Mile End Green** a drilling
ground for citizen soldiers, to the east of London | **lay** lodged 257 **Sir . . . show**
(an exhibition of archery was held annually at Mile End Green, called "Arthur's
show," in which each archer took the name of one of King Arthur's knights;
Shallow played the part of Sir Dagonet, Arthur's fool) 258 **quiver** nimble | **piece**
firearm 259–60 **'a would . . . you in** he was skillful at firing and then running
around to the rear rank of musketeers to reload while the next rank fired, and so on

would 'a say, "Bounce,°" would 'a say, and away again
would 'a go, and again would 'a come. I shall ne'er see such
a fellow.

FALSTAFF   These fellows will do well, Master Shallow. God
keep you, Master Silence. I will not use many words with   265
you. Fare you well, gentlemen both. I thank you. I must a
dozen mile tonight. Bardolph, give the soldiers coats.

SHALLOW   Sir John, the Lord bless you! God prosper your
affairs! God send us peace! At your return, visit our house;
let our old acquaintance be renewed. Peradventure I will   270
with ye to the court.

FALSTAFF   'Fore God, would you would.

SHALLOW   Go to; I have spoke at a word.° God keep you.

FALSTAFF   Fare you well, gentle gentlemen.

Exit [Shallow with Silence]

On, Bardolph; lead the men away.   275

[Exeunt Bardolph, recruits, etc.]

As I return, I will fetch off° these justices. I do see the
bottom of Justice Shallow. Lord, Lord, how subject we old
men are to this vice of lying! This same starved justice hath
done nothing but prate to me of the wildness of his youth
and the feats he hath done about Turnbull Street,° and every   280
third word a lie, duer° paid to the hearer than the Turk's
tribute.° I do remember him at Clement's Inn like a man
made after supper of a cheese paring. When 'a was naked,
he was, for all the world, like a forked radish, with a head
fantastically carved upon it with a knife. 'A was so forlorn°   285
that his dimensions to any thick° sight were invisible.° 'A
was the very genius° of famine, yet lecherous as a monkey,
and the whores called him mandrake.° 'A came ever in the
rearward of the fashion, and sung those tunes to the
overscutched huswives° that he heard the carmen° whistle,   290

261 **Bounce** bang   273 **I have . . . word** I mean what I say   276 **fetch off** get the
better of   280 **Turnbull Street** a street in Clerkenwell, ill-reputed   281 **duer** more
promptly   281–2 **Turk's tribute** tribute money paid annually to the Sultan of
Turkey by merchants and others   285 **forlorn** meager, thin   286 **thick** imperfect |
invisible (some editors retain the reading of the Quarto and the Folio, "invincible,"
as meaning "invisible" or "indeterminable")   287 **genius** spirit, personification
288 **mandrake** root of a plant, said to resemble the body of a man   290 **overscutched
huswives** outworn and often-whipped prostitutes | **carmen** wagoners

and sware they were his fancies or his good-nights.° And now is this Vice's dagger° become a squire, and talks as familiarly of John o' Gaunt as if he had been sworn brother° to him, and I'll be sworn 'a ne'er saw him but once in the tilt-yard,° and then he burst his head° for crowding among 295 the marshal's men. I saw it, and told John o' Gaunt he beat his own name,° for you might have thrust him° and all his apparel into an eelskin; the case° of a treble hautboy° was a mansion for him, a court. And now has he land and beefs.° Well, I'll be acquainted with him if I return, and 't shall go 300 hard but I'll make him a philosopher's two stones to me.° If the young dace° be a bait for the old pike, I see no reason in the law of nature but I may snap at him. Let time shape, and there an end.   [*Exit*]

ACT 4
SCENE 1

Enter the Archbishop [of York], Mowbray, [Lord] Bardolph,
Hastings, [and others,] within the Forest of Gaultree

ARCHBISHOP What is this forest called?
HASTINGS 'Tis Gaultree Forest, an't° shall please Your Grace.
ARCHBISHOP Here stand, my lords, and send discoverers° forth
  To know° the numbers of our enemies.

291 fancies . . . good-nights impromptu love songs and serenades (of which he claimed authorship) **292 Vice's dagger** (the Vice, or comic character of the morality plays, was sometimes armed with a wooden dagger) **293 sworn brother** companion in arms who has taken a chivalric oath to share his fortunes **295 tilt-yard** tournament ground at Westminster | **he burst his head** he, Shallow, had his head beaten so that he bled **296–7 beat his own name** was thrashing a gaunt person **297 him** Shallow **298 case** instrument case | **hautboy** ancestor of the oboe (the *treble hautboy* was the smallest and narrowest of this family of instruments) **299 beefs** oxen **300–1 and 't . . . to me** and with any kind of luck I'll be able to turn Shallow into my philosopher's stone, supposedly able to change ordinary metal into gold and preserved youth and health (*two stones* also suggests "testicles") **302 dace** small fish used for live bait

4.1. Location: Yorkshire. Gaultree Forest. Summary: The rebels meet the Earl of Westmorland and argue over the moral nature of their acts. The Earl convinces the Archbishop that his complaints will be answered, together with a full pardon, though Mowbray is suspicious.
2 an't if it **3 discoverers** scouts **4 know** learn

HASTINGS We have sent forth already.

ARCHBISHOP   'Tis well done.   5
My friends and brethren in these great affairs,
I must acquaint you that I have received
New-dated letters from Northumberland,
Their cold° intent, tenor, and substance, thus:
Here doth he wish his person, with such powers°   10
As might hold sortance° with his quality,°
The which he could not levy. Whereupon
He is retired, to ripe his growing fortunes,°
To Scotland, and concludes in hearty prayers
That your attempts may overlive° the hazard   15
And fearful meeting of their opposite.°

MOWBRAY Thus do the hopes we have in him touch ground°
And dash themselves to pieces.

Enter Messenger

HASTINGS   Now, what news?

MESSENGER West of this forest, scarcely off a mile,
In goodly form comes on the enemy,   20
And, by the ground they hide, I judge their number
Upon or near the rate° of thirty thousand.

MOWBRAY The just proportion that we gave them out.°
Let us sway on° and face them in the field.

ARCHBISHOP What well-appointed° leader fronts° us here?   25

Enter Westmorland

MOWBRAY I think it is my lord of Westmorland.

WESTMORLAND Health and fair greeting from our general,
The Prince, Lord John and Duke of Lancaster.

ARCHBISHOP
Say on, my lord of Westmorland, in peace,
What doth concern your coming.°

WESTMORLAND   Then, my lord,   30
Unto Your Grace do I in chief address

---

9 **cold** dispiriting, gloomy 10 **powers** forces 11 **hold sortance** accord | **quality** rank 13 **ripe . . . fortunes** let his fortunes grow and ripen 15 **overlive** survive 16 **opposite** adversary 17 **touch ground** hit bottom 22 **rate** total 23 **The just . . . out** the precise number that we estimated 24 **sway on** advance 25 **well-appointed** well-armed | **fronts** confronts 30 **What . . . coming** what your coming means

The substance of my speech. If that° rebellion
Came like itself, in base and abject routs,°
Led on by bloody° youth, guarded° with rags,
And countenanced° by boys and beggary,°   35
I say, if damned commotion° so appeared
In his true, native, and most proper shape,
You, reverend father, and these noble lords
Had not been here to dress the ugly form
Of base and bloody insurrection   40
With your fair honors. You, Lord Archbishop,
Whose see° is by a civil° peace maintained,
Whose beard the silver hand of peace hath touched,
Whose learning and good letters° peace hath tutored,
Whose white investments figure° innocence,   45
The dove and very blessèd spirit of peace,
Wherefore do you so ill translate° yourself
Out of the speech of peace that bears such grace
Into the harsh and boist'rous tongue° of war,
Turning your books to graves, your ink to blood,   50
Your pens to lances, and your tongue divine
To a loud trumpet and a point of war?°
ARCHBISHOP   Wherefore do I this? So the question stands.
Briefly to this end: we° are all diseased,
And with our surfeiting and wanton° hours   55
Have brought ourselves into a burning fever,
And we must bleed° for it; of which disease
Our late King Richard, being infected, died.
But, my most noble lord of Westmorland,
I take not on me here as° a physician,   60
Nor do I as an enemy to peace
Troop in the throngs of military men,
But rather show° awhile like fearful war

32 **If that** if   33 **routs** mobs   34 **bloody** passionate | **guarded** adorned, trimmed
35 **countenanced** supported | **beggary** beggars   36 **commotion** tumult, sedition
42 **see** diocese | **civil** orderly, law-abiding   44 **good letters** scholarship   45 **invest-ments figure** vestments symbolize   47 **translate** (1) change from one language to another (2) transform   49 **tongue** language   52 **point of war** signal of war   54 **we** the whole commonwealth   55–79 **And . . . wrong** (omitted from the Quarto probably because of censorship, since these lines plead the cause of rebellion; also ll. 103–39)   55 **wanton** self-indulgent   57 **bleed** (1) be bled by a doctor (2) bleed in war   60 **take . . . as** do not now undertake the role of   63 **show** appear

To diet rank minds, sick of happiness,°
And purge th'obstructions which begin to stop   65
Our very veins of life. Hear me more plainly.
I have in equal balance° justly° weighed
What wrongs our arms may do, what wrongs we suffer,
And find our griefs° heavier than our offenses.
We see which way the stream of time doth run,   70
And are enforced from our most quiet there°
By the rough torrent of occasion,°
And have the summary of all our griefs,
When time shall serve, to show in articles;°
Which long ere this we offered to the King,   75
And might by no suit gain our audience.
When we are wronged and would unfold our griefs,
We are denied access unto his person
Even by those men that most have done us wrong.°
The dangers of the days but newly gone,   80
Whose memory is written on the earth
With yet-appearing blood, and the examples
Of every minute's instance,° present now,
Hath put us in these ill-beseeming° arms,
Not to break peace, or any branch of it,   85
But to establish here a peace indeed,
Concurring both in name and quality.°
WESTMORLAND   Whenever yet was your appeal denied?
Wherein have you been gallèd° by the King?
What peer hath been suborned to grate on° you,   90
That you should seal this lawless bloody book
Of forged rebellion with a seal divine°
And consecrate commotion's bitter edge?°

---

64 To . . . happiness to deny excess to those who are bloated with indolent luxury
67 equal balance balanced scales | justly exactly   69 griefs grievances   71 our . . .
there our greatest quiet therein, in the stream of time   72 occasion circumstances
74 articles specified items   83 Of . . . instance presented every minute   84 ill-
beseeming unsuitable, inappropriate   87 Concurring . . . quality a peace that will be
both in name and in fact   89 gallèd injured, made sore with chafing   90 suborned
. . . on induced to annoy, harass   91–2 That . . . divine that you should put your
seal of approval on this lawless and forged rebellion, much as if a bishop were
to license a seditious book   93 And . . . edge and sanctify the cruel sword-edge
of sedition

ARCHBISHOP   My brother general, the commonwealth;
  To brother born unhouseled cruelty   95
  I make my quarrel in particular.°
WESTMORLAND   There is no need of any such redress;
  Or if there were, it not belongs to you.
MOWBRAY   Why not to him in part,° and to us all
  That feel the bruises of the days before,   100
  And suffer the condition of these times
  To lay a heavy and unequal° hand
  Upon our honors?
WESTMORLAND   O my good Lord Mowbray,
  Construe the times to° their necessities,°
  And you shall say indeed it is the time,   105
  And not the King, that doth you injuries.
  Yet for your part, it not appears to me
  Either from the King or in the present time
  That you should have an inch of any ground
  To build a grief on. Were you not restored   110
  To all the Duke of Norfolk's seigniories,°
  Your noble and right well remembered father's?
MOWBRAY   What thing, in honor, had my father lost,
  That need to be revived and breathed° in me?
  The King that loved him, as the state° stood then,   115
  Was force perforce° compelled to banish him;
  And then that Henry Bolingbroke and he,
  Being mounted and both rousèd in their seats,°
  Their neighing coursers daring of the spur,°
  Their armèd staves in charge,° their beavers° down,   120
  Their eyes of fire sparkling through sights° of steel,

94–6 My brother . . . particular (the text is corrupt here, but the general sense seems to be: the grievances of my brother-Englishmen and the cruelty shown to my blood brother Scroop [who was executed at Bristol by Henry IV; see *1 Henry IV*, 1.3.269] provoke me to make this cause my own; *unhouseled* means "denied extreme unction")   **99 Why . . . part** why shouldn't redress belong in some measure to the Archbishop for the killing of his brother, Scroop   **102 unequal** unjust   **104 to** according to | **their necessities** that which is necessary in a time of disorder and civil strife   **111 seigniories** properties, estates   **114 breathed** given the breath of life   **115 state** condition of things   **116 force perforce** willy-nilly (for the banishment of Mowbray by Richard II, see *Richard II*, 1.1 and 1.3)   **118 rousèd . . . seats** raised in their saddles   **119 daring of the spur** eager to be urged on   **120 armèd . . . charge** lances ready for the charge | **beavers** movable visors of helmets   **121 sights** eye slits

And the loud trumpet blowing them together,
Then, then, when there was nothing could have stayed
My father from the breast of Bolingbroke,
Oh, when the King did throw his warder° down—   125
His own life hung upon the staff he threw—
Then threw he down himself and all their lives
That by indictment and by dint of sword°
Have since miscarried under Bolingbroke.

WESTMORLAND
You speak, Lord Mowbray, now you know not what.   130
The Earl of Hereford° was reputed then
In England the most valiant gentleman.
Who knows on whom fortune would then have smiled?
But if your father had been victor there,
He ne'er had borne it out of Coventry;°   135
For all the country in a general voice
Cried hate upon him, and all their prayers and love
Were set on Hereford, whom they doted on,
And blessed, and graced, indeed more than the King.
But this is mere digression from my purpose.   140
Here come I from our princely general
To know your griefs, to tell you from His Grace
That he will give you audience; and wherein°
It shall appear that your demands are just,
You shall enjoy them, everything set off°   145
That might so much as think you° enemies.

MOWBRAY   But he hath forced us to compel this offer,
And it proceeds from policy, not love.

WESTMORLAND   Mowbray, you overween° to take it so.
This offer comes from mercy, not from fear.   150
For, lo, within a ken° our army lies,
Upon mine honor, all too confident
To give admittance to a thought of fear.
Our battle° is more full of names° than yours,

---

125 **warder** staff of command   128 **That . . . sword** that either through the
miscarriage of justice or by the brute force of the sword   131 **Earl of Hereford**
Bolingbroke, later King Henry IV   135 **borne . . . Coventry** carried away the prize
from Coventry, where the trial by combat was to have been held   143 **wherein**
wherever   145 **set off** set aside   146 **think you** make you seem   149 **overween** are
arrogant or presumptuous   151 **a ken** sight   154 **battle** army | **names** noble names

Our men more perfect in the use of arms,   155
Our armor all as strong, our cause the best.
Then reason will° our hearts should be as good.
Say you not then our offer is compelled.
MOWBRAY   Well, by my will° we shall admit no parley.°
WESTMORLAND   That argues but the shame of your offense.   160
A rotten case° abides° no handling.
HASTINGS   Hath the Prince John a full commission,
In very ample virtue° of his father,
To hear and absolutely to determine
Of what conditions we shall stand upon?°   165
WESTMORLAND   That is intended° in the General's name.°
I muse° you make so slight a question.
ARCHBISHOP [*giving a document*]
Then take, my lord of Westmorland, this schedule,
For this contains our general grievances.
Each several article herein redressed,   170
All members of our cause, both here and hence,
That are insinewed to this action,
Acquitted by a true substantial form
And present execution of our wills
To us and to our purposes confined,   175
We come within our awful banks again°
And knit our powers to the arm of peace.
WESTMORLAND   This will I show the General. Please you, lords,
In sight of both our battles° we may meet,
And either end in peace—which God so frame!°—   180
Or to the place of difference° call the swords
Which must decide it.
ARCHBISHOP   My lord, we will do so.

                                             Exit Westmorland

---

157 reason will it stands to reason that   **159 by my will** as far as I'm concerned |
admit no parley agree to no conference   **161 case** (1) container (2) cause | **abides**
tolerates   **163 very ample virtue** full authority   **164–5 To hear . . . upon?** to hear our
grievances and be able to make a final decision regarding the terms we insist upon?
166 intended understood, implied | **name** title   **167 muse** wonder   **170–6 Each . . .
again** provided that each separate article herein is redressed, and that all members
who are joined together in this action are pardoned, both here and henceforward, by
a formal agreement and by immediate satisfaction of our demands as regards us and
our intents, we will return into the bounds of respect imposed by our reverence for
royal authority   **179 battles** armies   **180 frame** bring about   **181 difference** conflict

MOWBRAY   There is a thing within my bosom tells me
That no conditions of our peace can stand.
HASTINGS   Fear you not that. If we can make our peace   185
Upon such large° terms and so absolute
As our conditions shall consist° upon,
Our peace shall stand as firm as rocky mountains.
MOWBRAY   Yea, but our valuation° shall be such
That every slight and false-derivèd cause,   190
Yea, every idle, nice, and wanton° reason,
Shall to the King taste of this action,
That, were our royal faiths martyrs in love,°
We shall be winnowed with so rough a wind
That even our corn° shall seem as light as chaff   195
And good from bad find no partition.°
ARCHBISHOP   No, no, my lord. Note this: the King is weary
Of dainty and such picking° grievances;
For he hath found to end one doubt° by death
Revives two greater in the heirs of life,°   200
And therefore will he wipe his tables° clean
And keep no telltale to his memory
That may repeat and history° his loss
To new remembrance. For full well he knows
He cannot so precisely° weed this land   205
As his misdoubts° present occasion.
His foes are so enrooted with his friends
That, plucking to unfix an enemy,
He doth unfasten so and shake a friend.
So that this land, like an offensive wife   210
That hath enraged him on to offer strokes,
As he is striking, holds his infant up
And hangs resolved correction° in the arm
That was upreared to execution.

---

186 large liberal   **187 consist** insist   **189 our valuation** the King's estimation of us
191 idle . . . wanton foolish, petty, and frivolous   **193 That . . . love** so that even if
our allegiance to the King were as strong as the devotion of martyrs   **195 corn**
grain, wheat   **196 partition** distinction   **198 picking** fastidious, trivial   **199 doubt**
danger, source of fear   **200 heirs of life** those who survive   **201 tables** tablets,
notebooks   **203 history** record, chronicle   **205 precisely** thoroughly   **206 misdoubts**
suspicions   **213 hangs resolved correction** interrupts in mid-action the punishment
that was intended

HASTINGS   Besides, the King hath wasted all his rods°   215
On late° offenders, that he now doth lack
The very instruments of chastisement,
So that his power, like to a fangless lion,
May offer, but not hold.°
ARCHBISHOP   'Tis very true.
And therefore be assured, my good Lord Marshal,   220
If we do now make our atonement° well,
Our peace will, like a broken limb united,
Grow stronger for the breaking.
MOWBRAY   Be it so.
Here is returned my lord of Westmorland.

Enter Westmorland

WESTMORLAND
The Prince is here at hand. Pleaseth° Your Lordship   225
To meet His Grace just distance° 'tween our armies.
MOWBRAY
Your Grace of York, in God's name then set forward.
ARCHBISHOP   Before,° and greet His Grace.—My lord, we come.

ACT 4
SCENE 2

Enter Prince John [of Lancaster] and his army

PRINCE JOHN
You are well encountered here, my cousin° Mowbray.
Good day to you, gentle° Lord Archbishop,
And so to you, Lord Hastings, and to all.

---

215 **wasted . . . rods** exhausted the supply of whipping rods, spent all his punishments   216 **late** other recent   219 **offer . . . hold** threaten violence but not hold fast   221 **atonement** reconciliation   225 **Pleaseth** may it please   226 **just distance** halfway   228 **Before** go before

4.2. Location: This scene is apparently continuous with the previous scene. In the Quarto, Prince John and his army enter before the last two lines of 4.1. Summary: Hal's brother, Prince John, accepts the rebels' claims, but once they disband their forces, he and Westmorland surprise them, arresting them for treason and sending them to their deaths. (In some editions this action is part of 4.1, with succeeding scenes renumbered accordingly.)

1 **cousin** (normal address of royal family to a duke)   2 **gentle** noble

My lord of York, it better showed with you°
When that your flock, assembled by the bell,   5
Encircled you to hear with reverence
Your exposition on the holy text
Than now to see you here an iron man,°
Cheering a rout° of rebels with your drum,
Turning the word° to sword and life to death.   10
That man that sits within a monarch's heart
And ripens in the sunshine of his favor,
Would he° abuse the countenance° of the King,
Alack, what mischiefs might he set abroach°
In shadow of such greatness!° With you, Lord Bishop,   15
It is even° so. Who hath not heard it spoken
How deep you were within the books of God,°
To us the speaker° in his parliament,
To us th'imagined voice of God himself,
The very opener and intelligencer°   20
Between the grace, the sanctities, of heaven
And our dull workings?° Oh, who shall believe
But you misuse the reverence of your place,
Employ the countenance and grace of heav'n
As a false favorite doth his prince's name,   25
In deeds dishonorable? You have ta'en up,°
Under the counterfeited zeal of God,
The subjects of His substitute,° my father,
And both against the peace of heaven and him
Have here up-swarmed° them.
ARCHBISHOP   Good my lord of Lancaster,   30
  I am not here against your father's peace;
  But, as I told my lord of Westmorland,
  The time misordered° doth, in common sense,°

---

4 it . . . you it showed you to better advantage   **8 iron man** (1) warrior clad in armor (2) merciless fighter   **9 rout** mob   **10 the word** the word of God, the Scriptures   **13 Would he** if he should choose to | **countenance** favor   **14 set abroach** set aflowing, begin   **15 In shadow . . . greatness** furtively, not in the open *sunshine* of the King's favor (l. 12)   **16 even** just   **17 within . . . God** (1) versed in works of divinity (2) in God's good graces   **18 speaker** spokesman for God, just as the Speaker of Parliament spoke in the name of the King   **20 opener and intelligencer** interpreter and messenger   **22 dull workings** imperfect human perceptions   **26 ta'en up** enlisted   **28 His substitute** God's deputy   **30 up-swarmed** raised up in swarms   **33 time misordered** disorders of the time | **in common sense** as anyone can see

Crowd us and crush us to this monstrous form
To hold our safety up. I sent Your Grace   35
The parcels° and particulars of our grief,°
The which hath been with scorn shoved from the court,
Whereon this Hydra° son of war is born,
Whose dangerous eyes° may well be charmed asleep
With grant of our most just and right desires,   40
And true obedience, of this madness cured,
Stoop tamely to the foot of majesty.
MOWBRAY   If not, we ready are to try our fortunes
To the last man.
HASTINGS   And though° we here fall down,
We have supplies° to second our attempt;   45
If they miscarry,° theirs° shall second them,
And so success° of mischief shall be born,
And heir from heir shall hold this quarrel up
Whiles England shall have generation.°
PRINCE JOHN
You are too shallow, Hastings, much too shallow,   50
To sound the bottom of the aftertimes.°
WESTMORLAND   Pleaseth° Your Grace to answer them directly
How far forth you do like their articles.
PRINCE JOHN   I like them all, and do allow° them well,
And swear here, by the honor of my blood,   55
My father's purposes have been mistook,
And some about him have too lavishly°
Wrested his meaning and authority.
My lord, these griefs shall be with speed redressed,
Upon my soul, they shall. If this may please you,   60
Discharge your powers° unto their several° counties,
As we will ours; and here between the armies
Let's drink together friendly and embrace,

---

36 parcels items, details | **grief** grievances   **38 Hydra** (the Lernaean Hydra was a
fabulous monster with several heads; when one was cut off, others grew in its place)
39 eyes (the image here conflates Hydra with Argus, Juno's watchful guard with
one hundred eyes, who was charmed asleep by Mercury's music)   **44 though** even
if   **45 supplies** forces in reserve   **46 miscarry** come to grief | **theirs** their
reinforcements   **47 success** succession   **49 generation** issue, offspring   **51 sound . . .
aftertimes** predict what the future will bring (*sound the bottom* means "plumb the
depths")   **52 Pleaseth** May it please   **54 allow** approve, sanction   **57 lavishly**
loosely, negligently   **61 powers** forces | **several** respective

That all their eyes may bear those tokens home
Of our restorèd love and amity.   65
ARCHBISHOP   I take your princely word for these redresses.
PRINCE JOHN   I give it you, and will maintain my word,
  And thereupon I drink unto Your Grace.
                              [*They drink together, and embrace*]
HASTINGS   Go, Captain, and deliver to the army
  This news of peace. Let them have pay, and part.°   70
  I know it will well please them. Hie thee, Captain.
                                            [*Exit a Captain*]
ARCHBISHOP   To you, my noble lord of Westmorland.
WESTMORLAND
  I pledge Your Grace; and, if you knew what pains
  I have bestowed to breed this present peace,
  You would drink freely. But my love to ye   75
  Shall show itself more openly hereafter.
ARCHBISHOP   I do not doubt you.
WESTMORLAND   I am glad of it.
  Health to my lord and gentle cousin, Mowbray.
MOWBRAY   You wish me health in very happy season,°
  For I am on the sudden something° ill.   80
ARCHBISHOP   Against° ill chances men are ever merry,
  But heaviness foreruns the good event.°
WESTMORLAND   Therefore be merry, coz,° since sudden sorrow
  Serves to say thus, "Some good thing comes tomorrow."
ARCHBISHOP   Believe me, I am passing° light in spirit.   85
MOWBRAY   So much the worse, if your own rule be true.
                                            Shout [*within*]
PRINCE JOHN
  The word of peace is rendered.° Hark, how they shout!
MOWBRAY   This had been° cheerful after victory.
ARCHBISHOP   A peace is of the nature of a conquest,
  For then both parties nobly are subdued,   90
  And neither party loser.
PRINCE JOHN [*to Westmorland*]   Go, my lord,

---

70 **part** depart   79 **in . . . season** at an opportune moment   80 **something**
somewhat   81 **Against** when about to face   82 **heaviness . . . event** sadness comes
over men prior to a happy outcome   83 **coz** cousin, kinsman   85 **passing**
surpassingly   87 **rendered** proclaimed   88 **had been** would have been

And let our army be dischargèd too.

                    [Exit Westmorland]

And, good my lord, so please you, let our trains°
March by us, that we may peruse the men
We should have coped withal.°

ARCHBISHOP   Go, good Lord Hastings,   95
And ere they be dismissed, let them march by.

                      [Exit Hastings]

PRINCE JOHN   I trust, lords, we shall lie° tonight together.

                   Enter Westmorland

Now cousin, wherefore° stands our army still?

WESTMORLAND   The leaders, having charge° from you to stand,
Will not go off until they hear you speak.   100

PRINCE JOHN   They know their duties.

                     Enter Hastings

HASTINGS *[to the Archbishop]*
My lord, our army is dispersed already.
Like youthful steers unyoked, they take their courses
East, west, north, south, or, like a school broke up,
Each hurries toward his home and sporting-place.   105

WESTMORLAND   Good tidings, my lord Hastings, for the which
I do arrest thee, traitor, of high treason.
And you, Lord Archbishop, and you, Lord Mowbray,
Of capital° treason I attach° you both.

MOWBRAY   Is this proceeding just and honorable?   110

WESTMORLAND   Is your assembly so?

ARCHBISHOP
Will you thus break your faith?

PRINCE JOHN   I pawned° thee none.
I promised you redress of these same grievances
Whereof you did complain, which, by mine honor,
I will perform with a most Christian care.   115
But for° you rebels, look° to taste the due
Meet° for rebellion and such acts as yours.

93 **trains** followers, armies   95 **coped withal** encountered, fought with   97 **lie** lodge (with perhaps a hidden suggestion of "tell untruths")   98 **wherefore** why   99 **charge** command   109 **capital** punishable by death | **attach** arrest   112 **pawned** pledged   116 **for** as for | **look** expect   117 **Meet** fitting

Most shallowly° did you these arms° commence,
Fondly° brought here and foolishly sent hence.—
Strike up our drums; pursue the scattered stray.°   120
God, and not we, hath safely fought today.
Some guard these traitors to the block of death,
Treason's true bed and yielder-up of breath.

[*Exeunt*]

ACT 4
SCENE 3

Alarum. Excursions.° Enter Falstaff
[and Sir John Coleville, meeting]

FALSTAFF What's your name, sir? Of what condition° are you,
and of what place?

COLEVILLE I am a knight, sir, and my name is Coleville of the
Dale.

FALSTAFF Well, then, Coleville is your name, a knight is your   5
degree, and your place the Dale. Coleville shall be still
your name, a traitor your degree, and the dungeon your
place, a place deep enough; so shall you be still Coleville of
the Dale.°

COLEVILLE Are not you Sir John Falstaff?   10

FALSTAFF As good a man as he, sir, whoe'er I am. Do ye yield,
sir, or shall I sweat for you? If I do sweat, they are the drops°
of thy lovers,° and they weep for thy death. Therefore rouse
up fear and trembling, and do observance° to my mercy.

---

118 shallowly without due consideration | **arms** hostilities   **119 Fondly** foolishly
120 stray stragglers

4.3. Location: Gaultree Forest, as before. The scene is continuous. **Summary:** A
rebel surrenders to Falstaff, who makes much of his triumph. Prince John reacts
coolly to Falstaff's antics, and after he leaves, Falstaff diagnoses his problem as a
lack of wine.

0.1 *Alarum. Excursions* trumpet call and sallies of troops (here engaged in pursuing
the scattered stragglers [4.2.120] in the wake of the arrest of the rebel leaders)

1 condition rank   **7–9 dungeon . . . Dale** (Falstaff jests that a deep dungeon can be
thought of as a kind of *dale* or pit)   **12 drops** tears   **13 lovers** friends   **14 observance**
reverence, homage

COLEVILLE I think you are Sir John Falstaff, and in that 15
thought yield me.

FALSTAFF I have a whole school of tongues in this belly of mine,
and not a tongue of them all speaks any other word but my
name.° An I had but a belly of any indifferency,° I were°
simply the most active fellow in Europe. My womb,° my 20
womb, my womb undoes me. Here comes our general.

Enter [Prince] John [of Lancaster],
Westmorland, [Blunt,] and the rest

PRINCE JOHN The heat° is past; follow no further now.
Call in the powers, good cousin Westmorland.
                    [Exit Westmorland. Sound] retreat
Now, Falstaff, where have you been all this while?
When everything is ended, then you come. 25
These tardy tricks of yours will, on my life,
One time or other break some gallows' back.

FALSTAFF I would be sorry, my lord, but it should be thus.° I
never knew yet but rebuke and check° was the reward of
valor. Do you think me a swallow, an arrow, or a bullet? 30
Have I, in my poor and old motion, the expedition° of
thought? I have speeded hither with the very extremest inch°
of possibility. I have foundered nine score and odd posts,°
and here, travel-tainted as I am, have in my pure and
immaculate valor taken Sir John Coleville of the Dale, a 35
most furious knight and valorous enemy. But what of that?
He saw me and yielded, that I may justly say, with the hook-
nosed fellow of Rome,° "I came, saw, and overcame."

PRINCE JOHN It was more of his courtesy than your deserving.

FALSTAFF I know not. Here he is, and here I yield him. And I 40
beseech Your Grace, let it be booked° with the rest of this
day's deeds, or, by the Lord, I will have it in a particular
ballad° else,° with mine own picture on the top on't,

17–19 I have . . . name (Falstaff jests that his belly eloquently identifies him; *school*
means "large number") **19 indifferency** moderate size **│ were** would be **20 womb**
belly **22 heat** hot pursuit **28 but . . . thus** if it were otherwise (it is fitting, Falstaff
wryly says, that valor is never properly recognized, because that is how the world
goes) **29 check** reprimand **31 expedition** speed **32 very extremest inch** fullest extent
33 foundered . . . posts lamed at least 180 post-horses **37–8 hook-nosed . . . Rome**
Julius Caesar **41 booked** recorded by the chroniclers **42–3 a particular ballad** a
broadside ballad written and published on this particular episode **43 else** otherwise

Coleville kissing my foot. To the which course if I be
enforced, if you do not all show like gilt twopences to me,°   45
and I in the clear sky of fame o'ershine you as much as the
full moon doth the cinders of the element,° which show like
pins' heads to° her, believe not the word of the noble.
Therefore let me have right, and let desert mount.°
PRINCE JOHN   Thine's too heavy to mount.   50
FALSTAFF   Let it shine, then.
PRINCE JOHN   Thine's too thick° to shine.
FALSTAFF   Let it do something, my good lord, that may do me
good, and call it what you will.
PRINCE JOHN   Is thy name Coleville?   55
COLEVILLE   It is, my lord.
PRINCE JOHN   A famous rebel art thou, Coleville.
FALSTAFF   And a famous true subject took him.
COLEVILLE   I am, my lord, but as my betters are
That led me hither. Had they been ruled by me,°   60
You should have won them dearer° than you have.
FALSTAFF   I know not how they sold themselves. But thou, like
a kind fellow, gavest thyself away gratis, and I thank thee
for thee.

Enter Westmorland

PRINCE JOHN   Now, have you left pursuit?   65
WESTMORLAND   Retreat is made and execution stayed.°
PRINCE JOHN   Send Coleville with his confederates
To York, to present° execution.
Blunt, lead him hence, and see you guard him sure.
                    [*Exit Blunt with Coleville*]
And now dispatch we° toward the court, my lords.   70
I hear the King my father is sore sick.
Our news shall go before us to His Majesty,
Which, cousin,° you shall bear to comfort him,
And we with sober° speed will follow you.

45 **if . . . to me** if you do not all look like counterfeit coins (literally, twopenny pieces
gilded to resemble half-crowns worth thirty pence each) in comparison with me
47 **cinders . . . element** stars   48 **to** compared with   49 **desert mount** merit ascend,
be promoted   52 **thick** (1) opaque, dim (2) heavy   60 **been ruled by me** listened to
my advice   61 **dearer** at greater military cost   66 **Retreat . . . stayed** the order for
withdrawal has been sounded, and the slaughter has been stopped   68 **present**
immediate   70 **dispatch we** let us hasten   73 **cousin** Westmorland   74 **sober** deliberate

FALSTAFF   My lord, I beseech you give me leave to go through   75
Gloucestershire, and, when you come to court, stand my
good lord° in your good report.

PRINCE JOHN   Fare you well, Falstaff. I, in my condition,°
Shall better speak of you than you deserve.

[Exeunt all but Falstaff]

FALSTAFF   I would you had but the wit; 'twere better than your   80
dukedom. Good faith, this same young sober-blooded boy
doth not love me, nor a man cannot make him laugh. But
that's no marvel; he drinks no wine. There's never none of
these demure boys come to any proof,° for thin drink doth so
overcool their blood, and making many fish meals, that they   85
fall into a kind of male greensickness,° and then, when they
marry, they get wenches.° They are generally fools and
cowards, which some of us should be too, but for
inflammation.° A good sherris sack° hath a twofold
operation in it. It ascends me° into the brain, dries me there   90
all the foolish and dull and crudy vapors° which environ it,
makes it apprehensive,° quick, forgetive,° full of nimble,
fiery, and delectable shapes, which, delivered o'er to the
voice, the tongue, which is the birth, becomes excellent wit.°
The second property of your excellent sherris is the warming   95
of the blood, which, before cold and settled, left the liver°
white and pale, which is the badge of pusillanimity and
cowardice. But the sherris warms it and makes it course°
from the innards to the parts' extremes.° It illumineth the
face, which as a beacon gives warning to all the rest of this   100
little kingdom, man, to arm; and then the vital commoners
and inland petty spirits muster me all to their captain, the
heart,° who, great and puffed up with this retinue, doth any
deed of courage; and this valor comes of sherris. So that skill

76–7 **stand my good lord** act as my patron   78 **condition** function as commander
84 **come to any proof** stand up well under testing, turn out well   86 **greensickness** a
kind of anemia thought to affect young women   87 **get wenches** beget girls
89 **inflammation** spirits inflamed by liquor | **sherris sack** sherry   90 **ascends me**
ascends (*me* is used colloquially, as also in l. 102)   91 **crudy vapors** curdled
exhalations (ascending from the body to the brain, thereby obstructing it)
92 **apprehensive** quick to perceive | **forgetive** inventive   94 **wit** verbal dexterity
96 **liver** (thought to be the seat of courage)   98 **course** run   99 **the parts' extremes**
the body's various extremities   101–3 **and then . . . heart** and then the vital spirits
that function in the body's interior, like troops of commoners all rally to the support
of their leader, the heart

in the weapon is nothing without sack, for that sets it a- 105
work, and learning a mere hoard of gold kept by a devil till
sack commences it and sets it in act and use.° Hereof comes
it that Prince Harry is valiant, for the cold blood he did
naturally inherit of his father, he hath, like lean,° sterile, and
bare land, manured, husbanded,° and tilled with excellent 110
endeavor of drinking good and good store° of fertile sherris,
that he is become very hot and valiant. If I had a thousand
sons, the first human° principle I would teach them should be
to forswear thin potations° and to addict themselves to sack.

Enter Bardolph

How now, Bardolph?   115
BARDOLPH   The army is discharged all and gone.
FALSTAFF   Let them go. I'll through Gloucestershire, and there
   will I visit Master Robert Shallow, Esquire. I have him
   already tempering° between my finger and my thumb, and
   shortly will I seal with° him. Come away.   120

[Exeunt]

ACT 4
SCENE 4

Enter the King, Warwick, Thomas Duke of Clarence,
Humphrey [Duke] of Gloucester, [and others]

KING   Now, lords, if God doth give successful end
   To this debate° that bleedeth at our doors,
   We will our youth° lead on to higher fields°

106–7 and learning . . . use *and learning is a mere heap of uselessly acquired*
knowledge, a secret horde guarded over by some evil spirit, until wine releases its
potential (as at a university commencement) and transforms that potential into
intellectual adventurousness 109 lean *barren* 110 husbanded *cultivated* 111 good
and good store *good quality and plenty* 113 human *(1) mundane, worldly (2) manly*
(3) humane (so spelled in the Quarto) 114 potations *drinks* 119 tempering
softening (like a piece of wax) 120 seal with *shape him to my purposes; seal a*
bargain with (continuing the metaphor of sealing wax)

4.4. Location: King Henry's court at Westminster. The Jerusalem Chamber (adjoining
Westminster Abbey), so called for its various inscriptions concerning Jerusalem.
Summary: His health failing, King Henry longs for his crusade to the Holy Land
and worries about Hal. He collapses despite welcome news that the rebellion has
been crushed.
2 debate *strife* 3 our youth *our young men* | higher fields *a crusade to Palestine*

And draw no swords but what° are sanctified.
Our navy is addressed,° our power collected,   5
Our substitutes° in absence well invested,°
And everything lies level° to our wish.
Only we want° a little personal strength,
And pause us till these rebels now afoot
Come underneath the yoke of government.   10
WARWICK Both which we doubt not but Your Majesty
    Shall soon enjoy.
KING   Humphrey, my son of Gloucester,
    Where is the Prince your brother?
GLOUCESTER I think he's gone to hunt, my lord, at Windsor.
KING And how accompanied?
GLOUCESTER   I do not know, my lord.   15
KING Is not his brother Thomas of Clarence with him?
GLOUCESTER No, my good lord, he is in presence here.
CLARENCE What would my lord and father?
KING Nothing but well to thee, Thomas of Clarence.
    How chance thou art not with the Prince thy brother?   20
    He loves thee, and thou dost neglect him, Thomas;
    Thou hast a better place in his affection
    Than all thy brothers. Cherish it, my boy,
    And noble offices° thou mayst effect°
    Of mediation, after I am dead,   25
    Between his greatness and thy other brethren.
    Therefore omit° him not, blunt not his love,
    Nor lose the good advantage of his grace°
    By seeming cold or careless of his will.
    For he is gracious, if he be observed.°   30
    He hath a tear for pity and a hand
    Open as day for meting° charity.
    Yet notwithstanding, being incensed, he is flint,°
    As humorous° as winter, and as sudden
    As flaws congealèd° in the spring of day.°   35

---

4 **what** those that 5 **addressed** ready, prepared 6 **substitutes** deputies | **invested** appointed, empowered 7 **level** conformable 8 **want** lack 24 **offices** functions | **effect** perform, accomplish 27 **omit** neglect 28 **grace** favor 30 **observed** paid proper respect, humored 32 **meting** meting out, distributing 33 **flint** both in hardness and in giving off sparks 34 **humorous** capable of change in mood 35 **flaws congealèd** snow squalls | **spring of day** early morning

His temper,° therefore, must be well observed.
Chide him for faults, and do it reverently,
When you perceive his blood inclined to mirth;
But, being moody,° give him time and scope,
Till that his passions, like a whale on ground,   40
Confound° themselves with working.° Learn this, Thomas,
And thou shalt prove a shelter to thy friends,
A hoop of gold to bind thy brothers in,
That the united vessel of their blood,
Mingled with venom of suggestion—   45
As, force perforce, the age will pour it in—
Shall never leak, though it do work as strong
As aconitum or rash gunpowder.°
CLARENCE   I shall observe him with all care and love.
KING   Why art thou not at Windsor with him, Thomas?   50
CLARENCE   He is not there today; he dines in London.
KING   And how accompanied? Canst thou tell that?
CLARENCE   With Poins and other his continual followers.
KING   Most subject is the fattest° soil to weeds,
And he, the noble image of my youth,   55
Is overspread with them. Therefore my grief
Stretches itself beyond the hour of death.
The blood weeps from my heart when I do shape
In forms imaginary th'unguided days
And rotten times that you shall look upon   60
When I am sleeping with my ancestors.
For when his headstrong riot hath no curb,
When rage and hot blood are his counselors,
When means and lavish° manners meet together,
Oh, with what wings shall his affections° fly   65
Towards fronting peril and opposed decay!°

---

36 temper disposition 39 moody angry 41 Confound exhaust, consume |
working exertion 43–8 A hoop . . . gunpowder (the King urges Thomas to act like
a hoop of gold binding his brothers one to another, so that the chalice of kinship in
which their bloods are combined may never leak, even when their enemies will
attempt to pour into it the poison of mistrust; *suggestion* means "suspicion";
aconitum is a strong poison extracted from monkshood; *rash* means "quick-
acting") 54 fattest richest 64 lavish unrestrained, licentious 65 affections
inclinations 66 fronting . . . decay danger and ruin that confront him

WARWICK My gracious lord, you look beyond° him quite.
The Prince but studies his companions
Like a strange° tongue, wherein, to gain the language,
'Tis needful that the most immodest word   70
Be looked upon and learned, which, once attained,
Your Highness knows, comes to no further use
But to be known and hated. So, like gross terms,°
The Prince will in the perfectness of time
Cast off his followers, and their memory   75
Shall as a pattern or a measure live
By which His Grace must mete° the lives of other,°
Turning past evils to advantages.
KING 'Tis seldom when the bee doth leave her comb
In the dead carrion.°

Enter Westmorland

                Who's here? Westmorland?   80
WESTMORLAND Health to my sovereign, and new happiness
Added to that that I am to deliver!
Prince John your son doth kiss Your Grace's hand.
Mowbray, the Bishop Scroop, Hastings, and all
Are brought to the correction of your law.   85
There is not now a rebel's sword unsheathed,
But Peace puts forth her olive everywhere.
The manner how this action hath been borne
Here at more leisure may Your Highness read,
With every course in his° particular.°   90
                      [He gives a document]
KING Oh, Westmorland, thou art a summer bird,
Which ever in the haunch° of winter sings
The lifting up° of day.

Enter Harcourt

            Look, here's more news.

---

67 look beyond go too far in judging   **69 strange** foreign   **73 like gross terms** just
as with coarse expressions   **77 mete** measure, appraise | **other** others   **79–80 'Tis
. . . carrion** rarely does the bee that has made a honeycomb in dead carrion abandon
that honeycomb; the Prince will not forsake his corrupt delights   **90 course . . .
particular** event or phase set forth in detail | **his** its   **92 haunch** latter end   **93 lifting
up** dawn

HARCOURT   From enemies heaven keep Your Majesty,
    And, when they stand against you, may they fall   95
    As those that I am come to tell you of!
    The Earl Northumberland and the Lord Bardolph,
    With a great power of English and of Scots,
    Are by the sheriff of Yorkshire overthrown.
    The manner and true order of the fight   100
    This packet, please it you, contains at large.°
                                       [He gives letters]
KING   And wherefore should these good news make me sick?
    Will Fortune never come with both hands full,
    But write her fair words still° in foulest letters?
    She either gives a stomach° and no food—   105
    Such are the poor, in health; or else a feast
    And takes away the stomach—such are the rich
    That have abundance and enjoy it not.
    I should rejoice now at this happy news,
    And now my sight fails and my brain is giddy.   110
    Oh, me! Come near me. Now I am much ill.
               [The King swoons. Several come to his aid]
GLOUCESTER   Comfort, Your Majesty!
CLARENCE   O my royal father!
WESTMORLAND   My sovereign lord, cheer up yourself, look up.
WARWICK   Be patient, princes. You do know these fits
    Are with His Highness very ordinary.   115
    Stand from him, give him air; he'll straight be well.
CLARENCE   No, no, he cannot long hold out these pangs.
    Th'incessant care and labor of his mind
    Hath wrought the mure° that should confine it in
    So thin that life looks through and will break out.   120
GLOUCESTER   The people fear° me, for they do observe
    Unfathered heirs and loathly births of nature.°
    The seasons change their manners, as° the year
    Had found some months asleep and leapt them over.

---

101 at large in full   **104 still** always   **105 stomach** appetite   **119 wrought the mure** worn the wall   **121 fear** frighten   **121–2 they . . . nature** they take note of ominous signs, such as parthenogenic and other unnatural births   **123 as** as if

CLARENCE The river° hath thrice flowed, no ebb between, 125
    And the old folk, time's doting chronicles,
    Say it did so a little time before
    That our great-grandsire, Edward,° sicked° and died.
WARWICK Speak lower, princes, for the King recovers.
GLOUCESTER This apoplexy will certain be his end. 130
KING I pray you, take me up and bear me hence
    Into some other chamber. Softly, pray.

ACT 4
SCENE 5

[The King is borne to another part of the stage, to bed]

KING Let there be no noise made, my gentle friends,
    Unless some dull and favorable° hand
    Will whisper music to my weary spirit.
WARWICK Call for the music in the other room.
KING Set me the crown upon my pillow here. 5
CLARENCE His eye is hollow, and he changes much.
WARWICK Less noise, less noise!
                [The crown is placed on the King's pillow]

                        Enter [Prince] Harry

PRINCE   Who saw the Duke of Clarence?
CLARENCE I am here, brother, full of heaviness.°
PRINCE How now, rain° within doors, and none abroad?
    How doth the King? 10
GLOUCESTER Exceeding ill.
PRINCE Heard he the good news yet? Tell it him.
GLOUCESTER He altered much upon the hearing it.

---

125 river Thames (Holinshed records this event as having happened on October 12, 1412)   **128 Edward** Edward III | **sicked** fell sick

4.5. Location: The scene is continuous. Summary: Hal watches at his father's bedside and, thinking him dead, takes the crown. The King awakens, accuses Hal bitterly, and predicts the destruction of the realm. Hal begs and receives forgiveness from his father, who also advises him about rulership. The King asks to be returned to the Jerusalem room, whose name he claims fulfills a prophesy about his death.
2 dull and favorable soothing and kindly   **8 heaviness** sadness   **9 rain** tears

PRINCE   If he be sick with joy, he'll recover without physic.°

WARWICK

    Not so much noise, my lords. Sweet Prince, speak low.   15

    The King your father is disposed to sleep.

CLARENCE   Let us withdraw into the other room.

WARWICK   Will't please Your Grace to go along with us?

PRINCE   No, I will sit and watch here by the King.

            [*Exeunt all but the Prince and the King*]

    Why doth the crown lie there upon his pillow,   20

    Being so troublesome a bedfellow?

    O polished perturbation,° golden care,

    That keep'st the ports° of slumber open wide

    To many a watchful° night! Sleep with it° now;

    Yet not° so sound and half so deeply sweet   25

    As he whose brow with homely biggen° bound

    Snores out the watch of night.° O majesty,

    When thou dost pinch thy bearer, thou dost sit

    Like a rich armor worn in heat of day,

    That scald'st with safety.° By his gates of breath°   30

    There lies a downy feather which stirs not.

    Did he suspire,° that light and weightless down

    Perforce must move.—My gracious lord! My father!—

    This sleep is sound indeed. This is a sleep

    That from this golden rigol° hath divorced   35

    So many English kings. Thy due from me

    Is tears and heavy sorrows of the blood,°

    Which nature, love, and filial tenderness

    Shall, O dear father, pay thee plenteously.

    My due from thee is this imperial crown,   40

    Which, as immediate from° thy place and blood,

    Derives itself° to me. [*He puts on the crown*] Lo, where it sits,

    Which God shall guard. And put the world's whole strength°

---

14 physic medicine   **22 perturbation** cause of perturbation   **23 ports** gates   **24 watchful** wakeful | **Sleep with it** may you (King Henry) sleep even with this symbol of care beside you   **25 Yet not** yet your sleep will nonetheless not be   **26 biggen** nightcap   **27 Snores . . . night** snores the night through   **30 scald'st with safety** burns while providing safety | **gates of breath** lips and nose   **32 suspire** breathe   **35 rigol** circle, crown   **37 blood** (1) heart (2) kinship   **41 as immediate from** as I am next in line to   **42 Derives itself** descends   **43 put . . . strength** if all the strength in the world were put

Into one giant arm, it shall not force
This lineal° honor from me. This from thee   45
Will I to mine leave, as 'tis left to me.   *Exit*
KING [*awakening*]   Warwick! Gloucester! Clarence!

      Enter Warwick, Gloucester, Clarence, [and others]

CLARENCE   Doth the King call?
WARWICK   What would Your Majesty?
KING   Why did you leave me here alone, my lords?
CLARENCE   We left the Prince my brother here, my liege,   50
Who undertook to sit and watch by you.
KING   The Prince of Wales? Where is he? Let me see him.
He is not here.
WARWICK   This door is open; he is gone this way.
GLOUCESTER
He came not through the chamber where we stayed.   55
KING   Where is the crown? Who took it from my pillow?
WARWICK   When we withdrew, my liege, we left it here.
KING   The Prince hath ta'en it hence. Go seek him out.
Is he so hasty that he doth suppose
My sleep my death?   60
Find him, my lord of Warwick; chide him hither.
                         [*Exit Warwick*]
This part° of his conjoins° with my disease
And helps to end me. See, sons, what things you are!
How quickly Nature falls into revolt
When gold becomes her object!   65
For this the foolish overcareful fathers
Have broke their sleep with thoughts,°
Their brains with care, their bones with industry;
For this they have engrossèd° and piled up
The cankered° heaps of strange-achievèd° gold;   70
For this they have been thoughtful° to invest
Their sons with arts and martial exercises—
When, like the bee, tolling° from every flower,

---

45 **lineal** inherited   62 **part** act | **conjoins** unites, joins   67 **thoughts** cares
69 **engrossèd** amassed   70 **cankered** rusting and malignant | **strange-achievèd** won
by unusual effort or means, or in distant lands   71 **thoughtful** careful   73 **tolling**
taking as toll, collecting

Our thighs packed with wax, our mouths with honey,
We bring it to the hive, and like the bees   75
Are murdered for our pains.° This bitter taste
Yields his engrossments to the ending father.°

Enter Warwick

Now, where is he that will not stay so long
Till his friend sickness have determined me?°
WARWICK   My lord, I found the Prince in the next room,   80
Washing with kindly° tears his gentle cheeks,
With such a deep° demeanor in great sorrow
That Tyranny, which never quaffed but blood,°
Would, by beholding him, have washed his knife°
With gentle eyedrops. He is coming hither.   85
KING   But wherefore did he take away the crown?

Enter [Prince] Harry [with the crown]

Lo, where he comes. Come hither to me, Harry.—
Depart the chamber; leave us here alone.

Exeunt [Warwick and the rest]

PRINCE   I never thought to hear you speak again.
KING   Thy wish was father, Harry, to that thought.   90
I stay too long by thee; I weary thee.
Dost thou so hunger for mine empty chair°
That thou wilt needs° invest thee with my honors
Before thy hour be ripe? Oh, foolish youth,
Thou seek'st the greatness that will overwhelm thee.   95
Stay but a little, for my cloud of dignity°
Is held from falling with so weak a wind°
That it will quickly drop. My day is dim.
Thou hast stol'n that which after some few hours

75–6 and like . . . pains (compare Bartholomew, *De Proprietatibus Rerum*: "bees that are unobedient to the king, they deem themselves by their own doom for to die by the wound of their own sting")   **76–7 This . . . father** his stored-up treasures yield this bitter taste to the dying father   **79 Till . . . me?** till sickness, befriending him, has put an end to me?   **81 kindly** natural, filial   **82 deep** intense   **83 That . . . blood** that even the personified spirit of Cruelty, despite its insatiable thirst for blood   **84 his knife** (a conventional attribute of personifications like Revenge and Wrath)   **92 chair** throne   **93 wilt needs** must   **96 cloud of dignity** earthly greatness, as evanescent as a cloud   **97 so weak a wind** the King's failing breath, compared to the wind that was thought to hold up the clouds

Were thine without offense, and at my death   100
Thou hast sealed up my expectation.°
Thy life did manifest thou loved'st me not;
And thou wilt have me die assured of it.
Thou hid'st a thousand daggers in thy thoughts,
Which thou hast whetted on thy stony heart,   105
To stab at half an hour of my life.
What, canst thou not forbear° me half an hour?
Then get thee gone and dig my grave thyself,
And bid the merry bells ring to thine ear
That thou art crownèd, not that I am dead.   110
Let all the tears that should bedew my hearse
Be drops of balm° to sanctify thy head.
Only compound° me with forgotten dust;
Give that which gave thee life unto the worms.
Pluck down my officers, break my decrees,   115
For now a time is come to mock at form.°
Harry the Fifth is crowned. Up, vanity!°
Down, royal state!° All you sage counselors, hence!
And to the English court assemble now,
From every region, apes of idleness!°   120
Now, neighbor confines,° purge you of your scum.
Have you a ruffian that will swear, drink, dance,
Revel the night, rob, murder, and commit
The oldest sins the newest kind of ways?
Be happy; he will trouble you no more.   125
England shall double gild his treble guilt;
England shall give him office, honor, might;
For the fifth Harry from curbed license plucks
The muzzle of restraint,° and the wild dog
Shall flesh his tooth° on every innocent.   130
O my poor kingdom, sick with civil blows!

100–1 and at . . . expectation and now that I am dying you have confirmed my worst fears   **107 forbear** spare   **112 balm** consecrated oil used in anointing the King at his coronation   **113 compound** mix   **116 form** ceremony, orderly usages **117 vanity** folly   **118 state** ceremony   **120 apes of idleness** foolishly idle hangers-on   **121 neighbor confines** neighboring countries   **128–9 For . . . restraint** for Harry the Fifth unmuzzles the unlawful licentiousness and vice that have hitherto been restrained (*curbed*)   **130 flesh his tooth on** plunge his teeth into the flesh of (to *flesh* means "to initiate into bloodshed," "to make an animal eager for prey by the taste of blood")

When that my care could not withhold thy riots,°
What wilt thou do when riot is thy care?°
Oh, thou wilt be a wilderness again,
Peopled with wolves, thy old inhabitants!   135
PRINCE [*kneeling and returning the crown*]
      Oh, pardon me, my liege! But for° my tears,
The moist impediments unto my speech,
I had° forestalled this dear° and deep rebuke
Ere you with grief had spoke and I had heard
The course of it so far. There is your crown;   140
And He that wears the crown immortally
Long guard it yours! If I affect° it more
Than as your honor and as your renown,
Let me no more from this obedience° rise,
Which my most inward true and duteous spirit   145
Teacheth this prostrate and exterior bending.
God witness with me, when I here came in,
And found no course° of breath within Your Majesty,
How cold it struck my heart! If I do feign,
Oh, let me in my present wildness die   150
And never live to show th'incredulous world
The noble change that I have purposèd!
Coming to look on you, thinking you dead,
And dead almost, my liege, to think you were,
I spake unto this crown as having sense,°   155
And thus upbraided it: "The care on thee depending°
Hath fed upon the body of my father;
Therefore, thou best of gold art worst of gold.
Other, less fine in carat, is more precious,
Preserving life in med'cine potable;°   160
But thou, most fine, most honored, most renowned,
Hast eat° thy bearer up." Thus, my most royal liege,

---

132 **When . . . riots** when even the care I took to maintain discipline could not rein in your disorders of civil strife   133 **care** inclination, concern   136 **But for** were it not for   138 **had** would have | **dear** severe, grievous (because deeply felt emotionally)   142 **affect** desire   144 **obeisance** kneeling posture   148 **course** current   155 **as having sense** as if it were capable of sense impressions   156 **The care . . . depending** the worry that comes from maintaining you   160 **med'cine potable** potable gold, an elixir, thought from Galen's time to possess magical powers to cure   162 **eat** eaten (pronounced "et")

Accusing it, I put it on my head,
To try with it,° as with an enemy
That had before my face murdered my father,   165
The quarrel of a true inheritor.°
But if it did infect my blood with joy
Or swell my thoughts to any strain° of pride,
If any rebel or vain spirit of mine
Did with the least affection° of a welcome   170
Give entertainment to the might of it,°
Let God forever keep it from my head
And make me as the poorest vassal is
That doth with awe and terror kneel to it!
KING   Oh, my son,   175
God put it in thy mind to take it hence,
That thou mightst win the more thy father's love,
Pleading so wisely in excuse of it!
Come hither, Harry, sit thou by my bed,
          [*The Prince rises and sits by the bed*]
And hear, I think, the very latest° counsel   180
That ever I shall breathe. God knows, my son,
By what bypaths and indirect crook'd ways
I met this crown, and I myself know well
How troublesome it sat upon my head.
To thee it shall descend with better quiet,   185
Better opinion,° better confirmation,
For all the soil° of the achievement goes
With me into the earth. It seemed in me
But as an honor snatched with boist'rous° hand,
And I had many living to upbraid   190
My gain of it by their assistances,
Which daily grew to quarrel and to bloodshed,
Wounding supposèd peace. All these bold fears°
Thou see'st with peril I have answerèd,

---

164 **To try with it** to dispute with it (also suggesting "try it on")   166 **The quarrel
. . . inheritor** (the Prince, as the son and heir of a murdered man, has a quarrel to
settle with the murderer, the crown)   168 **strain** feeling, tendency   170 **affection**
inclination   171 **Give . . . of it** show appreciation or desire for the power it
represents   180 **latest** last   186 **opinion** public support, reputation   187 **soil** stain
189 **boist'rous** violent   193 **fears** objects of fear

For all my reign hath been but as a scene   195
Acting that argument.° And now my death
Changes the mood,° for what in me was purchased°
Falls upon thee in a more fairer sort;°
So° thou the garland° wear'st successively.°
Yet, though thou stand'st more sure than I could do,   200
Thou art not firm enough, since griefs are green,°
And all my friends,° which thou must make thy friends,
Have but their stings and teeth newly ta'en out,
By whose fell working° I was first advanced
And by whose power I well might lodge° a fear   205
To be again displaced. Which to avoid,
I cut them off, and had a purpose now
To lead out many to the Holy Land,
Lest rest and lying still might make them look
Too near unto my state.° Therefore, my Harry,   210
Be it thy course to busy giddy minds
With foreign quarrels, that action, hence borne out,°
May waste° the memory of the former days.
More would I, but my lungs are wasted so
That strength of speech is utterly denied me.   215
How I came by the crown, O God forgive,
And grant it may with thee in true peace live!

PRINCE   My gracious liege,
  You won it, wore it, kept it, gave it me.
  Then plain and right must my possession be,   220
  Which I with more than with a common pain°
  'Gainst all the world will rightfully maintain.

Enter [Prince John of] Lancaster, [Warwick, and others]

KING   Look, look, here comes my John of Lancaster.
PRINCE JOHN   Health, peace, and happiness to my royal father!

195–6 hath been . . . argument has seemed like a drama enacting that theme (of rebellion)   **197 mood** state of mind; mode, musical key | **purchased** acquired rather than inherited   **198 sort** manner, way   **199 So** thus | **garland** crown | **successively** by right of succession   **201 griefs are green** grievances are fresh   **202 friends** former allies   **204 fell working** ruthless efforts   **205 lodge** harbor   **209–10 look . . . state** examine too skeptically my regal claim   **212 action . . . out** military action, conducted in other lands   **213 waste** efface, obliterate   **221 pain** effort

KING Thou bring'st me happiness and peace, son John;   225
  But health, alack, with youthful wings is flown
  From this bare withered trunk. Upon thy sight°
  My worldly business makes a period.°
  Where is my lord of Warwick?
PRINCE   My lord of Warwick!

[*Warwick comes forward*]

KING Doth any name particular belong   230
  Unto the lodging° where I first did swoon?
WARWICK 'Tis called Jerusalem, my noble lord.
KING Laud be to God! Even there my life must end.
  It hath been prophesied to me many years
  I should not die but in Jerusalem,   235
  Which vainly I supposed the Holy Land.
  But bear me to that chamber; there I'll lie.
  In that Jerusalem shall Harry die.

[*Exeunt, bearing the King in his bed*]

ACT 5
SCENE 1

Enter Shallow, Falstaff, and Bardolph [and Page]

SHALLOW By Cock and pie,° sir, you shall not away tonight.—
  What, Davy, I say!
FALSTAFF You must excuse me, Master Robert Shallow.
SHALLOW I will not excuse you, you shall not be excused,
  excuses shall not be admitted, there is no excuse shall serve,   5
  you shall not be excused.—Why, Davy!

[*Enter Davy*]

227 **Upon thy sight** at the very moment of my seeing you   228 **makes a period**
comes to an end   231 **lodging** room, chamber
5.1. Location: Gloucestershire. Shallow's house. Summary: Shallow hosts Falstaff,
hoping to use his influence at court, even as Falstaff hopes to use him, most
immediately, as the source of anecdotes to entertain Hal.
1 **By Cock and pie** (a mild oath, meaning "by God and the ordinal or book of
services for the Church")

DAVY   Here, sir.

SHALLOW   Davy, Davy, Davy, Davy, let me see, Davy, let me see, Davy, let me see. Yea, marry, William cook,° bid him come hither.—Sir John, you shall not be excused.   10

DAVY   Marry, sir, thus: those precepts° cannot be served. And, again, sir: shall we sow the headland° with wheat?

SHALLOW   With red wheat,° Davy. But for William cook—are there no young pigeons?

DAVY   Yes, sir. Here is now the smith's note° for shoeing and   15 plow irons.   [*He gives a paper*]

SHALLOW   Let it be cast° and paid.—Sir John, you shall not be excused.

DAVY   Now, sir, a new link° to the bucket° must needs be had. And sir, do you mean to stop any of William's wages about   20 the sack he lost at Hinckley° fair?

SHALLOW   'A shall answer° it. Some pigeons, Davy, a couple of short-legged hens, a joint of mutton, and any pretty little tiny kickshaws,° tell William cook.

[*Davy and Shallow confer privately*]

DAVY   Doth the man of war stay all night, sir?   25

SHALLOW   Yea, Davy. I will use him well. A friend i'th' court is better than a penny in purse. Use his men well, Davy, for they are arrant knaves, and will backbite.

DAVY   No worse than they are backbitten,° sir, for they have marvelous° foul linen.   30

SHALLOW   Well conceited,° Davy. About thy business, Davy.

DAVY   I beseech you, sir, to countenance° William Visor of Wo'ncot against Clement Perkes o'th' Hill.

SHALLOW   There is many complaints, Davy, against that Visor. That Visor is an arrant knave, on my knowledge.   35

DAVY   I grant Your Worship that he is a knave, sir; but yet, God forbid, sir, but a knave should have some countenance at his

---

9 **William cook** William the cook   11 **precepts** writs, summonses   12 **headland** strip of unplowed land at the edge of a field to allow for the turning of the plow   13 **red wheat** a variety of red-tinged wheat planted late in the summer   15 **note** bill   17 **cast** added up   19 **link** chain | **bucket** yoke or pail   21 **Hinckley** market town not far from Coventry, famous for its fairs   22 **answer** pay for   24 **kickshaws** fancy dishes (from the French *quelque chose*)   29 **backbitten** (with pun on "bitten by vermin")   30 **marvelous** marvelously   31 **Well conceited** ingeniously punned   32 **countenance** favor

friend's request. An honest man, sir, is able to speak for himself, when a knave is not. I have served Your Worship truly, sir, this eight years; an I cannot once or twice in a   40
quarter bear out° a knave against an honest man, I have little credit with Your Worship. The knave is mine honest friend, sir; therefore, I beseech you, let him be countenanced.

SHALLOW   Go to,° I say he shall have no wrong. Look about,°
Davy.   [*Exit Davy*]   45
Where are you, Sir John? Come, come, come, off with your boots.—Give me your hand, Master Bardolph.

BARDOLPH   I am glad to see Your Worship.

SHALLOW   I thank thee with all my heart, kind Master Bardolph. [*To the Page*] And welcome, my tall° fellow. —   50
Come, Sir John.

FALSTAFF   I'll follow you, good Master Robert Shallow.
                                         [*Exit Shallow*]
Bardolph, look to our horses.
                           [*Exeunt Bardolph and Page*]
If I were sawed into quantities,° I should make four dozen of such bearded hermits' staves° as Master Shallow. It is a   55
wonderful thing to see the semblable coherence° of his men's spirits and his. They, by observing of him, do bear themselves like foolish justices; he, by conversing° with them, is turned into a justice-like servingman. Their spirits are so married in conjunction with the participation of   60
society° that they flock together in consent, like so many wild geese. If I had a suit to Master Shallow, I would humor his men with the imputation of being near° their master; if to his men, I would curry with° Master Shallow that no man could better command his servants. It is certain that either   65
wise bearing or ignorant carriage° is caught, as men take diseases, one of another. Therefore let men take heed of

41 bear out support   **44 Go to** (an expression of remonstrance) | **Look about** get busy   **50 tall** brave (but also with an ironic witticism about the Page's small stature)   **54 quantities** pieces   **55 hermits' staves** staffs or canes belonging to hermits and, like them, thin as a rail   **56 semblable coherence** close correspondence   **58 conversing** associating   **60–1 married . . . society** united by close association   **63 with . . . near** by implying that I am friendly with, or that they enjoy the confidence of (probably the latter)   **64 curry with** flatter   **66 carriage** demeanor, behavior

their company. I will devise matter enough out of this
Shallow to keep Prince Harry in continual laughter the
wearing out of six fashions, which is four terms, or two   70
actions,° and 'a shall laugh without intervallums.° Oh, it is
much that a lie with a slight oath and a jest with a sad° brow
will do with a fellow that never had the ache in his
shoulders!° Oh, you shall see him° laugh till his face be like
a wet cloak ill laid up.°   75

SHALLOW [*within*]   Sir John!

FALSTAFF   I come, Master Shallow, I come, Master Shallow.

[*Exit*]

ACT 5
SCENE 2

Enter Warwick [and the] Lord Chief Justice [meeting]

WARWICK   How now, my Lord Chief Justice, whither away?°

CHIEF JUSTICE   How doth the King?

WARWICK   Exceeding well.° His cares are now all ended.

CHIEF JUSTICE
   I hope, not dead.

WARWICK   He's walked the way of nature,°
   And to our purposes he lives no more.   5

CHIEF JUSTICE   I would His Majesty had called me with him.
   The service that I truly° did his life
   Hath left me open to all injuries.

70–1 **six . . . actions** six changes in the fashion of clothing, which occupies the same
time as the four terms of court (Michaelmas, Hilary, Easter, and Trinity, all in all
comprising one legal year), or two lawsuits (which proceed slowly at the rate of only
two a year)   71 **intervallums** intervals between terms of court   72 **sad** serious
73–4 **a fellow . . . shoulders** someone who is youthfully inexperienced in the troubles
and complexities of this world and hence gullible   74 **him** Prince Hal   75 **ill laid
up** carelessly put away wet so that it wrinkles

5.2. **Location: Westminster. The royal court. Summary:** The Lord Chief Justice
expects the worst with Hal's ascension to the kingship, but his debut as Henry V
reassures him and the princely brothers of his virtuous sincerity.
1 **whither away?** where are you going?   3 **well** at peace   4 **walked . . . nature** died
7 **truly** loyally

WARWICK Indeed I think the young King loves you not.

CHIEF JUSTICE I know he doth not, and do arm myself　　　10
　　To welcome the condition of the time,
　　Which cannot look more hideously upon me
　　Than I have drawn it in my fantasy.

Enter [Prince] John [of Lancaster], Thomas [of Clarence], and
Humphrey [of Gloucester, with] Westmorland, [and others]

WARWICK Here come the heavy issue° of dead Harry.
　　Oh, that the living Harry had the temper°　　　15
　　Of he, the worst° of these three gentlemen!
　　How many nobles then should hold their places
　　That must strike sail to spirits of vile sort!°

CHIEF JUSTICE O God, I fear all will be overturned.

PRINCE JOHN Good morrow, cousin Warwick, good morrow.　　20

GLOUCESTER, CLARENCE Good morrow, cousin.

PRINCE JOHN We meet like men that had forgot° to speak.

WARWICK We do remember, but our argument°
　　Is all too heavy to admit much talk.

PRINCE JOHN Well, peace be with him that hath made us heavy!　25

CHIEF JUSTICE Peace be with us, lest we be heavier!

GLOUCESTER O good my lord, you have lost a friend indeed,
　　And I dare swear you borrow not that face
　　Of seeming sorrow; it is sure your own.

PRINCE JOHN Though no man be assured what grace to find,°　　30
　　You stand in coldest° expectation.
　　I am the sorrier; would 'twere otherwise.

CLARENCE Well, you must now speak Sir John Falstaff fair,°
　　Which swims against your stream of quality.°

CHIEF JUSTICE Sweet princes, what I did I did in honor,　　35
　　Led by th'impartial conduct of my soul,
　　And never shall you see that I will beg
　　A ragged and forestalled remission.°

14 heavy issue grieving sons　**15 temper** disposition　**16 he, the worst** the least
worthy　**18 That . . . sort** who now must humble themselves before despicable
people, like ships lowering their sails in token of submission　**22 forgot** forgotten
how　**23 argument** subject　**30 grace to find** favor he will find　**31 coldest** most
comfortless　**33 speak . . . fair** speak courteously to Sir John Falstaff　**34 swims . . .
quality** runs counter to your natural inclination and position　**38 A . . . remission** a
half-hearted (beggarly) pardon, which is sure to be refused or whose effect is gone
before it is granted

If truth and upright innocency fail me,
I'll to the King my master that is dead   40
And tell him who hath sent me after him.
WARWICK   Here comes the Prince.

    Enter the Prince [as King Henry the Fifth] and Blunt

CHIEF JUSTICE   Good morrow, and God save Your Majesty!
KING   This new and gorgeous garment, majesty,
Sits not so easy on me as you think.   45
Brothers, you mix your sadness with some fear.
This is the English, not the Turkish court;
Not Amurath° an Amurath succeeds,
But Harry Harry. Yet be sad, good brothers,
For, by my faith, it very well becomes you.   50
Sorrow so royally in you appears
That I will deeply put the fashion on
And wear it in my heart. Why then, be sad,
But entertain no more of it, good brothers,
Than a joint burden laid upon us all.   55
For° me, by heaven, I bid you be assured,
I'll be your father and your brother too.
Let me but bear your love, I'll bear your cares.
Yet weep that Harry's dead, and so will I;
But Harry lives that shall convert those tears   60
By number into hours of happiness.°
PRINCES   We hope no otherwise from Your Majesty.
KING   You all look strangely on me. [*To the Chief Justice*]
                                And you most.
You are, I think, assured I love you not.
CHIEF JUSTICE   I am assured, if I be measured rightly,   65
Your Majesty hath no just cause to hate me.
KING   No?
How might a prince of my great hopes forget
So great indignities you laid upon me?
What? Rate,° rebuke, and roughly send to prison   70

---

48 Amurath a Turkish sultan who, upon succeeding his father, had his brothers strangled   **56 For** as for   **61 By . . . happiness** for each of our many tears, there will be an hour of happiness   **70 Rate** chide

Th'immediate heir of England? Was this easy?°
May this be washed in Lethe° and forgotten?
CHIEF JUSTICE   I then did use° the person of your father;
The image of his power lay then in me.
And in th'administration of his law,   75
Whiles I was busy for the commonwealth,
Your Highness pleasèd to forget my place,
The majesty and power of law and justice,
The image of the King whom I presented,°
And struck me in my very seat of judgment;   80
Whereon, as an offender to your father,
I gave bold way to my authority
And did commit° you. If the deed were ill,
Be you contented, wearing now the garland,°
To have a son set your decrees at naught,   85
To pluck down justice from your awful° bench,
To trip the course of law and blunt the sword
That guards the peace and safety of your person,
Nay, more, to spurn at your most royal image
And mock your workings in a second body?°   90
Question your royal thoughts, make the case yours;
Be now the father and propose° a son,
Hear your own dignity so much profaned,
See your most dreadful laws so loosely slighted,
Behold yourself so by a son disdained,   95
And then imagine me taking your part
And in your power soft° silencing your son.
After this cold considerance° sentence me,
And, as you are a king, speak in your state°
What I have done that misbecame my place,   100
My person, or my liege's sovereignty.
KING   You are right° justice, and you weigh this well.
   Therefore still bear the balance° and the sword;

---

71 easy of small importance, easily forgotten   **72 Lethe** the river of forgetfulness in Hades   **73 use** represent   **79 presented** represented   **83 commit** to prison   **84 garland** crown   **86 awful** awe-inspiring   **90 And . . . body** and ridicule your justice as administered by your representative or deputy   **92 propose** imagine, suppose   **97 soft** gently   **98 cold considerance** calm reflection   **99 state** royal capacity   **102 right** true, ideal   **103 balance** scales (which, along with the sword, were emblematic of justice)

And I do wish your honors may increase,
Till you do live to see a son of mine   105
Offend you and obey you, as I did.
So shall I live to speak my father's words:
"Happy am I, that have a man so bold
That dares do justice on my proper° son;
And not less happy, having such a son   110
That would deliver up his greatness so
Into the hands of justice." You did commit me;
For which I do commit into your hand
Th'unstainèd sword that you have used° to bear,
With this remembrance,° that you use the same   115
With the like bold, just, and impartial spirit
As you have done 'gainst me. There is my hand.
You shall be as a father to my youth.
My voice shall sound° as you do prompt mine ear,
And I will stoop and humble my intents   120
To your well-practiced wise directions.
And, princes all, believe me, I beseech you:
My father is gone wild into his grave,
For in his tomb lie my affections,°
And with his spirits° sadly° I survive,   125
To mock the expectation of the world,
To frustrate prophecies, and to raze out
Rotten opinion, who° hath writ me down
After my seeming.° The tide of blood° in me
Hath proudly° flowed in vanity° till now;   130
Now doth it turn and ebb back to the sea,
Where it shall mingle with the state of floods°
And flow henceforth in formal majesty.
Now call we our high court of Parliament.
And let us choose such limbs of noble counsel   135

---

109 proper own   **114 have used** have been accustomed   **115 remembrance**
reminder, admonition   **119 sound** speak   **123–4 My . . . affections** my wildness,
having disappeared with my father's death, is buried along with my father   **125 spirits**
soul, spiritual heritage | **sadly** soberly   **128 who** which   **129 After my seeming**
according to what I appeared to be | **blood** passion   **130 proudly** overbearingly |
vanity folly   **132 state of floods** majesty of the ocean

That the great body of our state may go
In equal rank° with the best-governed nation;
That war, or peace, or both at once, may be
As things acquainted and familiar to us,

[*To Chief Justice*]

In which you, father, shall have foremost hand.   140
Our coronation done, we will accite,°
As I before remembered,° all our state.°
And, God consigning° to my good intents,
No prince nor peer shall have just cause to say,
God shorten Harry's happy life one day!   *Exeunt*   145

ACT 5
SCENE 3

[*A table and chairs are set out.*] *Enter Sir John*
[*Falstaff*], *Shallow, Silence, Davy, Bardolph,* [*and the*]
Page. [*Davy provides food and wine*]

SHALLOW   Nay, you shall see my orchard, where, in an arbor,
we will eat a last year's pippin° of mine own grafting, with a
dish of caraways,° and so forth. Come, cousin Silence. And
then to bed.

FALSTAFF   'Fore God, you have here a goodly dwelling and a   5
rich.

SHALLOW   Barren, barren, barren. Beggars all, beggars all, Sir
John. Marry, good air. Spread,° Davy, spread, Davy. Well
said,° Davy.

FALSTAFF   This Davy serves you for good uses. He is your   10
servingman and your husband.°

SHALLOW   A good varlet, a good varlet,° a very good varlet, Sir
John. By the Mass, I have drunk too much sack at supper. A

136–7 go . . . rank march side by side   **141 accite** summon   **142 remembered**
mentioned | **state** peers, nobility   **143 consigning to** sanctioning

5.3. Location: Gloucestershire. Shallow's orchard. **Summary:** Pistol brings Falstaff
news of Henry IV's death, and he and his companions eagerly set out for London
filled with great expectations.

2 pippin a kind of apple   **3 caraways** (pastries made with caraway seeds were often
eaten with apples)   **8 Spread** spread the cloth   **8–9 Well said** well done (also in l. 46)
11 husband steward   **12 varlet** (1) servant (2) rascal

good varlet. Now sit down, now sit down. Come, cousin.

SILENCE Ah, sirrah, quoth 'a,° we shall   15
  [*sings*] "Do nothing but eat, and make good cheer,
       And praise God for the merry year,
       When flesh° is cheap and females dear,
       And lusty lads roam here and there
       So merrily,   20
       And ever among° so merrily."

FALSTAFF There's a merry heart, good Master Silence! I'll give
  you a health° for that anon.

SHALLOW Give Master Bardolph some wine, Davy.

DAVY [*to the guests*] Sweet sir, sit.—I'll be with you anon.—   25
  Most sweet sir, sit. Master Page, good master Page, sit.
  Proface!° What you want° in meat,° we'll have in drink. But
  you must bear.° The heart's all.°

                                                         [*They sit. Exit Davy*]

SHALLOW Be merry, Master Bardolph, and, my little soldier
  there, be merry.   30

SILENCE [*sings*]
       "Be merry, be merry, my wife has all,
       For women are shrews, both short and tall.
       'Tis merry in hall when beards wags all,°
       And welcome merry Shrovetide.°
       Be merry, be merry."   35

FALSTAFF I did not think Master Silence had been a man of this
  mettle.°

SILENCE Who, I? I have been merry twice and once° ere now.

                                                                    Enter Davy

DAVY [*to the guests*] There's a dish of leather-coats° for you.

SHALLOW Davy!   40

DAVY Your Worship? I'll be with you straight. [*To Falstaff*] A
  cup of wine, sir?

---

15 **quoth 'a** said he   18 **flesh** meat (with sexual suggestion)   21 **ever among** all the
while   22–3 **give you a health** drink you a toast   27 **Proface** (formula of welcome
to a meal, meaning "may it do you good") | **want** lack | **meat** food   28 **bear** be
patient | **The heart's all** a spirit of hospitality is what counts; don't judge us by the
lavishness of the entertainment but by our good will   33 **beards wags all** all the
beards wag up and down (as men talk and laugh)   34 **Shrovetide** three-day period
of merrymaking before Ash Wednesday and Lent   37 **mettle** spirit   38 **twice and
once** now and again   39 **leather-coats** russet apples

SILENCE [*sings*]
> "A cup of wine that's brisk and fine,
> And drink unto thee, leman° mine,
> And a merry heart lives long-a." 45

FALSTAFF   Well said, Master Silence.

SILENCE   And we shall be merry; now comes in the sweet o'th' night.

FALSTAFF   Health and long life to you, Master Silence.

SILENCE [*sings*]
> "Fill the cup, and let it come,° 50
> I'll pledge you a mile to th' bottom.°"

SHALLOW   Honest Bardolph, welcome. If thou want'st anything, and wilt not call, beshrew thy heart.° [*To the Page*] Welcome, my little tiny thief, and welcome indeed, too. I'll drink to Master Bardolph, and to all the cabileros° 55 about London.

DAVY   I hope to see London once ere I die.

BARDOLPH   An I might see you there, Davy!

SHALLOW   By the Mass, you'll crack° a quart together, ha, will you not, Master Bardolph? 60

BARDOLPH   Yea, sir, in a pottle pot.°

SHALLOW   By God's liggens,° I thank thee. The knave will stick by thee, I can assure thee that. 'A will not out,° 'a; 'tis true bred.

BARDOLPH   And I'll stick by him, sir. 65

SHALLOW   Why, there spoke a king. Lack nothing; be merry. (*One knocks at door.*) Look who's at door there, ho! Who knocks?   [*Davy goes to the door*]

FALSTAFF [*to Silence*]   Why, now you have done me right.°

SILENCE [*sings*]
> "Do me right, 70
> And dub me knight,
>   Samingo.°"

Is't not so?

44 **leman** sweetheart   50 **let it come** pass it around   51 **a mile to th' bottom** even if the cup were a mile deep   52–3 **If . . . heart** if you want something and don't ask for it, you deserve a mild curse   55 **cabileros** cavaliers, gallants   59 **crack** consume   61 **pottle pot** two-quart tankard   62 **By God's liggens** (an oath, perhaps "by God's little eyelid")   63 **out** drop out   69 **done me right** kept up with me in drinking   72 **Samingo** (a corruption of "Sir Mingo," the titular knight of a French drinking song; derived from the Latin *mingo*, "I urinate"—a result of much drinking)

FALSTAFF 'Tis so.

SILENCE Is't so? Why then, say an old man can do somewhat.° 75

DAVY [*returning*] An't please Your Worship, there's one Pistol come from the court with news.

FALSTAFF From the court? Let him come in.

Enter Pistol

How now, Pistol?

PISTOL Sir John, God save you! 80

FALSTAFF What wind blew you hither, Pistol?

PISTOL Not the ill wind which blows no man to good. Sweet knight, thou art now one of the greatest men in this realm.

SILENCE By'r Lady, I think 'a be, but° goodman° Puff of Bar'son. 85

PISTOL Puff?
Puff i'thy teeth, most recreant° coward base!—
Sir John, I am thy Pistol and thy friend,
And helter-skelter have I rode to thee,
And tidings do I bring, and lucky joys, 90
And golden times, and happy news of price.°

FALSTAFF I pray thee now, deliver them like a man of this world.°

PISTOL A foutre° for the world and worldlings base!
I speak of Africa° and golden joys. 95

FALSTAFF O base Assyrian° knight, what is thy news?
Let King Cophetua° know the truth thereof.

SILENCE [*sings*] "And Robin Hood, Scarlet, and John.°"

PISTOL Shall dunghill curs confront the Helicons°?
And shall good news be baffled?° 100
Then, Pistol, lay thy head in Furies' lap.°

---

75 **somewhat** something 84 **but** except (Silence interprets *greatest* in the sense of "heaviest") | **goodman** yeoman 87 **recreant** faithless, base 91 **price** great value 92–3 **a man . . . world** an ordinary man using plain ordinary speech 94 **foutre** (from the French *foutre*, "fornicate"; a scornful phrase) 95 **Africa** (fabled for its wealth) 96 **Assyrian** (Falstaff adopts Pistol's high-flown style and metrics) 97 **Cophetua** (King Cophetua married a beggar maid, according to the popular ballad "King Cophetua and the Beggar Maid"; more inflated rhetoric) 98 **"And . . . John"** (a scrap from another ballad) 99 **Helicons** poets (Mount Helicon was the abode of the Muses) Pistol takes umbrage at the drunken interruption of his poetically phrased announcement 100 **baffled** confounded, foiled 101 **lay . . . lap** (Pistol appeals his wrong to the avenging goddesses of classical mythology)

SHALLOW   Honest gentleman, I know not your breeding.°

PISTOL   Why then, lament therefor.°

SHALLOW   Give me pardon, sir. If, sir, you come with news from
the court, I take it there's but two ways: either to utter them   105
or conceal them. I am, sir, under the King, in some authority.

PISTOL   Under which king, Besonian?° Speak, or die.

SHALLOW   Under King Harry.

PISTOL   Harry the Fourth, or Fifth?

SHALLOW   Harry the Fourth.

PISTOL   A foutre for thine office!—
Sir John, thy tender lambkin now is king;   110
Harry the Fifth's the man. I speak the truth.
When Pistol lies, do this, and fig° me like
The bragging Spaniard.

FALSTAFF   What, is the old King dead?

PISTOL   As nail in door. The things I speak are just.   115

FALSTAFF   Away, Bardolph, saddle my horse! Master Robert
Shallow, choose what office thou wilt in the land, 'tis thine.
Pistol, I will double-charge° thee with dignities.

BARDOLPH   Oh, joyful day! I would not take a knighthood for
my fortune.   120

PISTOL   What, I do bring good news?

FALSTAFF   Carry Master Silence to bed.

                              [*Silence is carried off*]
Master Shallow, my lord Shallow—be what thou wilt, I am
fortune's steward—get on thy boots. We'll ride all night.—
Oh, sweet Pistol!—Away, Bardolph!   [*Exit Bardolph*]   125
Come, Pistol, utter more to me, and withal devise something
to do thyself good. Boot, boot,° Master Shallow! I know
the young King is sick for me. Let us take any man's horses;
the laws of England are at my commandment. Blessed are
they that have been my friends, and woe to my Lord Chief   130
Justice!

---

102 **breeding** parentage, rank   103 **therefor** for that   107 **Besonian** low, beggarly
rascal (from Italian *bisogno*, "need")   112 **fig** insult with a vulgar gesture,
consisting of thrusting the thumb between the index and middle fingers (the gesture
was thought to originate in Spain, as l. 113 suggests; it means much the same as
foutre, ll. 94 and 109)   118 **double-charge** (with a play on Pistol's name)   127 **Boot,
boot** put on your riding boots

PISTOL   Let vultures vile seize on his lungs also!
"Where is the life that late I led?"° say they.
Why, here it is. Welcome these pleasant days!

Exeunt

ACT 5
SCENE 4

Enter Beadle and three or four officers
[dragging in Hostess Quickly and Doll Tearsheet]

HOSTESS   No, thou arrant knave! I would to God that I might
die, that I might have thee hanged. Thou hast drawn my
shoulder out of joint.

BEADLE   The constables have delivered her over to me, and she
shall have whipping cheer,° I warrant her. There hath been a   5
man or two killed about her.°

DOLL   Nuthook,° nuthook, you lie! Come on, I'll tell thee
what, thou damned tripe-visaged° rascal, an the child I go
with° do miscarry, thou wert better thou hadst struck thy
mother, thou paper-faced° villain!   10

HOSTESS   Oh, the Lord, that Sir John were come! He would
make this a bloody day to somebody. But I pray God the
fruit of her womb miscarry!°

BEADLE   If it do, you shall have a dozen of cushions again; you
have but eleven now.° Come, I charge you both, go with me,   15
for the man is dead that you and Pistol beat amongst you.

DOLL   I'll tell you what, you thin man in a censer,° I will have
you as soundly swinged° for this—you bluebottle° rogue,

---

133 **"Where . . . led"** (fragment of a poem or ballad)

5.4. Location: London. A street. Summary: Quickly and Doll Tearsheet are arrested for violent crimes at the tavern.

5 **whipping cheer** a whipping for supper   6 **about her** (1) in her company (2) on her account   7 **Nuthook** hook for pulling down branches in nutting; here, a constable   8 **tripe-visaged** sausage-faced   8–9 **go with** am pregnant with (Doll implies that the father of the child, perhaps Falstaff, will retaliate if the child is aborted by rough handling)   10 **paper-faced** pale   13 **miscarry** (the Hostess must mean just the opposite of this)   15 **eleven now** (the Beadle accuses Doll of using one of the cushions to make her appear pregnant; pregnant women were spared execution)   17 **thin . . . censer** figure of a man on the lid of a censer or incense burner, embossed in low relief   18 **swinged** thrashed | **bluebottle** (an allusion to the Beadle's blue coat)

you filthy famished correctioner, if you be not swinged, I'll
forswear half-kirtles.° 20
BEADLE   Come, come, you she knight-errant,° come.
HOSTESS   Oh, God, that right should thus overcome might!°
Well, of sufferance° comes ease.
DOLL   Come, you rogue, come, bring me to a justice.
HOSTESS   Ay, come, you starved bloodhound. 25
DOLL   Goodman death, goodman bones!
HOSTESS   Thou atomy,° thou!
DOLL   Come, you thin thing, come, you rascal!°
BEADLE   Very well.   [*Exeunt*]

ACT 5
SCENE 5

Enter [Grooms as] strewers of rushes°

FIRST GROOM   More rushes, more rushes!
SECOND GROOM   The trumpets have sounded twice.
THIRD GROOM   'Twill be two o'clock ere they come from
the coronation. Dispatch,° dispatch.   [*Exeunt*]

*Trumpets sound, and the King and his train
pass over the stage. After them enter Falstaff,
Shallow, Pistol, Bardolph, and the Boy [Page]*

FALSTAFF   Stand here by me, Master Shallow; I will make the   5
King do you grace.° I will leer° upon him as 'a comes by, and
do but mark the countenance that he will give me.
PISTOL   God bless thy lungs, good knight!

---

20 half-kirtles skirts   **21 she knight-errant** a streetwalker working at night (with a
mocking comparison to some heroine of a romance)   **22 right . . . might** (the
Hostess gets this backward)   **23 sufferance** suffering (suffering now promises a
better future, since one's luck is bound to change)   **27 atomy** (for "anatomy,"
skeleton; an *atomy* is an "atom," "speck")   **28 rascal** (1) lean deer (2) scoundrel

5.5. Location: A public place near Westminster Abbey. Summary: Falstaff prepares
his greatest performance only to be crushed by cold rejection. The new King,
however, is applauded by Prince John and the Lord Chief Justice, who anticipate a
heroic future.

0.1 *rushes* straw often used as floor covering   **4 Dispatch** hurry   **6 grace** honor |
leer glance invitingly

FALSTAFF   Come here, Pistol, stand behind me.—Oh, if I had
had time to have made new liveries,° I would have   10
bestowed° the thousand pound I borrowed of you.° But 'tis
no matter; this poor show° doth better. This doth infer° the
zeal I had to see him.

SHALLOW   It doth so.

FALSTAFF   It shows my earnestness of affection—   15

SHALLOW   It doth so.

FALSTAFF   My devotion—

SHALLOW   It doth, it doth, it doth.

FALSTAFF   As it were, to ride day and night, and not to
deliberate, not to remember, not to have patience to shift   20
me°—

SHALLOW   It is best, certain.

FALSTAFF   But to stand stained with travel and sweating with
desire to see him, thinking of nothing else, putting all affairs
else in oblivion, as if there were nothing else to be done but 25
to see him.

PISTOL   'Tis *semper idem*, for *obsque hoc nihil est*.° 'Tis all in
every part.°

SHALLOW   'Tis so, indeed.

PISTOL   My knight, I will inflame thy noble liver°   30
And make thee rage.
Thy Doll, and Helen° of thy noble thoughts,
Is in base durance° and contagious° prison,
Haled° thither
By most mechanical° and dirty hand.   35
Rouse up Revenge from ebon° den with fell Alecto's° snake,
For Doll is in.° Pistol speaks naught but truth.

FALSTAFF   I will deliver her.
                    [*Shouts within, and the trumpets sound*]

---

10 new liveries new outfits bearing the King's insignia   **11 bestowed** spent | **you**
Justice Shallow   **12 poor show** appearing in inferior garments | **infer** imply   **20–1 shift
me** change my apparel   **27 *semper . . . est*** "always the same," for "apart from this
there is nothing" (Pistol approvingly rephrases Falstaff's dedication to put his
loyalty to the Prince above all else) *Obsque* is an error for *absque*   **27–8 'Tis . . .
part** (a very free translation of the Latin)   **30 liver** (the seat of the passions)
32 Helen Helen of Troy, the type of womanly beauty   **33 durance** imprisonment |
contagious pestilential   **34 Haled** dragged   **35 mechanical** menial, base   **36 ebon**
black | **Alecto** one of the Furies, who were depicted with snakes twined in their hair
37 in in prison

PISTOL   There roared the sea, and trumpet-clangor sounds.

Enter the King and his train,
[the Lord Chief Justice among them]

FALSTAFF   God save Thy Grace, King Hal, my royal Hal!   40
PISTOL
   The heavens thee guard and keep, most royal imp° of fame!
FALSTAFF   God save thee, my sweet boy!
KING   My Lord Chief Justice, speak to that vain° man.
CHIEF JUSTICE [*to Falstaff*]
   Have you your wits? Know you what 'tis you speak?
FALSTAFF   My King! My Jove! I speak to thee, my heart!   45
KING   I know thee not, old man. Fall to thy prayers.
   How ill white hairs becomes a fool and jester!
   I have long dreamt of such a kind of man,
   So surfeit-swelled,° so old, and so profane,
   But being awaked I do despise my dream.   50
   Make less thy body hence,° and more thy grace;
   Leave gormandizing.° Know the grave doth gape
   For thee thrice wider than for other men.
   Reply not to me with a fool-born jest.
   Presume not that I am the thing I was,   55
   For God doth know, so shall the world perceive,
   That I have turned away my former self;
   So will I those that kept me company.
   When thou dost hear I am as I have been,
   Approach me, and thou shalt be as thou wast,   60
   The tutor and the feeder of my riots.
   Till then, I banish thee, on pain of death,
   As I have done the rest of my misleaders,
   Not to come near our person by ten mile.
   For competence of life° I will allow you,   65
   That lack of means enforce you not to evils.
   And, as we hear you do reform yourselves,
   We will, according to your strengths and qualities,
   Give you advancement.—Be it your charge, my lord,

---

41 imp scion   **43 vain** foolish   **49 surfeit-swelled** swollen from gluttony   **51 hence** henceforth   **52 gormandizing** gluttonous feeding   **65 competence of life** modest allowance

To see performed the tenor of my word.   70
Set on.   [*Exeunt King and his train*]

FALSTAFF   Master Shallow, I owe you a thousand pound.

SHALLOW   Yea, marry, Sir John, which I beseech you to let me
have home with me.

FALSTAFF   That can hardly be, Master Shallow. Do not you grieve   75
at this. I shall be sent for in private to him. Look you, he must
seem thus to the world. Fear not your advancements; I will be
the man yet that shall make you great.

SHALLOW   I cannot perceive how, unless you give me your
doublet and stuff me out with straw. I beseech you, good Sir   80
John, let me have five hundred of my thousand.

FALSTAFF   Sir, I will be as good as my word. This that you heard
was but a color.°

SHALLOW   A color that I fear you will die° in, Sir John.

FALSTAFF   Fear no colors.° Go with me to dinner. Come,   85
Lieutenant Pistol, come, Bardolph. I shall be sent for soon
at night.°

*Enter [the Lord Chief] Justice and
Prince John [of Lancaster, with officers]*

CHIEF JUSTICE   Go carry Sir John Falstaff to the Fleet.°
Take all his company along with him.

FALSTAFF   My lord, my lord—   90

CHIEF JUSTICE   I cannot now speak. I will hear you soon.—
Take them away.

PISTOL   *Si fortuna me tormenta, spero me contenta.*°
                    Exeunt [all but Prince John and the Chief Justice]

PRINCE JOHN   I like this fair proceeding of the King's.
He hath intent his wonted° followers   95
Shall all be very well provided for,
But all are banished till their conversations°
Appear more wise and modest to the world.

CHIEF JUSTICE   And so they are.

---

83 **color** pretense (but Shallow uses the word to mean *collar*, "hangman's noose")
84 **die** (1) be hanged (2) be dyed   85 **colors** standards or flags (of the enemy); "fear
not," says Falstaff   86–7 **soon at night** early in the evening   88 **Fleet** a famous
London prison   93 *Si . . . contenta* (see the note for 2.4.160)   95 **wonted** accustomed
97 **conversations** conduct

PRINCE JOHN   The King hath called his parliament, my lord.   100
CHIEF JUSTICE   He hath.
PRINCE JOHN   I will lay odds that, ere this year expire,
We bear our civil swords and native fire°
As far as France. I heard a bird so sing,
Whose music, to my thinking, pleased the King.   105
Come, will you hence?   [*Exeunt*]

EPILOGUE

[*Enter Epilogue*]

EPILOGUE
First, my fear; then, my curtsy;° last, my speech. My fear is
your displeasure; my curtsy, my duty; and my speech, to beg
your pardons. If you look for a good speech now, you undo
me, for what I have to say is of mine own making, and what
indeed I should say will, I doubt,° prove mine own marring.   5
But to the purpose, and so to the venture. Be it known to
you, as it is very well, I was lately here in the end of a
displeasing play,° to pray your patience for it and to promise
you a better. I meant indeed to pay you with this, which, if
like an ill venture° it come unluckily home, I break,° and   10
you, my gentle creditors, lose. Here I promised you I would
be, and here I commit my body to your mercies. Bate me
some° and I will pay you some and, as most debtors do,
promise you infinitely.
    If my tongue cannot entreat you to acquit me, will you   15
command me to use my legs?° And yet that were but light

103 **civil . . . fire** our weapons used recently in civil war

Epilogue. Summary: Shakespeare ends ten plays with epilogues, many soliciting the audience's approval. This one is best known for two intriguing comments about Falstaff: the first promising his return in *Henry V*—a promise left unfulfilled—and the second, a tactful disclaimer about his historical referent. [See note at ll. 27–8 and Contexts, pp. 372–77.]

1 **curtsy** bow, obeisance 5 **doubt** fear 8 **displeasing play** (identification is uncertain) 10 **ill venture** unlucky sending out of merchant vessels | **break** (1) break my promise (2) become bankrupt 12–3 **Bate me some** let me off from some portion of the debt 16 **use my legs** perform the jig that normally concluded performances in the public theaters

payment, to dance out of your debt. But a good conscience will make any possible satisfaction, and so would I. All the gentlewomen here have forgiven me. If the gentlemen will not, then the gentlemen do not agree with the gentlewomen, which was never seen before in such an assembly.   20

One word more, I beseech you. If you be not too much cloyed with fat meat, our humble author will continue the story, with Sir John in it,° and make you merry with fair Katharine of France. Where, for anything I know, Falstaff   25 shall die of a sweat,° unless already 'a be killed with your hard opinions; for Oldcastle died a martyr, and this is not the man.° My tongue is weary; when my legs are too,° I will bid you good night; and so I kneel down before you, but, indeed, to pray for the Queen.   [*Exit Epilogue*]   30

---

24 Sir John in it (Shakespeare evidently originally intended to introduce Falstaff into *Henry V*; instead, only his death is reported there in 2.1 and 2.3)   **26 sweat** plague, fever, or venereal disease   **27–8 Oldcastle . . . man** Falstaff was not intended to resemble Sir John Oldcastle, the Lollard venerated by 16th-c. Puritans as a martyr for their beliefs (this statement may have been intended to placate Lord Cobham, descendant of Oldcastle, whose resentment of Shakespeare's use of the Oldcastle name in an earlier version of the *Henry IV* plays may have led to the change of the name to Falstaff)   **28 when . . . too** when my legs are tired from dancing the jig

CONTEXTS

Shakespeare's Historical Sources

Reading Shakespeare's historical sources reveals his textual agility. As he selects, rearranges, and transforms agents and events for the sake of dramatic construction and characterization, he is inspired in part by the sources themselves, which invite appropriation. Far from being a monolithic background, the varied representational modes of these materials—prose chronicle, poetic narrative, moral drama, conduct book—keep in play different forms of coherence and improvise on details borrowed from each other. Even individual texts involve juxtapositions, divergent points of view, and ambiguities, dynamics suggestive to a playwright whose very craft thrives on competing perspectives and conflicting desires.

This malleability touches a paradox central to Renaissance thought about the boundaries between fact and imagination, rigorous account and constructed fiction. Modern scholars sometimes argue that such discursive segregation was just emerging and cite the multiple senses of "history" itself as a narrative, whether true or imaginary. Some of Shakespeare's titles show this—*The most excellent Historie of the Merchant of Venice*, for example. But rather than implying a casual undifferentiation, the mingling of fact and invention created a good deal of self-consciousness for historical writers, and readers and writers with even a passing knowledge of classical philosophy or the rhetorical tradition were aware of the epistemological effect (for good or ill) of bending, universalizing, or shuffling accounts of the past. Some, like Sir Philip Sidney, exploit this uncertainty with a subversively skeptical wit. A historical poet or playwright might be expected to observe restraint—not reverse the results of important battles (unlike Rumor, the demonic poet-chorus who begins *Part Two*)—yet the same writer might alter the chronology or significance of the battles, fabricate speeches, devise companions for the major figures, rework the major figures themselves, or even interweave the occasional new one, such as the Bastard, who outshines the historical figures for much of Shakespeare's *King John*.

The best-known additions to the *Henry IV* plays appear with Falstaff and the tavern world, but impressive effects also stem from minor revisions, or from bits of what we might loosely call "found art." Consider Shakespeare's introduction of the King to us. In Raphael Holinshed's *Chronicles*, the report of Henry IV's bloody conflict with the rebel Glendower in Wales breaks off for other foreign and domestic news of 1401: a visit by the Emperor of Constantinople seeking support for his conflict with the Turks, and the enforcement of religious orthodoxy at home. Having delivered the report, Holinshed returns to Wales, with its civil bloodshed, waste, and the King's guilty conscience about Mortimer. Such disjunctive presentation is in the nature of a chronicle, a form that is typically organized by temporal sequence rather than by continuing or analytical narrative. Shakespeare exploits the fortuitous juxtaposition of Henry IV's domestic and foreign affairs. The King first appears exhausted by civil conflict. In his longing to end bloodshed at home, he dreams of a Crusade against the Turk that will restore unity to his land and purge his own guilt about his dubious accession. But he acknowledges now is not the time, and his reverie is broken off by renewed reports of battlefield butchery and the Percies' anger over his strategic indifference to Mortimer. What Holinshed presents primarily as a sequence of discrete, outward events Shakespeare fashions into a dramatic character—his aspirations, his frustrations, and his guilt-driven machinations.

No less intriguing is Shakespeare's exploitation of a small change introduced by Samuel Daniel: the altering of Hotspur's age to match Prince Hal's. Daniel doesn't do much with his suggestive innovation, other than to coordinate it with his larger analogy of civil war and fraternal conflict. For Shakespeare, the adjustment of age enables a multidimensional motif of warring doubles—a complex mythic, political, and psychological dance in *Part One*. He has King Henry wish his son and Hotspur had been exchanged at birth (1.1.85–89); though the characters have never met, they mock each other at a distance, Hal lampooning Hotspur's restless aggression (2.4.94–102),

Hotspur mocking Hal's "madcap" behavior (4.1.94–97). When Hal prepares for combat, he appropriates, according to Vernon, Hotspur's own soaring, chivalric fantasy (4.1.100), inflaming the latter into deadly (and some think, erotic) fascination with his *alter ego*:

> Come, let me taste my horse,
> Who is to bear me like a thunderbolt
> Against the bosom of the Prince of Wales.
> Harry to Harry shall, hot horse to horse,
> Meet and ne'er part till one drop down a corse.
> (4.1.119–23)

Vernon will later tell Hotspur that Hal challenged him as "a brother should a brother dare," and when Hal does finally triumph, he fulfills his vow to crop Hotspur's "honors," even as he reciprocates by hiding Hotspur's mangled face with his "favors." In these violent reciprocities, Shakespeare lures us into imagining an English foundational myth to match the fratricidal myth of Romulus and Remus and the foundation of Rome.

History offers Shakespeare an expressive vocabulary through its contradictory uses and emotional registers. Providential historians were still intent to discover divine intent, a "theater of God's judgments," to use the ubiquitous and dramatically suggestive phrase. Humanist educators and rhetoricians could be providentialist this way, but they also viewed history as a source of concrete ethical lessons and *exempla*, notable images of virtue and vice to be stored in the memory for imitation or caution. And the more purely pragmatic might see in the past lessons of ambiguous import, strategies for worldly success irrespective of morality—teaching the necessity of ruthless opportunism as well as virtue, or even opportunism as a kind of *virtù*, to invoke Machiavelli's pregnant term.[1]

Amidst these didactic interests, the Renaissance sense of the past could also be more subtly philosophical and psychological—a way to manage anxiety in a fluctuating, unpredictable world. Civil war, religious reversals, and economic shifts sharpened for the Tudors what people have always known, even in times of relative

---

[1]See Machiavelli selections in the Contexts sections "Authority, Resistance, Rebellion" and "The Theater of the World."

peace or metaphysical stability, about mutable fortune. History—an exceptionally popular subject with a wide readership in Shakespeare's day—revived images of energetic and glorious ancestors, providing a sense of purpose and stability for those seeking to legitimate institutional or individual identities. But history also reminded its readers with images of dissolution of what Henry IV darkly calls "the revolution of the times." Historical imagination in the Renaissance, whether meditating on Alexander, Rome, or Stonehenge, traces any culture to inevitable dust and ruins.

In the *Henry IV* plays, Shakespeare conveys these multiple, historical meanings, not only in the utterances of his several characters but also in the conflicts of a single mind—whether on stage or in its spectator.

Raphael Holinshed (c. 1525–1580)

Shakespeare turned to Raphael Holinshed's Chronicles of England, Scotland, and Ireland *(2nd ed., 1587) throughout his career, for the English history plays and for later tragedies:* King Lear, Macbeth, *and parts of* Cymbeline. *The work of about a dozen writers, this massive volume is named after Holinshed, a contributor to and general editor of the first edition, even though he died years before the revised and expanded second edition appeared.*

The Chronicles *presents a mode of historical writing already on the wane in the late sixteenth century: chronological, year-by-year reports. It also features wholesale ingesting of documents and sections of other histories (sometimes named, sometimes not), juxtaposed events, and conflicting points of view. Modern readers used to consign this work to the realm of "compilation" or "agglomeration"; E. M. W. Tillyard, for one, called it "chaotic." Recently, however, critics have found a special value in its procedure, regarding it as the "collaboration" of a syndicate of writers, suggestive for its very "multivocality" (see Patterson 1994). Holinshed's chief English antecedent, Edward Hall's* Union of the Two Noble and Illustrious Families of Lancaster and York *(1548), also used by Shakespeare (and liberally integrated into Holinshed), though diverse in its own way, is governed by a more unified, providential (and politically orthodox) narrative: God's punishment of England for overthrowing Richard II, then the renewal of*

His promise with the rise of the Tudors. While such providentialism is important in the Chronicles, *with additional moralizing and political orthodoxy injected by Abraham Fleming in the revised edition, greater weight is given to "secondary" causes: social, economic, legal, religious, and cultural accounts, including the material realities of daily life. Furthermore, its eyewitness accounts of and contradictory commentary on major events produce an effect Holinshed himself appears to have prized, saying in his Preface that for uncertain cases, he has decided "to show the diversity" of his sources rather than "overruling them and using a peremptory censure, to frame them to agree to my liking, leaving it nevertheless to each man's judgment to control them as he seeth cause."*

Shakespeare accepts and extends the invitation. The introduction to this Contexts section mentioned some of his alterations. Two others should be noted. In Holinshed, the Prince's courage at Shrewsbury is clear, but the real hero is the King, who personally slays thirty-six foes. This trumps even the combined body count of Shakespeare's two comic hyperboles: Hal's mock-Hotspur ("Some fourteen . . . a trifle, a trifle" [Part One, 2.4.100–101]) and Falstaff's tall tale ("Eleven buckram men" [Part One, 2.4.204]). In Holinshed, furthermore, it is the King who magnanimously pardons the Earl of Douglas.

Shakespeare not only elevates the Prince's role but also inserts the matter of his battlefield "redemption" in Part One, *a fulfillment of his earlier submission and vow to his father in 3.2 (though Shakespeare "forgets" both these moments when crafting their deathbed reconciliation in* Part Two). *In* Part One *Shakespeare imports matter from later times, following Holinshed in some details while altering others. In Holinshed, the Prince's falling out and reunion with his father does not appear before or even at Shrewsbury (1403), but rather tracks across the following decade (up to 1412). During these years, according to Holinshed, certain "servants" maliciously informed the King both of Hal's misbehavior and of his increasing popularity among the nobility, a potential threat to the King's authority. True to his method, however, Holinshed also reports alternative views of the son's high-spirited "recreations" as "not offensive." (Modern historians note that as the King grew sickly, the ambitious Prince became a political power. When one of his followers, Henry Beaufort, proposed that the King abdicate in 1411, the angered monarch dismissed Hal from the Council. [See Bullough 1958, 4:251.] Holinshed does allude, at the coronation of Henry V in 1412, to his earlier banishment from court, attributed, however, to a mythical altercation with the Chief Justice.) Shakespeare orchestrates several of these views—in the King's suspicious reproaches, in the tavern play ("Depose me?"), in Hal's care to minimize the damage caused by his high-jinx, in his injured (and somewhat disingenuous) self-defense against malicious gossip, in the King's comment about Hal's forced absence from Council, as well as in the overarching Prodigal Son pattern (from Luke 15.11–24).*

from *Holinshed's Chronicles of England, Scotland, and Ireland* (1587)

Materials for *Henry IV, Part One*

[*Glendower begins his rebellion*]

[1400] In the king's absence, whilst he was forth of the realm in Scotland against his enemies, the Welshmen took occasion to rebel under the conduct of their captain Owen Glendower, doing what mischief they could devise, unto their English neighbors. This Owen Glendower was the son to an esquier[1] of Wales, named Griffth Vichan. . . . He was set to study the laws of the realm and became an utter barrister, or an apprentice of the law (as they term him), and served Richard at Flint Castle, when he was taken by Henry, Duke of Lancaster, though others have written that he served this King Henry the Fourth before he came to attain the crown, in room of an esquier, and after, by reason of variance that rose betwixt him and the Lord Reginald Grey of Ruthin, about the lands which he claimed to be his by right of inheritance. When he saw that he might not prevail, finding no such favor in his suit as he looked for, he first made war against the said Lord Grey, wasting his lands and possessions with fire and sword, cruelly killing his servants and tenants. The king, advertised of such rebellious exploits enterprised by the said Owen and his unruly complices, determined to chastise them as disturbers of his peace, and so with an army entered into Wales, but the Welshmen with their captain withdrew into the mountains of Snowdon, so to escape the revenge which the King meant towards them. The King therefore did much hurt in the countries with fire and sword, slaying diverse that with weapon in

---

[1]Probably Old French for "esquire," a member of the higher order of gentry, "ranking immediately below a knight"; "a landed proprietor"; as well as an officer "in the service of a king or nobleman," as in its next usage, below (*OED*). Another tradition stresses that Glendower was of noble birth; during his revolt, in 1406, he named himself "Owain, Prince of Wales" in a letter to Charles VI of France.

hand came forth to resist him, and so with a great booty of beasts and cattle he returned.

[*Foreign affairs and orthodoxy at home*]

[1401] The emperor of Constantinople coming into England to sue for aid against the Turks was met by the king on Blackheath upon the feast day of Saint Thomas the apostle, and brought unto London with great honor. The King bare all his charges, presenting him with gifts at his departure, meet for such an estate. After the feast of the Epiphany, a parliament was held, in which an act was made against those that held opinions in religion contrary to the received doctrine of the church of Rome, ordaining that wheresoever any of them were found and proved to set forth such doctrine they should be apprehended and delivered to the bishop their diocesane,[2] and if they stood stiffly in their opinions, and would not be reformed, they should be delivered to the secular power, to be burnt to ashes.

[*Glendower and portents*]

[1402] In the month of March appeared a blazing star,[3] first between the east part of the firmament and the north, flashing forth fire and flames round about it, and lastly shooting forth fiery beams towards the north, foreshowing (as was thought) the great effusion of blood that followed, about the parts of Wales and Northumberland. For much about the same time, Owen Glendower (and his Welshmen) fought with the Lord Grey of Ruthin, coming forth to defend his possessions, which the same Owen wasted and destroyed: and as the fortune of that day's work fell out, the Lord Grey was taken prisoner, and many of his men were slain. This hap lifted the Welshmen into high pride, and increased marvellously their wicked and presumptuous attempts.

[*War in Wales: "shameful villainy" and guilty King*]

Owen Glendower, according to his accustomed manner, robbing and spoiling within the English borders, caused all the forces of the shire of Hereford to assemble together against them, under the conduct

---

[2]Religious overseer of their jurisdiction.
[3]Halley's comet.

of Edmund Mortimer, Earl of March. But coming to try the matter by battle, whether by treason or otherwise, so it fortuned, that the English power was discomfited, the Earl taken prisoner, and above a thousand of his people slain in the place. The shameful villainy used by the Welshwomen towards the dead carcasses was such as honest ears would be ashamed to hear and continent tongues to speak thereof.[4] The dead bodies might not be buried without great sums of money given for liberty to convey them away.

The King was not hasty to purchase the deliverance of the Earl of March, because his title to the crown was well-enough known, and therefore suffered him to remain in miserable prison, wishing both the said Earl and all other of his lineage out of this life, with God and his saints in heaven so they had been out of the way, for then all had been well enough as he thought.[5] But to let these things pass, the King this year sent his eldest daughter Blanch, accompanied with the Earl of Somerset, the Bishop of Worcester, the Lord Clifford, and others into Alamanie,[6] which brought her

---

[4]Graphic details of the Welshwomen's "shameful villainy" are recounted in the *Chronicles*, in Abraham Fleming's digression for the year 1405. After warning readers that their deeds were worse than the brutality of the Scythian queen, Tamyris, or of Marc Antony's wife, Fulvia (who had Cicero's head and hands cut off and his tongue cut out to "prick it all over with pins and needles"), Fleming's account moves from castration to further grotesquerie:

> yet did the women of Wales cut off their privities, and put one part therof into the mouths of every dead man, in such sort that the cullions [testicles] hung down to their chins; and not so contented they did cut off their noses and thrust them into their tails as they lay on the ground mangled and defaced. This was a very ignominious deed, and a worse not committed among the barbarous: which though it make the reader to read it, and the hearer to hear it, ashamed: yet because it was a thing done in open sight, and left testified in history, I see little reason why it should not be imparted in our mother tongue to the knowledge of our own countrymen, as well as unto strangers in a language unknown. And thus much by way of notifying the inhumanity and detestable demeanor of those Welshwomen, after the conflict between the English and the Welsh, whereof desultory mention is made before. . . .

Recent critical speculation about this gruesome episode in Holinshed and Shakespeare has stressed male anxiety about female effacement of heroism, identity, and historical mission, linking it to the pacifist sentiments of Lady Mortimer in *Part One* and Lady Percy in *Part*s *One* and *Two*. This episode might serve just as well, however, to contrast the monstrous warfare on all sides to the humane pacifism of the Ladies that has been shunted aside.

[5]A marginal comment in Holinshed's text notes at this point: "The suspicion of K. Henry grounded upon a guilty conscience."

[6]Germany.

to Cologne, and there with great triumph she was married to William, Duke of Bavaria, son and heir to Lewis, the Emperor. About mid of August, the King, to chastise the presumptuous attempts of the Welshmen, went with a great power of men into Wales to pursue the captain of the Welsh rebel Owen Glendower, but in effect he lost his labor; for Owen conveyed himself out of the way into his known lurking places, and (as was thought) through art [of] magic, he caused such foul weather of winds, tempest, rain, snow and hail to be raised for the annoyance of the King's army that the like had not been heard of; in such sort, that the King was constrained to return home, having caused his people yet to spoil and burn a great part of the country.

[*Hotspur defeats Scottish force at Holmedon*]

The Scots, under the leading of Patric Hepborne of the Hales, the younger, entering into England was overthrown at Nesbit in the marches, as in the Scottish chronicle ye may find more at large. This battle was fought the two and twentieth of June, in this year of our Lord, 1402.

Archibald, Earl Douglas, sore displeased in his mind for this overthrow, procured a commission to invade England, and that to his cost, as ye may likewise read in the Scottish histories. For at a place called Holmedon, they were so fiercely assailed by the Englishmen, under the leading of the Lord Percy, surnamed Henry Hotspur, and George, Earl of March, that with violence of the English shot they were quite vanquished and put to flight, on the Rood Day in harvest, with a great slaughter made by the Englishmen. . . . [O]f prisoners among others were these: Mordake, Earl of Fife, son to the Governor; Archibald, Earl Douglas, which in the fight lost one of his eyes; Thomas, Earl of Murray; Robert, Earl of Angus; (and as some writers have) the Earls of Athol and Menteith, with five hundred other of meaner degrees. . . .

[*Mortimer joins forces with the mysterious Glendower*]

Edmund Mortimer, Earl of March, prisoner with Owen Glendower, whether for irksomeness of cruel captivity or fear of death or for what other cause, it is uncertain, agreed to take part with Owen against the King of England and took to wife the daughter of the said Owen.

Strange wonders happened (as men reported) at the nativity of this man, for the same night he was born, all his father's horses in the stable were found to stand in blood up to the bellies.

[*The Percies turn against King Henry*]

[1403] Henry, Earl of Northumberland, with his brother Thomas, Earl of Worcester, and his son, the Lord Henry Percy, surnamed Hotspur, which were to King Henry in the beginning of his reign both faithful friends and earnest aiders, began now to envy his wealth and felicity; and especially they were grieved because the King demanded of the Earl and his son such Scottish prisoners as were taken at Holmedon and Nesbit: for of all the captives which were taken in the conflicts fought in those two places, they were delivered to the King's possession only Mordake, Earl of Fife, the Duke of Albany's son, though the King did divers and sundry times require deliverance of the residue, and that with great threatenings; wherewith the Percies, being sore offended, for that they claimed them as their own proper prisoners and their peculiar prize, by the counsel of the Lord Thomas Percy, Earl of Worcester, whose study was ever (as some write) to procure malice and set things in a broil, came to the King unto Windsor (upon a purpose to prove him) and there required of him that either by ransom or otherwise he would cause to be delivered out of prison Edmund Mortimer, Earl of March, their cousin german, whom (as they reported) Owen Glendower kept in filthy prison, shackled with irons, only for that he took his part and was to him faithful and true.

The King began not a little to muse at this request and not without cause; for indeed it touched him somewhat near, sith this Edmund was son to Roger, Earl of March, son to the Lady Philip, daughter of Lionel, Duke of Clarence, the third son of King Edward the Third; which Edmund, at King Richard's going into Ireland, was proclaimed heir apparent to the crown and realm; whose aunt called Eleanor, the Lord Henry Percy had married; and therefore King Henry could not well hear that any man should be earnest about the advancement of that lineage.[7] The King, when he had

---

[7]This lineage is inaccurate, conflating two Edmund Mortimers. It makes for a more concentrated drama, however, and is followed by Shakespeare. See "Selective Genealogy" (pp. xxx–xxxi).

studied on the matter, made answer that the Earl of March was not taken prisoner for his cause nor in his service but willingly suffered himself to be taken, because he would not withstand the attempts of Owen Glendower and his complices, and therefore he would neither ransom him nor relieve him.

The Percies with this answer and fraudulent excuse were not a little fumed, insomuch that Henry Hotspur said openly: "Behold, the heir of the realm is robbed of his right, and yet the robber with his own will not redeem him." So in this fury the Percies departed, minding nothing more than to depose King Henry from the high type of his royalty and to place in his seat their cousin Edmund, Earl of March, whom they did not only deliver out of captivity but also (to the high displeasure of King Henry) entered in league with the foresaid Owen Glendower. Herewith they, by their deputies in the house of the Archdeacon of Bangor, divided the realm amongst them, causing a tripartite indenture to be made and sealed with their seals, by the covenants whereof, all England from Severn and Trent south and eastward was assigned to the Earl of March; all Wales and the lands beyond Severn westward were appointed to Owen Glendower; and all the remnant from Trent northward to the Lord Percy.

This was done (as some have said) through a foolish credit given to a vain prophecy, as though King Henry was the moldwarp,[8] cursed of God's own mouth, and they three were the dragon, the lion, and the wolf, which should divide this realm between them. Such is the deviation (saith Hall[9]) and not divination of those blind and fantastical dreams of the Welsh prophesiers. King Henry, not knowing of this new confederacy, and nothing less minding than that which after happened, gathered a great army to go again into Wales, whereof the Earl of Northumberland and his son were advertised by the Earl of Worcester, and with all diligence raised all the power they could make, and sent to the Scots which before were taken prisoners at Holmedon for aid of men, promising to the Earl of Douglas the town of Berwick and a part of Northumberland, and to other Scottish lords great lordships and seignories, if they obtained the upper hand. The Scots, in hope of gain and desirous to

[8]A European mole; a stupid and shiftless person.
[9]Edward Hall, chronicler cited in headnote.

be revenged of their old griefs, came to the Earl with a great company well appointed.

[*Propaganda, rumor, argument*]

The Percies, to make their part seem good, devised certain articles by the advice of Richard Scroop, Archbishop of York, brother to the Lord Scroop, whom King Henry had caused to be beheaded at Bristol. These articles being shown to diverse noblemen and other states of the realm, moved them to favor their purpose, insomuch that many of them did not only promise to the Percies aid and succor by words, but also by their writings and seals confirmed the same. Howbeit, when the matter came to trial, the most part of the confederates abandoned them, and at the day of the conflict left them alone. Thus after that the conspirators had discovered themselves, the Lord Henry Percy, desirous to proceed in the enterprise, upon trust to be assisted by Owen Glendower, the Earl of March, and others, assembled an army of men-of-arms and archers forth of Cheshire and Wales. Incontinently, his uncle Thomas Percy, Earl of Worcester, that had the government of the Prince of Wales, who as then lay at London in secret manner, conveyed himself out of the Prince's house, and coming to Stafford (where he met his nephew), they increased their power by all ways and means they could devise. The Earl of Northumberland himself was not with them but, being sick, had promised upon his amendment to repair unto them (as some write) with all convenient speed.

These noblemen, to make their conspiracy to seem excusable, besides the articles above mentioned, sent letters abroad, wherein was contained that their gathering of an army tended to none other end but only for the safeguard of their own persons and to put some better government in the commonwealth. For whereas taxes and tallages[10] were daily levied under pretense to be employed in defense of the realm, the same were vainly wasted and unprofitably consumed; and where through the slanderous reports of their enemies the King had taken a grievous displeasure with them, they durst not appear personally in the King's presence, until the prelates and barons of the realm had obtained of the King license for them to come and purge themselves before him, by lawful trial of their

---

[10]Tolls, customs duties.

peers, whose judgment (as they pretended) they would in no wise refuse. Many that saw and heard these letters did commend their diligence and highly praised their assured fidelity and trustiness towards the commonwealth.

But the King, understanding their cloaked drift, devised (by what means he might) to quiet and appease the commons and deface their contrived forgeries; and therefore he wrote an answer to their libels that he marveled much, sith the Earl of Northumberland and the Lord Henry Percy, his son, had received the most part of the sums of money granted to him by the clergy and commonalty for defense of the marches, as he could evidently prove what should move them to complain and raise such manifest slanders. And whereas he understood that the Earls of Northumberland and Worcester and the Lord Percy had by their letters signified to their friends abroad that, by reason of the slanderous reports of their enemies, they durst not appear in his presence without the mediation of the prelates and nobles of the realm, so as they required pledges whereby they might safely come afore him to declare and allege what they had to say in proof of their innocency, he protested by letters sent forth under his seal that they might safely come and go, without all danger or any manner of endamagement to be offered to their persons.

But this could not satisfy those men but that, resolved to go forwards with their enterprise, they marched towards Shrewsbury upon hope to be aided (as men thought) by Owen Glendower and his Welshmen, publishing abroad throughout the countries on each side that King Richard was alive, whom if they wished to see, they willed them to repair in armor unto the castle of Chester, where (without all doubt) he was at that present and ready to come forward. This tale being raised, though it were most untrue, yet it bred variable motions in men's minds, causing them to waver so as they knew not to which part they should stick; and verily, divers were well affected towards King Richard, specially such as had tasted of his princely bountifulness, of which there was no small number. And to speak a truth, no marvel it was if many envied the prosperous state of King Henry, sith it was evident enough to the world that he had with wrong usurped the crown, and not only violently deposed King Richard but also cruelly procured his death; for the which, undoubtedly, both he and his posterity tasted such troubles as put them still in danger of their states, till their direct succeeding line was quite rooted out by the contrary faction, as in Henry the Sixth and Edward the Fourth it may appear.

[*Forces gather at Shrewsbury*]

But now to return where we left. King Henry, advertised of the proceedings of the Percies, forthwith gathered about him such power as he might make, and being earnestly called upon by the Scot, the Earl of March,[11] to make haste and give battle to his enemies, before their power by delaying of time should still too much increase, he passed forward with such speed that he was in sight of his enemies, lying in camp near to Shrewsbury, before they were in doubt of any such thing, for the Percies thought that he would have stayed at Burton-upon-Trent till his council had come thither to him to give their advice what he were best to do. But herein the enemy was deceived of his expectation, sith the King had great regard of expedition and making speed for the safety of his own person whereunto the Earl of March incited him, considering that in delay is danger and loss in lingering, as the poet in the like case saith:

> *Tolle moras, nocuit semper differre paratis,*
> *Dum trepidant nullo firmatae robore partes.*[12]

By reason of the King's sudden coming in this sort, they stayed from assaulting the town of Shrewsbury, which enterprise they were ready at that instant to have taken in hand, and forthwith the Lord Percy (as a captain of high courage) began to exhort the captains and soldiers to prepare themselves to battle, sith the matter was grown to that point that by no means it could be avoided, so that (said he): "This day shall either bring us all to advancement and honor, or else, if it shall chance us to be overcome, shall deliver us from the King's spiteful malice and cruel disdain; for playing the

[11]Here, George Dunbar, Earl of March of Scotland, not Edmund, the rival claimnant.

[12]From Lucan's *Civil War* (a.k.a. *Pharsalia*), 1.280–81: "While the other side in panic has not fortified its strength / end delay! Procrastination always harms the men prepared for action" (tr. S. H. Braund).

men (as we ought to do), better it is to die in battle for the common-wealth's cause than through cowardlike fear to prolong life, which after shall be taken from us by sentence of the enemy."

Hereupon the whole army, being in number about fourteen thousand chosen men, promised to stand with him so long as life lasted. There were with the Percies as chieftains of this army: the Earl of Douglas, a Scottish man; the Baron of Kinderton; Sir Hugh Browne and Sir Richard Vernon, knights, with diverse other stout and right valiant captains. Now when the two armies were encamped, the one against the other, the Earl of Worcester and the Lord Percy with their complices sent the articles (whereof I spake before) by Thomas Caiton and Thomas Salvain, esquiers to King Henry, under their hands and seals, which articles in effect charged him with manifest perjury, in that (contrary to his oath received upon the evangelists at Doncaster, when he first entered the realm after his exile) he had taken upon him the crown and royal dignity, imprisoned King Richard, caused him to resign his title and, finally, to be murdered. Diverse other matters they laid to his charge: as levying of taxes and tallages, contrary to his promise; infringing of laws and customs of the realm; and suffering the Earl of March to remain in prison without travailing to have him delivered. All which things they, as procurers and protectors of the common-wealth, took upon them to prove against him, as they protested unto the whole world.

King Henry, after he had read their articles, with the defiance which they annexed to the same, answered the esquiers that he was ready with dint of sword and fierce battle to prove their quarrel false and nothing else than a forged matter, not doubting but that God would aid and assist him in his righteous cause against the disloyal and false forsworn traitors. The next day in the morning early, being the even of Mary Magdalen, they set their battles in order on both sides, and now, whilst the warriors looked when the token of battle should be given, the Abbot of Shrewsbury and one of the clerks of the privy seal were sent from the King unto the Percies to offer them pardon if they would come to any reasonable agreement. By their persuasions, the Lord Henry Percy began to give ear unto the King's offer and so sent with them his uncle, the Earl of Worcester, to declare unto the King the causes of those troubles and to require some effectual reformation in the same.

[*Worcester's deception and the Battle of Shrewsbury*]

It was reported for a truth that now, when the King had condescended unto all that was reasonable at his hands to be required and seemed to humble himself more than was meet for his estate, the Earl of Worcester (upon his return to his nephew) made relation clean contrary to that the King had said, in such sort that he set his nephew's heart more in displeasure towards the King than ever it was before, driving him by that means to fight whether he would or not; then suddenly blew the trumpets, the King's part crying S[t] George upon them, the adversaries cried "Esperance Percy," and so the two armies furiously joined. The archers on both sides shot for the best game, laying on such load with arrows that many died and were driven down that never rose again.

The Scots (as some write), which had the fore ward on the Percies' side, intending to be revenged of their old displeasures done to them by the English nation, set so fiercely on the King's fore ward, led by the Earl of Stafford, that they made the same draw back, and had almost broken their adversaries' array. The Welshmen also, which before had lain lurking in the woods, mountains, and marshes, hearing of this battle toward, came to the aid of the Percies and refreshed the wearied people with new succors. The King, perceiving that his men were thus put to distress, what with the violent impression of the Scots and the tempestuous storms of arrows that his adversaries discharged freely against him and his people, it was no need to will him to stir; for suddenly, with his fresh battle, he approached and relieved his men, so that the battle began more fierce than before. Here the Lord Henry Percy and the Earl Douglas, a right stout and hardy captain, not regarding the shot of the King's battle nor the close order of the ranks, pressing forward together bent their whole forces towards the King's person, coming upon him with spears and swords so fiercely that the Earl of March the Scot, perceiving their purpose, withdrew the King from that side of the field (as some write) for his great benefit and safeguard (as it appeared), for they gave such a violent onset upon them that stood about the King's standard that, slaying his standard-bearer, Sir Walter Blunt, and overthrowing the standard, they made slaughter of all those that stood about it, as the Earl of Stafford, that day made by the King Constable of the realm, and divers other.

The Prince that day holp[13] his father like a lusty young gentleman; for although he was hurt in the face with an arrow, so that

[13] Helped.

diverse noblemen that were about him would have conveyed him forth of the field, yet he would not suffer them so to do, lest his departure from amongst his men might haply have stricken some fear into their hearts; and so, without regard of his hurt, he continued with his men and never ceased either to fight where the battle was most hot or to encourage his men where it seemed most need. This battle lasted three long hours with indifferent fortune on both parts, till at length the King, crying "Saint George victory," brake the array of his enemies and adventured so far that (as some write) the Earl Douglas strake him down and at that instant slew Sir Walter Blunt and three others appareled in the King's suit and clothing, saying: "I marvel to see so many kings thus suddenly arise one in the neck of another." The King indeed was raised and did that day many a noble feat of arms, for as it is written, he slew that day with his own hands six and thirty persons of his enemies. The other on his part, encouraged by his doings, fought valiantly and slew the Lord Percy, called Sir Henry Hotspur. To conclude, the King's enemies were vanquished and put to flight, in which flight the Earl of Douglas, for haste, falling from the crag of a high mountain, brake one of his cullions[14] and was taken, for his valiantness, of the King frankly and freely delivered.

There was also taken the Earl of Worcester, the procurer and setter forth of all this mischief, Sir Richard Vernon, and the Baron of Kinderton, with diverse other. There were slain upon the King's part, besides the Earl of Stafford, to the number of ten knights: Sir Hugh Shirley, Sir John Clifton, Sir John Cokaine, Sir Nicholas Gawsey, Sir Walter Blunt, Sir John Claverley, Sir John Macy of Podington, Sir Hugh Mortimer, and Sir Robert Gawsey, all the which received the same morning the order of knighthood; Sir Thomas Wendesley was wounded to death and so passed out of this life shortly after. There died in all upon the King's side sixteen hundred, and four thousand were grievously wounded. On the contrary side were slain, besides the Lord Percy, the most part of the knights and esquiers of the county of Chester, to the number of two hundred, besides yeomen and footmen; in all there died of those that fought on the Percies' side about five thousand. This battle was fought on Mary Magdalen Even, being Saturday. Upon the Monday following, the Earl of Worcester, the Baron of Kinderton, and Sir Richard

---

[14]Testicles.

Vernon, knights, were condemned and beheaded. The Earl's head was sent to London, there to be set on the bridge.

[*Estrangement and reconciliation of Prince and King*]

[1412] . . . The Lord Henry, Prince of Wales, eldest son to King Henry, got knowledge that certain of his father's servants were busy to give informations against him, whereby discord might arise betwixt him and his father; for they put into the King's head not only what evil rule (according to the course of youth) the Prince kept, to the offense of many, but also what great resort of people came to his house, so that the court was nothing furnished with such a train as daily followed the Prince. These tales brought no small suspicion into the King's head, lest his son would presume to usurp the Crown, he being yet alive, through which suspicious jealousy it was perceived that he favored not his son, as in times past he had done.

The Prince, sore offended with such persons as, by slanderous reports, sought not only to spot his good name abroad in the realm but to sow discord also betwixt him and his father, wrote his letters into every part of the realm to reprove all such slanderous devices of those that sought his discredit. And to clear himself the better, that the world might understand what wrong he had to be slandered in such wise, about the feast of Peter and Paul, to wit, the nine and twentieth day of June, he came to the court with such a number of noblemen and other his friends that wished him well, as the like train had been seldom seen repairing to the court at any one time in those days. He was appareled in a gown of blue satin full of small eyelet holes, at every hole the needle hanging by a silk thread with which it was sewed. About his arm he wore a hound's collar set full of SS of gold, and the tirets likewise being of the same metal.[15]

The court was then at Westminster where, he being entered into the hall, not one of his company durst once advance himself further than the fire in the same hall, notwithstanding they were earnestly requested by the lords to come higher; but they, regarding what they had in commandment of the Prince, would not presume to do

---

[15]The meaning of this strange garb is unclear. A couple of guesses are made at the analogous moment in *The Famous Victories*, excerpted later in this section.

in any thing contrary thereunto. He himself, only accompanied with those of the King's house, was straight admitted to the presence of the King his father, who being at that time grievously diseased, yet caused himself in his chair to be borne into his privy chamber, where in the presence of three or four persons in whom he had confidence, he commanded the Prince to show what he had to say concerning the cause of his coming.

The Prince, kneeling down before his father, said: "Most redoubted and sovereign lord and father, I am at this time come to your presence as your liege man and as your natural son, in all things to be at your commandment. And where I understand you have in suspicion my demeanor against your Grace, you know very well that if I knew any man within this realm of whom you should stand in fear, my duty were to punish that person, thereby to remove that grief from your heart. Then how much more ought I to suffer death, to ease your Grace of that grief which you have of me, being your natural son and liege man; and to that end I have this day made myself ready by confession and receiving of the sacrament. And therefore I beseech you, most redoubted lord and dear father, for the honor of God, to ease your heart of all such suspicion as you have of me and to dispatch me here before your knees with the same dagger" [and withal he delivered unto the King his dagger, in all humble reverence, adding further that his life was not so dear to him that he wished to live one day with his displeasure] "and therefore in thus ridding me out of life and yourself from all suspicion, here in presence of these lords and before God at the day of the general judgment, I faithfully protest clearly to forgive you."

The King, moved herewith, cast from him the dagger and, embracing the Prince, kissed him and with shedding tears confessed that indeed he had him partly in suspicion, though now (as he perceived) not with just cause, and therefore, from thenceforth no misreport should cause him to have him in mistrust, and this he promised of his honor. So by his great wisdom was the wrongful suspicion which his father had conceived against him removed and he restored to his favor. And further, where he could not but grievously complain of them that had slandered him so greatly, to the defacing not only of his honor but also putting him in danger of his life, he humbly besought the King that they might answer their unjust accusation; and in case they were found to have forged such matters upon a malicious purpose, that then they might suffer some punishment for their faults, though not to the full of that they had deserved. The King, seeming to grant his reasonable desire, yet told him that he must tarry a parliament that such offenders might be punished by judgment of their peers; and so for that time he was dismissed, with great love and signs of fatherly affection.

Thus were the father and the son reconciled, betwixt whom the said pickthanks[16] had sown division, insomuch that the son, upon a vehement conceit of unkindness sprung in the father, was in the way to be worn out of favor. Which was the more likely to come to pass by their informations that privily charged him with riot and other uncivil demeanor unseemly for a prince. Indeed, he was youthfully given, grown to audacity, and had chosen him companions agreeable to his age, with whom he spent the time in such recreations, exercises, and delights as he fancied. But yet (it should seem by the report of some writers) that his behavior was not offensive or at least tending to the damage of anybody, sith he had a care to avoid doing of wrong and to tender his affections within the tract of virtue, whereby he opened unto himself a ready passage of good liking among the prudent sort and was beloved of such as could discern his disposition, which was in no degree so excessive as that he deserved in such vehement manner to be suspected. In whose dispraise I find little but to his praise very much. . . .

Materials for *Henry IV, Part Two*

[*The King's fear*]

[1401] . . . One night, as the King was going to bed, he was in danger to have been destroyed; for some naughty traitorous persons had conveyed into his bed a certain iron made with smith's craft, like a caltrop,[1] with three long pricks, sharp and small, standing upright in such sort that when he had laid him down and that the weight of his body should come upon the bed, he should have been thrust in with those pricks and peradventure slain; but as God would, the King, not thinking of any such thing, chanced yet to feel

---

[16]One who seeks favor by flattery or telling tales. (Shakespeare's use of this word in *1 Henry IV* 3.2 is evidence of his use of the 1587 edition of Holinshed.)

---

[1]An iron ball with jutting spikes, thrown on a field to obstruct cavalry.

and perceive the instrument before he laid him down and so escaped the danger. Howbeit, he was not so soon delivered from fear; for he might well have his life in suspicion and provide for the preservation of the same, sith perils of death crept into his secret chamber and lay lurking in the bed of down where his body was to be reposed and to take rest. Oh what a suspected state therefore is that of a king holding his regiment with the hatred of his people, the heartgrudgings of his courtiers, and the peremptory practices of both together! Could he confidently compose or settle himself to sleep for fear of strangling? Durst he boldly eat and drink without dread of poisoning? Might he adventure to show himself in great meetings or solemn assemblies without mistrust of mischief against his person intended? What pleasure or what felicity could he take in his princely pomp, which he knew by manifest and fearful experience to be envied and maligned to the very death? The state of such a King is noted by the poet in Dionysius, as in a mirror, concerning whom it is said,

> Districtus ensis cui super impia
> Cervice pendet, non Siculae dapes
> Dulcem elaborabunt saporem,
> Non avium cytharaeq. cantus.[2]

[*The Archbishop as rebel*]

[1405] But at the same time, to his further disquieting, there was a conspiracy put in practice against him at home by the Earl of Northumberland, who had conspired with Richard Scroop, Archbishop of York, Thomas Mowbray Earl Marshal, son to Thomas Duke of Norfolk, who for the quarrel betwixt him and King Henry had been banished (as ye have heard), the Lords Hastings, Falconbridge, Bardolph, and divers others. It was appointed that they should meet all together with their whole power upon Yorkswold,

[2]From Horace's *Odes* 3.1, on the "sword of Damocles," suspended by a thread over the head of the flattering Damocles to dramatize to him how fearful was the life of the king. The stanza quoted here has been translated by Niall Rudd as: "For the man who has a naked sword hanging over his unholy neck, no Sicilian banquets will provide a sweet taste; no music of birds or lyre will bring back his sleep." We may suppose that Shakespeare had Horace's original in mind as well as Holinshed's excerpt, since Horace's succeeding lines, "The gentle sleep that countrymen enjoy does not despise their lowly cottages. . . ." informs the King's lament in Shakespeare.

at a day assigned, and that the Earl of Northumberland should be chieftain, promising to bring with him a great number of Scots. The Archbishop, accompanied with the Earl Marshal, devised certain articles of such matters, as it was supposed that not only the commonalty of the realm but also the nobility found themselves grieved with, which articles they showed first unto such of their adherents as were near about them and after sent them abroad to their friends further off, assuring them that for redress of such oppressions they would shed the last drop of blood in their bodies, if need were.

The Archbishop, not meaning to stay after he saw himself accompanied with a great number of men that came flocking to York to take his part in this quarrel, forthwith discovered[3] his enterprise, causing the articles aforesaid to be set up in the public streets of the city of York and upon the gates of the monasteries, that each man might understand the cause that moved him to rise in arms against the King, the reforming whereof did not yet appertain unto him. Hereupon knights, esquires, gentlemen, yeomen, and other of the commons as well of the city, towns, and countries about, being allured either for desire of change or else for desire to see a reformation in such things as were mentioned in the articles, assembled together in great numbers. And the Archbishop, coming forth amongst them clad in armor, encouraged, exhorted and (by all means he could) pricked them forth to take the enterprise in hand and manfully to continue in their begun purpose, promising forgiveness of sins to all them whose hap it was to die in the quarrel. And thus not only all the citizens of York but all other in the countries about that were able to bear weapon came to the Archbishop and the Earl Marshal. Indeed, the respect that men had to the Archbishop caused them to like the better of the cause, since the gravity of his age, his integrity of life and incomparable learning with the reverent aspect of his amiable personage moved all men to have him in no small estimation.

[*The Gaultree Stratagem*]

The King, advertised[4] of these matters, meaning to prevent them, left his journey into Wales and marched with all speed toward the north parts. Also, Ralph Neville, Earl of Westmoreland, that was

---

[3]Revealed, made public.
[4]Informed.

not far off, together with the Lord John of Lancaster, the King's son, being informed of this rebellious attempt, assembled together such power as they might make, and together with those which were appointed to attend on the said Lord John to defend the borders against the Scots . . . made forward against the rebels, and coming into a plain within the forest of Gaultree, caused their standards to be pitched down in like sort as the Archbishop had pitched his, over against them, being far stronger in number of people than the other, for (as some write) there were of the rebels at the least twenty thousand men.

When the Earl of Westmoreland perceived the force of the adversaries, and that they lay still and attempted not to come forward upon him, he subtly devised how to quell their purpose and forthwith dispatched messengers unto the Archbishop to understand the cause, as it were, of that great assembly, and for what cause (contrary to the King's peace) they came so in armor. The Archbishop answered that he took nothing in hand against the King's peace, but that whatsoever he did tended rather to advance the peace and quiet of the commonwealth than otherwise. And where he and his company were in arms, it was for fear of the King, to whom he could have no free access by reason of such a multitude of flatterers as were about him. And therefore he maintained that his purpose to be good and profitable, as well for the King himself as for the realm, if men were willing to understand a truth. And herewith he showed forth a scroll in which the articles were written whereof before ye have heard.

The messengers, returning to the Earl of Westmoreland, showed him what they had heard and brought from the Archbishop. When he had read the articles, he showed in word and countenance outwardly that he liked of the Archbishop's holy and virtuous intent and purpose, promising that he and his would prosecute the same in assisting the Archbishop, who, rejoicing hereat, gave credit to the Earl and persuaded the Earl Marshal (against his will as it were) to go with him to a place appointed for them to commune together. Here, when they were met with like number on either part, the articles were read over, and, without any more ado, the Earl of Westmoreland and those that were with him agreed to do their best to see that a reformation might be had according to the same.

The Earl of Westmoreland, using more policy than the rest: "Well," said he, "then our travel is come to the wished end; and where our people have been long in armor, let them depart home to their wonted trades and occupations. In the meantime, let us drink together in sign of agreement that the people on both sides may see it and know that it is true that we be light at a point." They had no sooner shaken hands together but that a knight was sent straightways from the Archbishop to bring word to the people that there was peace concluded, commanding each man to lay aside his arms and to resort home to their houses. The people, beholding such tokens of peace as shaking of hands and drinking together of the lords in loving manner, they, being already wearied with the unaccustomed travail of war, brake up their field and returned homewards. But, in the meantime, whilst the people of the Archbishop's side withdrew away, the number of the contrary part increased, according to order given by the Earl of Westmoreland. And yet the Archbishop perceived not that he was deceived until the Earl of Westmoreland arrested both him and the Earl Marshal with divers other. Thus saith Walsingham.

But others write somewhat otherwise of this matter, affirming that the Earl of Westmoreland, indeed, and the Lord Ralph Evers procured the Archbishop and the Earl Marshal to come to a communication with them upon a ground just in the midway betwixt both the armies, where the Earl of Westmoreland in talk declared to them how perilous an enterprise they had taken in hand so to raise the people and to move war against the King, advising them therefore to submit themselves without further delay unto the King's mercy and his son the Lord John, who was present there in the field with banners spread, ready to try the matter by dint of sword if they refused this counsel. And therefore he willed them to remember themselves well, and, if they would not yield and crave the King's pardon, he bade them do their best to defend themselves.

Hereupon as well the Archbishop as the Earl Marshal submitted themselves unto the King and to his son the Lord John that was there present and returned not to their army. Whereupon their troops scaled[5] and fled their ways, but, being pursued, many were taken, many slain, and many spoiled of that that they had about them and so permitted to go their ways. Howsoever the matter was handled, true it is that the Archbishop and the Earl Marshal were

---

[5]Split off into parts.

brought to Pomfret to the King, who in this meanwhile was advanced thither with his power, and from thence he went to York, whither the prisoners were also brought, and there beheaded the morrow after Whitsunday in a place without the city, that is to understand, the Archbishop himself, the Earl Marshal, Sir John Lampley, and Sir Robert Plumpton. Unto all which persons though indemnity were promised, yet was the same to none of them at any hand performed. By the issue hereof, I mean the death of the foresaid, but specially of the Archbishop. . . .

The Archbishop suffered death very constantly, insomuch as the common people took it he died a martyr, affirming that certain miracles were wrought as well in the field where he was executed as also in the place where he was buried. And immediately upon such bruits,[6] both men and women began to worship his dead carcass, whom they loved so much when he was alive, till they were forbidden by the King's friends, and for fear gave over to visit the place of his sepulture. The Earl Marshal's body, by the King's leave, was buried in the cathedral church, many lamenting his destiny. But his head was set on a pole aloft on the walls for a certain space, till by the King's permission (after the same had suffered many a hot, sunny day and many a wet shower of rain) it was taken down and buried together with the body.

After the King, accordingly as seemed to him good, had ransomed and punished by grievous fines the citizens of York (which had borne armor on their Archbishop's side against him), he departed from York with an army of thirty and seven thousand fighting men furnished with all provision necessary, marching northwards against the Earl of Northumberland. At his coming to Durham, the Lord Hastings, the Lord Falconbridge, Sir John Coleville of the Dale, and Sir John Griffith, being convicted of the conspiracy, were there beheaded.

[*The Death of King Henry IV*][7]

[1412] In this fourteenth and last year of King Henry's reign, a council was holden in the Whitefriars in London, at the which, among other things, order was taken for ships and galleys to be builded and

---

[6]Reports, rumors.

[7]This section appears shortly after the King's 1412 reconciliation with the Prince, material already mined by Shakespeare for *Part One*.

made ready and all other things necessary to be provided for a voyage which he meant to make into the Holy Land, there to recover the city of Jerusalem from the infidels. For it grieved him to consider the great malice of Christian princes, that were bent upon a mischievous purpose to destroy one another, to the peril of their own souls, rather than to make war against the enemies of the Christian faith, as in conscience (it seemed to him) they were bound.[8] He held his Christmas this year at Eltham, being sore vexed with sickness, so that it was thought sometime that he had been dead. Notwithstanding, it pleased God that he somewhat recovered his strength again, and so passed that Christmas with as much joy as he might.

[1413] The morrow after Candlemas day began a Parliament, which he had called at London, but he departed this life before the same Parliament was ended, for now that his provisions were ready and that he was furnished with sufficient treasure, soldiers, captains, victuals, munitions, tall ships, strong galleys, and all things necessary for such a royal journey as he pretended[9] to take into the Holy Land, he was eftsoons taken with a sore sickness, which was not a leprosy stricken by the hand of God (saith Master Hall), as foolish friars imagined, but a very apoplexy[10] of the which he languished till his appointed hour, and had none other grief nor malady, so that what man ordaineth, God altereth at his good will and pleasure, not giving place more to the prince than to the poorest creature living, when He seeth His time to dispose of him this way or that, as to His omnipotent power and Divine Providence seemeth expedient. During this last sickness, he caused his crown (as some write) to be set on a pillow at his bed's head, and suddenly his pangs so sore troubled him that he lay as though all his vital spirits had been from him departed. Such as were about him, thinking verily that he had been departed, covered his face with a linen cloth.

The Prince, his son, being hereof advertised, entered into the chamber, took away the crown, and departed. The father, being suddenly revived out of that trance, quickly perceived the lack of his crown, and, having knowledge that the Prince his son had taken it away, caused him to come before his presence, requiring of him what he meant, so to misuse himself. The Prince with a good audacity

---

[8] Ironists should note that this will be Henry V's dilemma in his French wars.

[9] Intended.

[10] A stroke, paralysis.

answered, "Sir, to mine and all men's judgments, you seemed dead in this world, wherefore I, as your next heir apparent, took that as mine own and not as yours."

"Well, fair son," said the King with a great sigh, "what right I had to it, God knoweth."

"Well," said the Prince, "if you die king, I will have the garland and trust to keep it with the sword against all mine enemies, as you have done."

Then said the King, "I commit all to God, and remember you to do well." With that he turned himself in his bed, and shortly after departed to God, in a chamber of the Abbot's of Westminster, called "Jerusalem," in the twentieth day of March, in the year 1413, and in the year of his age 46, when he had reigned thirteen years, five months and odd days, in great perplexity and little pleasure. . . .

We find that he was taken with his last sickness while he was making his prayers at Saint Edward's shrine, there as it were to take his leave, and so to proceed forth on his journey; he was so suddenly and grievously taken that such as were about him feared lest he would have died presently. Wherefore to relieve him (if it were possible) they bare him into a chamber that was next at hand, belonging to the Abbot of Westminster, where they laid him on a pallet before the fire and used all remedies to revive him. At length, recovering his speech and understanding, and perceiving himself in a strange place which he knew not, he willed to know if the chamber had any particular name, whereunto answer was made that it was called "Jerusalem." Then said the King, "lauds be given to the Father of Heaven, for now I know that I shall die here in this chamber, according to the prophecy of me declared, that I should depart this life in Jerusalem."

Whether this was true that so he spake, as one that gave too much credit to foolish prophecies and vain tales, or whether it was feigned, as in such cases it commonly happeneth, we leave it to the advised reader to judge.

[*Ambivalent summary of the King's reign*]

The King was of a mean stature, well proportioned, and formally compact, quick and lively, and of a stout courage. In his latter days he showed himself so gently, that he got more love amongst the nobles and the people of this realm, than he had purchased malice and evil will in the beginning.

But yet to speak a truth, by his proceedings, after he had attained to the crown, what with such taxes, tallages, subsidies, and exactions as he was constrained to charge the people with; and what by punishing such as moved with disdain to see him usurp the crown (contrary to the oath taken at his entering into this land, upon his return from exile) did at sundry times rebel against him, he won himself more hatred, than in all his lifetime (if it had been longer by many years than it was) had been possible for him to have weeded out and removed. And yet doubtless, worthy were his subjects to taste of that bitter cup, since they were so ready to join and clap hands with him, for the deposing of their rightful and natural prince King Richard, whose chief fault rested only in that, that he was too bountiful to his friends, and too merciful to his foes. . . .

[*The coronation and reformation of Henry V*]

He [Henry V] was crowned the ninth of April, being Passion Sunday, which was a sore, ruggie, and tempestuous day, with wind, snow and sleet, that men greatly marveled thereat, making diverse interpretations what the same might signify. But this King even at first appointing with himself to show that in his person princely honors should change public manners, he determined to put on him the shape of a new man. For whereas aforetime he had made himself a companion unto misruly mates of dissolute order and life, he now banished them all from his presence (but not unrewarded or else unpreferred), inhibiting them upon a great pain not once to approach, lodge, or sojourn within ten miles of his court or presence; and in their places he chose men of gravity, wit, and high policy, by whose wise counsel he might at all times rule to his honor and dignity, calling to mind how once, to high offense of the King his father, he had with his fist stricken the Chief Justice for sending one of his minions (upon desert) to prison, when the Justice stoutly commanded himself also straight to ward, and he (then Prince) obeyed.[11] The King after expelled him out of his Privy Council, banished him the court, and made the Duke of Clarence (his younger brother) President of Council in his stead.

---

[11]This notorious anecdote is alluded to but unstaged by Shakespeare; it is treated explicitly in *The Famous Victories* and in Elyot's *The Governor*.

Samuel Daniel (1562–1619)

Samuel Daniel was regarded by his contemporaries as a major poet on the level of Edmund Spenser and Sir Philip Sidney. Though some complained about the abstractness and lack of action in his work, Daniel's probing intelligence and varied achievements—love sonnets, verse epistles, philosophical debate, literary criticism, closet drama, historical narrative—have long drawn critical admiration. Like Holinshed's Chronicles, *but with more calculated, literary self-consciousness, Daniel's texts play perspectives against each other to highlight conflicting interests, sometimes with dispassionate objectivity, but also to provoke sympathy for those caught up in political and emotional turmoil.*

The Civil Wars *went through several versions, appearing first as* The First Four Books of the Civil Wars *(1595), the one used by Shakespeare and modernized here, and again in 1599, 1601, and 1609; but it remained unfinished. Written in* ottava rima *stanzas—abababcc—the verse form of Italian epic romances by Ariosto (*Orlando Furioso, *1516) and Tasso (*Gerusalemme Liberata, *1581), it also draws on the classical models of Homer, Virgil, and especially Lucan's first-century epic about civil war (*De bello civili, *also known as the* Pharsalia*). Like Lucan, who regards civil war as self-wounding conflict—"kin facing kin," and "javelins threatening javelins"—Daniel, beginning with his first stanza, often shapes his material into a collision of symmetrical forces:*

> I sing the civil wars, tumultuous broils
> And bloody factions of a mighty land,
> Whose people haughty, proud with foreign spoils,
> Upon themselves turn back their conquering hand;
> Whilst kin their kin, brother the brother foils,
> Like ensigns all against like ensigns band,
> Bows against bows, the Crown against the crown,
> Whilst all pretending right, all right's thrown down.

This shaping involved that important innovation of matching Hotspur's age to the Prince's (Hotspur was two years older than Hal's father). Shakespeare may have been influenced as well by other aspects of The Civil Wars: *a melancholy sense of time's wastefulness (featured in much of Daniel's work); the troubled conscience of Henry IV, especially on his deathbed (where Daniel has him on the verge of abdicating); and the inescapable, moral culpability of all involved in civil warfare. As the epic speaker laments, "valor here is vice, here manhood sin, / The forward'st hands doth O least honor win" (3.106).*

from *The First Four Books of the Civil Wars Between the Two Houses of Lancaster and York* (1595)

Materials for *Henry IV, Part One*

from The Third Book

86

And yet new Hydras[1] lo, new heads appear
T'afflict that peace reputed then so sure,
And gave him much to do, and much to fear,
And long and dangerous tumults did procure,
And those even of his chiefest followers were   685
Of whom he might presume him most secure,
Who whether not so graced or so preferred
As they expected, these new factions stirred.

87

The Percies were the men, men of great might,
Strong in alliance, and in courage strong   690
That thus conspire, under the pretense to right
The crookèd courses they had suffered long:
Whether their conscience[2] urged them or despite,
Or that they saw the part they took was wrong,
Or that ambition hereto did them call,   695
Or others envied grace, or rather all.

88

What cause soever were, strong was their plot,
Their parties great, means good, th' occasion fit:
Their practice close, their faith suspected not,
Their states far off and they of wary wit: 700
Who with large promises draw in the Scot
To aid their cause; he likes, and yields to it,

---

[1] A mythical, snake-like monster with seven, or fifty, or more heads, often representing envy or rebellion; difficult to kill because it regenerated its heads as soon as they were chopped off. Henry IV is himself ironically compared to the Hydra by Douglas in *1 Henry IV*, 5.4.

[2] Probably, guilty conscience for helping to overthrow Richard II.

Not for the love of them or for their good,
But glad hereby of means to shed our blood.

89

   Then join they with the Welsh, who fitly trained   705
And all in arms under a might head
Great Glendow'r, who long warred, and much attained,
Sharp conflicts made, and many vanquishèd:
With whom was Edmund Earl of March retained
Being first his prisoner, now confederèd,   710
A man the King much feared, and well he might
Lest he should look whether his crown stood right.[3]

90

   For Richard, for the quiet of the state,
Before he took those Irish wars in hand
About succession doth deliberate,   715
And finding how the certain right did stand,
With full consent this man did ordinate
The heir apparent in the Crown and land:
Then judge if this the King might nearly touch,
Although his might were small, his right being much.   720

91

   With these the Percies them confederate,
And as three heads they league in one intent,
And instituting a Triumvirate
Do part the land in triple government:
Dividing thus among themselves the state,   725
The Percies should rule all the North from Trent
And Glendow'r Wales: the Earl of March should be
Lord of the South from Trent; and thus they 'gree.

92

   Then those two helps which still such actors find—
Pretense of common good, the King's disgrace—   730

[3]See "Selective Genealogy," nn. 2 and 3.

Doth fit their course, and draw the vulgar mind
To further them and aid them in this case:
The King they accused for cruel, and unkind
That did the state, and Crown, and all deface;
A perjured man that held all faith in scorn,   735
Whose trusted oaths had others made forsworn.

93

    Besides the odious detestable act
Of that late murdered king they aggravate,
Making it his that so had willed the fact
That he the doers did remunerate: 740
And then such taxes daily doth exact
That were against the orders of the state,
And with all these or worse they him assailed
Who late of others with the like prevailed.

94

    Thus doth contentious proud mortality   745
Afflict each other and itself torment:
And thus O thou, mind-tort'ring misery,
Restless ambition, born in discontent,
Turn'st and retossest with iniquity
The unconstant courses frailty did invent: 750
And foul'st fair order and defil'st the earth
Fost'ring up war, father of blood and dearth.

95

    Great seemed the cause, and greatly, too, did add
The peoples' love thereto, these crimes rehearsed,
That many gathered to the troops they had   755
And many more do flock from coasts dispersed:[4]
But when the King had heard these news so bad,
Th' unlookt for dangerous toil more nearly pierced;
For bent t'wards Wales t'appease those tumults there,
H' is forced divert his course, and them forbear.   760

[4]From various parts of the realm.

96

Not to give time unto th' increasing rage
And gathering fury, forth he hastes with speed,
Lest more delay or giving longer age
To th' evil grown, it might the cure exceed:
All his best men at arms, and leaders sage   765
All he prepared he could, and all did need;
For to a mighty work thou goest, O King,
To such a field that power to power shall bring.

97

There shall young Hotspur with a fury led
Meet with thy forward[5] son as fierce as he:[6]   770
There warlike Worcester long experienced
In foreign arms, shall come t' encounter thee:
There Douglas to thy Stafford shall make head:
There Vernon for thy valiant Blunt shall be:
There shalt thou find a doubtful bloody day,   775
Though sickness keep Northumberland away.

98

Who yet reserved, though after quit for this,
Another tempest on thy head to raise,
As if still-wrong revenging *Nemesis*
Did mean t' afflict all thy continual days: 780
And yet this field he happily might miss
For thy great good, and therefore well he stays:
What might his force have done being joined thereto
When that already gave so much to do?[7]

[5]Ardent, zealous, aggressive.

[6]Hotspur's anticipation of his meeting with Hal transforms him into a young opponent, contributing to their symmetry.

[7]The stanza concludes that Henry was fortunate Northumberland could not attend, yet also suggests Henry's guilt has not been expiated; Nemesis, the goddess of retribution, may be protracting his punishment.

99

The swift approach and unexpected speed   785
The King had made upon this new-raised force
In th' unconfirmed troops much fear did breed,
Untimely hind'ring their intended course;
The joining with the Welsh they had decreed
Was hereby stopped, which made their part the worse, 790
Northumberland with forces from the North
Expected to be there, was not set forth.

100

And yet undaunted Hotspur seeing the King
So near approached leaving the work in hand
With forward speed his forces marshaling,   795
Sets forth his farther coming to withstand:
And with a cheerful voice encouraging
By his great spirit his well emboldened band,
Brings a strong host of firm resolvèd might,
And placed his troops before the King in sight.   800

101

"This day," saith he, "O faithful valiant friends,
Whatever it doth give, shall glory give:
This day with honor frees our state, or ends
Our misery with fame, that still shall live,
And do but think how well this day he spends   805
That spends his blood his country to relieve:
Our holy cause, our freedom, and our right,
Sufficient are to move good minds to fight.

102

"Besides th' assurèd hope of victory
That we may even promise on our side   810
Against this weak-constrainèd company,
Whom force and fear, not will and love doth guide
Against a prince whose foul impiety
The heavens do hate, the earth cannot abide,

Our number being no less, our courage more,   815
What need we doubt if we but work therefore."

103

This said, and thus resolved even bent[8] to charge
Upon the King, who well their order viewed
And careful noted all the form at large
Of their proceeding, and their multitude: 820
And deeming better if he could discharge
The day with safety, and some peace conclude,
Great proffers sends of pardon, and of grace
If they would yield, and quietness embrace.

104

But this refused,[9] the King with wrath incensed   825
Rage against fury doth with speed prepare:
And "O," saith he, "though I could have dispensed
With this day's blood, which I have sought to spare
That greater glory might have recompensed
The forward worth of these that so much dare,   830
That we might honor had by th' overthrown,
That th' wounds we make, might not have been our own.

105

"Yet since that other men's iniquity
Calls on the sword of wrath against my will,
And that themselves exact this cruelty,   835
And I constrainèd am this blood to spill:
Then on my masters, on courageously
True-hearted subjects against traitors ill,
And spare them not who seek to spoil us all,
Whose foul confusèd end soon see you shall."   840

[8]Prepared, like an aimed weapon or strung bow.

[9]Daniel, departing from Holinshed, avoids mentioning Worcester's duplicity, but he
hints at it in stanza 109, and is more explicit in the revised *Civil Wars* of 1607 (4.42).

106

Straight moves with equal motion equal rage
The like incensèd armies unto blood,
One to defend, another side to wage
Foul civil war, both vows their quarrel good:
Ah too much heat to blood doth now enrage   845
Both who the deed provokes and who withstood,
That valor here is vice, here manhood sin,
The forward'st hands doth O least honor win.

107

But now begin these fury-moving sounds
The notes of wrath that music brought from hell,   850
The rattling drums which trumpets voice confounds,
The cries, th' encouragements, the shouting shrill;
That all about the beaten air rebounds,
Thund'ring confusèd, murmurs horrible,
To rob all sense except the sense to fight: 855
Well hands may work, the mind hath lost his sight.

108

O war! begot in pride and luxury,
The child of wrath and of dissension,
Horrible good; mischief necessary,
The foul reformer of confusion,   860
Unjust-just scourge of our iniquity,
Cruel recurrer of corruption:
O that these sin-sick states in need should stand
To be let blood with such a boist'rous hand!

109

And O how well thou hadst been spared this day   865
Had not wrong-counseled Percy been perverse,
Whose young undangered hand now rash makes way
Upon the sharpest fronts of the most fierce:
Where now an equal fury thrusts to stay
And rebeat-back that force and his disperse,   870

Then these assail, then those chase back again,
Till stayed with new-made hills of bodies slain.

110

There lo that new-appearing glorious star
Wonder of Arms, the terror of the field,
Young Henry, laboring where the stoutest are,   875
And even the stoutest forces back to yield,
There is that hand bold'ned to blood and war
That must the sword in woundrous[10] actions wield:
But better hadst thou learned with others' blood
A less expense to us, to thee more good.   880

111

Hadst thou not there lent present speedy aid
To thy endangered father nearly tired,
Whom fierce encountring Douglas overlaid,
That day had there his troublous life expired:
Heroical courageous Blunt arrayed   885
In habit like as was the King attired
And deemed for him, excused that fate with his,
For he had what his lord did hardly miss.[11]

[10]Some read a pun (wound/wondrous); in 1609 Daniel revises to "wondrous" (4.48).

[11]Using decoys to protect a king was practical; but like Shakespeare, Daniel saw a metaphor, and in 1609 made it a patriotic, metaphysical conceit ("he" in the first line is Hotspur's ally Douglas):

> And three, with fiery courage, he assails;
> Three, all as Kings adorned in royal wise;
> And each successive after other quails;
> Still wond'ring, whence so many Kings should rise.
> And, doubting lest his hand or eye-sight fails,
> In these confounded, on a fourth he flies,
> And him unhorses too: whom had he sped,
> He then all Kings, in him, had vanquishèd.
>
> For Henry had divided, as it were,
> The person of himself, into four parts;
> To be less known, and yet known everywhere,
> The more to animate his people's hearts:
> Who, cheered by his presence, would not spare
> To execute their best and worthiest parts.
> But which, two special things effected are;
> His safety, and his subjects' better care.   (4.50–51)

112

For, thought a king, he would not now disgrace
The person then supposed, but princelike shows   890
Glorious effects of worth that fit his place,
And fighting dies, and dying overthrows:
Another of that forward name and race[12]
In that hot work his valiant life bestows,
Who bare the standard of the King that day,   895
Whose colors overthrown did much dismay.

113

And dear it cost, and O much blood is shed
To purchase thee this losing victory
O travailed King: yet hast thou conquerèd
A doubtful day, a mighty enemy: 900
But O what wounds, what famous worth lies dead!
That makes the winner look with sorrowing eye,
Magnanimous Stafford lost that much had wrought,
And valiant Shirley who great glory got.

114

Such wreck of others' blood thou didst behold,   905
O furious Hotspur, ere thou lost thine own!
Which now once lost that heat in thine waxed cold,
And soon became thy army overthrown;
And O that this great spirit, this courage bold,
Had in some good cause been rightly shown!   910
So had not we thus violently then
Have termed that rage, which valor should have been.

---

[12]There were two Blunts killed by Douglas (cf. *2 Henry IV* 1.1).

Materials for *Henry IV, Part Two*

from The Third Book

115

But now the King retires him to his peace,
A peace much like a feeble sick man's sleep
(Wherein his waking pains do never cease   915
Though seeming rest his closed eyes doth keep),
For, O, no peace could ever so release
His intricate turmoils and sorrows deep,
But that his cares kept waking all his life
Continue on till Death conclude the strife.   920

116

Whose herald, Sickness, being sent before
With full commission to denounce his end,
And Pain, and Grief, enforcing more and more,
Besieged the hold that could not long defend,
And so consumed all that emboldening store   925
Of hot gain-striving blood that did contend,
Wearing the wall so thin that now the mind
Might well look through, and his frailty find.

117

When, lo, as if the vapors vanished were,
Which heat of boiling blood and health did breed   930
(To cloud the sense that nothing might appear
Unto the thought, that which it was indeed),
The lightened soul began to see more clear
How much it was abused,[1] and notes with heed
The plain discovered falsehood open laid   935
Of ill persuading flesh that so betrayed.

[1]Deluded, misused.

118

And lying on his last afflicted bed
Where Death and Conscience both before him stand,
The one holding out a book, wherein he read
In bloody lines the deeds of his own hand;   940
The other shows a glass, which figured
An ugly form of foul corrupted sand—
Both bringing horror in the highest degree
With what he was, and what he straight should be.

119

Which seeing, all confused, trembling with fear,   945
He lay awhile, as overthrown in spirit,
At last commands some that attending were
To fetch the crown and set it in his sight,
On which with fixed eye and heavy cheer
Casting a look, "O God," saith he, "what right   950
I had to thee my soul doth now conceive—
Thee, which with blood I got, with horror leave.

120

"Wert thou the cause my climbing care was such
To pass those bounds nature and law ordained?
Is this that good which promised so much,   955
And seemed so glorious ere it was attained?
Wherein was never joy but gave a touch
To check my soul to think how thou were gained,
And now, how do I leave thee unto mine,
Which it is dread to keep, death to resign?"   960

121

With this the soul, rapt wholly with the thought
Of such distress, did so attentive weigh
Her present horror, whilst, as if forgot,
The dull, consumed body senseless lay,
And now as breathless quite, quite dead is thought,   965
When, lo, his son comes in, and takes away

The fatal crown from thence, and out he goes
As if unwilling longer time to lose.

122

   And whilst that sad confused soul doth cast
Those great accounts of terror and distress,   970
Upon this counsel it doth light at last
How she[2] might make the charge of horror less,
And finding no way to acquit that's past,
But only this, to use some quick redress
Of acted wrong, with giving up again   975
The crown to whom it seemed to appertain.

123

   Which found, lightened with some small joy she lies,
Rouses her servants that dead-sleeping lay
(The members of her house) to exercise
One feeble duty more during her stay;   980
And, opening those dark windows, he espies
The crown for which he looked was borne away,
And, all aggrieved with the unkind offense,
He caused him bring it back that took it thence.

124

   To whom (excusing his presumptuous deed   985
By the supposing him departed quite)
He said, "O son, what needs thee make such speed
Unto that care, where fear exceeds thy right,
And where his sin whom thou shalt now succeed
Shall still upbraid thy inheritance of might,   990
And if thou canst live, and live great from woe
Without this careful travail—let it go."

125

   "Nay, father, since your fortune did attain
So high a stand, I mean not to descend,"

[2]His soul.

Replies the Prince, "as if what you did gain   995
I were of spirit unable to defend.
Time will appease them well that now complain,
And ratify our interest in the end.
What wrong hath not continuance quite outworn?
Years make that right which never was so born."   1000

126

"If so, God work his pleasure," said the King,
"And, O, do thou contend with all thy might
Such evidence of virtuous deeds to bring,
That well may prove our wrong to be our right,
And let the goodness of the managing   1005
Rase[3] out the blot of foul attaining quite,
That discontent may all advantage miss
To wish it otherwise than now it is.

127

"And since my death my purpose doth prevent
Touching this sacred war I took in hand   1010
(An action wherewithal my soul had meant
T'appease my God and reconcile my land)
To thee is left to finish my intent,
Who, to be safe, must never idly stand,
But some great actions entertain thou still   1015
To hold their minds who else will practice ill.

128

"Thou hast not that advantage by my reign
To riot it (as they whom long descent
Hath purchased love by custom), but with pain
Thou must contend to buy the world's content.   1020
What their birth gave them, thou hast yet to gain
By thine own virtues and good government,
And that unless thy worth confirm the thing
Thou canst not be the father to a king.

[3]Erase, scrape.

129

"Nor art thou born in those calm days, where rest   1025
Hath brought a sleepy, sluggish security,
But in tumultuous times, where minds addressed
To factions are inured to mutiny,
A mischief not by force to be suppressed
Where rigor still begets more enmity.   1030
Hatred must be beguiled with some new course
Where states are strong, and princes doubt their force."

130

This and much more, affliction would have said
Out of the experience of a troublous reign,
For which his high desires had dearly paid   1035
The interest of an ever-toiling pain,
But that this all-subduing power here stayed
His faltering tongue and pain r'inforced again
And cut off all the passages of breath
To bring him quite under the state of death.   1040

The Famous Victories of Henry the Fifth

The anonymous play, The Famous Victories, *inspires modern curiosity largely for its relation to the three Shakespearean plays dramatizing this monarch's legendary progress from wild youth to moral convert to warrior King. Throughout the trilogy, Shakespeare appears to borrow from or allude to relevant (and sometimes scandalous) episodes.*

Though the importance of The Famous Victories *as one of the first secular history plays is uncontested (some even claiming that it is an early work by Shakespeare), it often inspires witty and invidious comparisons. A. R. Humphreys notes its significance but dismisses its "imbecile" patchwork: reading it is like "going through the* Henry IV–Henry V *sequence in a bad dream, so close to Shakespeare is it in fragments, so worlds removed in skill." Yet it was quite popular in its own day, and the fragmentary quality may be the result of textual corruption—a memorial reconstruction or abridged acting version of a fuller (now lost) two-part sequence—or just the mark of a different aesthetic in playtexts aimed at brisk, effective action. The play we have was first published in 1598 but was probably written before 1588, the death date of the famous Elizabethan clown, Richard Tarlton, who (anecdotal evidence suggests) played the role of Derick. Though we are not sure what version Shakespeare saw or read,* The Famous Victories *survives as a vigorous sample of Elizabethan political drama and provides a glimpse of Shakespeare's dramatic choices.*

    Continuing a dramatic tradition that juxtaposed serious and comic material (for instance, The Second Shepherds' Play*),* The Famous Victories *stages a tale of political and paternal woe interspersed with farcical truancy and self-indulgence. The Prince's rowdy cohorts, called "knights," appear with antics similar to those in Shakespeare's version but without the individuating features: Shakespeare's subtle sketching of a resentful Ned Poins and the imaginative exuberance of Falstaff/Oldcastle (see the Contexts section "The Fascination of Falstaff") are scarcely evident in this play's Ned or its John Oldcastle. Hal himself is coarser, both in his excesses and in his apparent conversion—though one might see in his swaggering a reflection (and trivializing) of genuinely subversive tendencies in the late sixteenth century: if the King were dead, he twice tells his companions, "we would be all Kings." This thuggish Prince, however, has none of Hal's mysterious recesses. He gloats openly over his special privileges and receives and gives roughhouse beatings (including the notorious striking of the Chief Justice, only alluded to by Shakespeare but here enacted twice, the second time in a brief, parodic play-within-the-play). Worst of all, he threatens the realm with anarchy when he ascends the throne. What would become, in Shakespeare's* Henry IV, Part Two, *the dying King's dread of English culture reverting to savagery is here a bully's gleeful hope. His reformation is equally stark, though with momentary, dramatic tension. A menacing figure with dagger drawn, the Prince abruptly becomes a conscience-stricken convert; but whether that conversion occurs offstage, just before scene vi, or after he enters and hears his father's reproach, is not clear. The chroniclers Stow and Holinshed use the dagger only as a sign of Hal's reverence, as he offers his life to prove his submission to his father. The* Famous Victories *stages a murkier moment, and one critic (Champion 1990) even suggests it may be a charade by the Prince who decides inheritance is a surer path to an uncontested throne than regicide.*

    The modernized selection here provides the first half of the play, scenes relevant to Henry IV, Parts One *and* Two, *up to the rejection of Oldcastle and company. (The rest pertains to the French wars, material relevant for* Henry V.*) Although much of the 1598 quarto is set in the form of verse, I follow modern consensus of treating the play as prose. I have altered the speech prefix for the protagonist (referred to as*

"Hen. 5" in the original) to "Prince," though I have retained "Jockey" for John Oldcastle. (He is variously labeled "Iockey," "Ioc.," "Iock.," or "Ioh. Old." "Jockey" is a diminutive form of "John" or "Jack," often contemptuous; by the seventeenth century it could refer to a vagabond, trickster, or cheat, "from the character attributed to horse-dealers" [OED].)

from *The Famous Victories of Henry the Fifth Containing the Honorable Battle of Agincourt* (pre-1588?; pub. 1598)

[SCENE i]

Enter the young Prince, Ned, and Tom.

PRINCE Come away, Ned and Tom.

BOTH Here, my lord.

PRINCE Come away, my lads. Tell me, sirs, how much gold have you got?

NED Faith, my lord, I have got five hundred pound. 5

PRINCE But tell me, Tom, how much hast thou got?

TOM Faith, my lord, some four hundred pound.

PRINCE Four hundred pounds! Bravely spoken, lads! But tell me, sirs, think you not that it was a villainous part of me to rob my father's receivers?[1] 10

NED Why no, my lord, it was but a trick of youth.

PRINCE Faith, Ned, thou sayest true. But tell me, sirs, whereabouts are we?

TOM My lord, we are now about a mile off London.

PRINCE But, sirs, I marvel that Sir John Oldcastle comes not 15 away.

Zounds, see where he comes!

Enter Jockey [Sir John Oldcastle].

How now, Jockey, what news with thee?

JOCKEY Faith, my lord, such news as passeth; for the town of Deptford is risen with hue and cry after your man which 20 parted from us the last night and has set upon and hath robbed a poor carrier.[2]

---

[1]Treasury officials.

[2]One who transports commodities.

PRINCE   Zounds! The villain that was wont to spy out our booties?[3]

JOCKEY   Aye, my lord; even the very same.   25

PRINCE   Now, base-minded rascal, to rob a poor carrier! Well, it skills not;[4] I'll save the base villain's life. Ay, I may. But tell me, Jockey, wherabout be the receivers?

JOCKEY   Faith, my lord, they are hard by; but the best is, we are ahorseback and they be afoot, so we may escape them.   30

PRINCE   Well, if the villains come, let me alone with them! But tell me, Jockey, how much got'st thou from the knaves? For I am sure I got something; for one of the villains so belammed[5] me about the shoulders, as I shall feel it this month.   35

JOCKEY   Faith, my lord, I have got a hundred pound.

PRINCE   A hundred pound! Now, bravely spoken, Jockey. But come, sirs, lay all your money before me. Now, by heaven, here is a brave show! But, as I am true gentleman, I will have the half of this spent tonight. But, sirs, take up your bags;   40
here comes the receivers. Let me alone.

Enter two Receivers.

FIRST RECEIVER   Alas, good fellow, what shall we do? I dare never go home to the Court, for I shall be hanged. But look, here is the young Prince. What shall we do?

PRINCE   How now, you villains! What are you?   45

FIRST RECEIVER   Speak you to him.

SECOND RECEIVER   No, I pray, speak you to him.

PRINCE   Why, how now, you rascals, why speak you not?

FIRST RECEIVER   Forsooth, we be—Pray, speak you to him.

PRINCE   Zounds, villains, speak, or I'll cut off your heads!   50

SECOND RECEIVER   Forsooth, he can tell the tale better than I.

FIRST RECEIVER   Forsooth, we be your father's receivers.

PRINCE   Are you my father's receivers? Then I hope ye have brought me some money.

FIRST RECEIVER   Money? Alas, sir, we be robbed.   55

---

[3]Helped to arrange robberies.
[4]Makes no difference.
[5]Thrashed.

PRINCE   Robbed! How many were there of them?

FIRST RECEIVER   Marry, sir, there were four of them; and one of them had Sir John Oldcastle's bay hobby,[6] and your black nag.[7]

PRINCE   Gog's[8] wounds! How like you this Jockey? Blood, you 60 villains! My father robbed of his money abroad, and we robbed in our stables! But tell me, how many were there of them?

FIRST RECEIVER   If it please you, there were four of them; and there was one about the bigness of you. But I am sure I so belammed 65 him about the shoulders that he will feel it this month.

PRINCE   Gog's wounds, you lammed them fairly, so that they have carried away your money. [*To Jockey, et al.*] But come, sirs, what shall we do with the villains?

RECEIVERS   I beseech your Grace, be good to us. 70

NED   I pray you, my Lord, forgive them this once.

[PRINCE.]   Well, stand up and get you gone. And look that you speak not a word of it; for if there be, zounds, I'll hang you and all your kin!

Exit [*Receivers*].

Now, sirs, how like you this? Was not this bravely done? For 75 now the villains dare not speak a word of it, I have so feared them with words. Now, whither shall we go?

ALL   Why, my lord, you know our old hostess at Faversham?[9]

PRINCE   Our hostess at Faversham? Blood, what shall we do there? We have a thousand pound about us and we shall go 80 to a petty ale-house? No, no! You know the old tavern in Eastcheap;[10] there is good wine. Besides, there is a pretty wench that can talk well, for I delight as much in their tongues as any part about them.

ALL   We are ready to wait upon your Grace. 85

---

[6]Small or middle-sized reddish-brown horse; a pony.

[7]Small riding horse or pony.

[8]Distorted version of "God's," used in oaths to avoid blasphemy.

[9]Town near the main London road.

[10]Probably the notorious tavern well known to Elizabethans (though nonexistent in Prince Henry's day) that also appears in Shakespeare's *Henry IV, Parts One* and *Two*.

PRINCE Gog's wounds! Wait? We will go all together; we are all fellows. I tell you, sirs, and[11] the King, my father, were dead, we would be all kings. Therefore, come away.

NED Gog's wounds, bravely spoken, Harry!

[Exeunt.]

[SCENE ii]

Enter John Cobbler, Robin Pewterer,
Lawrence Costermonger.[1]

JOHN All is well here; all is well, masters.

LAWRENCE How say you, neighbor John Cobbler? I think it best that my neighbor, Robin Pewterer, went to Pudding Lane End, and we will watch here at Billingsgate Ward. How say you, neighbor Robin? How like you this? 5

ROBIN Marry well, neighbors; I care not much if I go to Pudding Lane's End. But, neighbors, and you hear any ado about me, make haste; and if I hear any ado about you, I will come to you. *Exit Robin.*

LAWRENCE Neighbor, what news hear you of the young Prince? 10

JOHN Marry, neighbor, I hear say he is a toward young Prince; for, if he meet any by the highway, he will not let[2] to—talk with him. I dare not call him thief, but sure he is one of these taking[3] fellows.

LAWRENCE Indeed, neighbor, I hear say he is as lively a young 15
Prince as ever was.

JOHN Ay, and I hear say if he use it long, his father will cut him off from the crown. But, neighbor, say nothing of that!

LAWRENCE No, no, neighbor, I warrant you!

JOHN Neighbor, methinks you begin to sleep. If you will, we 20
will sit down; for I think it is about midnight.

---

[11]If.

---

[1]These three characters are members of the "watch" (i.e., watchmen, sentinels). They are named after their usual occupations: a cobbler repairs shoes; a costermonger sells fruit ("costard" = apple).

[2]Hesitate (the dash indicates that John catches himself before speaking ill of the Prince).

[3]The pun (at once "stealing" and "attractive," "fetching") makes the point indirectly.

LAWRENCE   Marry, content, neighbor; let us sleep.

Enter Derick, roving.

DERICK   Who,[4] who there, who there?   *Exit Derick.*

Enter Robin.

ROBIN   Oh, neighbors, what mean you to sleep and such ado in
the streets?   25

BOTH   How now, neighbor, what's the matter?

Enter Derick again.

DERICK   Who there, who there, who there?

JOHN   Why, what ailst thou? Here is no horses.

DERICK   O, alas, man, I am robbed! Who there! Who there!

ROBIN   Hold him, Neighbor Cobbler.   *[John holds him.]*   30

JOHN   Why, I see thou art a plain clown.[5]

DERICK   Am I a clown? Zounds, masters, do clowns go in silk
apparel? I am sure all we gentlemen-clowns in Kent scant go
so well. Zounds! You know clowns very well! Hear you, are
you Master Constable? And you be, speak, for I will not   35
take it at his hands.

JOHN   Faith, I am not Master Constable; but I am one of his
bad[6] officers, for he is not here.

DERICK   It is not Master Constable here? Well, it is no matter.
I'll have the law at his hands.   40

JOHN   Nay, I pray you, do not take the law of us.

DERICK   Well, you are one of his beastly officers.

JOHN   I am one of his bad officers.

DERICK   Why then, I charge thee, look to him!

JOHN   Nay, but hear ye, sir; you seem to be an honest fellow,   45
and we are poor men; and now 'tis night, and we would be
loath to have anything ado; therefore, I pray thee, put it up.[7]

DERICK   First, thou sayst true; I am an honest fellow—and a
proper handsome fellow, too! And you seem to be poor men;

---

[4]Sometimes emended here and at l. 27 to "Whoa" because of John's remark
about horses at l. 28. But John has already shown himself to be a punster, and
may be indulging in verbal slapstick.

[5]Either rustic or comedian.

[6]Appointed.

[7]Put away your weapon.

therefore I care not greatly. Nay, I am quickly pacified. But 50
and you chance to spy the thief, I pray you, lay hold on him.

ROBIN   Yes, that we will, I warrant you.

DERICK   Tis a wonderful thing to see how glad the knave is,
now I have forgiven him.

JOHN   Neighbors, do ye look about you. How now, who's there? 55

Enter the Thief.

THIEF   Here is a good fellow. I pray you, which is the way to
the old tavern in Eastcheap?

DERICK   Whoop hollo! Now, Gadshill,[8] knowest thou me?

THIEF   I know thee for an ass.

DERICK   And I know thee for taking fellow upon Gad's Hill in 60
Kent. A bots[9] light upon ye!

THIEF   The whoreson villain would be knocked.

DERICK   Villain! Masters, and ye be men, stand to him and take
his weapon from him. Let him not pass you!

JOHN   My friend, what make you abroad now? It is too late to 65
walk now.

THIEF   It is not too late for true men to walk.

LAWRENCE   We know thee not to be a true man.

THIEF   Why, what do you mean to do with me? Zounds! I am
one of the King's liege people.[10] 70

DERICK   Hear you, sir, are you one of the King's liege people?

THIEF   Ay, marry am I, sir! What say you to it?

DERICK   Marry, sir, I say you are one of the King's filching people.

JOHN   Come, come, let's have him away.

THIEF   Why, what have I done? 75

ROBIN   Thou hast robbed a poor fellow, and taken away his
goods from him.

THIEF   I never saw him before.

DERICK   Masters, who comes here?

Enter the Vintner's Boy.

---

[8]Derick names the thief for Gad's Hill, a frequent place for robberies. Shakespeare does the same in *1 Henry IV*, 2.1. This character is also named Cutbert
Cutter, for his occupation as a "cutpurse," i.e., a thief, and his ruthlessness as a
"cutthroat."

[9]A horse disease (Bullough 1958).

[10]Sworn servants.

BOY   How now, Goodman Cobbler!   80

JOHN   How now, Robin, what makes thou abroad at this time
of night?

BOY   Marry, I have been at the Counter;[11] I can tell such news
as never you have heard the like.

JOHN   What is that, Robin? What is the matter?   85

BOY   Why, this night, about two hours ago, there came the
young Prince, and three or four more of his companions,
and called for wine good store; and then they sent for a
noise[12] of musicians, and were very merry for the space of
an hour; then, whether their music liked them not, or   90
whether they had drunk too much wine or no, I cannot tell,
but our pots flew against the walls; and then they drew their
swords and went into the street and fought, and some took
one part and some took another; but for the space of half an
hour there was such a bloody fray as passeth! And none   95
could part them until such time as the Mayor and Sheriff
were sent for; and then, at the last, with much ado, they
took them; and so the young Prince was carried to the
Counter; and then, about one hour after, there came a messenger from the court in all haste from the King for my Lord   100
Mayor and the Sheriff—but for what cause I know not.

JOHN   Here is news indeed, Robert!

LAWRENCE   Marry, neighbor, this news is strange, indeed! I
think it best neighbor, to rid our hands of this fellow first.

THIEF   What mean you to do with me?   105

JOHN   We mean to carry you to the prison, and there to remain
till the sessions day.

THIEF   Then, I pray you, let me go to the prison where my
master is.

JOHN   Nay, thou must go to the country prison, to Newgate.[13]   110
Therefore, come away.

THIEF [*To Derick*]   I prithee, be good to me, honest fellow.

DERICK   Ay, marry, will I; I'll be very charitable to thee, for I will
never leave thee—till I see thee on the gallows.

[*Exeunt.*]

[11]A London prison.

[12]Band.

[13]Another London prison.

[SCENE iii]

*Enter Henry the Fourth, with the Earl of Exeter,
and the Lord of Oxford.*[1]

OXFORD   And please your Majesty, here is my Lord Mayor and
the Sheriff of London to speak with your Majesty.

HENRY IV   Admit them to our presence.

Enter the Mayor and the Sheriff.

Now, my good Lord Mayor of London, the cause of my
sending for you at this time is to tell you of a matter which I   5
have learned of my Council. Herein I understand that you
have committed my son to prison without our leave and
license. What although he be a rude youth and likely to give
occasion, yet you might have considered that he is a prince,
and my son, and not to be hauled to prison by every subject.   10

MAYOR   May it please your Majesty to give us leave to tell our
tale?

HENRY IV   Or else, God forbid; otherwise you might think me
an unequal judge, having more affection to my son than to
any rightful judgement.   15

MAYOR   Then I do not doubt but we shall rather deserve commendations at your Majesty's hands than any anger.

HENRY IV   Go to, say on.

MAYOR   Then, if it please your Majesty, this night, betwixt two
and three of the clock in the morning, my lord the young   20
Prince, with a very disordered company, came to the old tavern in Eastcheap; and whether it was that their music liked
them not, or whether they were overcome with wine, I know
not, but they drew their swords and into the street they went;
and some took my lord the young Prince's part, and some   25
took the other; but betwixt them there was such a bloody
fray for the space of half an hour that neither watchmen nor
any other could stay them till my brother the Sheriff of London and I were sent for; and at the last, with much ado, we
stayed them; but it was long first, which was a great disqui-   30
eting to all your loving subjects thereabouts. And then, my
good Lord, we knew not whether your Grace had sent them

[1]Corbin and Sedge (1991) retitle the Earl as Duke.

to try us whether we would do justice, or whether it were of their own voluntary will or not; we cannot tell. And therefore, in such a case, we knew not what to do. But for our own safe-guard we sent him to ward, where he wanteth nothing that is fit for his Grace and your Majesty's son. And thus most humbly beseeching your Majesty to think of our answer.

HENRY IV   Stand aside until we have further deliberated on your answer.

Exit Mayor [and Sheriff].

Ah, Harry, Harry! Now thrice accursed Harry, that hath gotten a son which with grief will end his father's days. Oh my son! A prince thou art, ay, a prince indeed, and to deserve imprisonment. And well have they done, and like faithful subjects. Discharge them, and let them go.

EXETER   I beseech your Grace, be good to my lord, the young Prince.

HENRY IV   Nay, nay, tis no matter; let him alone.

OXFORD   Perchance the Mayor and the Sheriff have been too precise[2] in this matter.

HENRY IV   No, they have done like faithful subjects. I will go myself to discharge them and let them go.

Exeunt omnes.

[SCENE iv]

Enter Lord Chief Justice, Clerk of the Office, the Jailer, John Cobbler, Derick, and the Thief.

JUSTICE   Gaoler, bring the prisoner to the bar.

DERICK   Hear you, my lord; I pray you, bring the bar to the prisoner.

JUSTICE   Hold thy hand up at the bar.

THIEF   Here it is, my lord.

JUSTICE   Clerk of the Office, read his indictment.

CLERK   What is thy name?

THIEF   My name was known before I came here, and shall be when I am gone, I warrant you.

JUSTICE   Ay, I think so; but we will know it better before thou go.

---

[2]Strict, exacting.

DERICK   Zounds! And you do but send to the next jail, we are
sure to know his name; for this is not the first prison he hath
been in, I'll warrant you.

CLERK   What is thy name?

THIEF   What need you to ask, and have it in writing?   15

CLERK   Is not thy name Cutbert Cutter?

THIEF   What the devil need you ask, and know it so well?

CLERK   Why then, Cutbert Cutter, I indict thee, by the name of
Cutbert Cutter, for robbing a poor carrier the 20th day of
May last past, in the fourteenth year of the reign of our Sov-   20
ereign Lord, King Henry the Fourth, for setting upon a poor
carrier upon Gad's Hill in Kent, and having beaten and
wounded the said carrier, and taken his goods from him.

DERICK   Oh, masters, stay there! Nay, let's never belie the man,
for he hath not beaten and wounded me also, but he hath   25
beaten and wounded my pack, and hath taken the great
raze[1] of ginger that Bouncing Bess with the jolly buttocks
should have had. That grieves me most.

JUSTICE   Well, what sayest thou? Art thou guilty or not guilty?

THIEF   Not guilty, my lord.   30

JUSTICE   By whom wilt thou be tried?

THIEF   By my lord the young Prince, or by myself, whether you
will.

              Enter the young Prince, with Ned and Tom.

PRINCE   Come away, my lads. Gog's wounds, ye villain, what
make you here? I must go about my business myself and you   35
must stand loitering here?

THIEF   Why, my lord, they have bound me and will not let me go.

PRINCE   Have they bound thee, villain? Why, how now, my lord?

JUSTICE   I am glad to see your Grace in good health.

PRINCE   Why, my lord, this is my man. 'Tis marvel you knew   40
him not long before this. I tell you, he is a man of his
hands.[2]

THIEF   Ay, Gog's wounds, that I am! Try me who dare!

---

[1]Root.

[2]A good fighter; Poins says the same of himself in *2 Henry IV*, 2.2.

JUSTICE   Your grace shall find small credit by acknowledging
him to be your man.   45
PRINCE   Why, my lord, what hath he done?
JUSTICE   And it please your Majesty, he hath robbed a poor
carrier.
DERICK   Hear you, sir; marry, it was one Derick, Goodman
Hobling's man, of Kent.   50
PRINCE   What! Was't you, button-breech? Of my word, my
lord, he did it but in jest.
DERICK   Hear you, sir, is it your man's quality to rob folks in
jest? In faith, he shall be hanged in earnest.
PRINCE   Well, my lord, what do you mean to do with my man?   55
JUSTICE   And please your Grace, the law must pass on him
according to justice; then he must be executed.
PRINCE   Why, then, belike you mean to hang my man?
JUSTICE   I am sorry that it falls out so.
PRINCE   Why, my lord, I pray ye, who am I?   60
JUSTICE   And please your Grace, you are my lord the young
Prince, our king that shall be after the decease of our Sover-
eign Lord, King Henry the Fourth, whom God grant long to
reign!
PRINCE   You say true, my lord. And you will hang my man?   65
JUSTICE   And like your Grace, I must needs do justice.
PRINCE   Tell me, my lord, shall I have my man?
JUSTICE   I cannot, my lord.
PRINCE   But will you not let him go?
JUSTICE   I am sorry that his case is so ill.   70
PRINCE   Tush! Case me no casings! Shall I have my man?
JUSTICE   I cannot, nor I may not, my lord.
PRINCE   Nay? And "I shall not", say; and then I am answered.
JUSTICE   No.
PRINCE   No! Then I will have him.   75

He giveth him a box on the ear.

NED   Gog's wounds, my lord, shall I cut off his head?
PRINCE   No. I charge you, draw not your swords. But get you
hence. Provide a noise of musicians. Away, begone!

Exeunt [*Ned and Tom*].

JUSTICE   Well, my lord, I am content to take it at your hands.

PRINCE Nay, if you be not, you shall have more!   80

JUSTICE Why, I pray you, my lord, who am I?

PRINCE You, who knows not you? Why, man, you are Lord Chief Justice of England.

JUSTICE Your Grace hath said truth; therefore, in striking me in this place you greatly abuse me; and not me only but also 85 your father, whose lively person here in this place I do represent. And therefore to teach you what prerogatives mean, I commit you to the Fleet³ until we have spoken with your father.

PRINCE Why, then, belike you mean to send me to the Fleet! 90

JUSTICE Ay, indeed; and therefore carry him away.

        Exeunt the Prince with the Officers.

JUSTICE Jailer, carry the prisoner to Newgate again until the next 'sizes.

Jailer. At your commandment, my lord, it shall be done.

     [*Exeunt all except Derick and John Cobbler.*]

DERICK [*To the audience*] Zounds, masters, here's ado when 95 princes must go to prison! Why, John, didst ever see the like?

JOHN O Derick, trust me, I never saw the like!

DERICK Why, John, thou mayst see what princes be in choler. A judge a box on the ear! I'll tell thee, John, O John, I would not have done it for twenty shillings. 100

JOHN No, nor I. There had been no way but one with us—we should have been hanged.

DERICK Faith, John, I'll tell thee what; thou shalt be my Lord Chief Justice, and thou shalt sit in the chair; and I'll be the young Prince, and hit thee a box on the ear; and then thou 105 shalt say, "To teach you what prerogatives mean, I commit you to the Fleet."

JOHN Come on; I'll be your judge! But thou shalt not hit me hard?

DERICK No, no.   110

    [*John Cobbler takes the Justice's seat.*]

---

³A London prison used by government officials (later notorious as a debtors' prison).

JOHN   What hath he done?

DERICK   Marry, he hath robbed Derick.

JOHN   Why, then, I cannot let him go.

DERICK   I must needs have my man.

JOHN   You shall not have him!   115

DERICK   Shall I not have my man? Say "No" and you dare! How say you? Shall I not have my man?

JOHN   No, marry, shall you not!

DERICK   Shall I not, John?

JOHN   No, Derick.   120

DERICK   Why, then, take you that [*Boxes his ear.*] till more come! Zounds, shall I not have him?

JOHN   Well, I am content to take this at your hand. But, I pray you, who am I?

DERICK   Who art thou? Zounds, dost not know thyself?   125

JOHN   No.

DERICK   Now away, simple fellow. Why, man, thou art John the Cobbler.

JOHN   No, I am my Lord Chief Justice of England.

DERICK   Oh, John, mass, thou sayst true, thou art indeed.   130

JOHN   Why, then, to teach you what prerogatives mean, I commit you to the Fleet.

DERICK   Well, I will go; but i'faith, you gray-beard knave, I'll course you.

                           Exit. And straight enters again.

Oh, John, come, come out of thy chair. Why, what a clown 135 wert thou to let me hit thee a box on the ear! And now thou seest they will not take me to the Fleet. I think that thou art one of these worenday[4] clowns.

JOHN   But I marvel what will become of thee.

DERICK   Faith, I'll be no more a carrier.   140

JOHN   What wilt thou do, then?

DERICK   I'll dwell with thee and be a cobbler.

JOHN   With me? Alas, I am not able to keep thee. Why, thou wilt eat me out of doors.

DERICK   Oh, John! No, John; I am none of these great slouch- 145 ing fellows that devour these great pieces of beef and brews.

---

[4]Workaday, ordinary (Bullough 1958).

Alas, a trifle serves me—a woodcock, a chicken, or a capon's leg, or any such little thing serves me.

JOHN   A capon! Why, man, I cannot get a capon once a year— except it be at Christmas, at some other man's house; for we 150 cobblers be glad of a dish of roots.

DERICK   Roots! Why, are you so good at rooting?[5] Nay, cobbler, we'll have you ringed.[6]

JOHN   But, Derick,

> Though we be so poor,   155
> Yet will we have in store
> A crab in the fire,
> With nut-brown ale
> That is full stale,
> Which will a man quail   160
> And lay in the mire.

DERICK   A bots on you! And be but for your ale, I'll dwell with you. Come, let's away as fast as we can.

Exeunt.

[SCENE v]

Enter the young Prince (released from prison),
with Ned and Tom.

PRINCE   Come away, sirs. Gog's wounds, Ned, didst thou not see what a box on the ear I took my Lord Chief Justice?

TOM   By Gog's blood, it did me good to see it. It made his teeth jar in his head!

Enter Sir John Oldcastle.

PRINCE   How now, Sir John Oldcastle, what news with you?   5

JOCKEY   I am glad to see your Grace at liberty. I was come, I, to visit you in prison.

PRINCE   To visit me? Didst thou not know that I am a prince's son? Why, 'tis enough for me to look into a prison, though I come not in myself. But here's such ado nowadays, here's 10 prisoning, here's hanging, whipping, and the devil and all! But I tell you, sirs, when I am king we will have no such

[5]Rooting in the earth, like a pig.
[6]Ringed through the nose, like a pig.

things. But, my lads, if the old King, my father, were dead, we would be all kings.

JOCKEY   He is a good old man; God take him to his mercy the 15 sooner!

PRINCE   But, Ned, so soon as I am king, the first thing I will do shall be to put my Lord Chief Justice out of office, and thou shalt be my Lord Chief Justice of England.

NED   Shall I be Lord Chief Justice? By Gog's wounds, I'll be the 20 bravest Lord Chief Justice that ever was in England.

PRINCE   Then, Ned, I'll turn all these prisons into fence-schools,[1] and I will endue thee with them, with lands to maintain them withal. Then I will have a bout with my Lord Chief Justice. Thou shalt hang none but pick-purses, and 25 horse-stealers, and such base-minded villains; but that fellow that will stand by the highway side courageously with his sword and buckler and take a purse, that fellow, give him commendations. Beside that, send him to me, and I will give him an annual pension out of my exchequer to maintain him 30 all the days of his life.

JOCKEY   Nobly spoken, Harry! We shall never have a merry world till the old King be dead.

NED   But whither are ye going now?

PRINCE   To the court; for I hear say my father lies very sick. 35

TOM   But I doubt he will not die.

PRINCE   Yet will I go thither; for the breath shall be no sooner out of his mouth but I will clap the crown on my head.

JOCKEY   Will you go to the court with that cloak so full of needles? 40

PRINCE   Cloak, eyelet-holes, needles, and all was of mine own divising; and therefore I will wear it.

TOM   I pray you, my lord, what may be the meaning thereof?[2]

PRINCE   Why, man, 'tis a sign that I stand upon thorns till the crown be on my head. 45

JOCKEY   Or that every needle might be a prick to their hearts that repine at your doings?

---

[1]Fencing schools.

[2]Tom's question has been asked by many. There are several historical accounts of the Prince's strange garb, but its significance is unclear. The fictional Prince and Oldcastle give their interpretations in the next lines.

PRINCE   Thou sayst true, Jockey. But there's some will say the
          young Prince will be a "well toward young man" and all this
          gear, that I had as lief they would break my head with a pot,   50
          as to say any such thing.[3] But we stand prating here too long. I
          must needs speak with my father; therefore, come away.

                    [*They rap at the court-gate. Enter a Porter.*]

PORTER   What a rapping keep you at the King's court-gate?
PRINCE   Here's one that must speak with the King.
PORTER   The King is very sick, and none must speak with him.   55
PRINCE   No? You rascal, do you not know me?
PORTER   You are my lord, the young Prince.
PRINCE   Then go and tell my father that I must, and will, speak
          with him.
NED   Shall I cut off his head?   60
PRINCE   No, no. Though I would help you in other places, yet I
          have nothing to do here. What, you are in my father's Court!
                                                              [*Exit Porter.*]
NED   I will write him in my tables; for so soon as I am made
          Lord Chief Justice I will put him out of his office.

                                                  The trumpet sounds.

PRINCE   Gog's wounds, sirs, the King comes. Let's all stand aside.   65

                    Enter the King with the Lord of Exeter.

HENRY IV   And is it true, my lord, that my son is already sent to
            the Fleet? Now, truly, that man is more fitter to rule the
            realm than I; for by no means could I rule my son, and he, by
            one word, hath caused him to be ruled. Oh, my son, my son,
            no sooner out of one prison but into another! I had thought   70
            once, whiles I had lived, to have seen this noble realm of
            England flourish by thee, my son; but now I see it goes to
            ruin and decay.   *He weepeth.*

                              Enter Lord of Oxford.

_____

[3]"Some" already suspect the Prince's delinquency is an act, claiming he is a
promising ("toward") youth. Cf. this casual remark and Hal's complex soliloquy in *1 Henry IV*, 1.2.

OXFORD And please your Grace, here is my Lord, your son, that cometh to speak with you. He saith he must and will   75
speak with you.

HENRY IV Who? My son Harry?

OXFORD Ay, and please your Majesty.

HENRY IV I know wherefore he cometh. But look that none come with him.   80

OXFORD A very disordered company, and such as make very ill rule in your Majesty's house.

HENRY IV Well, let him come; but look that none come with him.   *He goeth.*

OXFORD And please your Grace, my Lord the King sends for you.   85

PRINCE Come away, sirs; let's go all together.

OXFORD And please your Grace, none must go with you.

PRINCE Why I must needs have them with me; otherwise I can do my father no countenance.[4] Therefore, come away.

OXFORD The King your father commands there should none   90
come.

PRINCE Well, sirs, then be gone, and provide me three noise of musicians.[5]

Exeunt Knights.

[SCENE vi]

Enter the Prince, with a dagger in his hand.

HENRY IV Come, my son; come on, a God's name! I know wherefore thy coming is. Oh, my son, my son, what cause hath ever been that thou shouldst forsake me, and follow this vile and reprobate company, which abuseth youth so manifestly? Oh, my son, thou knowest that these thy doings   5
will end thy father's days. (*He weeps.*) Ay, so, so, my son, thou fearest not to approach the presence of thy sick father in that disguised sort. I tell thee, my son, that there is never a needle in thy cloak but it is a prick to my heart, and never an eyelet-hole but it is a hole to my soul; and wherefore thou   10
bringest that dagger in thy hand I know not, but by conjecture. (*He weeps.*)

[4]Appropriate respect.
[5]Trio of musicians.

PRINCE   My conscience accuseth me,[1] most sovereign Lord, and
well-beloved father, to answer first to the last point, that is,
whereas you conjecture that this hand and this dagger shall   15
be armed against your life, no! Know, my beloved father, far
be the thoughts of your son—"son," said I? an unworthy
son for so good a father!—but far be the thoughts of any
such pretended mischief. And I most humbly render it to
your Majesty's hand; and live, my Lord and Sovereign, for   20
ever! And with your dagger-arm show like vengeance upon
the body of that—"your son," I was about say, and dare not,
ah, woe is me therefore!—that, your wild slave. 'Tis not the
crown that I come for, sweet father, because I am unworthy.
And those vile and reprobate companions I abandon and   25
utterly abolish their company forever! Pardon, sweet father,
pardon, the least thing and most desired. And this ruffianly
cloak I here tear from my back, and sacrifice it to the devil,
which is master of all mischief. Pardon me, sweet father, pardon me! Good my Lord of Exeter, speak for me. Pardon me!   30
Pardon, good father! Not a word? —Ah, he will not speak
one word! Ah, Harry, now thrice-unhappy Harry! But what
shall I do? I will go take me into some solitary place, and
there lament my sinful life; and when I have done, I will lay
me down and die.   35

Exit.

HENRY IV   Call him again! Call my son again!

[*Enter Prince.*]

PRINCE   And doth my father call me again? Now Harry, happy
be the time that thy father calleth thee again!

[*He kneels.*]

HENRY IV   Stand up, my son; and do not think thy father, but at
the request of thee, my son, I will pardon thee. And God   40
bless thee, and make thee his servant.

---

[1]Some editors set this clause as an aside, to indicate sincerity; I retain the possibly ambiguous 1598 and 1617 version.

PRINCE   Thanks, good my Lord. And no doubt but this day, even this day, I am born new again.[2]

HENRY IV   Come, my son, and, lords, take me by the hands.

Exeunt omnes.

[SCENE vii]

Enter Derick [shouting at John Cobbler's wife within].

DERICK   Thou art a stinking whore, and a whoreson stinking whore. Dost think I'll take it at thy hands?

Enter John Cobbler, running.

JOHN   Derick, Derick, Derick! Hearest a'? Do, Derick, never while thou livest use that. Why, what will my neighbors say and thou go away so?   5

DERICK   She's an arrant whore, and I'll have the law on you, John.

JOHN   Why, what hath she done?

DERICK   Marry, mark thou, John. I will prove it, that I will.

JOHN   What wilt thou prove?

DERICK   That she called me into dinner. John, mark the tale   10 well, John; and, when I was set, she brought me a dish of roots and a piece of barrel butter[1] therein. And she is a very knave, and thou a drab if thou take her part.

JOHN   Hearest a', Derick, is this the matter? Nay, and it be no worse we will go home again, and all shall be amended.   15

DERICK   Oh, John, hearest a', John, is all well?

JOHN   Ay, all is well.

DERICK   Then I'll go home before, and break all the glass windows.

[Exeunt.]

[SCENE viii]

Enter the King with his Lords.

HENRY IV   Come, my lords. I see it boots me not to take any physic, for all the physicians in the world cannot cure me; no, not one. But, good my lords, remember my last will and

---

[2]"Except a man be born again, he cannot see the Kingdom of God" (John 3.3; cf. 1 Peter 1.23).

---

[1]Old salt butter (Bullough 1958).

testament concerning my son; for truly, my lords, I do not
think but he will prove as valiant and victorious a king as   5
ever reigned in England.

BOTH   Let heaven and earth be witness between us if we
accomplish not thy will to the uttermost.

HENRY IV   I give you most unfeigned thanks. Good my lords,
draw the curtains, and depart my chamber awhile; and   10
cause some music to rock me asleep.

Exeunt Lords.

He sleepeth. Enter the Prince.

PRINCE   Ah, Harry, thrice-unhappy, that hath neglect so long
from visiting of thy sick father! I will go. Nay, but why do I
not go to the chamber of my sick father to comfort the
melancholy soul of his body? "His soul," said I? Here is his   15
body, indeed, but his soul is whereas it needs no body. Now,
thrice-accursed Harry, that hath offended thy father so
much! And could not I crave pardon for all? O my dying
father! Curst be the day wherein I was born, and accursed
be the hour wherein I was begotten! But what shall I do? If   20
weeping tears, which come too late, may suffice the negli-
gence neglected to some,[1] I will weep day and night until the
fountain be dry with weeping.

Exit [with the crown].

Enter Lord[s] of Exeter and Oxford.

EXETER   Come easily, my lord, for waking of the King.

HENRY IV [*Waking.*]   Now, my lords?   25

OXFORD   How doth your Grace feel yourself?

HENRY IV   Somewhat better after my sleep. But, my good lords,
take off my crown. Remove my chair a little back, and set
me right.

BOTH LORDS   And please your Grace, the crown is taken away.   30

HENRY IV   The crown taken away! Good my Lord of Oxford,
go see who hath done this deed.

[*Exit Oxford.*]

---

[1]The confusing wording is emended by Bullough (1958), but its general sense is
clear as it stands. The Prince vows to compensate for his past delinquency with
profound mourning.

No doubt 'tis some vile traitor that hath done it to deprive
my son. They that would do it now would seek to scrape
and scrawl for it after my death.   35

Enter Lord of Oxford with the Prince.

OXFORD   Here, and please your Grace, is my lord the young
Prince with the crown.

HENRY IV   Why, how now, my son? I had thought the last time I
had you in schooling I had given you a lesson for all; and do
you now begin again? Why, tell me, my son, dost thou think   40
the time so long that thou wouldst have it before the breath
be out of my mouth?

PRINCE   Most Sovereign Lord and well-beloved father, I came
into your chamber to comfort the melancholy soul of your
body; and finding you at that time past all recovery, and   45
dead, to my thinking—God is my witness—and what should
I do, but with weeping tears lament the death of you, my
father? And after that, seeing the crown, I took it. And tell
me, my father, who might better take it than I, after your
death? But seeing you live, I most humbly render it into your   50
Majesty's hands; [*Giving him the crown, kneeling*] and the
happiest man alive that my father lives. And live, my Lord
and father, forever!

HENRY IV   Stand up, my son. Thine answer hath sounded well
in mine ears; for I must need confess that I was in a very   55
sound sleep, and altogether unmindful of thy coming. But
come near, my son, and let me put thee in possession whilst I
live, that none deprive thee of it after my death.

PRINCE   Well may I take it at your Majesty's hands; but it shall
never touch my head so long as my father lives.   60

He taketh the crown.

HENRY IV   God give thee joy, my son. God bless thee, and make
thee his servant, and send thee a prosperous reign! For God
knows, my son, how hardly I came by it, and how hardly I
have maintained it.

PRINCE   Howsoever you came by it, I know not; but now I have   65
it from you, and from you I will keep it. And he that seeks to
take the crown from my head, let him look that his armour

be thicker than mine, or I will pierce him to the heart, were it
harder than brass or bullion.

HENRY IV Nobly spoken, and like a king! Now trust me, my   70
lords, I fear not but my son will be as warlike and victorious
a Prince as ever reigned in England.

BOTH LORDS His former life shows no less.

HENRY IV Well, my lords, I know not whether it be for sleep, or
drawing near of drowsy summer of death, but I am very   75
much given to sleep. Therefore, good my lords, and my son,
draw the curtains; depart my chamber; and cause some
music to rock me asleep.

Exeunt omnes.

The King dieth.

[SCENE ix]

Enter the Thief.

THIEF Ah, God, I am now much like to a bird which hath
escaped out of the cage; for so soon as my Lord Chief Justice
heard that the old King was dead, he was glad to let me go
for fear of my lord the young Prince. But here comes some of
his companions. I will see and I can get anything of them for   5
old acquaintance.

Enter Knights, ranging.

TOM Gog's wounds, the King is dead!

JOCKEY Dead? Then, Gog's blood, we shall be all kings!

NED Gog's wounds, I shall be Lord Chief Justice of England.

TOM [*To Thief*] Why, how are you broken out of prison?   10

NED Gog's wounds, how the villain stinks!

JOCKEY Why, what will become of thee now? Fie upon him,
how the rascal stinks!

THIEF Marry, I will go and serve my master again.

TOM Gog's blood, dost think that he will have any such   15
scabbed knave as thou art? What, man, he is a king now.

NED Hold thee. Here's a couple of angels[1] for thee. And get
thee gone, for the King will not be long before he come this
way; and, hereafter, I will tell the King of thee.

Exit Thief.

[1]Gold coins.

JOCKEY   Oh, how it did me good to see the King when he was   20
crowned! Methought his seat was like the figure of heaven,
and his person like unto a god.

NED   But who would have thought that the King would have
changed his countenance so?

JOCKEY   Did you not see with what grace he sent his embassage   25
into France to tell the French King that Harry of England
hath sent for the crown, and Harry of England will have it?

TOM   But 'twas but a little to make the people believe that he
was sorry for his father's death.

The trumpet sounds.

NED   Gog's wounds, the King comes! Let's all stand aside.   30

*Enter the King with the Archbishop [of Canterbury],
and the Lord of Oxford.*

JOCKEY   How do you, my Lord?

NED   How now, Harry? Tut, my Lord, put away these dumps.[2]
You are a king and all the realm is yours! What, man! Do
you not remember the old sayings? You know I must be
Lord Chief Justice of England. Trust me, my Lord, methinks   35
you are very much changed, and 'tis but with a little sorrowing to make folks believe the death of your father grieves
you—and 'tis nothing so.[3]

HENRY V   I prithee, Ned, mend thy manners, and be more mod-
ester in thy terms; for my unfeigned grief is not to be ruled   40
by thy flattering and dissembling talk. Thou sayst I am
changed; so I am indeed, and so must thou be, and that
quickly, or else I must cause thee to be changed.

JOCKEY   Gog's wounds! How like you this? Zounds, 'tis not so
sweet as music.   45

TOM   I trust we have not offended your Grace no way.

HENRY V   Ah, Tom, your former life grieves me, and makes me
to abandon and abolish your company forever. And therefore, not upon pain of death to approach my presence by ten
mile's space. Then, if I hear well of you, it may be I will do   50

---

[2]Melancholy, heavy state of mind.

[3]Contrast this advice to the subtler exchange with Ned about Hal's sorrow
over his father's sickness in *2 Henry IV*, 2.2.

somewhat for you; otherwise, look for no more favor at my
hands than at any other man's. And therefore, begone! We
have other matters to talk on.

                       Exeunt Knights.

Now, my good Lord Archbishop of Canterbury, what say
you to our embassage into France?   55

* * *

Sir Thomas Elyot (c. 1490–1546)

*Sir Thomas Elyot was a prominent humanist and courtier who studied
with Sir Thomas More and served under Henry VIII. His* Book Named
the Governor *was one of the most successful publications of the Tudor
era, setting out an ambitious educational program that sought to culti-
vate England's ruling elite and through it, the nation. The huge tome is
filled with vivid discussions—of political order, moral philosophy, the
importance of varied disciplines (including history) on cognitive development—and stocked with literary anecdotes and digressions, linguistic innovation, and so on. Especially important is the fable of Prince
Hal's wild youth—though in his transmission Elyot tempers the wildness, exemplifying the virtue of "placability" when Hal stops himself
just short of striking the Chief Justice. The blow will land in* The
Famous Victories *(see p. 279), but Hal's restraint in Elyot's story helps
shape Shakespeare's complex sense of irony. In the same chapter, Elyot
describes the consequences of implacable wrath through the anecdote
of Alexander the Great killing his dear friend Clitus, a classical exem-
plum that Shakespeare's Fluellen will summon in awkward, strained
praise of his King in* Henry V.

from *The Book Named the Governor*, Book 2, Chapter 6 (1531)

Placability . . . is properly where a man is by any occasion moved to
be angry, and notwithstanding, either by his own reason ingenerate
or by counsel persuaded, he ommiteth to be revenged, and oftentimes receiveth the transgressor once reconciled into more favor. . . .
For who, beholding a man in estimation of nobility and wisdom by
fury changed into an horrible figure, his face enfarced[1] with rancor,

---

[1]Swollen.

his mouth foul and imbossed,[2] his eyes wide staring and sparkling like fire, not speaking, but as a wild bull, roaring and braying out words despiteful and venomous. . . . Shall he not wish to be in such a man placability? . . .

The most renowned prince, King Henry the Fifth, late King of England, during the life of his father was noted to be fierce and of wanton courage. It happened that one of his servants whom he well favored, for felony by him committed, was arraigned at the King's Bench; whereof he being advertised, and incensed by light persons about him, in furious rage came hastily to the bar, where his servant stood as a prisoner, and commanded him to be ungyved[3] and set at liberty, whereat all men were abashed, reserved the Chief Justice, who humbly exhorted the Prince to be contented that his servant might be ordered according to the ancient laws of this realm, or if he would have him saved from the rigor of the laws, that he should obtain, if he might, of the King, his father, his gracious pardon; whereby no law or justice should be derogate. With which answer the Prince nothing appeased, but rather more inflamed, endeavored himself to take away his servant. The judge, considering the perilous example and inconvenience that might thereby ensue, with a valiant spirit and courage commanded the Prince upon his allegiance to leave the prisoner and depart his way. With which commandment the Prince, being set all in a fury, all chafed, and in a terrible manner, came up to the place of judgment—men thinking that he would have slain the judge, or have done to him some damage; but the judge sitting still, without moving, declaring the majesty of the King's place of judgment, and with an assured and bold countenance, had to the Prince these words following: "Sir, remember yourself; I keep here the place of the King, your sovereign lord and father, to whom ye owe double obedience, wherefore eftsoons[4] in his name I charge you desist your willfulness and unlawful enterprise, and from henceforth give good example to those which hereafter shall be your proper subjects. And now for your contempt and disobedience, go you to the prison of the King's Bench, whereunto I commit you; and remain ye there prisoner until

[2]Foaming.
[3]Unchained.
[4]Again.

the pleasure of the King, your father, be further known." With which words being abashed and also wondering at the marvellous gravity of that worshipful Justice, the noble Prince, laying his weapon apart, doing reverence, departed and went to the King's Bench as he was commanded. Whereat his servants disdaining, came and showed to the King all the whole affair. Whereat he a while studying after as a man all ravished with gladness, holding his eyes and hands up toward heaven, abraided,[5] saying with a loud voice, "O merciful God, how much am I, above all other men, bound to your infinite goodness; specially for that ye have given me a judge who feareth not to minister justice, and also a son who can suffer semblably and obey justice!"

[5]Cried out.

Authority,
Resistance, Rebellion

When Prince John and the Earl of Westmoreland confront the Archbishop of York in *Henry IV, Part Two*, they profess outrage that a man of the Church would foment rebellion rather than advance order, harmony, and obedience to authority. While some of Shakespeare's audience might have agreed, recalling St. Paul and Church homilies, others might have objected that the King himself was a usurper and that the rebels were supporting the apparently legitimate Mortimer. Division comes with the doctrine: questions of authority, theorized in the middle ages and debated anew throughout the sixteenth century, worried obsessively about the nature, conditions, and limits of proper obedience, its ambiguities inextricably linked to its foundation. Although characters in the *Henry IV* plays voice primarily secular concerns—personal and familial honor or political self-interest—for them, as for Tudor England, the secular can reach for religion or metaphysics when seeking justification or devising effective propaganda, intensifying rather than resolving the dispute.

The same reaching can be seen in modern Shakespeare criticism. In two influential studies written during and influenced by World War II—*The Elizabethan World Picture* (1943) and *Shakespeare's History Plays* (1944)—E. M. W. Tillyard argued that not only Shakespeare but also Renaissance culture in general relied on traditional, religious notions of obedience. Violent confrontation may be the stuff of political history and stage plays, but it is always defined by "the principle of order behind all the terrible manifestations of disorder." In a scheme traceable back to antiquity, creation is fundamentally hierarchical, each creature dutiful to its superiors and expecting the same from its inferiors. A repertoire of metaphors and analogies elaborate the elegant comprehensiveness to this "world picture," imagined variously as a linked chain, a cosmic dance, or a living organism, all with multiple levels of application. The planetary cosmos, the state, the human body each contains vertical elements within itself even as it reflects all other levels of being: the body as a small version (or microcosm) of the state, the state of the cosmos, and so on. Obedience is the key, with individual elements observing propriety for the sake of the whole. Self-willed anomaly is sinful disobedience. In Tillyard's argument, Elizabethans, influenced by chroniclers such as Edward Hall, viewed recent English history in this light. For them, the overthrow of Richard II in 1399 became a divisive Fall, disobedience against God's anointed that was punished by the anguish of civil war. Despite occasional kingly triumphs, it was fully healed only with the rise of the Tudors and Henry VII's marriage, unifying the houses of York and Lancaster.

Tillyard's thesis, for all its comprehensiveness, has since become a byword for reductive interpretation. Focusing on idealized dogma whose goal was to preserve the status quo, he endorsed an official myth at the cost of failing to do justice, historically or aesthetically, to a complex social reality and literature. William Empson and A. P. Rossiter were brilliant early critics of the flaws in Tillyard's thesis, and others have gone further in detailing its selective use of political and philosophical materials. While Tillyard could be a sharper critic than some of his recent detractors allow, much Renaissance literature, and Shakespeare's plays in particular, are often ironic about, if not subversive of, the broadly formulaic moralizing one finds in the "Tudor myth."

Scripture itself, modern historians note, gave Renaissance political theorists and writers mixed signals: "The Bible both exalted and disparaged kingship, characterized civil government as both divine and demonic, proclaimed the duty of unlimited obedience to civil authority and, by inference, incited the godly to rebellion and tyrannicide."[1] The Reformation and early-modern political tensions further fractured attitudes toward power. Absolutist apologetics coexisted with theories of limited monarchy and mixed government, even with defenses of outright resistance, all drawing on ancient and medieval texts as well as contemporary practice.

[1]Withrop S. Hudson, *John Ponet (1516?–1556): Advocate of Limited Monarchy* (Univ. of Chicago Press, 1942), p. 110.

Some treatises represent starkly polarized positions; others cautiously inch their way along a continuum of attitudes. The questions they raise are played out in literary works as well: Does all power descend from above to restrain human sin and corruption? Must one be categorically obedient to any ruler, assuming that tyrants are God's punishment on sinful subjects and that only divine authority may topple them? Or do tyrants forfeit their authority, justifying resistance, even violent rebellion, by those whom they have wronged? Who determines that forfeiture? Lower magistrates? The people as a whole? The individual believer? Might one even claim, as some radical Protestants did, that it is one's sacred duty, in obedience to a higher authority, to rebel against corrupt rulers? Or, shifting to a more secular angle: Does political life originate in some act of consent that may be withdrawn if human creativity and freedom are violated? Is consent even an issue? And, from the ruler's point of view: To what degree are violence, cunning, and dissimulation justifiable to preserve social order, prosperity, and happiness? Do ethics underlie politics, or do politics operate in a separate and harshly pragmatic world?[2]

St. Paul (d. c. 64 CE)

Author of substantial sections of the New Testament, Paul is the first major Christian theologian. This selection from his Epistle to the Romans widely influenced medieval and Renaissance discussions of obedience and political obligation. That it was repeatedly invoked (and wrestled with) by continental and English commentators with divergent political sympathies points to the latent complexity of Paul's demands. Though his social and moral vision is hierarchical and patriarchal, it also insists on the duty to love each other (verse 8), a Pauline dialectic

---

[2]Among numerous studies, see Ernst Cassirer, *The Myth of the State* (Yale Univ. Press, 1946); Julian H. Franklin, trans. and ed., *Constitutionalism and Resistance in the Sixteenth Century* (Pegasus, 1969); J. G. A. Pocock, *The Machiavellian Moment: Florentine Political Thought and the Atlantic Republican Tradition* (Princeton Univ. Press, 1975); Quentin Skinner, *The Foundations of Modern Political Thought*, 2 vols. (Cambridge Univ. Press, 1978); and *The Individual in Political Theory and Practice*, ed. Janet Coleman (Oxford Univ. Press, 1996). The latter three include extensive bibliographies.

similar to the demands for obedience from wives and slaves in Ephe-
sians chapters 5 and 6, each linking sternness to love and gentleness.

Often called "Shakespeare's Bible," the Geneva Bible (the text
here) was an English translation by Protestant exiles in Switzerland in
the late 1550s. Its copious marginal commentary further tempers
Paul's authoritarian tone by emphasizing reciprocity: "by which
words, the Magistrates themselves are put in mind of that duty which
they owe to their subjects."

from Epistle to the Romans, Chapter 13 (c. 54–58 CE)

1. Let every soul be subject unto the higher powers: for there is
no power but of God: and the powers that be, are ordained of God.

2. Whosoever therefore resisteth the power, resisteth the ordinance of God: and they that resist, shall receive unto themselves
condemnation.

3. For Magistrates are not to be feared for good works, but for
evil. Wilt though then be without fear of the power? do well: so
shalt thou have praise of the same.

4. For he that is the minister of God for thy wealth, but if thou
do evil, fear: for he beareth not the sword for nought: for he is the
minister of God to take vengeance on him that doeth evil.

5. Wherefore ye must be subject, not because of wrath only, but
also for conscience sake.

6. For, for this cause ye pay also tribute: for they are God's ministers, applying themselves for the same thing.

7. Give to all men therefore their duty: tribute, to whom ye owe
tribute: custom, to whom custom: fear, to whom fear: honor, to
whom ye owe honor.

8. Owe nothing to any man, but to love one another: for he that
loveth another, hath fulfilled the Law.

Niccolò Machiavelli (1469–1527)

Niccolò Machiavelli saw power both at close range and at an ironic
distance. When the ruling family of the Medici was driven out of Flo-
rence, Machiavelli was appointed secretary to the republican govern-
ment in 1498, and diplomatic missions put him in personal contact

with some of Europe's leading figures. With the Medicean return to power in 1512, Machiavelli was dismissed from office and later arrested, tortured, and exiled to his estate outside Florence. It was there that he wrote his most famous works, including the notorious Il principe *(The Prince), a handbook for rulers dedicated to Lorenzo de' Medici (grandson of Lorenzo the Magnificent), hoping to ingratiate himself with the new regime. Despite some minor success, he failed to secure a significant post either with them or with the republic, which was again restored in 1527.*

The Prince, *based on wide reading and experience, hovers between cold, brutal objectivity and an elusive sense of irony, its tone making disagreement inevitable among interpreters. Its ability to shock, however, was not lost on Renaissance readers. In an age when major theorists discussed kings and princes as "God's lieutenants," Machiavelli's blunt pragmatism, his spurning of utopian idealism (and minimizing of providence) in favor of politics as an art of necessity in a treacherous world earned it a place on the Papal Index of forbidden books for three hundred years.*

Of particular interest to Machiavelli (and to Shakespeare's history plays) is the action required of rulers lacking clear hereditary claims. Authority must be gained, and obedience insured, by the Prince's virtù—*variously signifying "vigor," "courage," "merit," "genius," "native ability," as well as "manly aggression" (*vir = *man)—in constant struggle with shifting fortune, sometimes gendered as a fickle mistress who must be dominated.[1] Such skill does not necessarily exclude the Ciceronian meaning of virtue as "moral excellence," if circumstances allow. But circumstances are undependable, and ruthless cunning is needed to "seize the occasion." Religion is intermittently treated with respect, but often peripherally, discussed mainly as appearance and valued as a means rather than an end. (In his* Discourses on Livy, *1.11–15, Machiavelli treats ancient religion as instrumental, a powerfully effective resource even among disbelieving rulers for political manipulation and wartime propaganda.)*

In the final chapter of The Prince, *Machiavelli justifies his emphasis—a need for strength and unity to liberate a divided Italy from foreign domination ("the Barbarians"). Although this work fascinated contemporary politicians in private and was later admired in some nationalistic circles, in Shakespeare's time Machiavelli was defamed as an atheist and patterned into a stage type called the "Machiavel," cousin to the gloating, amoral Vice figure.*

---

[1]"Fortune is a mistress, and it is necessary to keep her in obedience, to ruffle and force her. . . . as a mistress, she is a friend to young men because they are less respective, more rough, and command her with more boldness" (*The Prince*, ch. 25).

The selections presented here concern the gaining and maintenance of power. The opening excerpt sharpens our sense of the tension between Shakespeare's King Henry and his former allies, the Percy family, at the start of Part One. *Although Machiavelli disdains excessive ruthlessness, he ultimately weighs virtue and vice, cruelty and kindness, with cold calculation. See also the Contexts section, "The Theater of the World," for the ruler's proteanism and use of histrionic spectacle.*

I have modernized the text from Nicholas Machiavel's Prince. *Also, the* Life of Castruccio Castratani of Lucca *(1640, the first published English translation, by Edward Dacres).*

from *The Prince* (1513, pub. 1532)

from Chapter III: *Of Mixed Principalities*

Men do willingly change their Lords, believing to better their condition; and this belief causes them to take arms against him that rules over them, whereby they deceive themselves; because they find after by experience they have made it worse. . . . [The new ruler] cannot keep them [as] friends those who have seated [him] in [his new position], for not being able to satisfy them according to their expectations. . . .

It is to be noted that men must either be dallied and flattered withall, or else be quite crushed, for they revenge themselves of small damages, but of great ones they are not able, so that when wrong is done to any man, it ought so to be done, that it need fear no return of revenge again.

from Chapter VI: *Of new Principalities,*
that are conquered by one's own arms and valor

To come to these, who have by their own virtues, and not by fortune, attained to be Princes. . . . And examining their lives and action, it will not appear they had other help of fortune than the occasion, which presented them with the matter wherein they might introduce what form they then pleased. Without that occasion, the virtue of their mind had been extinguished; and without that virtue, the occasion had been offered in vain. . . . These occasions therefore made these men happy, and their excellent virtue made the occasion be taken notice of, whereby their country became ennobled, and exceeding fortunate.

from Chapter VIII: *Concerning those who*
by wicked means have attained to a Principality

[*Machiavelli considers a ruthless strategem used by the ancient
Sicilian, Agathocles, who rose from abject origins to the kingship when he called together Syracuse's senators and richest
men to a peaceful meeting, then had his soldiers kill them.*]

He then that should consider the actions and valor of this man
would not see any, or very few, things to be attributed unto Fortune, seeing that as is formerly said, not by anyone's favor, but by
the degree of service in war with many sufferings and dangers, in
which he had risen, he came to the Principality; and that he
maintained afterwards with so many resolute and hazardous
undertakings. Yet cannot this be termed virtue or valor to slay his
own citizens, betray his friends, to be without faith, without pity,
without religion, which ways are of force to gain dominion, but
not glory; for if Agathocles' valor be well weighed, in his venturing upon and coming off from dangers, and the greatness of his
courage, in supporting and mastering of adversities, no man can
see why he should be thought any way inferior even to the ablest
captains. Notwithstanding, his beastly cruelty and inhumanity
with innumerable wickednesses allow not that he should be cele-
brated among the most excellent men. . . . Some men might
doubt[2] from whence it should proceed that Agathocles, and such
like, after many treacheries and cruelties, could possibly live long
secure in his own country, and defend himself from his foreign
enemies, and that never any of his own citizens conspired against
him, seeing that by means of cruelty, many others have never
been able even in peaceable times to maintain their States, much
less in the doubtful times of war. I believe that this proceeds from
the well or ill using of those cruelties. They may be termed well
used (if it be lawful to say well of evil) that are put in practice
only once of necessity for security's sake, not insisting[3] therein
afterwards, but therein use made of them for the subjects' profit,
as much as may be. But those that are ill used are such as though
they be but few in the beginning, yet they multiply rather in time,

[2]Wonder.
[3]Continuing.

than diminish. They that take the first way, may with the help of God, and men's care, find some remedy for their state. . . . Whereupon it is to be noted, that in the laying hold of a State, the usuper thereof ought to run over and execute all his cruelties at once. . . .

Chapter XV: *Of Those Things in Respect Whereof Men and Especially Princes Are Praised or Dispraised*

It now remains that we consider what the conditions of a prince ought to be, and his terms of government over his subjects and towards his friends. And because I know that many have written hereupon, I doubt lest I, venturing also to treat thereof, may be branded with presumption, especially seeing I am like enough to deliver an opinion different from others. But my intent being to write for the advantage of him that understands me, I thought it fitter to follow the effectual truth of the matter than the imagination thereof. And many Principalities and Republics have been in imagination which neither have been seen nor known to be indeed, for there is such a distance between how men do live and how men ought to live that he who leaves that which is done for that which ought to be done learns sooner his ruin than his preservation. For that man who will profess honesty in all his actions must needs go to ruin among so many that are dishonest. Whereupon it is necessary for a prince, desiring to preserve himself, to be able to make use of that honesty and to lay it aside again as need shall require.[4]

Passing by, then, things that are only in imagination belonging to a prince, to discourse upon those that are really true, I say that all men, whensoever mention is made of them, and especially princes, because they are placed aloft in view of all, are taken notice of for some of these qualities which procure them either commendations or blame. And this is that some one is held liberal, some miserable[5] (miserable, I say, not covetous, for the covetous desire to have though it were by rapine, but a miserable man is he that too much forbears to make use of his own), some free givers, others extortioners; some cruel, others piteous; the one a league breaker, another

---

[4]Machiavelli bases his claim to bold originality on his refusal to idealize. Chief among the self-deluding, imaginary worlds he rejects is Plato's *Republic*.

[5]Miserly, not sorrowful.

faithful; the one effeminate and of small courage, the other fierce and courageous; the one courteous, the other proud; the one lascivious, the other chaste; the one of fair dealing, the other wily and crafty; the one hard, the other easy; the one grave, the other light; the one religious, the other incredulous, and suchlike.

I know that everyone will confess it were exceedingly praiseworthy for a Prince to be adorned with all these above-named qualities that are good. But because this is not possible, nor do human conditions admit such perfection in virtues, it is necessary for him to be so discreet that he know how to avoid the infamy of those vices which would thrust him out of his state and, if it be possible, beware of those also which are not able to remove him thence. But where it cannot be, let them pass with less regard. And yet, let him not stand much upon it, though he incur the infamy of those vices without which he can very hardly save the state, for if all be thoroughly considered, some things we shall find which will have the color and very face of virtue, and following them, they will lead thee to thy destruction; whereas some others, that shall as much seem vice, if we take the course they lead us, shall discover unto us the way to our safety and well-being.[6]

from Chapter XVII: *Of Cruelty and Clemency and Whether It Is Better to Be Beloved or Feared*

Descending afterwards unto the other fore-alleged qualities, I say that every prince should desire to be held pitiful and not cruel. Nevertheless ought he beware that he ill uses not this pity. Cesare Borgia was accounted cruel, yet had his cruelty redressed the disorders in Romania, settled in it union, and restored it to peace and fidelity—which, if it be well weighed, we shall see was an act of more pity than that of the people of Florence who to avoid the term of cruelty

---

[6]Machiavelli's view of the Prince as a complex of virtues and vices rejects the hopes lying behind works such as Baldassare Castiglione's *Book of the Courtier*, which imagines an idealized, universal man composed of all the best features that can be imitated. The passage grows increasingly dark, suggesting first that reputation is more important than conquering vice itself, and then that vice may prove as useful as virtue—and in some instances, more so—for the well-being of the state. The first English translator, Dacres, appends a disapproving note to this chapter, calling it a "blemish" and insisting that such "ambidexterity," advocating both virtue and vice, forgets that "politics presuppose ethics" (pp. 120–21).

suffered Pistoia to fall to destruction.[7] Wherefore a Prince ought not to regard the infamy of cruelty for to hold his subjects united and faithful. For by giving a very few proofs of himself the other way, he shall be held more pitiful than they who through their too much pity suffer disorders to follow, from whence arise murders and rapines, for these are wont to hurt an entire universality, whereas the executions practiced by a prince hurt only some particular. And among all sorts of Princes, it is impossible for a new Prince to avoid the name of cruel, because all new states are full of dangers. . . .

From hence arises a dispute whether it is better to be beloved or feared. I answer, a man would wish he might be the one and the other; but because hardly can they subsist both together, it is much safer to be feared than be loved, being that one of the two must needs fail.[8] For touching men, we may say this in general: they are unthankful, inconstant dissemblers; they avoid dangers and are covetous of gain. And whilst thou dost them good they are wholly thine—their blood, their fortunes, lives and children are at thy service, as is said before, when the danger is remote. But when it approaches, they revolt. And that Prince who wholly relies upon their words, unfurnished of all other preparations, goes to wrack, for the friendships that are got with rewards and not by the magnificence and worth of the mind are dearly bought indeed, but they will neither keep long nor serve well in time of need. And men do less regard to offend one that is supported by love than by fear. For love is held by a certainty of obligation which because men are mischievous is broken upon any occasion of their own profit. But fear restrains with a dread of punishment which never forsakes a man.

Yet ought a Prince cause himself to be beloved in such a manner that if he gains not love he may avoid hatred, for it may well stand

[7]Machiavelli had close contact with both examples. Cesare Borgia, son of Pope Alexander VI, was a prominent politician and soldier, known for his shrewdness and cruelty. (See the selection from *The Prince* in the "Theater of the World" section.) Machiavelli knew Borgia personally and often (though not always) mentions him with great admiration as a model figure. Borgia's success in Romagna is contrasted to the brutal, civil violence that raged unchecked in the town of Pistoia, a Florentine possession. Machiavelli was sent by Florence to investigate, but the city failed to intervene, with disastrous consequences.

[8]Machiavelli again sets himself in opposition to traditional wisdom. Contrast Cicero's treatment in *De officiis*, bk. II, chs. 7 and 8 (e.g., "For fear is but a poor safeguard of lasting power; while affection, on the other hand, may be trusted to keep it safe for ever," par. 23).

together that a man may be feared and not hated which shall never fail if he abstain from his subject's goods and their wives. And whensoever he should be forced to proceed against any of their lives, do it when it is to be done upon a just cause and apparent conviction. But above all things, forbear to lay his hands on other men's goods, for men forget sooner the death of their father than the loss of their patrimony. Moreover, the occasions of taking from men their goods do never fail and always he that begins to live by rapine finds occasion to lay hold upon other men's goods; but against men's lives they are seldomer found and sooner fail. But when a prince is abroad in the field with his army and hath a multitude of soldiers under his government, then is it necessary that he stands not much upon it though he be termed cruel, for unless he be so, he shall never have his soldiers live in accord one with another nor ever well-disposed to any brave piece of service. . . .

I conclude, then, returning to the purpose of being feared and beloved. Insomuch as men love their own pleasure and to serve their own turn, and their fear depends upon the prince's pleasure, every wise prince ought to ground upon that which is of himself and not upon that which is of another. Only this, he ought to use his best wits to avoid hatred, as was said. (STC 850:12)

from *Certain Sermons or Homilies* (1547; 1563 [1571])

The two books we call the "Tudor Homilies," together with a homily later added, are important evidence of the regulation of preaching during an era when religious views fluctuated by regime and sometimes by individual preacher. The Homilies *were intended for reading aloud in churches on successive Sundays across the land and as models for undertrained (or independent-minded) preachers to follow state-sanctioned doctrine.*

The Homilies *cover many practical moral and spiritual concerns: human misery, good works, love and charity, gluttony and drunkenness, holy matrimony, the fear of death. The two most often discussed today (in part because of their relevance to Shakespeare's history plays) employ doctrine for political ends. They are "An Exhortation Concerning Good Order and Obedience to Rulers and Magistrates" (1547), and the lengthier, rhetorically vehement "An Homily Against Disobedience and Willful Rebellion," commissioned by Elizabeth in the wake of the 1569 Northern Rebellion (first published in 1570 and*

appended to the second book of Homilies *early in 1571). The Northern Rebellion was led by descendents of the same Percy family in the*
Henry IV *plays, adding a topical relevance Shakespeare may have
expected his audience to grasp (see Campbell 1947, 229–37). The precise relevance of the "Homily Against Disobedience" for Shakespeare's
play, however, remains a matter of debate.*

from "An Exhortation Concerning Good Order and Obedience to Rulers and Magistrates" (1547)

from *The First Part*

Almighty God hath created and appointed all things in heaven,
earth and waters in a most excellent and perfect order. In heaven, he
hath appointed distinct orders and states of archangels and angels.
In earth, he hath assigned kings, princes, and other governors under
them, all in good and necessary order. The water above is kept and
raineth down in due time and season. The sun, moon, stars, rain-
bow, thunder, lightning, clouds and all birds of the air do keep their
order. The earth, trees, seeds, plants, herbs, corn, grass and all manner of beasts keep them in their order. All the parts of the whole
year, as winter, summer, months, nights and days, continue in their
order. All kinds of fishes in the sea, rivers and waters, with all foun-
tains, springs, yea, the seas themselves keep their comely course and
order. And man himself also hath all his parts, both within and
without, as soul, heart, mind, memory, understanding, reason,
speech, with all and singular corporal members of his body, in a
profitable, necessary and pleasant order. Every degree of people, in
their vocation, calling and office, hath appointed to them their duty
and order. Some are in high degree, some in low, some kings and
princes, some inferiors and subjects, priests and laymen, masters
and servants, fathers and children, husbands and wives, rich and
poor, and every one have need of other: so that in all things is to be
lauded and praised the goodly order of God, without the which no
house, no city, no commonwealth can continue and endure. For
where there is no right order, there reigneth all abuse, carnal liberty,
enormity, sin and Babilonical confusion. Take away kings, princes,
rulers, magistrates, judges and such states of God's order, no man
shall ride or go by the highway unrobbed, no man shall sleep in his
own house or bed unkilled, no man shall keep his wife, children and

possessions in quietness: all things shall be common, and there must needs follow all mischief and utter destruction, both of souls, bodies, goods and commonwealths. . . . Thus Saint Paul writeth to the Romans: Let every soul submit himself to the authority of the higher powers, for there is no power, but of God, the powers that be, ordained of God. . . . And here, good people, let us all mark diligently that it is not lawful for inferiors and subjects in any case to resist the superior powers, for St. Paul's words be plain, that whosoever resisteth shall get to themselves damnation: for whosoever resisteth, resisteth the ordinance of God. (STC 48:03)

from "An Homily Against Disobedience and Willful Rebellion" (1570; 1571)

from *The First Part*

As God, the creator and Lord of all things, appointed his angels and heavenly creatures in all obedience to serve and to honour his majesty, so was it his will that man, his chief creature upon the earth, should live under the obedience of him, his creator and Lord; and for that cause, God, as soon as he had created man, gave unto him a certain precept and law, which he, being yet in the state of innocency, and remaining in paradise, should observe as a pledge and token of his due and bounden obedience, with denunciation of death if he did transgress and break the said law and commandment. . . .

from *The Third Part*

As I have in the first part of this treatise showed unto you the doctrine of the Holy Scriptures as concerning the obedience of true subjects to their princes . . . so remaineth it now that I partly do declare unto you in this third part what an abominable sin against God and man rebellion is, and how dreadfully the wrath of God is kindled and inflamed against all rebels, and what horrible plagues, punishments, and deaths, and finally eternal damnation doth hang over their heads; as how on the contrary part good and obedient subjects are in God's favor, and be partakers of peace, quietness and security, with other God's manifold blessings in this world, and by his mercies through our savior Christ, of life everlasting also in the world to come. How horrible a sin against God and man rebellion is cannot possibly be expressed according unto the greatness thereof. For he that nameth rebellion nameth not a singular, or one only sin, as if theft, robbery, murder and such like, but he nameth the whole puddle and sink[1] of all sins against God and man, against his prince, his country, his countrymen, his parents, his children, his kinsfolks, his friends, and against all men universally. All sins, I say, against God and all men heaped together nameth he that nameth rebellion. For concerning the offence of God's majesty, who seeth not that rebellion riseth first by contempt of God and of his holy ordinances and laws, wherein he so straightly commandeth obedience, forbiddeth disobedience and rebellion? And besides the dishonor done by rebels unto God's holy name by their breaking of the oath made to their prince with the attestation of God's name and calling of his majesty to witness, who heareth not the horrible oaths and blasphemies of God's holy name that are used daily amongst rebels, that is either amongst them or heareth the truth of their behavior? Who knoweth not that rebels do not only themselves leave all works necessary to be done upon workdays undone, whiles they accomplish their abominable work of rebellion, and do compel other that would gladly be well occupied to do the same, but also how rebels do not only leave the sabbath day of the Lord unsanctified, the temple and church of the Lord unresorted unto, but also do by their works of wickedness most horribly profane and pollute the sabbath day, serving Satan, and by doing of his work making it the devil's day instead of the Lord's day? Besides that, they compel good men that would gladly serve the Lord assembling in his temple and church upon his day, as becometh the Lord's servants, to assemble and meet armed in the field to resist the fury of such rebels. Yea, and many rebels, lest they should leave any part of God's commandments in the first table[2] of his law unbroken or any sin against God undone, do make rebellion for the maintenance of their images and idols, and of their idolatry committed or to be committed by

---

[1]A befouled body of standing water is a standard figure for "moral defilement" or "false doctrine." "Sink" means sewer or cesspool. The compound "puddle and sink" (spelled "poodle and sink" in the original text) appears in earlier texts as well (*OED*).

[2]A probable reference to Augustine's division of the Ten Commandments into two groups: the first three written on the first tablet (or "table"), concerning duties toward God, and the next seven on the second tablet, concerning duties toward man. There are other traditions of division (4/6, 5/5), but the point is the perverse, encyclopedic diligence of rebellion that includes all sins and breaks all commandments (the second table is noted in the next paragraph).

them, and, in despite of God, cut and tear in sunder his Holy Word, and tread it under their feet, as of late ye know was done.[3]

As concerning the second table of God's law, and all sins that may be committed against man, who seeth not that they be all contained in rebellion? For first, the rebels do not only dishonor their prince, the parent of their country, but also do dishonor and shame their natural parents, if they have any, do shame their kindred and friends, do disherit[4] and undo forever their children and heirs. Thefts, robberies and murders, which of all sins are most loathed of most men, are in no men so much, not so perniciously and mischievously, as in rebels. For the most errant thieves and cruelest murderers that ever were, so long as they refrain from rebellion, as they are not many in number, so spreadeth their wickedness and damnation unto a few: they spoil but a few, they shed the blood but of few in comparison. But rebels are the cause of infinite robberies and murders of great multitudes, and of those also whom they should defend from the spoil and violence of others; and, as rebels are many in number, so doth their wickedness and damnation spread it self unto many. And if whoredom and adultery amongst such persons as are agreeable to such wickedness are (as they in deed be) most damnable, what are the forceable oppressions of matrons and men's wives, and the violating and deflowering of virgins and maids, which are most rife with rebels, how horrible and damnable, think you, are they? Now, besides that, rebels, by breach of their faith given and oath made to their prince, be guilty of most damnable perjury, it is wondrous to see what false colors and feigned causes, by slanderous lies made upon their prince and the counselors, rebels will devise to cloak their rebellion withall, which is the worst and most damnable of all false-witness-bearing that may be possible. For what should I speak of coveting or desiring of other men's wives, houses, lands, goods, and servants in rebels, who by their wills would leave unto no man anything of his own?

Thus you see that all God's laws are by rebels violated and broken, and that all sins possible to be committed against God or man be contained in rebellion: which sins, if a man list to name by the accustomed names of the seven capital or deadly sins, as pride, envy, wrath, covetousness, sloth, gluttony, and lechery, he shall find them all in

---

[3]The text acknowledges its occasion: the Northern Rebellion on behalf of the Catholic Mary Queen of Scots. Protestants often accused Catholics of idolatry.
[4]Disinherit.

rebellion, and amongst rebels. For first, as ambition and desire to be aloft, which is the property of pride, stirreth up many men's minds to rebellion, so cometh it of a Luciferian pride and presumption that a few rebellious subjects should set themselves up against the majesty of their prince, against the wisdom of the counselors, and the power and force of all nobility, and the faithful subjects and people of the whole realm. As for envy, wrath, murder and desire of blood, and covetousness of other men's goods, lands and livings, they are the inseparable accidents of all rebels, and peculiar properties that do usually sit up wicked men unto rebellion. Now such as by riotousness, gluttony, drunkenness, excess of apparel, and unthrifty games have wasted their own goods unthriftily, the same are most apt unto and most desirous of rebellion, whereby they trust to come by other men's goods unlawfully and violently. And where other gluttons and drunkards take too much of such meats and drinks as are served to tables, rebels waste and consume in short space all corn in barns, fields or elsewhere, whole granaries, whole storehouses, whole cellars, devour whole flocks of sheep, whole droves of oxen and kine. And as rebels that are married, leaving their own wives at home, do most ungraciously, so much more do unmarried men worse than any stallions or horses, being now by rebellion set at liberty from correction of laws which bridled them before, which abuse by force other men's wives and daughters and ravish virgins and maidens most shamefully, abominably and damnably. Thus all sins, by all names that sins may be named, and by all means that all sins may be committed and wrought, do all wholly upon heaps follow rebellion, and are to be found altogether among rebels.

[*A long passage follows, the first part describing disease and famine created by rebellion: the degraded diet, depleted supplies, and filthy living conditions ("they do lie in ordure and much filth in the hot weather") are aggravated by pestilence "sent directly from God." The homily goes on to denounce civil war as the worst of wars, and rebellion "far more abominable yet . . . than any civil war."*]

And therefore our saviour Christ denounceth desolation and destruction to that realm that by sedition and rebellion is divided in it self. Now as I have showed before that pestilence and famine, so is it yet more evident that all the calamities, miseries and mischiefs of war be far more grievous and do more follow rebellion than any other war, as being far worse than all other wars. For not only those ordinary and usual mischiefs and miseries of other wars do follow rebellion, as corn and other things necessary to man's use to be spoiled, houses, villages, towns, cities to be taken, sacked, burned and destroyed, not only many wealthy men but whole countries to be impoverished and utterly beggared, many thousands of men to be slain and murdered, women and maids to be violated and deflowered: things, when they are done by foreign enemies, we do much mourn, as we have great causes, yet are all these miseries without any wickedness wrought by any our countrymen. But when these mischiefs are wrought in rebellion by them that should be friends, by countrymen, by kinsmen, by those that should defend their country and countrymen from such miseries, the misery is nothing so great as is the mischief and wickedness when the subjects unnaturally do rebel against their prince, whose honor and life they should defend, though it were with loss of their own lives: countrymen to disturb the public peace and quietness of their country, for defense of whose quietness they should spend their lives; the brother to seek and often to work the death of his brother, the son of the father; the fathers to seek or procure the death of his sons, being at man's age, and by their faults to disinherit their innocent children and kinsmen their heirs forever, for whom they might purchase livings and lands, as natural parents do take care and pains and be at great costs and charges; and universal, instead of all quietness, joy and felicity, which do follow blessed peace and due obedience, to ring in all trouble, sorrow, disquietness of minds and bodies, and all mischief and calamities, to turn all good order upside down, to bring all good law in contempt and to tread them under feet, to oppress all virtue and honesty and all virtuous and honest persons, and to set all vice and wickedness and all vicious and wicked men at liberty, to work their wicked wills, which were before bridled by wholesome laws, to weaken, to overthrow and to consume the strength of the realm, their natural country, as well by the spending and wasting of the money and treasure of the prince and realm, as by murdering of the people of the same, their own countrymen, who should defend the honor of their prince and liberty of their country against the invasion of foreign enemies: and so finally to make their country, thus by their mischief weakened, ready to be a prey and spoil to all outward enemies that will invade it, to the utter and perpetual captivity, slavery and destruction of all their countrymen, their children, their friends, their kinfolks left alive, whom by their wicked rebellion they procure to be delivered into the hands of foreign enemies, as much as in them doth lie. In foreign wars our countrymen, in obtaining the victory, winneth the praise of valiantness; yea, and though they were overcome and slain, yet win they an honest commendation in this world, and dieth in a good conscience for serving God, their prince and their country, and be children of eternal salvation. But in rebellion, how desperate and strong soever they be, yet win they shame here in fighting against God, their prince and country, and therefore justly do fall headlong into hell if they die, and they be rewarded with shameful deaths, their heads and carcasses set upon poles, or hanged in chains, eaten with kites and crows, judged unworthy the honor of burial, and so their souls, if they repent not (as commonly they do not), the devil harrieth them into hell, in the midst of their mischief. For which dreadful execution Saint Paul showeth the cause of obedience, not only for fear of death, but also in conscience to Godward, for fear of eternal damnation in the world to come.

Wherefore, good people, let us as the children of obedience fear the dreadful execution of God and live in quiet obedience to be the children of everlasting salvation. For as heaven is the place of good obedient subjects, and hell the prison and dungeon of rebels against God and their prince, so is that realm happy where most obedience of subjects doth appear, being the very figure of heaven; and contrariwise, where most rebellions and rebels be, there is the express similitude of hell, and the rebels themselves are the very figures of fiends and devils, and their captain the ungracious pattern of Lucifer and Satan, the prince of darkness, of whose rebellion, as they be followers, so shall they of his damnation in hell undoubtedly be partakers; and as undoubtedly children of peace the inheritors of heaven with God the Father, God the Son, and God the Holy Ghost, to whom be all honor and glory for ever and ever. Amen. (STC 496:01)

John Ponet (1516?–1556)

John Ponet studied at Cambridge, surrounded by young Protestant humanists such as John Cheke, Roger Ascham, and Thomas Smith, and was himself highly regarded for his knowledge of classical Greek, mathematics, astronomy, and religion. Ordained a priest in 1536 and made a Doctor of Divinity in 1547, he enjoyed a close relationship with the Archbishop of Canterbury, Thomas Cranmer (a major contributor to the 1547 Homilies *and the 1549* Book of Common Prayer*), an association that furthered his career ambitions even as it enmeshed him in religious controversy. Ponet became Bishop of Rochester and Winchester, but with the accession in 1553 of the Catholic Queen Mary, he lost his positions. Cranmer was burned at the stake for treason. After the failure in 1554 of Wyatt's Rebellion (led by the son of the late poet against Queen Mary's council), in which Ponet may have taken part, he fled England as one of the Marian exiles, claiming he could do God greater service abroad. It was at Strasbourg that Ponet wrote his vivid* Short Treatise. *Though a product of religious upheaval, the treatise also advances a secular tone in theories about rebellion. As historian Michael Walzer notes, Calvinists usually call the tyrant an idolator, but Ponet also calls him a thief.[1] The excerpts below, from the early chapters of the treatise, show Ponet's range. Beginning with a universalist, theological framework, he develops a contractualist sense of politics, anticipated by Thomas Aquinas, that would, in turn, influence later writers on liberty. We also see Ponet's rhetorical alertness as he wrestles with traditional, coercive figures, such as the "body politic," for new ends.*

from *A Short Treatise of Politic Power* (1556)

from *Whereof politic power groweth, wherefore it was ordained, and the right use of the same, etc.*

As oxen, sheep, goats, and such other unreasonable creatures cannot for lack of reason rule themselves, but must be ruled by a more excellent creature, that is, man, so man, albeit he have reason, yet because through the fall of the first man, his reason is wonderfully corrupt, and sensuality hath gotten the overhand,[2] is not able by himself to rule himself, but must have a more excellent governor. The worldlings thought, this governor was their own reason. They thought they might by their own reason do what they lusted, not only in private things, but also in public. Reason they thought to be the only cause, that men first assembled together in companies, that

---

[1]See Michael Walzer, *The Revolution of the Saints: A Study in the Origins of Radical Politics* (Harvard Univ. Press, 1965), p. 103.

[2]Upper hand.

commonwealths were made, that policies were well governed and long continued. But men see that such were utterly blinded and deceived in their imaginations, their doings and inventions (seemed they never so wise) were so easily and so soon (contrary to their expectation) overthrown.

Where is the wisdom of the Grecians? Where is the fortitude of the Assyrians? Where is both the wisdom and force of the Romans become? All is vanished away, nothing almost left to testify that they were, but that which well declareth, that their reason was not able to govern them. Therefore were such as were desirous to know the perfect and only governor of all, constrained to seek further than themselves, and so at length to confess, that it was one God that ruled all. . . . He[3] hath taken upon Him the order and government of man his chief creature, and prescribed him a rule, how he should behave himself, what he should do, and what he may not do.

This rule is the law of nature, first planted and graft only in the mind of man, then after (for that his mind was through sin defiled, filled with darkness and encumbered with many doubts), set forth in writing in the decalogue or ten commandments, and after reduced by Christ our saviour to these two words: Thou shalt love thy lord God above all things, and thy neighbor as thy self. The latter part whereof he also thus expoundeth: whatsoever ye will that men do unto you, do ye even so to them.

[*The chapter then notes there was no corporal punishment at first, even for the "horrible murders" committed by Cain and Lamech. After the flood, however, God saw the need for greater severity and instituted "politic power and giveth authority to men to make more laws," providing the lawmakers themselves "set apart all affections" and "observe an equality in pains, that they be not greater or less, than the fault deserveth."*]

from *Whether Kings, princes, and other governors have an absolute power and authority over their subjects*

Princes are ordained to do good, not to do evil; to take away evil, not to increase it; to give example of well doing, not to be procurers

---

[3]God.

of evil; to procure the wealth and benefit of their subjects, and not to work their hurt or undoing. And in the empire where (by the civil laws) the emperors claim, that the people gave them their authority to make laws, albeit they have been willing, and often attempted to execute their authority, which some Pickthanks (to please them) say they have by the laws, yet have they been forced of themselves to leave off their enterprise. But such as be indifferent expounders of the laws, be of that mind that we before have declared: and therefore make this a general conclusion, and as it were a rule, that the emperor willing any thing to be done, there is no more to be done, than the laws permit to be done. For (say they) neither pope, Emperor, nor king may do any thing to the hurt of his people without their consent. King Antigonus' Chancellor, saying unto him that all things were honest and lawful to kings: ye say true (quoth the king) but to such kings as be beasts, barbarous and without humanity. But to true and good Princes, nothing is honest, but that is honest in deed, and nothing is just, but that is just in deed.

from *Whether Kings, princes, and other politic Governors be subject to God's laws, and the positive laws of their countries*

He that noteth the procedings of princes and governors in these our days, how ambitious they are to usurp others' dominions, and how negligent they be to see their own well governed, might think that they believe that either there is no God, or that He hath no care over the things of the world: or that they think themselves exempt from God's laws and power. But the wonderful overthrow of their devices (when they think themselves most sure and certain) is so manifest that it is not possible to deny, but that both there is a God, and that he hath care over the things of the world. . . .

For good and just laws of man be God's power and ordinances, and they[4] are but ministers of the laws, and not the law's self. And if they were exempt from the laws, and so it were lawful for them to do what them lusteth, their authority being of God, it might be said, that God allowed their tyranny, robbery of their subjects, killing them without law, and so God the author of evil: which were a great blasphemy.

[4]Kings and princes.

from *In what things, and how far subjects are bounden to obey their princes and governors*

As the body of man is knit and kept together in due proportion by the sinews, so is every commonwealth kept and maintained in good order by Obedience. But as if the sinews be too much racked and stretched out, or too much shrinked together, it breedeth wonderful pains and deformity in man's body: so if Obedience be too much or too little in a commonwealth, it causeth much evil and disorder. . . .

God is the highest power, yea the power of powers, from him is derived all power. . . . Whatsoever God commandeth man to do, he ought not to consider the matter, but straight to obey the commander. . . . But contrary, in man's commandments, men ought to consider the matter, and not the man. For all men whatsoever ministry or vocation they exercise, are but men, and so may err. We see councils against councils, parliaments against parliaments, commandment against commandment; this day one thing, tomorrow another. It is not the man's warrant that can discharge thee, but it is the thing itself that must justify thee. It is the matter that will accuse thee and defend thee: acquit thee, and condemn thee: when thou shalt come before the throne to the highest and everlasting power, where no temporal power will appear for thee, to make answer or to defend thee: but thou thyself must answer for thyself, and for what so ever thou hast done. And therefore Christian men ought well to consider, and weigh men's commandments, before they be hasty to do them, to see if they be contrary or repugnant to God's commandments and justice: which if they be, they are cruel and evil, and ought not to be obeyed. We have this special commandment from God the highest power, often repeated by the holy ghost. Forbear to do evil, and do that is good.

. . . [M]en ought to have more respect to their country, than to their prince: to the commonwealth, than to one person. For the country and commonwealth is a degree above the king. Next unto God men ought to love their country, and the whole commonwealth before any member of it: as kings and princes (be they never so great) are but members; and commonwealths may stand well enough and flourish, albeit there be no kings; but contrariwise without a commonwealth there can be no king. Commonwealths and realms may live when the head is cut off, and may put on a new head, that is, make them a new governor, when they see their old head seek too much his own will and not the wealth of the whole body, for the which he was only ordained. (STC 349:11)

Philippe du Plessis-Mornay (1549–1623)

French Protestants, known as Huguenots, were an important source of later sixteenth-century political theory. Although much of their work distanced itself from radical statements, some of it was bolder. After the St. Bartholomew's Day Massacre in 1572—in which thousands of Protestants were treacherously attacked and killed in Paris and surrounding villages—a surge of tracts justified rebellion. Most famous was the anonymous Vindiciae contra tyrannos *(The Defense of Liberty Against Tyrants), probably by Philippe du Plessis-Mornay, an important French diplomat and political advisor whose wide travels included England. Among his friends was poet Sir Philip Sidney, who partially translated one of his theological treatises. The* Vindiciae *invests the power to resist with elected magistrates, cautioning the individual tyrant-killer who feels divinely inspired that he must be certain that he is not deluded, that he has not "confuse[d] himself with God." Nonetheless, it advances a secular defense of rebellion, focusing on the tyrant's betrayal both of his covenant (foedus) with God and of his "compact" or "contract" (pactum) with his people—their general welfare as well as each individual's rights.*

from *Vindiciae contra tyrannos* (*The Defense of Liberty Against Tyrants*) (1579)

[S]eeing that the only will of God is always just, and that of men may be, and is, oftentimes unjust, who can doubt but that we must always obey God's commandments without any exception, and men's ever with limitation? But . . . there are many Princes in these days calling themselves Christians, who arrogantly assume an unlimited power, over which God himself hath no command, and that they have no want of flatterers, who adore them as Gods upon earth. . . .

Tyranny is not only a will, but the chief, and as it were the complement and abstract of vices. A Tyrant subverts the State, pillages the people, lays stratagems to entrap their lives, breaks promise with all, scoffs at the sacred obligation of a solemn oath, and therefore is he so much more vile than the vilest of usual malefactors, by how much offences committed against a generality, are worthy of greater punshment than those which concern only particular and private persons. . . .

There is ever, and in all places, a mutual and reciprocal obligation between the people and the Prince, the one promiseth to be a good and wise Prince, the other to obey faithfully, provided he govern justly. The people therefore is obliged to the Prince under condition: the Prince to the people simply and purely. Therefore if the Prince fail in his promise, the people is exempt from obedience, the contract is made void, the right of obligation of no force. . . .

It is therefore permitted the Officers of a Kingdom, either all, or some good number of them, to suppress a Tyrant. And it is not only lawful for them to do it, but their duty expressly requires it, and if they do it not, they can by no excuse color their baseness. For the electors, palatines, peers, and other officers of state must not think they were established only to make pompous parades and shows, when they are at the coronations of the King, habited in their robes of states, as if there were some masque or interlude to be represented, or as if they were that day to act the parts of Roland, Oliver, or Renaldo, and such other personages on a stage, or to counterfeit and revive the memory of the Knights of the Round Table, and after the dismissing of that day's assembly, to suppose they have sufficiently acquit themselves of their duty. . . .[1] These solemn rites and ceremonies were not instituted for vain ostentation, nor to pass as in a dumb show to please the spectators, nor in children's sports as it is with Horace, to create a King in jest. . . . (STC 1062:19)

---

[1]Roland (Italian, "Orlando"), Oliver, and Renaldo ("Rinaldo") are fictitious heroes from medieval and Renaissance romances. Debates about the historical veracity of Arthur continued throughout the 16th c.

Shakespeare's History Plays

Two actors in Shakespeare's company, John Heminges and Henry Condell, played a crucial role in establishing the English history play as a distinct category. Editing their late colleague's dramatic canon for publication seven years after his death, they (or someone working under them) introduced a tripartite organization reflected in the title: *Mr William Shakespeares Comedies, Histories and Tragedies*. Known today as the First Folio, this famous collection of thirty-six plays (half had already appeared in smaller quarto editions) proclaimed by its prefatory matter and its size the author's enduring, literary fame.

That fame today includes credit for having invented the new kind of play tucked between the classic, generic alternatives of comedy and tragedy, though critics generally concede a need for some qualification. There was already a tradition of plays about English history—John Skelton's *Magnificence* (1519) and John Bale's *King Johan* (1536, 1538, 1561), for example—which produced several offshoots: the anonymous *Famous Victories of Henry V* (c. 1586–94), *Thomas of Woodstock* (c. 1592–95), and *True Tragedy of Richard III* (c. 1594), all possible sources for Shakespeare, as well as Robert Greene's romantic *Scottish History of James IV* (c. 1591) and Christopher Marlowe's *Edward II* (c. 1592). But the early examples are really political morality plays, and despite their suggestive crossing of timeless allegory with concrete historicism, they only modestly prepare the stage for what was to come. The later works, with the exception of Marlowe's, lack the sophistication of the Folio's histories. The genre, moreover, has permeable boundaries. Shakespeare's *Richard III* and *Richard II* had originally been published in their respective 1597 quartos as tragedies, with *Richard III* still named a "Tragedy" on the Folio title page and running titles—this despite being grouped with the histories both in the Catalogue (i.e., Table of Contents) and in the volume. Further complicating the picture is the appearance of some comedies and tragedies in quarto as histories: *The Merchant of Venice* as *The most excellent Historie*; *King Lear* as the *True Chronicle Historie*; *Troilus and Cressida* as *The Historie* or *The Famous Historie*.

Some of this instability is due to the linguistic link between "history" and "story" (noted earlier in the section "Shakespeare's Historical Sources"), with the former being used broadly to denote a "relation of incidents . . . either true or imaginary," a written narrative of any sort, or a story represented dramatically (*OED* 1, 2, 6). Nonetheless, Heminges and Condell had something more specific in mind for their edition, and their categorization for Shakespeare endures, more or less, today: a set of ten quasi-factual dramas representing the foundations and fragmentations of English identity, spanning approximately 350 years of medieval and early Tudor conflict and consolidation. This choice excludes plays based on classical history (*Julius Caesar*, *Antony and Cleopatra*, *Coriolanus*) and those set in mythic or pre-Norman Britain (*King Lear*, *Macbeth*, *Cymbeline*), however much such plays might be based on chronicle material or reflect contemporary political concerns.

Some of Shakespeare's contemporaries elide the history genre altogether. In 1598, London resident and Cambridge-educated Francis Meres praised Shakespeare's versatility in two rather than three "kinds." Intent to give Shakespeare classical stature, Meres compares him to the comedian Plautus and the tragedian Seneca and names four (or five) of his histories as tragedies, *Richard II*, *Richard III*, *Henry IV* (no reference to which part), and *King John*. As late as 1709, scholarly editor and poet laureate Nicholas Rowe described the histories as tragedies "with a run or mixture of comedy amongst them." Even so, Shakespeare and his audience were clearly drawn to the Janus-like form of the history play. Whether spurred by a public appetite for the past, a patriotic surge after the defeat of the Spanish Armada in 1588, the publication of the second edition of Holinshed in 1587 and of Tacitus and Lucan in 1591, or a more pervasive national self-consciousness—by turns confident and anxious—history plays make up the majority of Shakespeare's productions in the Elizabethan half of his career.

Although it is hard not to think of these plays in relation to each other, we have no evidence that they were ever performed in sequence during Shakespeare's lifetime (a practice probably beginning in the nineteenth century). Some critics emphasize each play as distinct with a unique structure and see attempts to group them into "cycles" as covertly ideological, unfolding a providential design akin to medieval mystery plays. Most critics, however, approach the plays with what Lawrence Danson terms a "double consciousness": "behind the discrete plot of each play is another longer plot . . . even if we don't remember, the characters do."[1] Although all genres have intracanonical "memories"—*A Midsummer Night's Dream* more than once recalls *Romeo and Juliet*, and *Hamlet* intriguingly calls up *Julius Caesar*—history, a branch of knowledge springing from memory (as Francis Bacon noted), inevitably invokes prior texts. All drama exists in time, of course, but history most explicitly thematizes the way future prospects and shades of the past impinge on the present.

The extent of this formal and temporal expansion varies, however, according to what we are looking for. The two parts of *Henry IV* are an obvious twin set amid larger family groupings: these are the first and second "tetralogies" (a Greek term meaning "four discourses," first used in England for Greek drama and oratory), composed of, respectively, the three parts of *Henry VI* with *Richard III*; and *Richard II*, the two parts of *Henry IV*, and *Henry V*.

The sequencing is slightly tricky. The First Folio orders the histories according to content, not composition: amid the tetralogies, *Richard II* is the first; *Richard III* is last, and between them lie six *Henry* plays. Moreover, there are two, single histories outside the tetralogies: *King John* and *Henry VIII*. Since these treat the earliest and latest events of the full ten, they appear as bookends. Modern criticism, however, tends to discuss the plays in

---

[1]*Shakespeare's Dramatic Genres* (Oxford Univ. Press, 2000), pp. 89–90. For a recent criticism of "cycle," see Michael Hattaway, "The Shakespearean History Play," in *The Cambridge Companion to Shakespeare's History Plays*, ed. Hattaway (Cambridge Univ. Press, 2002), p. 9.

terms of Shakespeare's maturing career. *Henry VIII* was, in fact, the last written, but *King John* was written roughly between the two tetralogies. And as far as those central eight are concerned, Shakespeare wrote about later events first, then dramatized their causes in earlier events.

In the Folio, then, what critics now call the Second Tetralogy—more mature and sometimes honored as the "major tetralogy"—appears just after the initial *King John* because of its subject matter. It is followed by what is usually called the First Tetralogy, so-called for having been written earlier, but placed later because it represents later events. Shakespeare himself made imaginative use of this compositional order to reinforce the terrible irony of what Henry IV calls "the revolution of the times" (*Part Two*, 3.1.46). He ends *Henry V* on a heroic high note only to remind the audience of what they had already often seen on stage: the later history of *Henry VI*, which concerns the disastrous loss of all that Henry V accomplished.

Mr. WILLIAM
SHAKESPEARES
COMEDIES,
HISTORIES, &
TRAGEDIES.

Publi∫hed according to the True Originall Copies.

Martin. Droeshout. ∫culp∫it. London.

LONDON
Printed by I∫aac Iaggard, and Ed. Blount. 1623.

First Folio title page.

Catalogue from the First Folio

The Catalogue (table of contents) announces the First Folio's segregation of the plays into three kinds, dividing them with horizontal bars and paginating separately. The Histories are the most rigorously ordered, by subject chronology. The fact that the compositional sequence is ignored is in keeping with the whole. *The Tempest*, one of Shakespeare's last plays, appears first among the Comedies, and the Tragedies are similarly random. The modern grouping of late Romances does not exist, and one of them, *Pericles*, was not included in the Folio.

Folio Sequence with Dates of Historical Reign and Probable Composition		
Title	Reign of Titular King	Probably Composition
King John	1199–1216	1595–96
[Second Tetralogy]		
Richard II	1377–99	1595–97
Henry IV, Part One	1399–1413	1596–97
Henry IV, Part Two	1399–1413	1597–98
Henry V	1413–22	1599
[First Tetralogy]		
Henry VI, Part One	1422–61	1589–92
Henry VI, Part Two	1422–61	1589–91
Henry VI, Part Three	1422–61	1590–91
Richard III	1483–85	1592–93
Henry VIII	1509–47	1612–13

A C A T A L O G V E

of the feuerall Comedies, Hiftories, and Tragedies contained in this Volume.

COMEDIES.

![He] He *Tempeft*.	*Folio* 1.
The two *Gentlemen of Verona*.	20
The *Merry Wiues of Windfor*.	38
Meafure for Meafure.	61
The *Comedy of Errours*.	85
Much adoo about Nothing.	101
Loues Labour loft.	122
Midfommer Nights Dreame.	145
The *Merchant of Venice*.	163
As you Like it.	185
The *Taming of the Shrew*.	208
All is well, that Ends well.	230
Twelfe-Night, or what you will.	255
The *Winters Tale*.	304

HISTORIES.

The *Life and Death of King John*.	*Fol.* 1.
The *Life & death of Richard the fecond*.	23
The *Firft part of King Henry the fourth*.	46
The *Second part of K. Henry the fourth*.	74
The *Life of King Henry the Fift*.	69
The *Firft part of King Henry the Sixt*.	96
The *Second part of King Hen. the Sixt*.	120
The *Third part of King Henry the Sixt*.	147
The *Life & Death of Richard the Third*.	173
The *Life of King Henry the Eight*.	205

TRAGEDIES.

The *Tragedy of Coriolanus*.	*Fol.* 1.
Titus Andronicus.	31
Romeo and Juliet.	53
Timon of Athens.	80
The *Life and death of Julius Cæfar*.	109
The *Tragedy of Macbeth*.	131
The *Tragedy of Hamlet*.	152
King Lear.	283
Othello, the Moore of Venice.	310
Anthony and Cleopater.	346
Cymbeline King of Britaine.	369

First Folio Catalogue (1623).

William Shakespeare (1564–1616)

> *The* Henry IV *plays frequently look back to* Richard II, *the first play of the Second Tetralogy. The following passages are especially useful to recall when reading the later plays.*

from *Richard II* (1595)

from Act 2, Scene 3

[*Henry Bolingbroke (or Bullingbrooke), soon to become King Henry IV, returns to England despite being exiled. Reproached by his uncle, the Duke of York, for defying King Richard II's order and for gathering military support from the Percy family, Bolingbroke insists he has come back only for his lawful, family inheritance, which the King has ruthlessly appropriated. Hotspur will reflect sarcastically on this moment, and Bolingbroke's hypocritically concealed ambition, in* Henry IV, Part One *(4.3.54ff).*]

BOLINGBROKE   My gracious uncle, let me know my fault.
  On what condition[1] stands it and wherein?[2]
YORK   Even in condition of the worst degree:
  In gross rebellion and detested treason.
  Thou art a banished man, and here art come   110
  Before the expiration of thy time
  In braving[3] arms against thy sovereign.
BOLINGBROKE   As I was banished, I was banished Hereford;
  But as I come, I come for Lancaster.[4]
  And, noble uncle, I beseech Your Grace   115
  Look on my wrongs with an indifferent[5] eye.
  You are my father, for methinks in you
  I see old Gaunt alive. O, then, my father,
  Will you permit that I shall stand condemned[6]
  A wandering vagabond, my rights and royalties[7]   120

[1]Defect in me.

[2]In what does it consist.

[3]Defiant.

[4]Under the title of Lancaster and in order to claim it.

[5]Impartial.

[6]Condemned as.

[7]Privileges granted by the King.

Plucked from my arms perforce and given away
To upstart unthrifts?[8] Wherefore was I born?
If that my cousin king be King in England,
It must be granted I am Duke of Lancaster.
You have a son, Aumerle, my noble cousin;   125
Had you first[9] died, and he been thus trod down,
He should have found his uncle Gaunt a father
To rouse[10] his wrongs and chase them to the bay.[11]
I am denied[12] to sue my livery[13] here,
And yet my letters patents[14] give me leave.   130
My father's goods are all distrained[15] and sold,
And these, and all, are all amiss employed.
What would you have me do? I am a subject,
And I challenge law.[16] Attorneys are denied me,
And therefore personally I lay my claim   135
To my inheritance of free descent.[17]

from Act 4, Scene 1

[*After Bolingbroke pressures an emotionally unstable Richard to uncrown himself, York convinces himself that the abdication was voluntary and declares Bolingbroke (now Duke of Lancaster) as the new King. Disgusted by the charade, the Bishop of Carlisle defends conservative orthodoxy and prophesies the nightmare of civil chaos. His rhetoric would have reminded Shakespeare's audience of the "Homily Against Disobedience" as well as the eventual consequences of this usurpation: domestic conflict leading to the Wars of the Roses (the subject of Shakespeare's First Tetralogy). Northumberland's response to the Bishop's sermon enacts the*

---

[8]Spendthrifts.

[9]Before Gaunt.

[10]Chase from cover, expose.

[11]The extremity where the hunted animal turns on its pursuers.

[12]Denied the right.

[13]Sue for possession of hereditary rights.

[14]Letters from the King indicating Bolingbroke's legal rights.

[15]Seized officially.

[16]Claim my legal rights.

[17]By legal succession.

bloody, relativistic irony that so often dooms those stranded by the tides of political fortune.]

YORK   Great Duke of Lancaster, I come to thee
        From plume-plucked Richard, who with willing soul
        Adopts thee heir, and his high scepter yields   110
        To the possession of thy royal hand.
        Ascend his throne, descending now from him,
        And long live Henry, fourth of that name!
BOLINGBROKE   In God's name, I'll ascend the regal throne.
CARLISLE   Marry, God forbid!   115
        Worst[1] in this royal presence may I speak,
        Yet best beseeming me[2] to speak the truth.
        Would God that any in this noble presence
        Were enough noble to be upright judge
        Of noble Richard! Then true noblesse[3] would   120
        Learn him forbearance[4] from so foul a wrong.
        What subject can give sentence on his king?
        And who sits here that is not Richard's subject?
        Thieves are not judged but they are by[5] to hear,
        Although apparent[6] guilt be seen in them;   125
        And shall the figure[7] of God's majesty,
        His captain, steward, deputy elect,
        Anointed, crownèd, planted many years,
        Be judged by subject and inferior breath,
        And he himself not present? O, forfend[8] it God   130
        That in a Christian climate souls refined[9]
        Should show so heinous, black, obscene[10] a deed!
        I speak to subjects, and a subject speaks,

[1]Least in rank.
[2]Most befitting to me as a clergyman.
[3]Nobleness.
[4]Teach him to forbear.
[5]Condemned unless they are present.
[6]Manifest.
[7]Image.
[8]Forbid.
[9]Civilized people.
[10]Odious, repulsive.

Stirred up by God thus boldly for his king.
My lord of Hereford here, whom you call king,   135
Is a foul traitor to proud Hereford's king.
And if you crown him, let me prophesy:
The blood of English shall manure the ground
And future ages groan for this foul act;
Peace shall go sleep with Turks and infidels,   140
And in this seat of peace tumultuous wars
Shall kin with kin and kind with kind confound;[11]
Disorder, horror, fear, and mutiny
Shall here inhabit, and this land be called
The field of Golgotha[12] and dead men's skulls.   145
O, if you raise this house against this house,[13]
It will the woefullest division prove
That ever fell upon this cursèd earth.
Prevent it, resist it, let it not be so,
Lest child, child's children, cry against you woe!   150
NORTHUMBERLAND   Well have you argued, sir, and for your pains
Of[14] capital treason we arrest you here.
My lord of Westminster, be it your charge
To keep him safely till his day of trial.

from Act 5, Scene 1

[*Dethroned, Richard predicts to Northumberland that his alliance
with the new King will come to grief through mutual suspicion and
envy. A sickly Henry IV will recall this prophesy in his first appearance in* Henry IV, Part Two *(3.1.57ff).*]

KING RICHARD   Northumberland, thou ladder wherewithal   55
The mounding Bolingbroke ascends my throne,
The time shall not be many hours of age
More than it is ere foul sin, gathering head,[1]

[11]Shall destroy kinsmen by means of kinsmen and fellow countrymen by means of
fellow countrymen.

[12]Calvary, the hill outside of Jerusalem called "the place of dead men's skulls" (see
Mark 15.22 and John 19.17) where Jesus was crucified.

[13]Lancaster against York. (See Mark 3.25.)

[14]On a charge of.

[1]Gathering to a head.

Shall break into corruption.² Thou shalt think,
Though he divide the realm and give thee half,   60
It is too little, helping³ him to all;
He shall think that thou, which knowest the way
To plant unrightful kings, wilt know again,
Being ne'er so little urged another way,
To⁴ pluck him headlong from the usurpèd throne.   65
The love of wicked men converts⁵ to fear,
That fear⁶ to hate, and hate turns one or both⁷
To worthy⁸ danger and deservèd death.

from Act 5, Scene 3

[*The newly crowned Henry IV, who began* Richard II *as a bold, young man, appears near the end to have aged a generation, worrying about his "unthrifty son." His remarks about the latter's rowdiness and thieving, accompanied by "sparks of better hope," introduce to the tetralogy the well-known tradition of a "wild," then repentant, Prince Hal that will be explored in the two parts of* Henry IV. *It is worth noting that the "Percy" to whom King Henry complains is Hal's future rival, Hotspur.*]

KING HENRY   Can no man tell me of my unthrifty¹ son?
'Tis full three months since I did see him last.
If any plague hang over us, 'tis he.
I would to God, my lords, he might be found.
Inquire at London, 'mongst the taverns there,   5
For there, they say, he daily doth frequent
With unrestrainèd loose companions,
Even such, they say, as stand in narrow lanes

---

²Putrid matter, pus.
³Since you helped.
⁴How to.
⁵Changes.
⁶That fear changes.
⁷The new king or his partner, or both.
⁸Well-merited.

---

¹Profligate.

And beat our watch,[2] and rob our passengers[3]—
While he, young wanton[4] and effeminate[5] boy,   10
Takes on the[6] point of honor to support
So dissolute a crew.
PERCY   My lord, some two days since I saw the Prince,
And told him of those triumphs held[7] at Oxford.
KING HENRY   And what said the gallant?   15
PERCY   His answer was, he would unto the stews,[8]
And from the common'st creature pluck a glove,
And wear it as a favor, and with that[9]
He would unhorse the lustiest[10] challenger.
KING HENRY   As dissolute as desperate! Yet through both   20
I see some sparks of better hope, which elder years
May happily[11] bring forth.

from Act 5, Scene 6

[Richard II *ends here, with Henry lamenting the death of his prede-*
cessor. Although Henry did not directly order his murder, he strongly
implied his desire to an eager follower, Sir Pierce Exton, who quotes
the hint—"Have I no friend will rid me of this living fear?"—in 5.4.
According to Peter Ure, Shakespeare appears to have been the first to
link Henry's desire for pilgrimage to his guilt. This innovation ren-
ders him at once sympathetic and coldly manipulative. Henry will
reiterate his desire to go to the Holy Land in both parts of Henry IV.]

EXTON   Great King, within this coffin I present   30
Thy buried fear. Herein all breathless lies
The mightiest of thy greatest enemies,
Richard of Bordeaux, by me hither brought.

[2]Night watchmen.
[3]Passersby, wayfarers.
[4]Pampered youth.
[5]Self-indulgent.
[6]Makes it a.
[7]To be held.
[8]Brothels.
[9]Wearing that as a favor.
[10]Most vigorous and brave.
[11]With good fortune.

KING HENRY   Exton, I thank thee not, for thou hast wrought
　　A deed of slander[1] with thy fatal hand   35
　　Upon my head and all this famous land.
EXTON   From your own mouth, my lord, did I this deed.
KING HENRY   They love not poison that do poison need,
　　Nor do I thee. Though I did wish him dead,
　　I hate the murderer, love him murderèd.   40
　　The guilt of conscience take thou for thy labor,
　　But neither my good word nor princely favor.
　　With Cain[2] go wander through the shades of night,
　　And never show thy head by day nor light.
　　　　　　　　　　　　　　　　[*Exeunt Exton and attendants.*]
　　Lords, I protest my soul is full of woe   45
　　That blood should sprinkle me to make me grow.
　　Come mourn with me for what I do lament,
　　And put on sullen black incontinent.[3]
　　I'll make a voyage to the Holy Land
　　To wash this blood off from my guilty hand.   50
　　March sadly after. Grace[4] my mournings here
　　In weeping after this untimely bier.
　　　　　　　　　　　　　[*Exeunt in procession, following the coffin.*]

[1]A deed sure to arouse slanderous talk about the new King.

[2]Murderer of his brother Abel.

[3]Immediately.

[4]Dignify.

The Fascination of Falstaff

"I am not only witty in myself, but the cause that wit is in other men" (*Part Two*, 1.2.10). For critics and theatergoers, Falstaff is the most generous of egotists, but whether we accept his offering has always been the question. Few other fictional characters have attracted such opposing reactions of sympathy and condemnation, delivered in jest and earnest, with ringing eloquence and stinging rebuke—so much so that William Empson credits Falstaff with having started "the whole snowball of modern Shakespearean criticism . . . the first time a psychological paradox was dug out of a Shakespeare text" (*Essays on Shakespeare*, p. 38). In a two-play sequence crowded with striking, diverse, and complexly drawn figures, it is Falstaff who most often provokes efforts to take his measure.

For A. C. Bradley, Falstaff has an "inexplicable touch of infinity" that frustrates calculation by critics (and even by his author). Many twentieth-century efforts, however, reject (or defer) such appreciative terms to focus on long-known or newly excavated contexts—literary, religious, social, and historical. Varied materials, they remind us, went into making the Falstaff artifact and its environment: classical and medieval theatrical types including braggart soldiers, parasites, the Lord of Misrule, allegorical vices and tempters—among these last according to Hal, "that old white-bearded Satan" (*Part One*, 2.4.458). For some, these types fix Falstaff as a comic butt, moral abstraction, or some other conventional figure. For other critics, however, even these relatively clear-edged forms play across various, sometimes linked webs of significance: a religious fable of the soul's maturation; an anthropological view of the pleasures and limits of Carnival; a social view of the Elizabethan underworld; a political tale of princely education; a subversive burlesque (or recuperation) of official values; a psychological tale of libidinal excess curbed by the patriarchal superego; or all of the above, each a partial measure of this complex drama of human attraction, choice, and obligation.

Along with these conceptual schemes, specific political and religious histories have been brought to bear on Falstaff. Evidence not only from the two plays but also from contemporary and rival texts reveals that Shakespeare originally named Falstaff "Sir John Oldcastle." Hal still teasingly calls him "my old lad of the castle" in *Part One* (1.2.39), and the epilogue to *Part Two* appears to apologize to an offended party: "Oldcastle died a martyr, and this [Falstaff] is not the man." We are pretty sure that the name was changed because of complaints by influential descendents of Oldcastle's title, Lord Cobham,[1] but we still wonder about Shakespeare's original choice. Was "Oldcastle" an awkward blunder, merely following a source play, *The Famous Victories of Henry V* (see p. 267)? Or was Shakespeare's exploiting of an ongoing debate about the historical Oldcastle, regarded by some as an early friend and courageous ally of Henry, ruthlessly betrayed by churchmen into martyrdom and judged by others as an incorrigible heretic and political threat to the English monarch? If Shakespeare was deliberate, what do the *Henry IV* plays say about the cruelty of Elizabethan, and in particular Shakespeare's, sense of humor? Comic references to Hal's beefy companion as a "roasted Manningtree ox with the pudding in his belly" (*Part One*, 2.4.447) or dripping with fat ("he lards the lean earth" [*Part One*, 2.2.108]) become horrible (or rueful) when we recall that the historical Oldcastle was suspended in chains over an open fire and roasted to death (see Foxe's account, p. 374). The revision to "Falstaff" returns to, or at least echoes, the name of a supposed coward Shakespeare had used earlier, in *Henry VI, Part One*, a choice noted a few years later for its own unfairness as well as its anachronism (the historical "Fastolf" or "Fastolfe" was in his twenties when he fought at Harfleur and outlived Henry V by

---

[1]For recent summaries of the evidence and discussion, see Taylor 1985, Corbin and Sedge 1991, and Kastan 1999. Sir William Brooke, Lord Cobham, was Lord Chamberlain in 1596–97, i.e., contemporaneous with the first performances of *Henry IV, Part One*.

over forty years).[2] Whatever the motive, the new name proved to be fortunate, as the punning "Fall-staff" or "False-staff" not only implies battlefield cowardice and impotence but also spoofs the martial valor traditionally associated with Shakespeare's family name, "Shake-spear."

This Contexts section offers some frameworks for the fascination of Falstaff's dramatic appeal. One of these, largely invented for Falstaff himself, is character criticism. Modern scholars often dismiss this approach as sentimental, careless of the play's larger vision, better treated as a curious error of eighteenth- and nineteenth-century criticism, prone to fruitless conjectures. Such a critique argues that characters are linguistic constructions and thus parts of a larger web of meaning, not freestanding, independent beings with inner lives or imaginable, pre-dramatic biographies. This critique also likes to remind us that even as the word "character" derives from a Greek instrument for surface engraving, and, by extension, the distinctive mark so engraved, dramatic characters may have less to do with psychology than with socially visible inscription.

Yet, if the excesses of character studies form an easy target, the best of such criticism is more illuminating than polemic admits. The often perceptive and nuanced readings of Morgann, Hazlitt, and Bradley (excerpted here) continue to underlie a great deal of modern discussion and stage performance. And if Empson's linguistic analyses inspired some of the reaction against character studies, he too came to feel chastening should not lead to rejection and grew suspicious of "the drive against character-mongering in Shakespeare criticism." Defending Bradley from L. C. Knights's famous 1933 essay against character criticism ("How Many Children Had Lady Macbeth?"), Empson notes: "My impression is that good local uses of [Knights's] principle, to brush off some

---

[2]Often quoted by critics and editors is Richard James's c. 1625 letter reporting the question of a "young gentle lady": "How [the character] Sir John Falstaff, or Fastolf . . . could be dead in Harry the fifth's time and again live in the time of Harry the sixth to be banished for cowardice." She was either witty, unusually literal minded, or a useful fiction, allowing James to note Plato's antipathy to poetic license as well as the fact that "in Shakespeare's first show of Harry the fifth, the person with which he undertook to play a buffoon was not Falstaff, but Sir John Oldcastle, and that offence being worthily taken by personages descended from his title . . . the poet was put to make an ignorant shift of abusing Sir John Fastolfe, a man not inferior of virtue though not so famous in piety as the other. . . . " For further details about the letter, see Taylor 1985.

Frontispiece of Kirkman, *The Wits* (1662).

The enduring popularity of Falstaff, even during the closing of the theaters, is illustrated in this collection of truncated "drolls."

unduly greasy piece of habitual sentiment, were often found; but that no amount of tact in the critics could stave off for ever its inhumanity and wrongheadedness."[3]

Dramatic characters, of course, are representations. But Shakespeare's language creates the impression that these characters, especially Falstaff, are also representing themselves. Our sense of them as subjects as well as objects of language is, of course, an illusion, an *as if* whose permissiveness may lead to Hazlitt's engagement with characters "as if they were living persons, not fictions of the mind."[4] If, as A. R. Humphreys notes in his valuable overview, "Falstaff's vitality confused critics as to the difference between dramatic and real persons," this confusion is the play's strength. The paradox is shrewdly acknowledged in Humphrey's very caveat, through the indispensably evasive notion of "vitality"—an effect superbly discussed by the critics in this section.[5]

Key Statements

Samuel Johnson (1709–1784)

Critic, essayist, poet, and lexicographer, Dr. Johnson was a lifelong devotee of Shakespeare, the author most often quoted in his ground-breaking Dictionary *of 1755. Johnson's edition of Shakespeare's plays, fulfilling a plan first raised twenty years before, is best remembered for the extensive, opinionated, and powerful critical remarks in the Preface and the notes to the plays: their language, their moral challenges, their characters. Johnson's brief, enthusiastic remarks on Falstaff are rightly praised by J. Dover Wilson as a "complete and rounded little critical essay," (1953, p. 13), though we may be equally inclined to notice the angular, self-divided moral analysis that takes over once the opening apostrophe conjures Falstaff's powerfully imagined presence.*

---

[3]Empson 1996, p. 109.

[4]William Hazlitt, "On Shakespeare and Milton" (1818), in *The Selected Writings of William Hazlitt*, ed. Ducan Wu. Pickering and Chatto, 1998, vol. 2, p. 211.

[5]Humphreys 1961, rev. 1989, p. xliv. Humphreys later summarizes: "Falstaff, though immensely living, is not like any single real man. But he is symbolically like life itself" (xlv).

from *The Plays of William Shakespeare* (1765)

But Falstaff unimitated, unimitable Falstaff, how shall I describe thee? Thou compound of sense and vice; of sense which may be admired but not esteemed, of vice which may be despised, but hardly detested. Falstaff is a character loaded with faults, and with those faults which naturally produce contempt. He is a thief, and a glutton, a coward, and a boaster, always ready to cheat the weak, and prey upon the poor; to terrify the timorous and insult the defenceless. At once obsequious and malignant, he satirises in their absence those whom he lives by flattering. He is familiar with the prince only as an agent of vice, but of his familiarity he is so proud as not only to be supercilious and haughty with common men, but to think his interest of importance to the duke of Lancaster. Yet the man thus corrupt, thus despicable, makes himself necessary to the prince that despises him, by the most pleasing of all qualities, perpetual gaiety, by an unfailing power of exciting laughter, which is the more freely indulged, as his wit is not of the splendid or ambitious kind, but consists in easy escapes and sallies of levity, which make sport but raise no envy. It must be observed that he is stained with no enormous or sanguinary crimes, so that his licentiousness is not so offensive but that it may be borne for his mirth.

The moral to be drawn from this representation is, that no man is more dangerous than he that with a will to corrupt, hath the power to please; and that neither wit nor honesty ought to think themselves safe with such a companion when they see Henry seduced by Falstaff.

Elizabeth Montagu (1720–1800)

> *Dubbed "Queen of the Blues" by Johnson (by which he meant hostess of the Bluestockings, a group of literary women), Elizabeth Montagu wrote her* Essay *largely in response to Voltaire. Professing to admire Shakespeare's works, the French classicist charged that the plays were too irregular, coarse, and barbaric. Montagu's remarks include an important recognition of and effort to contain the potential scandal of Hal's attraction to Falstaff.*

from *Essay on the Writings and Genius of Shakespeare* (1769)

We cannot but suppose, that at the time it was written, many stories yet subsisted of the wild adventures of this Prince of Wales, and his idle companions. His subsequent reformation, and his conquests in France, rendered him a very popular character. . . . How happily therefore was the character of Falstaff introduced, whose wit and festivity in some measure excuse the Prince for admitting him into his familiarity, and suffering himself to be led by him into some irregularities. . . .

The Prince seems always diverted, rather than seduced by Falstaff; he despised his vices while he is entertained by his humour: and though Falstaff is for a while a stain upon his character, yet it is of a kind with those colors, which are used for a disguise in sort, being of such a nature as are easily washed out, without leaving any bad tincture. . . .

Whether Henry in the early part of his life was indulging a humor that inclined him to low and wild company, or endeavoring to acquire a deeper and more expensive knowledge of human nature, by a general acquaintance with mankind, it is the business of his historians to determine. But a critic must surely applaud the dexterity of Shakespeare for throwing this color over that part of his conduct, whether he seized on some intimations historians had given of that sort, or, of himself imagined so respectable a motive for the Prince's deviations from the dignity of his birth.

Maurice Morgann (1726–1802)

Maurice Morgann was a British Undersecretary of State whose expertise in American affairs involved him in important negotiations with Canada and, later, with the new United States. A liberal thinker, he wrote Plan for the Abolition of Slavery in the West Indies *(1772) during a hiatus in his political career, anticipating the early abolitionist works of John Wesley and Thomas Clarkson. Paradoxically described by contemporaries as both self-effacing and pompous, he was above all amusingly digressive and intellectually curious, qualities very much in evidence in his essay on Falstaff.*

Johnson, who sparred with Morgann on other occasions, found absurd his attempt to clear Falstaff of the charge of cowardice, and summaries or truncated anthologizing often highlight the willful outrageousness of Morgann's apologia. A longer selection, however, better reveals its often brilliant critical insights into the multiple responses evoked by the character. Sometimes regarded as proto-Romantic for its stress on subjective impression over moral judgment and for its praise of Shakespeare's genius, the Essay's *resourcefulness also aligns it with Renaissance and modern styles of reading against the grain. A confessedly "playful discussion"—its serio-comic tone and sophistical courtroom style throughout recall Sidney's* Defence of Poetry—the Essay *concedes from the start that the topic of Falstaff's courage is a mere pretext for pleasurable, critical exercise that inclines to "levity." The offhandedness frees Morgann to digress, to alternately assume and challenge stereotypes, and to explore, in a long, speculative footnote (included here), how Shakespeare's characters achieve a "roundedness" and "integrity" not found in those of his contemporary playwrights.*

from *An Essay on the Dramatic Character of Sir John Falstaff* (1777)

Preface

The following sheets were written in consequence of a friendly conversation, turning by some chance upon the character of Falstaff, wherein the writer, maintaining contrary to the general opinion, that, this character was not intended to be shown as a coward, he was challenged to deliver and support that opinion. . . . From the influence of the foregoing circumstances it is, that the writer has generally assumed rather the character and tone of an Advocate than of an Inquirer;—though if he had not first inquired and been convinced, he should never have attempted to have amused either himself or others with the subject. . . .

The vindication of Falstaff's Courage is truly no otherwise than the object of some old fantastic oak, or grotesque rock, may be the object of a morning's ride; yet being proposed as such, may serve to limit the distance, and shape the course: The real object is exercise, and the delight which a rich, beautiful, picturesque, and perhaps unknown country may excite from every side. . . .

On the Dramatic Character of Sir John Falstaff

We see this extraordinary character, almost in the first moment of our acquaintance with him, involved in circumstances of apparent dishonor, and we hear him familiarly called coward by his most intimate companions. We see him, on occasion of the robbery at Gads Hill, in the very act of running away from the Prince and Poins; and we behold him, on another of more honorable obligation, in open daylight, in battle, and acting in his profession as a soldier, escaping from Douglas even out of the world as it were, counterfeiting death and deserting his very existence; and we find him on the former occasion betrayed into those lies and braggadocioes which are the usual concomitants of cowardice in military men and pretenders to valor. These are not only in themselves strong circumstances, but they are moreover thrust forward, pressed upon our notice as the subject of our mirth, as the great business of the scene. No wonder therefore that the word should go forth that Falstaff is exhibited as a character of cowardice and dishonor.

What there is to the contrary of this, it is my business to discover. Much, I think, will presently appear; but it lies so dispersed, is so latent, and so purposely obscured that the reader must have some patience whilst I collect it into one body and make it the object of a steady and regular contemplation.

But what have we to do, may my readers exclaim, with principles so latent, so obscured? In dramatic composition the impression is the fact; and the writer who, meaning to impress one thing, has impressed another, is unworthy of observation. . . .

The reader will perceive that I distinguish between mental Impressions and the Understanding. I wish to avoid everything that looks like subtlety and refinement, but this is a distinction which we all comprehend. There are none of us unconscious of certain feelings or sensations of mind which do not seem to have passed through the Understanding—the effects, I suppose, of some secret influences from without, acting upon a certain mental sense, and producing feelings and passions in just correspondence to the force and variety of those influences on the one hand, and to the quickness of our sensibility on the other. Be the cause however what it may, the fact is undoubtedly so, which is all I am concerned in. And it is equally a fact, which every man's experience may avouch, that the Understanding and those feelings are frequently at variance. The latter often arise from the most minute circumstances, and frequently from such as the Understanding cannot estimate or even recognize, whereas the Understanding delights in abstraction and in general propositions which, however true considered as such, are very seldom (I had like to have said never) perfectly applicable to any particular case. And hence, among other causes, it is that we often condemn or applaud characters and actions on the credit of some logical process, while our hearts revolt and would fain lead us to a very different conclusion.

The Understanding seems for the most part to take cognizance of actions only, and from these to infer motives and character; but the sense we have been speaking of proceeds in a contrary course; and determines of actions from certain first principles of character, which seem wholly out of the reach of the Understanding. We cannot indeed do otherwise than admit that there must be distinct principles of character in every distinct individual: The manifest variety even in the minds of infants will oblige us to this. But what are these first principles of character? Not the objects, I am persuaded, of the Understanding; and yet we take as strong Impressions of them as if we could compare and assort them in a syllogism. We often love or hate at first sight; and indeed, in general, dislike or approve by some secret reference to these principles; and we judge even of conduct, not from any idea of abstract good or evil in the nature of actions, but by referring those actions to a supposed original character in the man himself. I do not mean that we talk thus; we could not indeed, if we would, explain ourselves in detail on this head; we can neither account for Impressions and passions, nor communicate them to others by words: Tones and looks will sometimes convey the passion strangely, but the Impression is incommunicable. The same causes may produce it indeed at the same time in many, but it is the separate possession of each, and not in its nature transferable: It is an imperfect sort of instinct, and proportionably dumb.—We might indeed, if we chose it, candidly confess to one another, that we are greatly swayed by these feelings, and are by no means so rational in all points as we could wish; but this would be a betraying of the interests of that high faculty, the Understanding, which we so value ourselves upon, and which we more peculiarly call our own. This, we think, must not be; and so we huddle up the matter, concealing it as much as possible, both from ourselves and others. . . .

But if there was one man in the world, who could make a more perfect draught of real nature, and steal such Impressions on his audience, without their special notice, as should keep their hold in spite of any error of their Understanding, and should thereupon venture to introduce an apparent incongruity of character and action, for ends which I shall presently endeavour to explain; such an imitation would be worth our nicest curiosity and attention. . . .

It is not to the courage only of Falstaff that we think these observations will apply: No part whatever of his character seems to be fully settled in our minds; at least there is something strangely incongruous in our discourse and affections concerning him. We all like Old Jack; yet, by some strange perverse fate, we all abuse him, and deny him the possession of any one single good or respectable quality. There is something extraordinary in this: It must be a strange art in Shakespeare which can draw our liking and good will towards so offensive an object. He has wit, it will be said; cheerfulness and humor of the most characteristic and captivating sort. And is this enough? Is the humor and gaiety of vice so very captivating? Is the wit, characteristic of baseness and every ill quality capable of attaching the heart and winning the affections? Or does not the apparency of such humor, and the flashes of such wit, by more strongly disclosing the deformity of character, but the more effectually excite our hatred and contempt of the man? And yet this is not our feeling of Falstaff's character. When he has ceased to amuse us, we find no emotions of disgust; we can scarcely forgive the ingratitude of the Prince in the new-born virtue of the King, and we curse the severity of that poetic justice which consigns our old good-natured delightful companion to the custody of the warden, and the dishonors of the Fleet. . . .

If then it should turn out, that this difficulty has arisen out of the Art of Shakespeare, who has contrived to make secret Impressions upon us of courage, and to preserve those Impressions in favor of a character which was to be held up for sport and laughter on account of actions of apparent cowardice and dishonor, we shall have less occasion to wonder, as Shakespeare is a Name which contains All of Dramatic artifice and genius. . . .

To me . . . it appears that the leading quality in Falstaff's character, and that from which all the rest take their color, is a high degree of wit and humor, accompanied with great natural vigor and alacrity of mind. This quality so accompanied, led him probably very early into life, and made him highly acceptable to society; so acceptable, as to make it seem unnecessary for him to acquire any other virtue. Hence, perhaps, his continued debaucheries and dissipations of every kind.—He seems, by nature, to have had a mind free of malice or any evil principle; but he never took the trouble of acquiring any good one. He found himself esteemed and beloved with all his faults; nay *for* his faults, which were all connected with humor, and for the most part, grew out of it. As he had, possibly, no vices but such as he thought might be openly professed, so he appeared more dissolute through ostentation. To the character of wit and humor, to which all his other qualities seem to have conformed themselves, he appears to have added a very necessary support, that of the profession of a soldier. He had from nature, as I presume to say, a spirit of boldness and enterprise; which in a military age, though employment was only occasional, kept him always above contempt, secured him an honorable reception among the great, and suited best both with his particular mode of humor and of vice. Thus living continually in society, nay even in taverns, and indulging himself, and being indulged by others, in every debauchery; drinking, whoring, gluttony, and ease; assuming a liberty of fiction, necessary perhaps to his wit, and often falling into falsity and lies, he seems to have set, by degrees, all sober reputation at defiance; and finding eternal resources in his wit, he borrows, shifts, defrauds, and even robs, without dishonor.—Laughter and approbation attend his greatest excesses; and being governed visibly by no settled bad principle or ill design, fun and humor account for and cover all. By degrees, however, and through indulgence, he acquires bad habits, becomes an humorist, grows enormously corpulent, and falls into the infirmities of age; yet never quits, all the time, one single levity or vice of youth, or loses any of that cheerfulness of mind, which had enabled him to pass through this course with ease to himself and delight to others; and thus, at last, mixing youth and age, enterprise and corpulency, wit and folly, poverty and expense, title and buffoonery, innocence as to purpose, and wickedness as to practice; neither incurring hatred by bad principle, or contempt by cowardice, yet involved in circumstances productive of imputation in both; a butt and a wit, a humorist and a man of humor, a touchstone and a laughing stock, a jester and a jest, has Sir John Falstaff, taken at that period of his life in which we see him, become the most perfect comic character that perhaps ever was exhibited. . . .

We will begin then, if the reader pleases, by inquiring what Impression the very vulgar had taken of Falstaff. . . .

The Hostess Quickly employs two officers to arrest Falstaff. On the mention of his name, one of them immediately observes "that it may chance to cost some of them their lives, for that he will stab." "Alas a day," says the Hostess, "take heed of him, he cares not what mischief he doth; if his weapon be out, he will foin like any devil; he will spare neither man, woman, or child." Accordingly, we find that when they lay hold on him he resists to the utmost of his power, and calls upon Bardolph, whose arms are at liberty, to draw. "Away, varlets, draw, Bardolph, cut me off the villain's head, throw the quean in the kennel." The officers cry, "a rescue, a rescue!" But the Chief Justice comes in and the scuffle ceases. In another scene, his wench Doll Tearsheet asks him "when he will leave fighting . . . and patch up his old body for heaven." This is occasioned by his drawing his rapier on great provocation, and driving Pistol, who is drawn likewise, downstairs and hurting him in the shoulder. To drive Pistol was no great feat, nor do I mention it as such; but upon this occasion it was necessary. "A rascal bragging slave," says he, "the rogue fled from me like quicksilver"—expressions which, as they remember the cowardice of Pistol, seem to prove that Falstaff did not value himself on the adventure. Even something may be drawn from Davy, Shallow's serving man, who calls Falstaff, in ignorant admiration, the man of war. I must observe here, and I beg the reader will notice it, that there is not a single expression dropped by these people or either of Falstaff's followers from which may be inferred the least suspicion of cowardice in his character, and this is I think such an implied negation as deserves considerable weight.

But to go a little higher, if indeed to consider Shallow's opinion be to go higher: it is from him, however, that we get the earliest account of Falstaff. He remembers him a page to Thomas Mowbray, Duke of Norfolk: "He broke," says he, "Schoggan's head at the court gate when he was but a crack thus high." Shallow throughout considers him as a great leader and soldier, and relates this fact as an early indication only of his future prowess. Shallow it is true is a very ridiculous character, but he picked up these impressions somewhere, and he picked up none of a contrary tendency. I want at present only to prove that Falstaff stood well in the report of common fame as to this point; and he was now near seventy years of age, and had passed in a military line through the active part of his life. At this period common fame may be well considered as the seal of his character—a seal which ought not perhaps to be broke open on the evidence of any future transaction.

But to proceed. Lord Bardolph was a man of the world, and of sense and observation. He informs Northumberland, erroneously indeed, that Percy had beaten the King at Shrewsbury. "The King," according to him, "was wounded; the Prince of Wales and the two Blunts slain, certain nobles (whom he names) had escaped by flight; and the brawn Sir John Falstaff was taken prisoner." But how came Falstaff into this list? Common fame had put him there. He is singularly obliged to common fame. But if he had not been a soldier of repute, if he had not been brave as well as fat, if he had been mere brawn, it would have been more germane to the matter if this lord had put him down among the baggage or the provender.

> [*Morgann pauses to make some general comments
> about Shakespeare's characterization*]

I cannot forsee the temper of the reader, nor whether he be content to go along with me in these kind of observations. Some of the incidents which I have drawn out of the Play may appear too minute, whilst yet they refer to principles, which may seem too general. Many points require explanation; something should be said of the nature of Shakespeare's Dramatic characters;[1] by what arts they were formed, and wherein they differ from those of other writers; something likewise more professedly of Shakespeare himself, and of the peculiar character of his genius. After such a review we may not perhaps think any consideration arising out of the Play, or out of general nature, either as too minute or too extensive.

Shakespeare is in truth, an author whose mimic creation agrees in general so perfectly with that of nature, that it is not only wonderful in the great, but opens another scene of amazement to the discoveries of the microscope. . . .

Shakespeare is a name so interesting, that it is excusable to stop a moment, nay it would be indecent to pass him without the tribute of some admiration. He differs essentially from all other writers: Him we may profess rather to feel than to understand; and it is safer to say, on many occasions, that we are possessed by him, than

---

[1]Morgann here appends a long footnote, virtually an essay in itself; I place it at the end of this essay (p. 350).

that we possess him. And no wonder;—He scatters the seeds of things, the principles of character and action, with so cunning a hand yet with so careless an air, and, master of our feelings, submits himself so little to our judgment, that every thing seems superior. We discern not his course, we see no connection of cause and effect, we are rapt in ignorant admiration, and claim no kindred with his abilities. All the incidents, all the parts, look like chance, whilst we feel and are sensible that the whole is design. His Characters not only act and speak in strict conformity to nature, but in strict relation to us; just so much is shewn as is requisite, just so much is impressed; he commands every passage to our heads and to our hearts, and moulds us as he pleases, and that with so much ease, that he never betrays his own exertions. We see these Characters act from the mingled motives of passion, reason, interest, habit and complection, in all their proportions, when they are supposed to know it not themselves; and we are made to acknowledge that their actions and sentiments are, from those motives, the necessary result. He at once blends and distinguishes every thing;—every thing is complicated, every thing is plain. . . .

[*Falstaff's behavior at Shrewsbury*]

We see him, after he had expended his rag-o-muffians, with sword and target in the midst of battle, in perfect possession of himself, and replete with humor and jocularity. He was, I presume, in some immediate personal danger, in danger also of a general defeat, too corpulent for flight; and to be led a prisoner was probably to be led to execution; yet we see him laughing and easy, offering a bottle of sack to the Prince instead of a pistol, punning, and telling him, "there was that which would sack a city."—"What, is it a time (says the Prince) to jest and dally now?" No, a sober character would not jest on such an occasion, but a coward could not; he would neither have the inclination or the power. And what could support Falstaff in such a situation? Not principle; he is not suspected of the point of honor; he seems indeed fairly to renounce it. "Honor cannot set a leg or an arm; it has no skill in surgery. What is it? a word only; mere air. It is insensible to the dead; and detraction will not let it live with the living." What then but a strong natural constitutional courage which nothing could extinguish or dismay? In the following passages the true character of Falstaff as to courage and principle is finely touched, and the different colors at once nicely blended and distinguished. "If Percy be alive, I'll pierce him. If he do come in my way, so. If he do not, if I come in his willingly, let him make a carbonado of me. I like not such grinning honor as Sir Walter hath; give me life, which, if I can save, so; if not, honor comes unlooked for, and there's an end." One cannot say which prevails most here, profligacy or courage; they are both tinged alike by the same humor, and mingled in one common mass; yet when we consider the superior force of Percy, as we must presently also that of Douglas, we shall be apt, I believe, in our secret heart to forgive him. These passages are spoken in soliloquy and in battle. If every soliloquy made under similar circumstances were as audible as Falstaff's, the imputation might perhaps be found too general for censure. These are among the passages that have impressed on the world an idea of cowardice in Falstaff; yet why? He is resolute to take his fate. If Percy do come in his way, so; if not, he will not seek inevitable destruction. He is willing to save his life, but if that cannot be, why, "honor comes unlooked for, and there's an end." This surely is not the language of cowardice. It contains neither the bounce or whine of the character. He derides, it is true, and seems to renounce that grinning idol of military zealots, honor. But Falstaff was a kind of military free-thinker, and has accordingly incurred the obloquy of his condition. He stands upon the ground of natural courage only and common sense, and has, it seems, too much wit for a hero. But let me be well understood. I do not justify Falstaff for renouncing the point of honor; it proceeded doubtless from a general relaxation of mind, and profligacy of temper. Honor is calculated to aid and strengthen natural courage and lift it up to heroism; but natural courage, which can act as such without honor, is natural courage still—the very quality I wish to maintain to Falstaff. And if without the aid of honor he can act with firmness, his portion is only the more eminent and distinguished. In such a character, it is to his actions, not his sentiments, that we are to look for conviction. But it may be still further urged in behalf of Falstaff that there may be false honor as well as false religion. It is true; yet even in that case candor obliges me to confess that the best men are most disposed to conform, and most likely to become the dupes of their own virtue. But it may however be more reasonably urged that there are particular tenets both in honor and religion which it is the grossness of folly not to question. . . .

We must remember that Falstaff had a double character. He was a wit as well as a soldier, and his courage, however eminent, was but the accessary; his wit was the principal, and the part which, if they should come in competition, he had the greatest interest in maintaining. Vain indeed were the licentiousness of his principles if he should seek death like a bigot yet without the meed of honor, when he might live by wit and increase the reputation of that wit by living. But why do I labor this point? It has been already anticipated, and our improved acquaintance with Falstaff will now require no more than a short narrative of the fact.

Whilst in the battle of Shrewsbury he is exhorting and encouraging the Prince who is engaged with the Spirit Percy—"Well said, Hal, to him, Hal"—he is himself attacked by the Fiend Douglas. There was no match; nothing remained but death or stratagem, grinning honor or laughing life. But an expedient offers, a mirthful one: take your choice, Falstaff, a point of honor or a point of drollery. It could not be a question. Falstaff falls, Douglas is cheated, and the world laughs. But does he fall like a coward? No, like a buffoon only; the superior principle prevails, and Falstaff lives by a stratagem growing out of his character to prove himself no counterfeit, to jest, to be employed, and to fight again. That Falstaff valued himself, and expected to be valued by others, upon this piece of saving wit is plain. It was a stratagem, it is true; it argued presence of mind; but it was moreover (what he most liked) a very laughable joke, and as such he considers it, for he continues to counterfeit after the danger is over that he may also deceive the Prince and improve the event into more laughter. He might, for ought that appears, have concealed the transaction; the Prince was too earnestly engaged for observation; he might have formed a thousand excuses for his fall; but he lies still and listens to the pronouncing of his epitaph by the Prince with all the waggish glee and levity of his character. The circumstance of his wounding Percy in the thigh, and carrying the dead body on his back like luggage, is indecent but not cowardly. . . .

The shame arising to Falstaff from the detection of mere lies would be temporary only, his character as to this point being already known and tolerated for the humor. Nothing therefore could follow but mirth and laughter and the temporary triumph of baffling a wit at his own weapons and reducing him to an absolute surrender, after which we ought not to be surprised if we see him rise again like a boy from play and run another race with as little dishonor as before. . . .

Though I have considered Falstaff's character as relative only to one single quality, yet so much has been said that it cannot escape the reader's notice that he is a character made up by Shakespeare wholly of incongruities—a man at once young and old, enterprising and fat, a dupe and a wit, harmless and wicked, weak in principle and resolute by constitution, cowardly in appearance and brave in reality, a knave without malice, a liar without deceit, and a knight, a gentleman, and a soldier without either dignity, decency, or honor. This is a character which, though it may be de-compounded, could not I believe have been formed, nor the ingredients of it duly mingled, upon any receipt whatever. It required the hand of Shakespeare himself to give to every particular part a relish of the whole, and of the whole to every particular part—alike the same incongruous, identical Falstaff, whether to the grave Chief Justice he vainly talks of his youth and offers to caper for a thousand, or cries to Mrs. Doll, "I am old, I am old," though she is seated on his lap and he is courting her for busses. How Shakespeare could furnish out sentiment of so extraordinary a composition, and supply it with such appropriated and characteristic language, humor and wit, I cannot tell; but I may however venture to infer, and that confidently, that he who so well understood the uses of incongruity, and that laughter was to be raised by the opposition of qualities in the same man and not by their agreement or conformity, would never have attempted to raise mirth by showing us cowardice in a coward unattended by pretense and softened by every excuse of age, corpulence, and infirmity. And of this we cannot have more striking proof than his furnishing this very character, on one instance of real terror, however excusable, with boast, braggadocio, and pretense exceeding that of all other stage cowards the whole length of his superior wit, humor, and invention.

Morgann's footnote, signaled on p. 346.

[1]The reader must be sensible of something in the composition of Shakespeare's characters, which renders them essentially different from those drawn by other writers. The characters of every Drama must indeed be grouped; but in the groups of other poets the parts

which are not seen, do not in fact exist. But there is a certain round-ness and integrity in the forms of Shakespeare, which give them an independence as well as a relation, insomuch that we often meet with passages, which tho' perfectly felt, cannot be sufficiently explained in words, without unfolding the whole character of the speaker: And this I may be obliged to do in respect to that of Lan-caster, in order to account for some words spoken by him in censure of Falstaff.—Something which may be thought too heavy for the text, I shall add here, as a conjecture concerning the composition of Shakespeare's characters: Not that they were the effect, I believe, so much of a minute and laborious attention, as of a certain compre-hensive energy of mind, involving within itself all the effects of sys-tem and of labour.

Bodies of all kinds, whether of metals, plants, or animals, are supposed to possess certain first principles of being, and to have an existence independent of the accidents, which form their magni-tude or growth: Those accidents are supposed to be drawn in from the surrounding elements, but not indiscriminately; each plant and each animal, imbibes those things only, which are proper to its own distinct nature, and which have besides such a secret relation to each other as to be capable of forming a perfect union and coa-lescence: But so variously are the surrounding elements mingled and disposed, that each particular body, even of those under the same species, has yet some peculiar of its own. Shakespeare appears to have considered the being and growth of the human mind as analogous to this system: There are certain qualities and capacities, which he seems to have considered as first principles; the chief of which are certain energies of courage and activity, according to their degrees; together with different degrees and sorts of sensibilities, and a capacity, varying likewise in the degree, of discernment and intelligence. The rest of the composition is drawn in from an atmosphere of surrounding things; that is, from the various influences of the different laws, religions and govern-ments in the world; and from those of the different ranks and inequalities in society; and from the different professions of men, encouraging or repressing passions of particular sorts, and induc-ing different modes of thinking and habits of life; and he seems to have known intuitively what those influences in particular were which this or that original constitution would most freely imbibe, and which would most easily associate and coalesce. But all these things being, in different situations, very differently disposed, and those differences exactly discerned by him, he found no difficulty in marking every individual, even among characters of the same sort, with something peculiar and distinct.—Climate and complexion demand their influence, '*Be thus when thou art dead, and I will kill thee, and love thee after,*' is a sentiment characteristic of, and fit only to be uttered by a Moor.

But it was not enough for Shakespeare to have formed his characters with the most perfect truth and coherence; it was further necessary that he should possess a wonderful facility of compressing, as it were, his own spirit into these images, and of giving alternate animation to the forms. This was not to be done from without; he must have felt every varied situation, and have spoken thro' the organ he had formed. Such an intuitive comprehension of things and such a facility, must unite to produce a Shakespeare. The reader will not now be surprised if I affirm that those characters in Shakespeare, which are seen only in part, are yet capable of being unfolded and understood in the whole; every part being in fact relative, and inferring all the rest. It is true that the point of action or sentiment, which we are most concerned in, is always held out for our special notice. But who does not perceive that there is a peculiarity about it, which conveys a relish of the whole? And very frequently, when no particular point presses, he boldly makes a character act and speak from those parts of the composition, which are inferred only, and not distinctly shewn. This produces a wonderful effect: it seems to carry us beyond the poet to nature itself, and gives an integrity and truth to facts and character, which they could not otherwise obtain: And this is in reality that art in Shakespeare, which being withdrawn from our notice, we more emphatically call nature. A felt propriety and truth from causes unseen, I take to be the highest point of Poetic composition. If the characters of Shakespeare are thus whole, and as it were original, while those of almost all other writers are mere imitation, it may be fit to consider them rather as Historic than Dramatic beings; and, when occasion requires, to account for their conduct from the whole of character, from general principles, from latent motives, and from policies not avowed.

William Hazlitt (1778–1830)

William Hazlitt devoted himself to painting as a young man but is remembered today for his penetrating essays and criticism, ranging across politics and philosophy as well as poetry and the arts. Strangely inward at times, he was nonetheless a pugnacious journalist (and, appropriately, author of the famous boxing essay "The Fight"), and he counted Coleridge, Wordsworth, Lamb, Keats, and Shelley among his friends. His Shakespearean criticism (an excerpt on Falstaff appears here) develops from previous critics but has its own vivacity. For a fuller sense of Hazlitt's keen appreciation of Shakespeare, see his "On Shakespeare and Milton," first an extremely well received public lecture, soon published in Lectures on the English Poets *(1818). For the general aesthetic underlying his praise of Falstaff, see his essay concerning painting, "On Gusto," which first appeared the previous year in* The Examiner *(1816).*

from *Characters of Shakespear's Plays* (1817)

Henry IV in Two Parts

Falstaff . . . is perhaps the most substantial comic character that ever was invented. Sir John carries a most portly presence in the mind's eye; and in him, not to speak it profanely, "we behold the fulness of the spirit of wit and humor bodily." We are as well acquainted with his person as his mind, and his jokes come upon us with double force and relish from the quantity of flesh through which they make their way, as he shakes his fat sides with laughter, or "lards the lean earth as he walks along." Other comic characters seem, if we approach and handle them, to resolve themselves into air, "into thin air"; but this is embodied and palpable to the grossest apprehension: it lies "three fingers deep upon the ribs," it plays about the lungs and diaphragm with all the force of animal enjoyment. His body is like a good estate to his mind, from which he receives rents and revenues of profit and pleasure in kind, according to its extent and the richness of the soil. Wit is often a meagre substitute for pleasurable sensation; an effusion of spleen and petty spite at the comforts of others, from feeling none in itself. Falstaff's wit is an emanation of a fine constitution; an exuberance of good-humor and good-nature; an overflowing of his love of laughter and good-fellowship; a giving vent to his heart's ease, and over-contentment with himself and others. He would not be in character, if he were not so fat as he is; for there is the greatest keeping in the boundless luxury of his imagination and the pampered self-indulgence of his physical appetites. He manures and nourishes his mind with jests, as he does his body with sack and sugar. He carves out his jokes, as he would a capon or a haunch of venison, where there is *cut and come again*; and pours out upon them the oil of gladness. His tongue drops fatness, and in the chambers of his brain "it snows of meat and drink." He keeps up perpetual holiday and open house, and we live with him in a round of invitations to a rump and dozen. Yet we are not to suppose that he was a mere sensualist. All this is as much in imagination as in reality. His sensuality does not engross and stupify his other faculties, but "ascends me into the brain, dries me there all the foolish and dull and crudy vapors which environ it, makes it apprehensive, quick, forgetive, full of nimble, fiery, and delectable shapes."[1] His imagination keeps up the ball after his senses have done with it. He seems to have even a greater enjoyment of the freedom from restraint, of good cheer, of his ease, of his vanity, in the ideal exaggerated description which he gives of them, than in fact. He never fails to enrich his discourse with allusions to eating and drinking, but we never see him at table. He carries his own larder about with him, and he is himself "a tun of man." His pulling out the bottle in the field of battle is a joke to show his contempt for glory accompanied with danger, his systematic adherence to his Epicurean philosophy in the most trying circumstances. Again, such is his deliberate exaggeration of his own vices, that it does not seem quite certain whether the account of his hostess's bill, found in his pocket, with such an out-of-the-way charge for capons and sack with only one half-penny-worth of bread, was not put there by himself as a trick to humor the jest upon his favorite propensities, and as a conscious caricature of himself. He is represented as a liar, a braggart, a coward, a glutton, &c., and yet we are not offended but delighted with him; for he is all these as much to amuse others as to gratify himself. He openly assumes all these characters to show the humorous part of them. The unrestrained indulgence of his own ease, appetites, and convenience, has neither malice nor hypocrisy in it. In a word, he is an actor in himself almost as much as upon the stage, and we no more object to the

---

[1][Part II., act iv., sc. 3]. [Hazlitt's note]

character of Falstaff in a moral point of view than we should think of bringing an excellent comedian, who should represent him to the life, before one of the police offices. We only consider the number of pleasant lights in which he puts certain foibles (the more pleasant as they are opposed to the received rules and necessary restraints of society), and do not trouble ourselves about the consequences resulting from them, for no mischievous consequences do result. Sir John is old as well as fat, which gives a melancholy retrospective tinge to the character; and by the disparity between his inclinations and his capacity for enjoyment, makes it still more ludicrous and fantastical.

The secret of Falstaff's wit is for the most part a masterly presence of mind, an absolute self-possession, which nothing can disturb. His repartees are involuntary suggestions of his self-love; instinctive evasions of everything that threatens to interrupt the career of his triumphant jollity and self-complacency. His very size floats him out of all his difficulties in a sea of rich conceits; and he turns round on the pivot of his convenience, with every occasion and at a moment's warning. His natural repugnance to every unpleasant thought or circumstance, of itself makes light of objections, and provokes the most extravagant and licentious answers in his own justification. His indifference to truth puts no check upon his invention, and the more improbable and unexpected his contrivances are, the more happily does he seem to be delivered of them, the anticipation of their effect acting as a stimulus to the gaiety of his fancy. The success of one adventurous sally gives him spirits to undertake another: he deals always in round numbers, and his exaggerations and excuses are "open, palpable, monstrous as the father that begets them." . . .

One of the topics of exulting superiority over others most common in Sir John's mouth is his corpulence and the exterior marks of good living which he carries about him, thus "turning his vices into commodity." He accounts for the friendship between the Prince and Poins, from "their legs being both of a bigness"; and compares Justice Shallow to "a man made after supper of a cheese-paring." There cannot be a more striking gradation of character than that between Falstaff and Shallow, and Shallow and Silence. It seems difficult at first to fall lower than the squire; but this fool, great as he is, finds an admirer and humble foil in his cousin Silence. Vain of his acquaintance with Sir John, who makes a butt of him, he exclaims, "Would, cousin Silence, that thou hadst seen that which this knight and I have seen!"—"Ay, Master Shallow, we have heard the chimes at midnight," says Sir John. To Falstaff's observation, "I did not think Master Silence had been a man of this mettle," Silence answers, "Who, I? I have been merry twice and once ere now." What an idea is here conveyed of a prodigality of living! What good husbandry and economical self-denial in his pleasures! What a stock of lively recollections! . . .

The truth is, that we never could forgive the Prince's treatment of Falstaff; though perhaps Shakespear knew what was best, according to the history, the nature of the times, and of the man. We speak only as dramatic critics. Whatever terror the French in those days might have of Henry V., yet, to the readers of poetry at present, Falstaff is the better man of the two. We think of him and quote him oftener.

A. C. Bradley (1851–1935)

Andrew Cecil Bradley, a professor at Oxford, remains the best-known Shakespearean critic largely but not exclusively on the strength of his Shakespearean Tragedy *(1904). Widely admired, copied, criticized, and parodied, Bradley offers both an ambitious theory of tragedy and extended lectures on four major examples—*Hamlet, Othello, King Lear, *and* Macbeth—*now sometimes called "the Bradleyan Four." For better or worse, he is often said to mark the culmination of character criticism, supposedly treating figures as if they had an autonomous, historical life, or the verisimilitude of novelistic figures, or, as in the essay presented here, a presence beyond the capacity of the play to contain them. Bradley's defenders note that detractors exaggerate his defects at the expense of the remarkable insights throughout his works, which have appealed to general readers as well as professional critics.*

The excerpt here is from a collection, Oxford Lectures on Poetry *(1909), which includes essays on Shakespeare, nineteenth-century literature, and Hegel's theory of tragedy. A still later essay, on* Coriolanus *(1912), is widely anthologized.*

from "The Rejection of Falstaff" (1902; 1909)

I do not propose to attempt a full account either of this character or of that of Prince Henry, but shall connect the remarks I have to make on them with a question which does not appear to have been satisfactorily discussed—the question of the rejection of Falstaff by the Prince on his accession to the throne. What do we feel, and what are we meant to feel, as we witness this rejection? And what does our feeling imply as to the characters of Falstaff and the new King? . . .

What are our feelings during this scene? They will depend on our feelings about Falstaff. If we have not keenly enjoyed the Falstaff scenes of the two plays, if we regard Sir John chiefly as an old reprobate, not only a sensualist, a liar, and a coward, but a cruel and dangerous ruffian, I suppose we enjoy his discomfiture and consider that the King has behaved magnificently. But if we *have* keenly enjoyed the Falstaff scenes, if we have enjoyed them as Shakespeare surely meant them to be enjoyed, and if, accordingly, Falstaff is not to us solely or even chiefly a reprobate and ruffian, we feel, I think, during the King's speech, a good deal of pain and some resentment; and when, without any further offense on Sir John's part, the Chief Justice returns and sends him to prison, we stare in astonishment. These, I believe, are, in greater or less degree, the feelings of most of those who really enjoy the Falstaff scenes (as many readers do not). Nor are these feelings diminished when we remember the end of the whole story, as we find it in *Henry V.*, where we learn that Falstaff quickly died, and, according to the testimony of persons not very sentimental, died of a broken heart. . . .

Now why did Shakespeare end his drama with a scene which, though undoubtedly striking, leaves an impression so unpleasant? . . .

What troubles us is not only the disappointment of Falstaff, it is the conduct of Henry. It was inevitable that on his accession he should separate himself from Sir John, and we wish nothing else. It is satisfactory that Sir John should have a competence, with the hope of promotion in the highly improbable case of his reforming himself. And if Henry could not trust himself within ten miles of so fascinating a companion, by all means let him be banished that distance: we do not complain. These arrangements would not have prevented a satisfactory ending: the King could have communicated his decision, and Falstaff could have accepted it, in a private interview rich in humor and merely touched with pathos. But Shakespeare has so contrived matters that Henry could not send a private warning to Falstaff even if he wished to, and in their public meeting Falstaff is made to behave in so infatuated and outrageous a manner that great sternness on the King's part was unavoidable. And the curious thing is that Shakespeare did not stop here. If this had been all we should have felt pain for Falstaff, but not, perhaps, resentment against Henry. But two things we do resent. Why, when this painful incident seems to be over, should the Chief Justice return and send Falstaff to prison? Can this possibly be meant for an act of private vengeance on the part of the Chief Justice, unknown to the King? No; for in that case Shakespeare would have shown at once that the King disapproved and cancelled it. It must have been the King's own act. This is one thing we resent; the other is the King's sermon. He had a right to turn away his former self, and his old companions with it, but he had no right to talk all of a sudden like a clergyman; and surely it was both ungenerous and insincere to speak of them as his "misleaders," as though in the days of Eastcheap and Gadshill he had been a weak and silly lad. We have seen his former self, and we know that it was nothing of the kind. He had shown himself, for all his follies, a very strong and independent young man, deliberately amusing himself among men over whom he had just as much ascendency as he chose to exert. Nay, he amused himself not only among them, but at their expense. In his first soliloquy—and first soliloquies are usually significant—he declares that he associates with them in order that, when at some future time he shows his true character, he may be the more wondered at for his previous aberrations. You may think he deceives himself here; you may believe that he frequented Sir John's company out of delight in it and not merely with this cold-blooded design; but at any rate he *thought* the design was his one motive. And, that being so, two results follow. He ought in honor long ago to have given Sir John clearly to understand that they must say good-bye on the day of his accession. And, having neglected to do this, he ought not to have lectured him as his misleader. It was not only ungenerous, it was dishonest. It looks disagreeably like an attempt to buy the praise of the respectable at the cost of honor and truth. And it succeeded. Henry *always* succeeded.

You will see what I am suggesting, for the moment, as a solution of our problem. I am suggesting that our fault lies not in our resentment at Henry's conduct, but in our surprise at it; that if we had read his character truly in the light that Shakespeare gave us, we should have been prepared for a display both of hardness and of policy at this point in his career. And although this suggestion does not suffice to solve the problem before us, I am convinced that in itself it is true. Nor is it rendered at all improbable by the fact that Shakespeare has made Henry, on the whole, a fine and very attractive character, and that here he makes no one express any disapprobation of the treatment of Falstaff. For in similar cases Shakespeare is constantly misunderstood. His readers expect him to mark in some distinct way his approval or disapproval of that which he represents; and hence where *they* disapprove and *he* says nothing, they fancy that he does *not* disapprove, and they blame his indifference, like Dr. Johnson, or at the least are puzzled. But the truth is that he shows the fact and leaves the judgment to them. And again, when he makes us like a character we expect the character to have no faults that are not expressly pointed out, and when other faults appear we either ignore them or try to explain them away. This is one of our methods of conventionalizing Shakespeare. We want the world's population to be neatly divided into sheep and goats, and we want an angel by us to say, "Look, that is a goat and this is a sheep," and we try to turn Shakespeare into this angel. His impartiality makes us uncomfortable: we cannot bear to see him, like the sun, lighting up everything and judging nothing. And this is perhaps especially the case in his historical plays, where we are always trying to turn him into a partisan. He shows us that Richard II. was unworthy to be king, and we at once conclude that he thought Bolingbroke's usurpation justified; whereas he shows merely, what under the conditions was bound to exist, an inextricable tangle of right and unright. Or, Bolingbroke being evidently wronged, we suppose Bolingbroke's statements to be true, and are quite surprised when, after attaining his end through them, he mentions casually on his death-bed that they were lies. Shakespeare makes us admire Hotspur heartily; and accordingly, when we see Hotspur discussing with others how large his particular slice of his mother-country is to be, we either fail to recognize the monstrosity of the proceeding, or, recognizing it, we complain that Shakespeare is inconsistent. Prince John breaks a tottering rebellion by practising a detestable fraud on the rebels. We are against the rebels, and have heard high praise of Prince John, but we cannot help seeing that his fraud is detestable; so we say indignantly to Shakespeare, "Why, you told us he was a sheep"; whereas, in fact, if we had used our eyes we should have known beforehand that he was the brave, determined, loyal, cold-blooded, pitiless, unscrupulous son of a usurper whose throne was in danger. . . .

[T]he natural conclusion is that Shakespeare *intended* us to feel resentment against Henry. And yet that cannot be, for it implies that he meant the play to end disagreeably; and no one who understands Shakespeare at all will consider that supposition for a moment credible. No; he must have meant the play to end pleasantly, although he made Henry's action consistent. And hence it follows that he must have intended our sympathy with Falstaff to be so far weakened when the rejection-scene arrives that his discomfiture should be satisfactory to us; that we should enjoy this sudden reverse of enormous hopes (a thing always ludicrous if sympathy is absent); that we should approve the moral judgment that falls on him; and so should pass lightly over that disclosure of unpleasant traits in the King's character which Shakespeare was too true an artist to suppress. Thus our pain and resentment, if we feel them, are wrong, in the sense that they do not answer to the dramatist's intention. But it does not follow that they are wrong in a further sense. They may be right, because the dramatist has missed what he aimed at. And this, though the dramatist was Shakespeare, is what I would suggest. In the Falstaff scenes he overshot his mark. He created so extraordinary a being, and fixed him so firmly on his intellectual throne, that when he sought to dethrone him he could not. The moment comes when we are to look at Falstaff in a serious light, and the comic hero is to figure as a baffled schemer; but we cannot make the required change, either in our attitude or in our sympathies. We wish Henry a glorious reign and much joy of his crew of hypocritical politicians, lay and clerical; but our hearts go with Falstaff to the Fleet, or, if necessary, to Arthur's bosom or wheresomever he is. . . .

Prince Hal never made such sport of Falstaff's person as he himself did. It is *he* who says that his skin hangs about him like an old lady's loose gown, and that he walks before his page like a sow that hath o'erwhelmed all her litter but one. And he jests at himself when he is alone just as much as when others are by. It is the same with his appetites. The direct enjoyment they bring him is scarcely so great as the enjoyment of laughing at this enjoyment; and for all his addiction to sack you never see him for an instant with a brain dulled by it, or a temper turned solemn, silly, quarrelsome, or pious.

The virtue it instills into him, of filling his brain with nimble, fiery, and delectable shapes—this, and his humorous attitude towards it, free him, in a manner, from slavery to it; and it is this freedom, and no secret longing for better things (those who attribute such a longing to him are far astray), that makes his enjoyment contagious and prevents our sympathy with it from being disturbed.

The bliss of freedom gained in humor is the essence of Falstaff. His humor is not directed only or chiefly against obvious absurdities; he is the enemy of everything that would interfere with his ease, and therefore of anything serious, and especially of everything respectable and moral. For these things impose limits and obligations, and make us the subjects of old father antic the law, and the categorical imperative, and our station and its duties, and conscience, and reputation, and other people's opinions, and all sorts of nuisances. I say he is therefore their enemy; but I do him wrong; to say that he is their enemy implies that he regards them as serious and recognizes their power, when in truth he refuses to recognize them at all. They are to him absurd; and to reduce a thing *ad absurdum* is to reduce it to nothing and to walk about free and rejoicing. This is what Falstaff does with all the would-be serious things of life, sometimes only by his words, sometimes by his actions too. . . .

No one in the play understands Falstaff fully, any more than Hamlet was understood by the persons round him. They are both men of genius. Mrs. Quickly and Bardolph are his slaves, but they know not why. "Well, fare thee well," says the hostess whom he has pillaged and forgiven; "I have known thee these twenty-nine years, come peas-cod time, but an honester and truer-hearted man—well, fare thee well." Poins and the Prince delight in him; they get him into corners for the pleasure of seeing him escape in ways they cannot imagine; but they often take him much too seriously. Poins, for instance, rarely sees, the Prince does not always see, and moralizing critics never see, that when Falstaff speaks ill of a companion behind his back, or writes to the Prince that Poins spreads it abroad that the Prince is to marry his sister, he knows quite well that what he says will be repeated, or rather, perhaps, is absolutely indifferent whether it be repeated or not, being certain that it can only give him an opportunity for humor. It is the same with his lying, and almost the same with his cowardice, the two main vices laid to his charge even by sympathizers. Falstaff is neither a liar nor a coward in the usual sense, like the typical cowardly boaster of comedy. He tells his lies either for their own humor, or on purpose to get himself into a difficulty. He rarely expects to be believed, perhaps never. He abandons a statement or contradicts it the moment it is made. There is scarcely more intent in his lying than in the humorous exaggerations which he pours out in soliloquy just as much as when others are by. Poins and the Prince understand this in part. You see them waiting eagerly to convict him, not that they may really put him to shame, but in order to enjoy the greater lie that will swallow up the less. But their sense of humor lags behind his. . . .

The main source, then, of our sympathetic delight in Falstaff is his humorous superiority to everything serious, and the freedom of soul enjoyed in it. But, of course, this is not the whole of his character. Shakespeare knew well enough that perfect freedom is not to be gained in this manner; we are ourselves aware of it even while we are sympathizing with Falstaff; and as soon as we regard him seriously it becomes obvious. His freedom is limited in two main ways. For one thing he cannot rid himself entirely of respect for all that he professes to ridicule. He shows a certain pride in his rank: unlike the Prince, he is haughty to the drawers, who call him a proud Jack. He is not really quite indifferent to reputation. When the Chief Justice bids him pay his debt to Mrs. Quickly for his reputation's sake, I think he feels a twinge, though to be sure he proceeds to pay her by borrowing from her. He is also stung by any thoroughly serious imputation on his courage, and winces at the recollection of his running away on Gadshill; he knows that his behavior there certainly looked cowardly, and perhaps he remembers that he would not have behaved so once. It is, further, very significant that, for all his dissolute talk, he has never yet allowed the Prince and Poins to *see* him as they saw him afterwards with Doll Tearsheet; not, of course, that he has any moral shame in the matter, but he knows that in such a situation he, in his old age, must appear contemptible—not a humorist but a mere object of mirth. And, finally, he has affection in him—affection, I think, for Poins and Bardolph, and certainly for the Prince; and that is a thing which he cannot jest out of existence. Hence, as the effect of his rejection shows, he is not really invulnerable. And then, in the second place, since he is in the flesh, his godlike freedom has consequences and conditions; consequences, for there is something painfully wrong with his great toe; conditions, for he cannot eat and drink for ever without money, and his purse suffers from consumption, a disease for which he can find no remedy. As the Chief Justice tells him, his means are very slender and his waste great; and his answer, "I would it were otherwise; I would my means were greater and my waist slenderer," though worth much money, brings none in. And so he is driven to evil deeds; not only to cheating his tailor like a gentleman, but to fleecing Justice Shallow, and to highway robbery, and to cruel depredations on the poor woman whose affection he has secured. All this is perfectly consistent with the other side of his character, but by itself it makes an ugly picture.

Yes, it makes an ugly picture when you look at it seriously. But then, surely, so long as the humorous atmosphere is preserved and the humorous attitude maintained, you do not look at it so. You no more regard Falstaff's misdeeds morally than you do the much more atrocious misdeeds of Punch or Reynard the Fox. You do not exactly ignore them, but you attend only to their comic aspect. This is the very spirit of comedy, and certainly of Shakespeare's comic world, which is one of make-believe, not merely as his tragic world is, but in a further sense—a world in which gross improbabilities are accepted with a smile, and many things are welcomed as merely laughable which, regarded gravely, would excite anger and disgust. The intervention of a serious spirit breaks up such a world, and would destroy our pleasure in Falstaff's company. Accordingly through the greater part of these dramas Shakespeare carefully confines this spirit to the scenes of war and policy, and dismisses it entirely in the humorous parts. Hence, if *Henry IV.* had been a comedy like *Twelfth Night*, I am sure that he would no more have ended it with the painful disgrace of Falstaff than he ended *Twelfth Night* by disgracing Sir Toby Belch.

But *Henry IV.* was to be in the main a historical play, and its chief hero Prince Henry. In the course of it his greater and finer qualities were to be gradually revealed, and it was to end with beautiful scenes of reconciliation and affection between his father and him, and a final emergence of the wild Prince as a just, wise, stern, and glorious King. Hence, no doubt, it seemed to Shakespeare that Falstaff at last must be disgraced, and must therefore appear no longer as the invincible humorist, but as an object of ridicule and even of aversion. And probably also his poet's insight showed him that Henry, as he conceived him, *would* behave harshly to Falstaff in order to impress the world, especially when his mind had been wrought to a high pitch by the scene with his dying father and the impression of his own solemn consecration to great duties.

This conception was a natural and a fine one; and if the execution was not an entire success, it is yet full of interest. Shakespeare's purpose being to work a gradual change in our feelings towards Falstaff, and to tinge the humorous atmosphere more and more deeply with seriousness, we see him carrying out this purpose in the Second Part of *Henry IV*. Here he separates the Prince from Falstaff as much as he can, thus withdrawing him from Falstaff's influence, and weakening in our minds the connection between the two. In the First Part we constantly see them together; in the Second (it is a remarkable fact) only once before the rejection. Further, in the scenes where Henry appears apart from Falstaff, we watch him growing more and more grave, and awakening more and more poetic interest; while Falstaff, though his humor scarcely flags to the end, exhibits more and more of his seamy side. This is nowhere turned to the full light in Part I.; but in Part II. we see him as the heartless destroyer of Mrs. Quickly, as a ruffian seriously defying the Chief Justice because his position as an officer on service gives him power to do wrong, as the pike preparing to snap up the poor old dace Shallow, and (this is the one scene where Henry and he meet) as the worn-out lecher, not laughing at his servitude to the flesh but sunk in it. Finally, immediately before the rejection, the world where he is king is exposed in all its sordid criminality when we find Mrs. Quickly and Doll arrested for being concerned in the death of one man, if not more, beaten to death by their bullies; and the dangerousness of Falstaff is emphasized in his last words as he hurries from Shallow's house to London, words at first touched with humor but at bottom only too seriously meant: "Let us take any man's horses; the laws of England are at my commandment. Happy are they which have been my friends, and woe unto my Lord Chief Justice." His dismissal to the Fleet by the Chief Justice is the dramatic vengeance for that threat.

Yet all these excellent devices fail. They cause us momentary embarrassment at times when repellent traits in Falstaff's character are disclosed; but they fail to change our attitude of humor into one of seriousness, and our sympathy into repulsion. And they were bound to fail, because Shakespeare shrank from adding to them the one device which would have ensured success. If, as the Second Part of *Henry IV.* advanced, he had clouded over Falstaff's humor so heavily that the man of genius turned into the Falstaff of the *Merry Wives*, we should have witnessed his rejection without a pang. This Shakespeare was too much of an artist to do—though even in this way he did something—and without this device he could not succeed. As I said, in the creation of Falstaff he overreached himself. He was caught up on the wind of his own genius, and carried so far that he could not descend to earth at the selected spot. It is not a misfortune that happens to many authors, nor is it one we can regret, for it costs us but a trifling inconvenience in one scene, while we owe to it perhaps the greatest comic character in literature. For it is in this character, and not in the judgment he brings upon Falstaff's head, that Shakespeare asserts his supremacy. To show that Falstaff's freedom of soul was in part illusory, and that the realities of life refused to be conjured away by his humor—this was what we might expect from Shakespeare's unfailing sanity, but it was surely no achievement beyond the power of lesser men. The achievement was Falstaff himself, and the conception of that freedom of soul, a freedom illusory only in part, and attainable only by a mind which had received from Shakespeare's own the inexplicable touch of infinity which he bestowed on Hamlet and Macbeth and Cleopatra, but denied to Henry the Fifth.

Three Literary Models

Braggart Soldier

Falstaff is often traced back to Plautus's braggart soldier (*miles gloriosus*), even though the numerous versions of this (originally Greek) type—a ridiculous boaster deluded by his own vanity—are significantly unlike Shakespeare's creation. As Morgann and others have noted, Falstaff is a self-conscious version of his ancestors: he may wildly exaggerate his exploits at Gadshill, shamelessly take credit for killing Hotspur, or proclaim his military reputation through all of Europe, but he also jokes at his own expense, inviting others to admire his outrageousness.

Titus Maccius Plautus (c. 251–184 BCE)

> *Together with Terence (whose Thraso is another famous literary braggart), the Roman Titus Maccius Plautus was one of the most widely admired and copied comic dramatists in Renaissance Europe. Shakespeare had already closely borrowed from two of his farces,* Amphitruo *and* Menaechmi, *for his* Comedy of Errors, *while the braggart-soldier type had been used by English playwrights as early as 1537, when the anonymous farce* Thersites *signaled an early influence of the classics on English drama.*

from *Miles Gloriosus* (*The Braggart Soldier*) (c. 205 BCE)

PYRGOPOLINICES (*the Braggart*) Take ye care that the lustre of my shield is more bright than the rays of the sun are wont to be at the time when the sky is clear; that when occasion comes, the battle being joined, 'mid the fierce ranks right opposite it may dazzle the eyesight of the enemy. But, I wish to console this sabre of mine, that it may not lament nor be downcast in spirits, because I have thus long been wearing it keeping holiday, which so longs right dreadfully to make havoc of the enemy. But where is Artotrogus?

ARTOTROGUS (*a flattering Parasite*) Here he is; he stands close by the hero, valiant and successful, and of princely form. Mars could not dare to style himself a warrior so great, nor compare his prowess with yours.

PYRGOPOLINICES Him you mean whom I spared on the Gorgonidonian plains, where Bumbomachides Clytomestoridysarchides, the grandson of Neptune, was the chief commander?

ARTOTROGUS I remember him; him, I suppose, you mean with the golden armor, whose legions you puffed away with your breath just as the wind blows away leaves or the reed-thatched roof.

PYRGOPOLINICES That, on my troth, was really nothing at all.

ARTOTROGUS Faith, that really was nothing at all in comparison with other things I could mention—[*aside*] which you never did. If any person ever beheld a more perjured fellow than this, or one more full of vain boasting, faith let him have me for himself, I'll resign myself for his slave. . . . (*The Parasite continues his flattery, recounting the Braggart's single-handed defeat of an elephant, then thousands of armed foes; further into this scene, he continues . . .*) I do remember this. In Cilicia there were a hundred and fifty men, a hundred in Cryphiolathronia, thirty at Sardis, sixty men of Macedon, whom you slaughtered altogether in one day.

PYRGOPOLINICES   What is the sum total of those men?
ARTOTROGUS   Seven thousand.
PYRGOPOLINICES   It must be as much: you keep the reckoning well.

. . . .

PALAESTRIO (*the clever slave, explaining the plot and characters to the audience*)   "Alazon" is the name, in Greek, of this Comedy; the same we call in Latin "the Braggart" (Gloriosus). This city is Ephesus; then, the Captain, my master, who has gone off hence to the Forum, a bragging, impudent, stinking fellow, brimful of lying and lasciviousness, says that all the women are following him of their own accord. Wherever he goes, he is the laughing stock of all; and so, the Courtesans here—since they make wry mouths at him, you may see the greater part of them with lips all awry.
(*The Comedies of Plautus*, tr. H. T. Riley, 2 vols. London, 1912.)

Allegories, Dramatic and Nondramatic

Allegorical morality plays were still being performed in England throughout the sixteenth century, and although their didactic conventions only partly explain Falstaff's function in the two *Henry IV* plays, they represent an important fund of materials out of which Shakespeare creates an evolving structure of revised and complicated expectations.

from *The Interlude of Youth*

An "interlude" is a brief theatrical entertainment, possibly staged between courses of a feast, though the term is much debated. In this example, an "everyman" figure, an abusive, narcissistic Youth, spurns Charity (spiritual love) for the sake of Riot, Pride, and Lechery. Riot's high-spirited estrangement of the "royal" lad from the "king" of virtues, as well as his remarks about thieving, escaping the gallows, fatness, and his final rejection by a chastened Youth (leaving the reprobate a bitter and broken old man), broadly anticipate Hal's relations with Falstaff and his kingly father.

from *The Interlude of Youth* (c. 1554)

Youth: I am goodly of person;
              I am peerless, wherever I come.
              My name is Youth, I tell thee,
              I flourish as the vine-tree
              Who may be likened unto me,
              In my youth and jollity?
              My hair is royal and bushed thick;
              My body pliant as a hazel stick

                 . . . .

              I am the heir of all my father's land,
              And it is come into my hand:
              I care for no more.

                 . . . .

              I wish my brother Riot would help me,
              For to beat Charity
              And his brother too.

Riot: Huffa! huffa! who calleth after me?
              I am Riot, full of jollity.
              My heart as light as the wind,
              And all on riot is my mind,
              Wheresoever I go.

                 . . . .

Youth: What! I weened[1] thou hadst been hanged,
              But I see thou art escaped,
              For it was told me here
              You took a man on the ear,
              That his purse in your bosom did fly,
              And so in Newgate[2] you did lie.

                 . . . .

              But, sir, how didst thou 'scape?

Riot: Verily, sir, the rope brake,
              And so I fell to the ground,

[1]Thought.
[2]Prison.

And ran away, safe and sound;
By the way I met with a courtier's lad,
And twenty nobles of gold in his purse he had:
I took the lad on the ear,
Beside his horse I felled him there:
I took his purse in my hand,
And twenty nobles therein I fand[3]
Lord, how I was merry!

Youth: God's fate! thou didst enough there
For to be made knight of the collar.

. . . .

[*After Youth returns from a tavern, he proclaims his kingship.*]

Youth: Aback! gallants, and look unto me,
And take me for your special,
For I am promoted to high degree,
By right I am king eternal;
Neither duke ne lord, baron ne knight,
That may be likened unto me,
They be subdued to me by right,
As servants to their masters should be.

[*Youth is, nevertheless, converted by the appeals of Charity and his brother, Humility, to the surprise of Pride and, especially, of a dismayed Riot.*]

Charity: Now thou must forsake Pride,
And all Riot set aside.

Pride: I will not him forsake,
Neither early ne late;
I ween'd he would not forsake me;
But if it will none otherwise be,
I will go my way.

Youth: Sir, I pray God be your speed,
And help you at your need.

Riot: I am sure thou wilt not forsake me,
Nor I will not forsake thee.

Youth: I forsake you also,
And will not have with you to do.

[3]Found.

Riot: And I forsake thee utterly:
           Fie on thee, caitiff, fie!
           Once a promise thou did me make,
           That thou would me never forsake,
           But now I see it is hard
           For to trust the wretched world;
           Farewell, masters, everyone.

. . . .

A Select Collection of Old English Plays,
ed. W. Carew Hazlitt (New York/London, 1874–1876)

Edmund Spenser (c. 1552–1599)

Shakespeare appears to have read Edmund Spenser's allegorical epic-romance The Faerie Queene, *especially the first three books, printed in 1590. In the first book, Spenser recounts the adventures of the Redcross Knight; in the excerpt presented here, the relatively inexperienced Knight has taken up residence at the House of Pride, a perverse court where the counsellors are personified sins, including the obese, sweaty Gluttony, carrying his trusty drinking can and harboring in his body "more diseases than his body knew for," as the doctor reports of Falstaff (*Part Two, 1.2*).*

from *The Faerie Queene*, Book I, Canto IV, Stanzas 21–23 (1590, 1596)

And by his side rode loathsome *Gluttony*
    Deformed creature, on a filthy swine,
    His belly was up-blown with luxury,
    And eke with fatness swollen were his eyne,°   *eyes*
    And like a crane his neck was long and fine,   185
    With which he swallowed up excessive feast;
    For want whereof poor people oft did pine;
    And all the way, most like a brutish beast,
He spewed up his gorge, that all did him detest.

In green vine leaves he was right fitly clad;   190
    For other clothes he could not wear for heat,

Of Gluttony.

All such therefore as peruert bee : and seekes to maintaine their estate:
Without repentance straight shall see : the endles woe and dreadfull gate.

¶ The signification.

THe two foremost excesse , the king mainteinaunce, the
Frier sufferance : and *Backus* the god of wyne : the Beare
force : the seruing man riot : and the Popishe priest careles
dyet.

F.ij.   Gluttonie

A Cristall Glasse of Christian Reformation, by Stephen Bateman
(1569): sig Fii (*Seven Deadly Sins: Gluttony*).

And on his head an ivy garland had,
From under which fast trickled down the sweat:
Still as he rode, he somewhat still did eat,
And in his hand did bear a boozing can,   195
Of which he supped so oft, that on his seat
His drunken corse° he scarce upholden can,   *body*
In shape and life more like a monster, than a man.

Unfit he was for any worldly thing,
    And eke° unable once to stir or go,   *also*   200
    Not meet to be of counsel to a king,
    Whose mind in meat and drink was drowned so,
    That from his friend he seldom knew his foe:
    Full of diseases was his carcass blue,
    And a dry dropsy through his flesh did flow: 205
    Which by misdiet daily greater grew:
Such one was *Gluttony*, the second of that crew.

From Oldcastle to Falstaff

John Foxe (1517–1587)

That John Foxe was born the same year Luther posted his 95 Theses is a coincidence too appropriate to ignore; his life's work and fame are founded on Reformation struggle and controversy. Already at work on a brief, Latin history of persecution and martyrdom of the Lollards (English predecessors of the Reformation), Foxe went into exile when the Catholic Mary came to the throne in 1553. He published his history on the continent the following year, greatly expanding it in 1559. Returning to England after Mary's death, he produced the epochal English version, Acts and Monuments of These Latter and Perilous Days *in 1563. Over the next twenty years, further expansions and revisions yielded massive editions, placing Marian persecution in a historical perspective of heroic martyrdom stretching back to the dawn of Christianity. Also known as the* Book of Martyrs, *Foxe's work was enormously influential for its vividly detailed history of suffering as well as for its sensational illustrations, and it was placed in cathedrals and parish churches throughout England. The book also inspired controversy, with charges and countercharges appearing from its own day down to nineteenth- and twentieth-century scholarly accounts, proclaiming the work to be either distorted, nationalistic propaganda or a scrupulous, historical treatment of primary documents and eyewitness testimony.*

Foxe's account of Sir John Oldcastle, Lord Cobham (c. 1378–1417), is based on (and credits) John Bale's Protestant narrative, which casts Oldcastle as a "valiant warrior" and "blessed martyr" against earlier but still potent views of him as a traitor and heretic. Spanning several years, it presents Henry V, despite his stern policy on religious orthodoxy, as more gentle and sympathetic to his old friend than the "fierce," "blood thirsty raveners" who persecute him, but it ultimately concedes Henry's loss of patience. Oldcastle's sharp-witted defense against those he names sophistical and idolatrous members of the "great Antichrist" is to no avail, and despite a daring escape and a few years' refuge in Wales, he is retaken and horribly executed.

The account presented here ends with a typological reading of his "terrible kind of death" to point readers beyond a limited "carnal" view of events; it claims to find in Oldcastle's being hauled over the flames a reminder of Elias (i.e., Elijah) taken up in a fiery chariot (2 Kings 2.12). The point is also made to head off what Foxe considers a superstitious (or malicious) rumor that Oldcastle expected to rise from the dead on the third day after his execution. Foxe's cautious account of Henry's role in the unjust execution may have influenced the Hostess's and Fluellen's oblique remarks about the King's share in Falstaff's death in Shakespeare's Henry V *(2.1; 4.7).*

from *Acts and Monuments* (*Book of Martyrs*) (1563)

And, upon the day appointed, he was brought out of the tower with his arms bound behind him, having a very cheerful countenance. Then was he laid upon a hurdle, as though he had been a most heinous traitor to the crown, and so drawn forth into Saint Giles' field, whereas they had set up a new pair of gallows. As he was coming to the place of execution, and was taken from the hurdle, he fell down devoutly upon his knees, desiring Almighty God to forgive his enemies. Then stood he up and beheld the multitude, exhorting them in most godly manner to follow the laws of God written in the Scriptures, and in any wise to beware of such teachers as they see contrary to Christ in their conversation and living, with many other special counsels. Then was he hanged up there by the middle in chains of iron, and so consumed alive in the fire, praising the name of God, so long as his life lasted. In the end, he commended his soul into the hands of God, and so departed hence most christianly, his body being resolved into ashes.

And this was done in the year of our Lord 1418, which was the fifth year of the reign of King Henry the Fifth, the people, there present, showing great dolor. How the priests that time fared, blasphemed, and accursed, requiring the people not to pray for him, but to judge him damned in hell because he departed not in the obedience of their Pope, it were too long to write.

The description of the horrible and cruell martirdome
of my Lorde Cobham, called syr Ihon Old Castle.

This terrible kinde of death, with galowes chaines, and fyre, appeareth not very precious in the eyes of men that be carnal, no more thã did the death of Chriſte whan he was hanged vp amonge theues. The rightuous ſeemeth to dye (ſaithe the wiſe man) in the ſyghte of them whyche are vnwiſe, and their end is taken for very deſtruction. Ungodly foles thinketh ther liues verye madneſſe, and there paſſage hence without all honoure. But thoughe they ſuffer paine before menne (ſaythe he) yet is their expectation ful of immortality. They are accounted for the children of God, and haue their inſt portion amonge the ſainctes. As gold in the for nace doth God try his elect, and as a moſt pleaſant brent offering receiueth he them to reaſt.

The more hard the paſſage be, the more glorious ſhall they appeare in the latter reſurrection . Not that the afflictions of this life are worthye of ſuche a gloriy, but that it is Gods heauenly pleaſure ſo to rewarde them. Neuer are the iudgementes and wayes of men, lyke vnto the iudgementes and wayes of God, but contrarye euermore, vnleſſe they be taught of him, In the latter time (ſayeth the Lorde vnto Daniell) ſhall many be choſen, proued, and pu rified by fyre, yet ſhal the vngodly liue wicked lye ſtill, and haue no vnderſtandinge that is of ſayth. By an aungell from heauen, was Ihõ earneſtlye commaunded to wryte: that bleſſed are the dead which hence departeth in the lord. Righte deare (ſayeth Dauid) in the ſyghte of God is the death of his true ſeruauntes. Thus reaſteth this valeaunte Chriſten knighte, ſyr Ihon Oldcaſtel vnder the aultare of G O D) whiche is Jeſus Chriſte, amonge that godlye company which in the kingdome of pacience, ſuffred greate tribulation with the Deathe of their bodies for his faithful word and teſtimo ny, abiding there with them , be fulfillinge of their whole nomber, and the full reſtauration of his electes. The which he graunte in effecte at this time appoynted, which is one God eter nall, Amen.

Thus haue you hard the whole matter concerning the martirdom of the good Lord Cobham, as we haue gath:red it partly out of the Colleaors of Ihon Bale and others. Nowe if there be any that require the old monuments of the biſhops them ſelues, which hadd the doinge in the matter for a further teſtimonye to ſatiſfy their mindes we haue here annered the Epiſtle of Thomas Arundel Archbiſhop of Cã terbury his perſecutor therwithal, thoughe it be not greatly neceſſary, for the hiſtory ſufficiently declared before, yet for thantiquity therof, we thought it not to be omitted.

Do.i.   The

Image of Oldcastle martyred, from Foxe, *Acts and Monuments* (1563).

This terrible kind of death, with gallows, chains, and fire, appeareth not very precious in the eyes of men that be carnal, no more than did the death of Christ, when he was hanged up among thieves. "The righteous seemeth to die" (saith the wise man) "in the sight of them which are unwise, and their end is taken for very destruction. Ungodly souls think their lives very madness, and their passage hence without all honor; but, though they suffer pains before men," saith he, "yet is their expectation full of immortality. They are accounted for the children of God, and have their portion among the saints. As gold in the furnace doth God try his elect, and as a most pleasant burnt offering, receiveth he them to rest."

The more hard the passage be, the more glorious shall they appear in the latter resurrection. Not that the afflictions of this life are worthy of such a glory, but that it is God's heavenly pleasure so to reward them. Never are the judgments and ways of men like unto the judgments and ways of God, but contrary evermore, unless they be taught of him. "In the latter time," saith the Lord unto Daniel, "shall many be chosen, proved, and purified by fire; yet shall the ungodly live wickedly still, and have no understanding that is of faith." By an angel from heaven was John earnestly commanded to write: that "blessed are the dead which hence departed in the Lord." "Right dear," saith David, "in the sight of God, is the death of his true servants." Thus rested this valiant Christian knight, Sir John Oldcastle, under the altar of God, which is Jesus Christ, among that godly company, which in the kingdom of patience, suffered great tribulation with the death of their bodies, for His faithful word and testimony, abiding there with them, He fulfilling of their whole number, and the full restoration of his elect. The which He grant in effect at this time appointed, which is one God eternal. Amen.

Thus have you heard the whole matter concerning the martyrdom of the good Lord Cobham, as we have gathered it partly out of the collections of John Bale and others. . . .

This is not to be forgotten, which is reported by many, that he should say: that he should die here on earth after the sort and manner of Elias[1], the which, whether it sprang of the common people without

---

[1]Elijah.

cause, or that it was foreshowed by him, I think it not without good consideration, or that it sprang not without some gift of prophecy, the end of the matter doth sufficiently prove. For, like as when Elias should leave this mortal life, he was carried by a fiery chariot into immortality; even so the order of this man's death, not being much unlike, followed the figure of his departure. For he, first of all, being lifted up upon the gallows, as into a chariot, and compassed enround[2] about with flaming fire, what other thing, I pray you, did this most holy martyr of Christ represent, than only a figure of a certain Elias, flying up into heaven. The which went up into heaven by a fiery chariot.

Michael Drayton (c. 1563–1631), Richard Hathaway (fl. 1597–1603), Anthony Munday (1560–1633), and Robert Wilson (d. 1600)

These four authors joined to write a play featuring Oldcastle for the Lord Admiral's Men, Shakespeare's leading competitor. It begins by scoring points at Shakespeare's expense, scolding his company, the Lord Chamberlain's Men, for their scurrilous portrait of a martyr and patriot. Falstaff/Oldcastle's biblical and pious parodies must have particularly rankled the more sober Protestants as well as the contemporary Lord Cobham. The brief Prologue, excerpted here, is a sonnet mostly in blank verse, until its concluding, stinging couplet.

from *The True and Honorable History of the Life of Sir John Oldcastle, Part One* (1600)

The Prologue

The doubtful[1] title, gentlemen, prefixed
Upon the argument we have in hand,
May breed suspense and wrongfully disturb
The peaceful quiet of your settled thoughts.   4

---

[2]Encompassed round.

---

[1]I.e., the "Honorable" of the title might provoke doubt in the spectator because of previous slanders against Oldcastle.

To stop this scruple let this brief suffice:
It is no pampered glutton we present,
No agèd counsellor to youthful sins;
But one whose virtues shone above the rest,   8
A valiant martyr and a virtuous peer,
In whose true faith and loyalty expressed
To his true sovereign and his country's weal,
We strive to pay that tribute of our love   12
Your favours merit. Let fair truth be graced,
Since forged invention former time defaced.

The Theater of the World

Theatrical imagery appears throughout the two parts of *Henry IV*. In *Part One*, Hal and Falstaff stage a tavern "play extempore" that anticipates and parodies the meeting of father and son (2.4); the King's rebuke of Hal is as much an acting lesson as a moral and political reproach (3.2); the multiple impersonations of the King at Shrewsbury ("What art thou, that counterfeitist the person of a king") is pragmatic strategy but also reflects a preoccupation with kingship as role-playing (5.4). *Part Two* continues the pattern, opening with Rumor treating the audience's very presence as an instance of the world's perverse appetite for "false reports." We soon hear Northumberland's histrionic outcry against the world as a "stage" that must end its "ling'ring act" (1.1), and later, the King's dying regret about his disputed legitimacy: "all my reign was but as a scene / Acting that argument" (4.5).

The comparison of the world to a stage, a trope often referred to as *theatrum mundi* (Latin: theater of the world), has roots in antiquity and flourished so vigorously in Renaissance philosophy, theology, and literature that it is regarded as a hallmark of the era.[1] Heard in the playhouse, it effects an uncanny self-reflexiveness, as if the plays were commenting on themselves as theater, even as they extend the stage production into a metaphor for social and political life.

---

[1]Of the many studies, see especially Ernst Robert Curtius, *European Literature and the Latin Middle Ages*, tr. Willard R. Trask (1953; rpt. Harper & Row, 1963), ch. 7, sec. 5; Anne Barton, *Shakespeare and the Idea of the Play* (Chatto & Windus, 1962); A. Bartlett Giamatti, "Proteus Unbound: Some Versions of the Sea God the Renaissance" and Thomas Greene, "The Flexibility of the Self in Renaissance Literature," both in Peter Demetz, Thomas Greene, and Lowry Nelson, Jr., eds., *The Disciplines of Criticism* (Yale Univ. Press, 1968); Stephen J. Greenblatt, *Sir Walter Ralegh: The Renaissance Man and His Roles* (Yale Univ. Press, 1973), ch. 2; and William J. Bouwsma, *John Calvin: A Sixteenth-Century Portrait* (Oxford Univ. Press, 1988), ch. 11.

These moments, sometimes called "metatheatrical," can represent a spectrum of attitudes—sometimes in paradoxical combination. An optimistic view finds the world a comprehensible, just structure ("the theater of God's judgments") within which the resourceful self can become a prudent, sophisticated, and flexible improviser of effective action. But such energy risks destabilizing human identity within a tense, sociopolitical world of unregulated opportunism. Deception and hypocrisy ("hypocrite" derives from the Greek word meaning "actor" as well as "dissembler") may lurk behind any seemingly sincere act or virtuous quality, and at a critical moment, the actor may find himself gazing into a void—sapped of joy and meaning, haunted by his own insubstantial dreams.

The trope is prominent throughout the Second Tetralogy where, Alvin Kernan argues, "man has . . . broken into a strange, new existence where he is free to slide back and forth along the vast scale of being, coming to rest at various points, but never knowing for certain just who and what he is" ("*The Henriad,*" 251). Royal pomp is splendidly ambiguous—its costuming, artistry, and ritual observances affirming its higher meaning through idealized fictions, yet subversively implying theatrical fakery. The consecrated role is both exalted and tormented by its own grandeur as the "Player King" confronts the prying eyes of a fickle audience. Both monarchs of Shakespeare's lifetime understood that they were, in Queen Elizabeth's terms, "set on stage in the sight and view of the world," or, as King James more unnervingly put it: "A king is as one set on a stage, whose smallest actions and gestures, all the people gazingly do behold."

The selections presented here show the expressive range of this metaphor—its exuberance and its melancholy—and include a few of Shakespeare's powerful evocations.

John of Salisbury (c. 1115–1180)

John was a prominent English thinker, diplomat, and churchman who became Bishop of Chartres. His work on political theory, Policraticus, *was widely read in the middle ages and Renaissance. Its many contributions include its development and transmission of the classical* theatrum mundi *metaphor—at once stage play and Roman festival—as an image for mutable worldliness as well as our scrutiny by Providential spectatorship.*

from *Polycraticus*, Book III (1159)

The different periods of time take on the character of shifts of scene. The individuals become subordinate to the acts as the play of mocking fortune unfolds itself in them. . . . [T]he end of all things is tragic, or if the name of comedy be preferred, I offer no objection provided that we are agreed that, as Petronius remarks, almost all the world is playing a part. . . . It is surprising how nearly coextensive with the world is the stage on which this endless, marvelous, incomparable tragedy, or if you will comedy, can be played. . . . [S]ince all are playing parts, there must be some spectators. Let no one complain that his acting is marked by none, for he is acting in the sight of God, of his angels, and of a few sages who are themselves spectators at these Circensian Games. (Pike 1938, pp. 172–80)

Giovanni Pico della Mirandola (1463–1494)

Giovanni Pico della Mirandola was an Italian Renaissance philosopher who sought to harmonize an array of traditions: Greek, Latin, Arabic, and Jewish; Platonic and Aristotelian; scholastic and humanist. His best-known work today is the Oration (on the Dignity of Man), *intended to introduce a public disputation concerning nine hundred philosophical and theological theses. Some of the theses were declared heretical by a papal commission, and the disputation never took place.*

The Oration *reflects the ambitious optimism that would soon embroil its young author in controversy. It begins by dismissing traditional explanations of man's intermediary status between nature and the supernatural. Instead, Pico's creation myth has a divine Architect constructing an elaborate cosmos of high, middle, and low orders, only to find He has run out of Ideas (or Archetypes) on which to model a human observer for His handiwork. God decides, then, to make man of "indeterminate nature" without a "fixed abode," turning lack into power by granting him a radical and unique capacity for self-transformation, pictured in myth, according to Pico, by the sea-god, Proteus.*

Later Renaissance uses of Proteus would be more ambivalent. Spanish humanist Ludovico Vives, inspired by Pico's tale, would write his own Fable About Man *featuring a human actor on Jupiter's cosmic stage, able to impersonate all things in the universe—even Jupiter himself—much to the gods' admiration, but also discomfort. More purely negative is Englishman Sir John Hayward's 1623 complaint that man abandons "the dignity of his proper nature" by giving up the image of God to become, like Proteus, a creature of "divers forms" whose liberty of will inclines him to various, beastly sensualities.*

from *Oration (on the Dignity of Man)* (1486)

". . . The nature of all other beings is limited and constrained within the bounds of laws prescribed by Us. Thou, constrained by no limits, in accordance with thine own free will, in whose hand We have placed thee, shalt ordain for thyself the limits of thy nature . . . as though the maker and molder of thyself, thou mayest fashion thyself in whatever shape thou shalt prefer. Thou shalt have the power to degenerate into the lower forms of life, which are brutish. Thou shalt have the power, out of thy soul's judgment, to be reborn into the higher forms, which are divine." . . . Who would not admire this our chameleon? Or who could more greatly admire aught else whatever? It is man who Asclepius of Athens,[1] arguing from his mutability of character and from his self-transforming nature, on just grounds says was symbolized by Proteus in the mysteries. (Cassirer 1956, p. 225)

Niccolò Machiavelli (1469–1527)

The two following selections, from chapters 7 and 18 of The Prince, *display the theatricality of power. In the first, a shrewd ploy achieves, through tragic "spectacle," several goals simultaneously, including a "purg[ing]" of the spectators' emotion. The anecdote of a leader deputizing a "hard cop" to do his dirty work, then turning on him, appears in different forms in Shakespeare—Machiavel Richard III's betrayal of his "other self," Buckingham, and more subtly, Duke Vincentio's various uses of Angelo in* Measure for Measure.

[1]Mythological son of Apollo, worshipped as hero and god of healing.

> *In the second instance, Machiavelli borrows from classical sources to counsel flexibility as a kind of shape-shifting, imitating the lion or the fox for strength or cunning. This is a prelude to a fuller discussion of the Prince's deceptive role-playing before a gullible public.*

from *The Prince* (1513, pub. 1532)

from Chapter VII: *Of new Principalities, gotten by fortune, and other men's forces*

The Duke, when he had taken Romagna, finding it had been under the hands of poor Lords who had rather pillaged their subjects than chastized or amended them, giving them more cause of discord, than of peace and union, so that the whole country was fraught with robberies, quarrels, and all other sorts of insolencies, thought the best way to reduce them to terms of pacification and obedience to a Princely power, was, to give them some good government, and therefore he set over them one Remiro D'Orco, a cruel, haughty man, to whom he gave an absolute power. The man in very short time settled peace and union amongst them with very great reputation. Afterwards the Duke thought such excessive authority serv'd not so well to his purpose, and doubting it would grow odious, he erected a civil judicature[1] in the midst of the country, where one excellent judge did preside, and thither every city sent their advocates and because he knew the rigors passed had bred some hatred against him, to purge the minds of those people, and to gain them wholly to himself, he purposed to show that if there was any cruelty used, it proceeded not from any order of his, but from the harsh disposition of his Officer. Whereupon laying hold on him, at this occasion, he caused his head to be struck off one morning early in the market place at Cesena, where he was left upon a gibbet, with a bloody sword by his side, the cruelty of which spectacle for a while satisfied and amazed those people.[2]

from Chapter XVIII: *In what manner Princes ought to keep their words*

How commendable in a Prince it is to keep his word and live with integrity, not making use of cunning and subtlety, everyone knows

---

[1]Court of justice.

[2]The translator assumes only a beheading: Machiavelli's Italian is more grimly suggestive, noting that the body was displayed "in dua pezzi" (in two pieces).

well. Yet we see by experience in these our days that those princes have effected great matters who have made small reckoning of keeping their words and have known by their craft to turn and wind men about and in the end have overcome those who have grounded upon the truth. You must then know there are two kinds of combating or fighting: the one by right of the laws the other merely by force. The first way is proper to men, the other is also common to beasts. But because the first many times suffices not, there is a necessity to make recourse to the second, wherefore it behooves a Prince to know how to make good use of that part which belongs to a beast as well as that which is proper to a man. This part hath been covertly showed to Princes by ancient writers who say that Achilles and many others of those ancient Princes were entrusted to Chiron the centaur to be brought up under his discipline. The moral of this, having for their teacher one that was half a beast and half a man, was nothing else but that it was needful for a prince to understand how to make his advantage of the one and the other nature because neither could subsist without the other.

A Prince, then, being necessitated to know how to make use of that part belonging to a beast, ought to serve himself of the conditions of the Fox and the Lion, for the Lion cannot keep himself from snares nor the Fox defend himself against the Wolves. He had need then be a Fox that he may beware of the snares, and a Lion that he may scare the Wolves. Those that stand wholly upon the Lion understand not well themselves.

And therefore a wise Prince cannot nor ought not keep his faith given when the observance thereof turns to disadvantage and the occasions that made him promise are past. For if men were all good, this rule would not be allowable; but being they are full of mischief and would not make it good to thee, neither art thou tied to keep it with them, nor shall a prince ever want lawful occasions to give color to this breach. Very many modern examples hereof might be alleged wherein might be showed how many peaces concluded and how many promises made have been violated and broken by the infidelity of Princes, and ordinary things have best succeeded with him that hath been nearest the Fox in condition. But it is necessary to understand how to set a good color upon this disposition and be able to feign and dissemble thoroughly. And men are so simple and yield so much to the present necessities that he who hath a mind to deceive shall always find another that will be deceived.

I will not conceal any one of the examples that have been of late. Alexander VI[3] never did anything else than deceive men and never meant otherwise, and always found whom to work upon. Yet never was there man would protest more effectually nor aver anything with more solemn oaths and observe them less than he. Nevertheless, his cozenages all thrived well with him, for he knew how to play this part cunningly. Therefore is there no necessity for a prince to be endowed with all these above-written qualities, but it behooves well that he seem to be so. Or rather I will boldly say this, that having these qualities and always regulating himself by them, they are hurtful, but seeming to have them, they are advantageous. As to seem pitiful, faithful, mild, religious, and of integrity and indeed to be so, provided withal thou beest of such a composition that if need require thee to use the contrary, thou canst and knowst how to apply thy self thereto. And it suffices to conceive this, that a Prince and especially a new Prince cannot observe all those things for which men are held good, he being often forced for the maintenance of his state to do contrary to his faith, charity, humanity, and religion. And therefore, it behooves him to have a mind so disposed as to turn and take advantage of all winds and fortunes, and, as formerly I said, not forsake the good while he can, but to know how to make use of the evil upon necessity.

A Prince, then, ought to have a special care that he never let fall any words but what are all seasoned with the five above-written qualities, and let him seem to him that sees and hears him, all pity, all faith, all integrity, all humanity, all religion. Nor is there anything more necessary for him to seem to have than this last quality, for all men in general judge thereof rather by the sight than by the touch. For every man may come to the sight of him, few come to the touch and feeling of him; every man may come to see what thou seemest, few come to perceive and understand what thou art; and those few dare not oppose the opinion of many who have the majesty of state to protect them. And in all men's actions, especially those of Princes wherein there is no judgment to appeal unto, men forbear to give their censures till the events and ends of things.

---

[3]Pope from 1492 to 1503.

Let a Prince therefore take the surest courses he can to maintain his life and state. The means shall always be thought honorable and commended by everyone, for the vulgar is overtaken with the appearance and event of a thing. And for the most part of people, they are but the vulgar. . . .

Sir Thomas More (1478–1535)

The greatest English humanist of the early sixteenth century, Sir Thomas More early in life translated a Latin biography of Pico, studied law, and despite his attraction to monastic life, entered the world of politics, rising to the powerful position of Lord Chancellor under Henry VIII. His disapproval of Henry's break with the Church of Rome led to More's execution in 1535.

Through the account of an exotic traveler, More's Utopia *presents a fantastic world, at once ideal and self-critical—its Greek name suggesting both "good place" and "no place," free of European greed and selfish corruption yet also ruthless in calibrated, and ironically self-interested, perfectionism. The account is prefaced, moreover, by an unresolved debate between the traveler and a fictive version of More himself about the value of public service. While the traveler insists on the futility of offering wise counsel to willful rulers, "More" uses theatrical metaphors to suggest a more flexible, pragmatic approach than the timeless, universal truths of scholastic philosophy.*

from *Utopia* (1516)

[Idealistic traveler (Raphael Hythloday) speaks first.]

"That is what I meant," quod [said] he, "when I said philosophy had no place among kings."

"Indeed," quod I, "this school philosophy hath not, which thinketh all things meet for every place. But there is another philosophy more civil, which knoweth . . . her own stage, and thereafter ordering and behaving herself in the play which she hath in hand, playeth her part accordingly with comeliness, uttering nothing out of due order and fashion. And this is the philosophy that you must use. Or else whiles a comedy of Plautus is playing, and the vile bondmen scoffing and trifling among themselves, if you should suddenly come upon the stage in a Philosopher's apparel and rehearse out of *Octavia* the place wherein Seneca disputeth with Nero:[1] had it not been better for you to have played the dumb person than by rehearsing that, which served neither for the time nor place, to have made such a tragical comedy or gamillaufry? For by bringing in other stuff that nothing appertaineth to the present matter, you must needs mar and pervert the play that is in hand, though the stuff that you bring be much better. What part soever you have taken upon you, play that as well as you can and make the best of it: And do not therefore disturb and bring out of order the whole matter, because that another, which is merrier and better, cometh to your remembrance. So the case standeth in a commonwealth, and so it is in the consultations of kings and princes. If evil opinions and naughty persuasions cannot be utterly and quite plucked out of their hearts . . . yet for this cause you must not leave and forsake the commonwealth."

Sir Walter Ralegh (c. 1554–1618)

Poet, politician, explorer, soldier, Sir Walter Ralegh's flamboyant and ultimately tragic career made him both an active participant in and a skeptical observer of the ruthless ambition and theatricalism of Elizabethan and Jacobean courts. Ranging from idealism to morbidity, his poetry is among the most spectacular of the English Renaissance. The poem presented here, a powerful distillation of Ralegh's pervasive use of the trope, exists in several versions.

"On the Life of Man" (pub. 1612)

What is our life? A play of passion,
Our mirth, the music of division,
Our mothers' wombs the tiring-houses be,
Where we are dressed for this short comedy,
Heaven, the judicious sharp spectator, is,   5
That sits and marks still who doth act amiss,
Our graves that hide us from the searching sun

---

[1]Plautus and Seneca, Latin writers of comic farce and tragedy, respectively, represent opposing extremes or the range of possibility. Compare Polonius's praise of the players' versatility in *Hamlet* (2.2): "Seneca cannot be too heavy, nor Plautus too light."

Are like drawn curtains when the play is done,
Thus march we playing to our latest rest,
Only we die in earnest, that's no jest.   10

William Shakespeare (1564–1616)

from *Henry VI, Part Three* (3.2) (c. 1592)

[*The following is part of a lengthy soliloquy by Richard of Gloucester who, in a later play, will be crowned King Richard III.
Descended from the medieval stage Vice, Shakespeare's great comic
villain here sounds the peculiar combination of psychological torment, ruthless obsessiveness, and high-spirited exuberance that
makes the role-player so complex a metaphor. Richard traces his
energy not from Pico's open indeterminacy but from cruel deformity, a "chaos" that embodies the play's larger social disorder. The
speech ends by citing names and types traditionally associated with
self-transforming, histrionic skills.*]

RICHARD

    Why, love forswore me in my mother's womb;
    And, for[1] I should not deal in her soft laws,
    She did corrupt frail nature with some bribe   155
    To shrink mine arm up like a withered shrub;
    To make an envious[2] mountain on my back,
    Where sits deformity to mock my body;
    To shape my legs of an unequal size;
    To disproportion me in every part,   160
    Like to a chaos, or an unlicked bear whelp[3]
    That carries no impression[4] like the dam.
    And am I then a man to be beloved?
    Oh, monstrous fault, to harbor such a thought!
    Then, since this earth affords no joy to me   165

---

[1]So that.

[2]Spiteful, detested.

[3](It was a popular notion that bears licked their shapeless newly born cubs into a
proper shape.)

[4]Shape.

But to command, to check,[5] to o'erbear[6] such
As are of better person[7] than myself,
I'll make my heaven to dream upon the crown,
And, whiles I live, t'account this world but hell,
Until my misshaped trunk that bears this head   170
Be round impalèd[8] with a glorious crown.
And yet I know not how to get the crown,
For many lives stand between me and home;[9]
And I—like one lost in a thorny wood,
That rends the thorns and is rent with the thorns,   175
Seeking a way and straying from the way,
Not knowing how to find the open air,
But toiling desperately to find it out—
Torment myself to catch the English crown;
And from that torment I will free myself   180
Or hew my way out with a bloody ax.
Why, I can smile, and murder whiles I smile,
And cry "Content" to that which grieves my heart,
And wet my cheeks with artificial tears,
And frame my face to all occasions.   185
I'll drown more sailors than the mermaid[10] shall;
I'll slay more gazers than the basilisk;[11]
I'll play the orator as well as Nestor,
Deceive more slyly than Ulysses[12] could,
And, like a Sinon,[13] take another Troy.   190
I can add colors to the chameleon,

[5]Control, rebuke.

[6]Dominate.

[7]Handsomer appearance.

[8]Encircled.

[9]The goal.

[10](Mermaids allegedly had the power to lure sailors to destruction by their singing or weeping.)

[11]Fabulous reptile said to kill by its gaze.

[12]Greek leaders in the Trojan War, noted, respectively, for aged wisdom and cunning.

[13]Greek warrior who allowed himself to be taken captive by the Trojans and who then, feigning resentment toward his Greek companions, persuaded Priam to bring the wooden horse within the city walls, by which Troy was taken.

Change shapes with Proteus[14] for advantages,[15]
And set the murderous Machiavel to school.[16]
Can I do this, and cannot get a crown?
Tut, were it farther off, I'll pluck it down.   *Exit.*

from *Richard II* (5.2) (c. 1595)

[The first play of Shakespeare's Second Tetralogy uses theatrical imagery to represent the Duke of York's shift in loyalty. The fickleness of the crowd as it cheers its new King and ignores the deposed one reminds York of the behavior of spectators at a theater. He stops short of acknowledging the unreality of the moment by insisting on a higher power scripting all.]

YORK
    As in a theater the eyes of men,
    After a well-graced actor leaves the stage,
    Are idly[1] bent on him that enters next,   25
    Thinking his prattle to be tedious,
    Even so, or with much more contempt, men's eyes
    Did scowl on gentle Richard. No man cried, "God save him!"
    No joyful tongue gave him his welcome home,
    But dust was thrown upon his sacred head—   30
    Which with such gentle sorrow he shook off,
    His face still combating with tears and smiles,
    The badges[2] of his grief and patience,
    That had not God for some strong purpose steeled
    The hearts of men, they must perforce[3] have melted,   35
    And barbarism itself have pitied him.
    But heaven hath a hand in these events,

---

[14]Old man of the sea, able to assume different shapes.

[15]To gain tactical advantage.

[16]Teach Machiavelli how to be ruthless. (In the popular imagination, Machiavelli was the archetype of ruthless political cunning and atheism.)

---

[1]Indifferently.

[2]Insignia, outward signs.

[3]Necessarily.

To whose high will we bound our calm contents.[4]
To Bolingbroke are we sworn subjects now,
Whose state[5] and honor I for aye allow.[6]   40

from *Henry V* (4.1) (c. 1599)

[*On the eve of Henry V's greatest military test, what would later be
called the Battle of Agincourt, the former Prince Hal broods about
the "idol ceremony" that provides the trappings for his Kingly
role. An "idol" is a phantasm or unsubstantial form, such as a
reflection in water, the term often used for the image of a false god,
or an adored image that usurps true worship. It would also be
heard in performance as "idle," i.e., empty, vain, useless, foolish
(cf. Hamlet on his antic disposition: "I must be idle"). Once
Henry is interrupted, however, he regathers his strength (like York
in* Richard II*) by invoking heavenly power.*]

KING HENRY V

And what have kings that privates[1] have not too,
Save ceremony, save general ceremony?
And what art thou, thou idol ceremony?
What kind of god art thou, that suffer'st more
Of mortal griefs than do thy worshipers?   240
What are thy rents? What are thy comings-in?[2]
O ceremony, show me but thy worth!
What is thy soul of adoration?[3]
Art thou aught else but place,[4] degree, and form,
Creating awe and fear in other men?   245
Wherein thou art less happy, being feared,
Than they in fearing.
What drink'st thou oft, instead of homage sweet,

---

[4]We bind ourselves to be calmly content.
[5]Royal title.
[6]Acknowledge.

---

[1]Private persons.
[2]Revenues.
[3]The essential quality that makes you so much admired.
[4]Rank.

But poisoned flattery? Oh, be sick, great greatness,
And bid thy ceremony give thee cure![5]   250
Thinks thou the fiery fever will go out
With titles blown from adulation?[6]
Will it give place to flexure and low bending?[7]
Canst thou, when thou command'st the beggar's knee,
Command the health of it? No, thou proud dream,   255
That play'st so subtly with a king's repose.
I am a king that find thee,[8] and I know
'Tis not the balm,[9] the scepter, and the ball,[10]
The sword, the mace,[11] the crown imperial,
The intertissued[12] robe of gold and pearl,   260
The farcèd[13] title running 'fore the king,
The throne he sits on, nor the tide of pomp
That beats upon the high shore of this world—
No, not all these, thrice-gorgeous ceremony,
Not all these, laid in bed majestical,   265
Can sleep so soundly as the wretched slave. . . .

from *As You Like It* (2.7) (c. 1599)

[*The deposed Duke Senior, exiled in the Forest of Arden, has just witnessed the desperate hunger of the romantic hero, Orlando, and moralizes with the malcontent satirist, Jaques, through an extended use of the theatrical metaphor. Orlando's entrance with Adam at the end of Jaques' famous speech could be taken either as proof of the melancholy theme or as a tempering of it through a display of community linking the human generations.*]

---

[5]Learn to cure yourself by being sick, by treating poisoned flattery and ceremoniousness as a medicine that will purge you of being in love with your own greatness.

[6]Do you really think that the fever of vain pride will be extinguished by speeches breathed by flatterers? (*Blown* also suggests "inflated.")

[7]Will the sickness yield to bowing and scraping?

[8]Experience greatness and am able to appraise its worth and limitations.

[9]Consecrating oil used to anoint a king in his coronation.

[10]Orb of sovereignty.

[11]Ceremonial staff.

[12]Interwoven.

[13]Stuffed (with pompous phrases).

DUKE SENIOR

Thou see'st we are not all alone unhappy.   135
This wide and universal theater
Presents more woeful pageants than the scene
Wherein we play in.

JAQUES   All the world's a stage,
And all the men and women merely players.
They have their exits and their entrances,   140
And one man in his time plays many parts,
His acts being seven ages. At first the infant,
Mewling[1] and puking in the nurse's arms.
Then the whining schoolboy, with his satchel
And shining morning face, creeping like snail   145
Unwillingly to school. And then the lover,
Sighing like furnace, with a woeful ballad
Made to his mistress' eyebrow. Then a soldier,
Full of strange oaths and bearded like the pard,[2]
Jealous[3] in honor, sudden, and quick in quarrel,   150
Seeking the bubble reputation
Even in the cannon's mouth. And then the justice,
In fair round belly with good capon[4] lined,
With eyes severe and beard of formal cut,
Full of wise saws[5] and modern instances;[6]   155
And so he plays his part. The sixth age shifts
Into the lean and slippered pantaloon,[7]
With spectacles on nose and pouch on side,
His youthful hose, well saved, a world too wide
For his shrunk shank;[8] and his big manly voice,   160
Turning again toward childish treble, pipes

[1]Crying with a catlike noise.

[2]Having bristling mustaches like the leopard's.

[3]Quick to anger in matters of honor.

[4]Rooster castrated to make the flesh more tender for eating (and often presented to judges as a bribe).

[5]Sayings.

[6]Commonplace illustrations.

[7]Ridiculous, enfeebled old man. (A stock type in Italian *commedia dell'arte*.)

[8]Calf.

And whistles in his[9] sound. Last scene of all,
That ends this strange, eventful history,
Is second childishness and mere oblivion,[10]
Sans[11] teeth, sans eyes, sans taste, sans everything.   165

Enter Orlando, with Adam

DUKE SENIOR
  Welcome. Set down your venerable burden
  And let him feed.

from *Hamlet* (2.2) (c. 1601)

[*Of all Shakespeare's plays,* Hamlet *is the most fully permeated with references to theater, the playhouse, and dramatic illusion, including the protagonist's early denigration of "actions that a man might play" in favor of "that within which passes show" (1.2.84–85). The following, however, is more optimistic, as Hamlet soliloquizes about the power of playacting to have real effects, in this case the exposure of hidden guilt. The anecdote to which Hamlet refers descends from Plutarch's* Lives *and Sir Philip Sidney's* An Apology for Poetry.]

HAMLET
              I have heard
  That guilty creatures sitting at a play   590
  Have by the very cunning[1] of the scene[2]
  Been struck so to the soul that presently[3]
  They have proclaimed their malefactions;
  For murder, though it have no tongue, will speak
  With most miraculous organ. I'll have these players   595
  Play something like the murder of my father
  Before mine uncle. I'll observe his looks;
  I'll tent him to the quick.[4] If 'a do blench,[5]

---

[9]Its.
[10]Total forgetfulness.
[11]Without.

---

[1]Art, skill.
[2]Dramatic presentation.
[3]At once.
[4]Probe the tender part of the wound, the core.
[5]Quail, flinch.

I'll know my course. The spirit that I have seen
May be the devil, and the devil hath power   600
T'assume a pleasing shape; yea, and perhaps,
Out of my weakness and my melancholy,
As he is very potent with such spirits,[6]
Abuses[7] me to damn me. I'll have grounds
More relative[8] than this. The play's the thing   605
Wherein I'll catch the conscience of the King.

from *Macbeth* (5.5) (c. 1606)

[*The tyrannical usurper, surrounded by approaching enemies, has
just learned of the death of his Queen.*]

MACBETH   She should have died hereafter;[1]
There would have been a time for such a word.
Tomorrow, and tomorrow, and tomorrow
Creeps in this[2] petty pace from day to day   20
To the last syllable of recorded time,
And all our yesterdays have lighted[3] fools
The way to dusty[4] death. Out, out, brief candle!
Life's but a walking shadow, a poor player
That struts and frets his hour upon the stage   25
And then is heard no more. It is a tale
Told by an idiot, full of sound and fury,
Signifying nothing.[5]

---

[6]Humors (of melancholy).

[7]Deludes.

[8]Cogent, pertinent.

---

[1]She would have died someday, or, she should have died at some more appropriate
time, freed from the relentless pressures of the moment.

[2]In at this.

[3](The metaphor is of a candle used to light one to bed, just as life is a brief transit for
wretched mortals to their deathbeds.)

[4](Since life, made out of dust, returns to dust.)

[5](For biblical echoes in this speech, see Psalms 18.28, 22.15, 90.9; Job 8.9, 14.1–2,
18.6.)

from *The Tempest* (4.1) (c. 1611)

[*Prospero's magical displays on his island have been taken by some critics to reflect Shakespeare's imaginative inventions within the "wooden O" of the Globe Theatre. Here, Prospero consoles his future son-in-law after dispelling the enchanting masque that was his wedding gift, but in terms that suggest his own troubled state of mind.*]

PROSPERO   You do look, my son, in a moved sort,[1]
As if you were dismayed. Be cheerful, sir.
Our revels[2] now are ended. These our actors,
As I foretold you, were all spirits and
Are melted into air, into thin air;   150
And, like the baseless fabric[3] of this vision,
The cloud-capped towers, the gorgeous palaces,
The solemn temples, the great globe[4] itself,
Yea, all which it inherit,[5] shall dissolve,
And, like this insubstantial pageant faded,   155
Leave not a rack[6] behind. We are such stuff
As dreams are made on,[7] and our little life
Is rounded[8] with a sleep. Sir, I am vexed.
Bear with my weakness. My old brain is troubled.
Be not disturbed with[9] my infirmity.   160
If you be pleased, retire[10] into my cell
And there repose. A turn or two I'll walk
To still my beating[11] mind.

[1]Troubled state, condition.

[2]Entertainment, pageant.

[3]Unsubstantial theatrical edifice or contrivance.

[4](With a glance at the Globe Theatre.)

[5]Who subsequently occupy it.

[6]Wisp of cloud.

[7]Of.

[8]Surrounded (before birth and after death), or crowned, rounded off.

[9]By.

[10]Withdraw, go.

[11]Agitated.

Further Reading

Auden, W. H. "The Prince's Dog," in *The Dyer's Hand*. Random House, 1962.

Barber, C. L. *Shakespeare's Festive Comedy: A Study of Dramatic Form and Its Relation to Social Custom*. Princeton Univ. Press, 1959.

Barish, Jonas A. "The Turning Away of Prince Hal." *Shakespeare Studies* 1 (1965): 9–17.

Bevington, David, ed. *Henry the Fourth, Parts I and II: Critical Essays*. Garland Publishing, 1986.

———. "Introduction." *Henry IV, Part 1*. Oxford Univ. Press, 1987.

Blanpied, John W. *Time and the Artist in Shakespeare's English Histories*. Univ. Delaware Press, 1983.

Bradley, A. C. "The Rejection of Falstaff," in *Oxford Lectures on Poetry*. Macmillan, 1909.

Bullough, Geoffrey, ed. *The Narrative and Dramatic Sources of Shakespeare*. 8 vols. Routledge Kegan Paul, 1958.

Burckardt, Sigurd. *Shakespearean Meanings*. Princeton Univ. Press, 1968.

Calderwood, James. *Metadrama in Shakespeare's Henriad: Richard II to Henry V*. Univ. California Press, 1979.

Campbell, Lily B. *Shakespeare's "Histories": Mirrors of Elizabethan Policy*. Huntington Library Publications, 1947.

Cassirer, Ernst, Paul Oskar Kristeller, and John Herman Randall, Jr., eds. *The Renaissance Philosophy of Man*. Univ. of Chicago Press, 1956.

Champion, Larry S. *"The Noise of Threatening Drum": Dramatic Strategy and Political Ideology in Shakespeare and the English Chronicle Plays*. Univ. Delaware Press, 1990.

Corbin, Peter, and Douglas Sedge, eds. *The Oldcastle Controversy: "Sir John Oldcastle, Part I" and "The Famous Victories of Henry V."* The Revels Plays Companion Library. Manchester Univ. Press, 1991.

Danson, Lawrence. *Shakespeare's Dramatic Genres.* Oxford Univ. Press, 2000.

Empson, William. *Some Versions of Pastoral.* New Directions, 1960.

———. "Falstaff" (revised from "Falstaff and Mr. Dover Wilson"), in *Essays on Shakespeare,* ed. David B. Pirie. Cambridge Univ. Press, 1986.

———. "L. C. Knights on A. C. Bradley," in *The Strengths of Shakespeare's Shrew: Essays, Memoirs and Reviews,* ed. John Haffenden. Sheffield Academic Press, 1996.

Greenblatt, Stephen. "Invisible Bullets," in *Shakespearean Negotiations.* Univ. California Press, 1988.

Highley, Christopher. "Wales, Ireland, and *1 Henry IV.*" *Renaissance Drama* ns 21 (1990): 91–114.

Hodgdon, Barbara. *The End Crowns All: Closure and Contradiction in Shakespeare's History.* Princeton Univ. Press, 1991.

Howard, Jean, and Phyllis Rackin. *Engendering a Nation: A Feminist Account of Shakespeare's English Histories.* Routledge, 1997.

Humphreys, A. R. "Introduction" to *The First Part of King Henry IV.* The Arden Edition of the Works of William Shakespeare, 1961; rev. Routledge, 1989.

———. "Introduction" to *The Second Part of King Henry IV.* Arden Edition, 1966; rev. Routledge, 1989.

Hunter, G. K. "Henry IV and the Elizabethan Two-Part Play." *Review of English Studies* 5 (1954): 236–48.

———, ed. *"Henry IV, Parts 1 and 2": A Casebook.* Macmillan, 1970.

Jenkins, Harold. *The Structural Problem in Shakespeare's Henry IV.* 1956; rpt. *Structural Problems in Shakespeare: Lectures and Essays by Harold Jenkins,* ed. Ernst Honigmann. Thomson Learning, 2001.

Kahn, Coppelia. *Man's Estate: Masculine Identity in Shakespeare.* Univ. California Press, 1981.

Kastan, David Scott. *Shakespeare and the Shapes of Time.* Univ. Press of New England, 1982.

———. "'The King hath many marching in his Coats,' or What did you do in the war, Daddy?" *Shakespeare Left and Right*, ed. Ivo Kamps. Routledge, 1991.

———. "'Killed with Hard Opinions': Oldcastle and Falstaff and the Reformed Text of *1 Henry IV*," in *Shakespeare After Theory*. Routledge, 1999.

Kelly, Henry Ansagar. *Divine Providence in the England of Shakespeare's Histories*. Harvard Univ. Press, 1970.

Kernan, Alvin B. "*The Henriad*: Shakespeare's Major History Plays." *Yale Review* 59 (1969): 3–32; rev. in *Modern Shakespearean Criticism*, ed. Alvin B. Kernan. Harcourt Brace, 1970.

Knights, L. C. "Time's Subjects: The Sonnets and *King Henry IV, Part II*," in *Some Shakespearean Themes* (1954); rpt. *Some Shakespearean Themes and an Approach to Hamlet*. Stanford Univ. Press, 1966.

Leggatt, Alexander. *Shakespeare's Political Drama: The History Plays and the Roman Plays*. Routledge, 1988.

Levy, F. J. *Tudor Historical Thought*. Huntington Library, 1967.

Lyons, Bridget Gellert, ed. *Chimes At Midnight / Orson Welles, Director*. Rutgers Univ. Press, 1988.

Mack, Maynard. "Introduction" to *The History of Henry IV [Part One]*. The Signet Classic Shakespeare. 1963; rpt. New American Library, 1987.

McCoy, Richard. *The Rites of Knighthood: The Literature and Politics of Elizabethan Chivalry*. Univ. California Press, 1989.

———. "'Thou Idol Ceremony': Elizabeth I, the *Henriad*, and the Rites of the English Monarchy," in *Urban Life in the Renaissance*, ed. Susan Zimmerman and Ron Weissman. Univ. Delaware Press, 1989.

McMillin, Scott. *Henry IV, Part One. Shakespeare in Performance*. Manchester Univ. Press, 1991.

Mullaney, Steven. *The Place of the Stage: License, Play and Power in Renaissance England*. Univ. Michigan Press, 1988.

Ornstein, Robert. *A Kingdom for a Stage: The Achievement of Shakespeare's History Plays*. Harvard Univ. Press, 1972.

Patterson, Annabel. *Reading Holinshed's Chronicles*. Univ. Chicago Press, 1994.

Pike, Joseph. *Frivolities of Courtiers and Footprints of Philosophers*. Univ. of Minnesota Press, 1938.

Quint, David. "Bragging Rights: Honor and Courtesy in Shakespeare and Spenser," in *Creative Imitation: New Essays on Renaissance Literature in Honor of Thomas M. Greene*, ed. David Quint. MRTF, 1992.

Rabkin, Norman. *Shakespeare and the Common Understanding*. The Free Press, 1967.

Ribner, Irving. *The English History Play in the Age of Shakespeare*. Princeton Univ. Press, 1957.

Righter (Barton), Ann. *Shakespeare and the Idea of the Play*. Chatto & Windus, 1962.

Rossiter, A. P. *Angels with Horns: Fifteen Lectures on Shakespeare*, ed. Graham Storey. Longman, 1961.

Saccio, Peter. *Shakespeare's English Kings: History, Chronicle, and Drama*. Oxford Univ. Press, 1977.

Taylor, Gary. "The Fortunes of Oldcastle." *Shakespeare Survey* 38 (1985): 85–100.

Tillyard, E. M. W. *Shakespeare's History Plays*. Chatto & Windus, 1944.

Wilders, John. *The Lost Garden: A View of Shakespeare's English and Roman History Plays*. Macmillan, 1978.

Wiles, David. *Shakespeare's Clowns: Actor and Text in the Elizabethan Playhouse*. Cambridge Univ. Press, 1987.

Wilson, John Dover. *The Fortunes of Falstaff*. 1943; Cambridge Univ. Press, 1953.

Yachnin, Paul. "History, Theatricality, and the 'Structural Problem' in the Henry IV Plays." *Philological Quarterly* 70 (1991): 163–79.

Young, David P., ed. *Twentieth Century Interpretations of Henry IV, Part Two: A Collection of Critical Essays*. Prentice-Hall, 1968.